Ulster Loyalism after the Good Friday Agreement

Also by Graham Spencer:

THE MEDIA AND PEACE (2005)

THE STATE OF LOYALISM IN NORTHERN IRELAND (2008)

Ulster Loyalism after the Good Friday Agreement

History, Identity and Change

Edited By

James W. McAuley
Associate Dean for Research and Enterprise and Professor of Political Sociology & Irish Studies, University of Huddersfield, UK

and

Graham Spencer
Reader in Politics, Conflict and the Media, University of Portsmouth, UK

palgrave
macmillan

First published 2011 by
PALGRAVE MACMILLAN

Palgrave Macmillan in the UK is an imprint of Macmillan Publishers Limited,
registered in England, company number 785998, of Houndmills, Basingstoke,
Hampshire RG21 6XS.

Palgrave Macmillan in the US is a division of St Martin's Press LLC,
175 Fifth Avenue, New York, NY 10010.

Palgrave Macmillan is the global academic imprint of the above companies
and has companies and representatives throughout the world.

Palgrave® and Macmillan® are registered trademarks in the United States,
the United Kingdom, Europe and other countries.

ISBN: 978–0–230–22885–6 hardback

This book is printed on paper suitable for recycling and made from fully
managed and sustained forest sources. Logging, pulping and manufacturing
processes are expected to conform to the environmental regulations of the
country of origin.

A catalogue record for this book is available from the British Library.

A catalog record for this book is available from the Library of Congress.

10 9 8 7 6 5 4 3 2 1
20 19 18 17 16 15 14 13 12 11

Printed and bound in Great Britain by
CPI Antony Rowe, Chippenham and Eastbourne

For Karen and Stephanie

Contents

Abbreviations

BNP	British National Party
CGP	Consultative Group on the Past
CLMC	Combined Loyalist Military Command
CTI	Conflict Transformation Initiative
DUP	Democratic Unionist Party
EACTF	East Antrim Conflict Transformation Forum
EBHCS	East Belfast Historical and Cultural Society
ECHR	European Convention on Human Rights
EPIC	Ex-Prisoners Interpretative Centre
GFA	Good Friday Agreement
IICD	Independent International Commission on Decommissioning
IMC	Independent Monitoring Commission
INLA	Irish National Liberation Army
IRA	Irish Republican Army
LVF	Loyalist Volunteer Force
NIWC	Northern Ireland Women's Coalition
PIRA	Provisional Irish Republican Army
PSNI	Police Service of Northern Ireland
PUP	Progressive Unionist Party
RHC	Red Hand Commando
RUC	Royal Ulster Constabulary
SDLP	Social Democratic and Labour Party
TUV	Traditional Unionist Voice
UDA	Ulster Defence Association
UDP	United Democratic Party also Ulster Democratic Party
UFF	Ulster Freedom Fighters
UPRG	Ulster Political Research Group
UUP	Ulster Unionist Party
UVF	Ulster Volunteer Force
WiP	Women into Politics

Contributors

Kevin Bean is a lecturer in Irish politics at the Institute of Irish Studies, University of Liverpool. His research interests include Provisional Republicanism, the development of state counterinsurgency strategies and the development of nationalism as a political force in contemporary Europe. His publications include *The New Politics of Sinn Féin* (2007).

Stephen Bloomer is a freelance researcher working in the community and voluntary sector in Northern Ireland. He was previously project co-ordinator of *The Other View* Magazine between 2006 and 2008. He is co-editor (with Aaron Edwards) of *Transforming the Peace Process in Northern Ireland: From Terrorism to Democratic Politics* (Irish Academic Press, 2008).

Kris Brown is currently an RCUK Post-Doctoral Fellow at the Transitional Justice Institute, University of Ulster. His research interests focus on commemoration, memory and memorialization in post-conflict Northern Ireland, especially themes relating to victimhood, the nature of the conflict, relations with the state, the use of political symbols and national identities.

Leigh-Ann Coffey is a doctoral candidate at Queen's University, Canada. She is the author of *The Planters of Luggacurran, Co. Laois: A Protestant Community, 1879–1927* (Dublin: Four Courts Press, 2006).

Aaron Edwards is a senior lecturer in Defence and International Affairs at the Royal Military Academy Sandhurst. His latest book is *A History of the Northern Ireland Labour Party: Democratic Socialism and Sectarianism* (Manchester University Press, 2009). He is co-editor (with Stephen Bloomer) of *Transforming the Peace Process in Northern Ireland: From Terrorism to Democratic Politics* (Irish Academic Press, 2008).

John G. D. Grieve is former Deputy Assistant Commissioner of the Metropolitan Police. In 2004 he was appointed as one of four commissioners to the Independent Monitoring Commission in Ireland. This body was drawn up to report on paramilitary activity, security measures and governmental standards in a new devolved Northern Ireland.

Lyndsey Harris is a lecturer in Criminology and Security Studies at Birmingham City University. Her research interests include terrorism and political violence, strategic theory and Northern Irish politics. She is an elected executive member of the Political Studies Association of the United Kingdom.

Thomas Hennessey is Reader in the department of history and American studies, Canterbury Christ Church University. He has written extensively on the conflict in Ireland, and his books include: *The Evolution of the Troubles 1970–72; Dividing Ireland: World War One and Partition; A History of Northern Ireland, 1920–96; The Northern Ireland Peace Process: Ending the Troubles?* His latest book (with C. Thomas) is, *Spooks: The Unofficial History of MI5* (Amberley, 2009).

Chris Hudson is a Unitarian Minister in All Souls Church, Belfast. He acted as a go-between with the UVF and the Dublin Government from 1993 until recently. He received an MBE for his leadership role with the Peace Train Organization in 1999. Chris worked as a trade union official in Dublin for 20 years before taking up his ministry in Belfast.

Roger Mac Ginty is a Reader at the School of International Relations, University of St Andrews. He is author of *No War, No Peace: The Rejuvenation of Stalled Peace Processes and Peace Accords*, co-editor (with John Darby) of *Contemporary Peacemaking: Conflict, Peace Processes and Post-War Reconstruction*, and co-author (with Andrew Williams) of *Conflict and Development*. He is editor of the Palgrave book series 'Rethinking Political Violence'.

James W. McAuley is Associate Dean for Research and Enterprise, and Professor of Political Sociology and Irish Studies in the School of Human and Health Sciences at the University of Huddersfield. He recently completed two major projects on Orangeism (with Jon Tonge), funded by the ESRC, and on former paramilitary prisoners (with Jon Tonge, Peter Shirlow and Catherine McGlynn), funded by the Leverhulme Trust. His latest book *Ulster's Last Stand? (Re)Constructing Unionism after the Peace Process* was published in 2010 by Irish Academic Press.

Catherine McGlynn is a senior lecturer in politics at the University of Huddersfield. Her PhD was on the politics of the Progressive Unionist Party. Since then she has been actively working on a variety of projects involving citizenship and national identity. Her latest book is *Abandoning Historical Conflict: Former Paramilitary Prisoners and Political Reconciliation in Northern Ireland* (with Peter Shirlow, Jon Tonge and Jim McAuley; Manchester University Press, 2010).

Andrew Mycock is a senior lecturer in politics at the University of Huddersfield. His key research and teaching interests focus on post-empire citizenship and national identity, particularly in the United Kingdom and the Russian Federation, and the impact of citizenship and history education programmes. He has published widely on the politics of 'Britishness' and recently completed a survey of the Orange Order membership with Jim McAuley and Jon Tonge.

Phillip Orr is a writer, researcher and drama practitioner who lives in Carrickfergus, Co Antrim. He has written about Ireland's experience of the Great War, the 1798 Rising and social issues within today's loyalist communities. Recently he has worked with the Ulster Scots Agency on local drama projects that reflect upon the Irish Protestant heritage.

Neil Southern graduated with First Class Hons from Queen's University Beflast with a BA in Politics and was awarded the Lemberger-Mettrick Prize for Politics. He completed his PhD on religion and politics with particular reference to the Democratic Unionist Party and has written widely on Northern Ireland.

Graham Spencer is Reader in Politics, Conflict and the Media at the University of Portsmouth. His book *The State of Loyalism in Northern Ireland* was published in 2008. He is currently working on the book *Protestant Identity and Peacemaking in Northern Ireland*.

Jonathan Tonge is Professor of Politics at the University of Liverpool and Head of the School of Politics and Communication Studies. He is also President of the Political Studies Association of the United Kingdom. Professor Tonge has written extensively on various aspects of British and Irish politics, including 14 books and dozens of journal articles and book chapters.

Introduction: Politics, Identity and Change in Contemporary Loyalism

Graham Spencer and James W. McAuley

Enter any mainstream bookshop in Northern Ireland and the image of loyalism that confronts the browser is ostensibly one of criminality and individualism. Publishers of books on loyalism seem to take particular interest in acts of violence and murder perpetrated by those who gain reputations not so much for their thinking, but for their actions. Accounts of this behaviour, through dramatic emphasis on menace and brutality, mean such books tend to sit better on the shelves of crime fiction, rather than politics or social history.

Though in recent years serious studies of loyalism reveal an image which moves beyond this stereotype by demonstrating a considered engagement with peace process politics and social change in Northern Ireland (McAuley 2010; Spencer 2008) and although there have been important previous examinations of loyalist paramilitarism, both from academic (Bruce 1992, 1994; Crawford 2003; Nelson 1984; Wood 2006) and journalistic perspectives (Cusack and McDonald 1997; McDonald and Cusack 2004; Taylor 1999), it is the criminal portrait which dominates popular understanding of loyalism and therefore which shapes the public imagination about what loyalism means and the 'realities' of being a loyalist (for examples of this, see Adair 2007; Caldwell and Robinson 2006; McDowell 2008).

Moreover, the image of mafia type criminality and irrational behaviour that pervades modern accounts of loyalist activity finds no real comparison in the world of republicanism, where public relations awareness and political and communal emphasis combine to promote an image of seriousness, consideration and purpose. The loyalist image can only help magnify these differences, reinforcing the intelligence and sophistication of the republican project while underlining loyalism's apparent lack of structure and obstructing its social and political relevance in the process.

While acknowledging the criminality of loyalism and the destructive role that loyalist paramilitarism has played in the Northern Ireland conflict, this collection of essays goes some way to challenging the criminal stereotype by considering the social, historical, political and cultural forces

1

that shape loyalist history and identity and it relates that combination of forces to how loyalism is adapting to the complex shift from conflict to tentative peace.

In that sense, the collection is an attempt to interact with a range of influences and concerns that impact on loyalist thinking and help determine subsequent responses to change. But, to do this, the editors believe it is important to draw not only from academic interpretation and assessment, but also from the experiences and actions of loyalists themselves, as well as those who work with them, to understand how loyalist communities function. Hopefully this combination of academic and practitioner approaches to what we might think of as 'the loyalist condition' will help the reader to appreciate the range of tensions and pressures which are being faced in the post-conflict Northern Ireland climate by loyalists, and contribute towards a timely understanding about how those tensions and pressures are being dealt with.

Significantly, the conflict provided a sense of resistance and purpose for loyalists that acted to define paramilitary identity and galvanize communities through a protectionist psychology, often referred to as a 'siege mentality'. This, to a large extent, offered some stability and definition in an otherwise unstable and violent society. But the end of violence does not mean the end of those communities who were engaged in such violence.

Rather it tends to correspond with a change of meaning (perhaps a crisis of meaning), a questioning of identity (perhaps a crisis of identity) and a reappraisal of history and purpose (perhaps a crisis of history and purpose) which can cause problems for those seeking to maintain cohesion in a climate which encourages movement away from traditional positions and convictions (sometimes leading to further resistance, violence and conflict by those fearful of losing status, authority and control, or by those who see the end of conflict as throwing into doubt personal loyalties, costs and reasons for suffrage).

As is well known, unlike republicanism, loyalism has not been able to establish a political project, which has gained public understanding, sympathy or credibility. Those within loyalism who have shown and continue to show considerable political ability and skill have been hamstrung by perceived associations with paramilitarism, which connects with broader negative Protestant unionist imaginations about loyalism itself. In Protestant unionist society more generally loyalism has struggled unsuccessfully to overcome such imaginations, and because of lacking evident social or political legitimacy has been unable to cultivate even marginal recognition that loyalists have important contributions to make to political and social stability (recent popular books about turf wars, gangs and criminal underworlds merely confirm this perceived illegitimacy).

Yet, as this collection seeks to show, the possibility for contributions in both spheres is not only possible but also crucial for maintaining the transition from conflict to non-conflict society and entrenching the non-conflict attitudes to support such transformation. To view loyalists as little more than criminals is to overlook the importance of loyalism in the transition process and risks ignoring the influence of communities who have the ability to reactivate conflict. This by itself is reason enough to take loyalists seriously and not exclude them from the wider social benefits of peace and stability.

In examining the meaning and nature of loyalism today this book sets out interrogate history, identity and change within loyalism since the peace process took hold (McAuley 2004c) and gained cross-party support with the Good Friday Agreement (GFA) of 1998. However, in order to understand identity and its complexity it is also necessary to account for the historical influences and precedents of identity formation and construction.

The opening two chapters of the book do this by exploring relations between British, Ulster and Irish identity influences on the loyalist consciousness. In Chapter 1, Thomas Hennessey brings to light variations in regional, national and patriotic points of identity and moves us towards comprehending the loyalist condition as infused by clusters of regional and national identities. Looking at the connection between an allegiance to notions of patriotism, Irishness and Britishness as factors, which shape the loyalist imagination, Hennessey opens the book with a direct challenge to any preconceived idea that loyalism functions only as a reactive presence sustained by a single desire to protect the Union.

This is followed in Chapter 2 by Leigh-Ann Coffe's assessment of southern loyalists and their historical tendency (1921–37) to support more inclusive adaptations in loyalist identity. Here, Coffe explores shifts in political ties between Britain and Britishness and highlights the relationship which came to shape comprehension of both British values and the Free State. What this chapter clearly reveals is an historical dimension within loyalism in Ireland, which sought to reconcile multiple influences rather than reinforce simplistic and narrow definitions of loyalist identity.

In Chapter 3, Roger Mac Ginty considers the significance of international actors on loyalism throughout the peace process. Looking at the negligible influence of America on loyalism Mac Ginty indicates that it is precisely because loyalism was not subject to international pressures (unlike republicanism) that it was able to show greater agency in the transition process. Importantly, Mac Ginty notes how dominant narratives of the peace process have tended to accept the role of international players rather too easily and uses the example of loyalism to challenge this assumption.

From here, in Chapter 4, Kevin Bean focuses on how loyalism has lost at the expense of the growing republican project. Bean considers how public images of sectarian loyalist action such as Drumcree and Holy Cross serve to reinforce nationalist prejudices, which have been used to support the credibility and importance of political republicanism. This chapter therefore raises important questions about how actions by loyalists reinforce imaginations about sectarianism, which their political opponents use and capitalize on.

Bean's analysis finds an interesting comparison with Chapter 5 where Graham Spencer interviews former Ulster Volunteer Force (UVF) volunteer, turned Progressive Unionist Party (PUP) representative and community worker Billy Hutchinson. In this chapter, Hutchinson talks about engagement in political negotiations, the politicization of paramilitary loyalism and the moves towards UVF transformation, which resulted in the decommissioning of UVF weapons in July 2009. Hutchinson details an important inside account of the transformation process, which the UVF has gone through and signifies the primacy of political engagement in order to bring about change.

Further elaboration of this area is dealt with in Chapter 6 where former trade union official, now clergyman, Chris Hudson describes his involvement with the UVF since the early 1990s. Hudson acted as an intermediary between the UVF and the Irish government throughout the most sensitive period of the peace process and provided an important link between the UVF leadership and the Irish. In providing a personal account of his involvement with the UVF and its transformation, Hudson produces a picture, which develops a number of points about transformation made by Hutchinson in the previous chapter. Hudson's narration brings us up to date with recent decommissioning and gives an invaluable explanation of how the UVF has slowly moved from paramilitarism to recognizing the value of politics and social change.

Chapter 7 by Lyndsey Harris looks at what she calls the 'strategic environment' of loyalist paramilitarism and how the leaderships of both the UVF and the UDA have taken variable approaches to transforming their paramilitary worlds. How strategy has been adopted and carried out requires examination of how loyalist leaderships have engaged with their respective communities and grassroots and Harris does this here.

In Chapter 8 by Aaron Edwards and Stephen Bloomer, attention is given to the internal dialogues and debates conducted inside the UVF and how the authors themselves assisted with the development of each. In highlighting the work of key UVF figures that drove the transformation process, Edwards and Bloomer also invite us to think about the role of the academic as facilitator to conflict transformation initiatives and in doing so invite us to more critically evaluate the function and use of academic enquiry in such a contentious and delicate area.

In Chapter 9, Andrew Mycock, Jonathan Tonge and James W. McAuley investigate relations between loyalism, Orangeism and Britishness. In particular, the authors are interested in how Britishness in this relationship draws on patterns of nationalism while absorbing civic and ethic values of exclusiveness. They explore how Orange identity interacts with British nationalism and outline how commonality and difference function through and within this nationalism.

Chapter 10 by Catherine McGlynn and James W. McAuley tackles the neglected study of the roles that women have played in the loyalist paramilitary campaign. Concluding that there is little evidence of gender equality in the involvement with paramilitary activity, McGlynn and McAuley explain how women come to be part of paramilitarism and they connect this relationship with the broader patriarchal nature of Northern Irish society and the social structure of the Protestant working-class communities within which paramilitarism is embedding.

The relationship with wider social forces also preoccupies Philip Orr, who in Chapter 11 reflects on the relationship between loyalism and the Protestant churches. Orr is very much concerned with the working class/ loyalist drift away from churches but also acknowledges the work carried out by loyalists who have a religious conviction. Looking at the involvement of transformative projects by individuals such as Billy Mitchell (former UVF volunteer and prisoner) Orr interrogates the tendency for Protestant self-criticism and views eroding support for the church as representative of an important underlying identity shift.

Having established historical and identity-based influences on loyalism the remaining chapters of the book address more specifically loyalist reactions and attitudes towards change and transformation. Chapter 12 looks at the problems faced by ex-prisoners trying to integrate with society and draws from the experiences of the ex-prisoner group, Ex-Prisoners Interpretative Centre (EPIC), and its director Tom Roberts to explain what those problems are and what needs to be done to help overcome them. Roberts highlights the marginalization and exclusion faced by ex-prisoners, who are themselves crucial for developing and facilitating conflict-prevention projects. Though acknowledged by the GFA, ex-prisoners remain dislocated from many of the social advantages and opportunities provided by peace and Roberts talks about the consequences of this dislocation.

An interesting comparison to this chapter is provided by Independent Monitoring Commission (IMC) Commissioner John Grieve, who in Chapter 13 explains how the IMC goes about monitoring paramilitarism as part of a remit to monitor the wider transition to democratic politics and institutional normalization in Northern Ireland. Grieve explains how the IMC operates and uses extracts from a series of Reports produced by the IMC to show how official monitoring functions as an important part of intelligence assessment in the process of change. The difference in style and presentation of this chapter is representative of the formal approach necessary while the IMC still exists and produces its Reports. Grieve's contribution is reflective of the IMC itself and the construction of the chapter must complement the legal obligations and expectations of the Commission while it continues to operate. The reader is asked to accept the rather formal nature of the chapter structure in this light. This is the first time the IMC has published such an explanation of how it monitors, recommends and Reports on areas such as paramilitarism. For this reason, it provides vital information about how such an official agency operates in the transformation of Northern Ireland. In Chapter 14, Neil Southern explores the relationship between political violence and decommissioning. Southern is interested in the extent to which republican violence has impacted on loyalism and concludes that the lack of a loyalist political project (and so political transformation and gains), along with the continued existence and actions of dissident republicans, made loyalist decommissioning especially difficult and that this was an act which should be recognized in that light.

Returning to this difficulty and the internal tensions and difficulties that persist, Chapter 15 consists of an interview between Graham Spencer and south Belfast UDA leader Jackie McDonald. In this interview McDonald explains the tensions and obstructions, which the UDA leadership have sought to address over recent years as well as arguing for a conclusive and decisive end to paramilitary structures and intent. Once a hardened paramilitary himself, McDonald now symbolizes the extent to which, at leadership level, there is a strategic aim to shift the UDA from a focus on community defence to a preoccupation with community politics.

The difficulty of shifting UDA consciousness from military to political strategy inevitably involves coping with new challenges for understanding memory, past loyalties and the cultivation of new organizational identity. The question of what role memory might play in a new Northern Ireland is elaborated in Chapter 16 by Kris Brown who seeks to frame memory as a space which allows for the re-negotiation of identity but only if related to the imperatives of the peace process. Notably, Brown explores how ceremony and murals tend to reinforce conflict identity and addresses this tendency in relation to the possibility of rethinking the function of memory not as dominated by the past but reoriented to the possibilities of the future.

In Chapter 17, Graham Spencer examines loyalist relations with the past by looking at loyalist attitudes towards apology, regret and change. Drawn from interviews with a number of loyalists, Spencer finds significant resistance to apology but a determination to avoid a return to conflict. This raises questions about the relationship between regret and lack of regret and points towards the need to think carefully about how open displays of regret can bring shame and other destructive consequences. Spencer suggests here that works towards peace, on the other hand, provide a far less contentious demonstration that attitudes have changed and perhaps have stronger and more significant impact for peace than a verbal articulation of sorrow.

Overall, this collection offers an introduction to the complexity of concerns, aspirations and influences, which effect loyalism in the post-GFA phase. The chapters challenge the simplistic, narrow, often depoliticized representations of loyalism that dominate the public mind and show loyalism not as a static monolith, but as a dynamic system of beliefs and attitudes that move with the flux of political and social change. Given the absence of rewards and gains that Sinn Féin has been able to acquire because of a very different reception within the wider republican–nationalist community, perhaps we might acknowledge that what loyalists have done is even more remarkable, while recognizing that this has come at the expense of unquantifiable levels of pain and suffering that have been both perpetrated and received.

Chapter 1
Historic Loyalism: Allegiance, Patriotism, Irishness and Britishness in Ireland

Thomas Hennessey

In Ireland the term 'loyalism' has been deployed in many guises – too many in fact. In the late twentieth century, by the climax of the conflict known as the Troubles, the term came to embody anyone who was part of, or linked with, Protestant organizations that used pro-state terrorism against Roman Catholics in Northern Ireland. But, less than a generation earlier, the term could equally apply to those who were 'traditional unionists' and opposed the reformist policies of Stormont governments. In this way the Reverend Dr Ian Paisley began political life as a 'loyalist' before entering the electoral mainstream and becoming a 'unionist'.

Yet, away from the definitional muddles of contemporary Northern Ireland, loyalism has been, at its core, a loyalty to the Crown: but, not necessarily the British Crown, rather the English Crown, the Irish Crown and, finally, the British Crown. This allegiance formed the basis the very of basis of not merely Irishness, but Englishness and, later, Britishness, itself. And, in Ireland, it was a key element of nationalist identity as well as unionist identity.

Loyalism in Irish history

The basis of historic loyalism is the fact that the Kingdom of Ireland and its successors (the United Kingdom of Great Britain and Ireland, and the United Kingdom of Great Britain and Northern Ireland) were, and are monarchical states. Republicanism was an alien form of government introduced into Ireland in 1798; indeed it was a minority sport until 1916.

In medieval terms it was the fact of being a kingdom, or some lesser, but effective unit of government, and of sharing a single law and government which promoted a sense of solidarity among its subjects and made them describe themselves as a people, irrespective of any relationship that can be traced between the medieval 'people' and its kingdom on the one hand, and the modern 'nation' on the other. The difficulty with avoiding 'national' in medieval contexts is the lack of an adjective derived from 'kingdom'.

Reynolds therefore adopts the word 'regnal' to describe that which pertained to a kingdom or kingdoms.

Reynolds describes race (largely translated *gens*) not as race, nor as tribe, but as 'a people'. A people might also serve as a neutral translation of both *natio* and *populus*. There is, argues Reynolds, no foundation for the belief that the word nation was seldom used in the middle ages except to describe the *nationes* into which university students were divided. Reynolds suggests that the term was used much more widely and often as a synonym for *gens*. Like a *gens* or *natio*, a *populus* was thought of as a community of custom, descent and government; a people.

One of the most important political developments for the centuries after 900 was that in many areas the loyalties of kingship came to coincide with the solidarities of supposed common descent and law. Kingdoms came to be seen as identical, not inevitably but sufficiently often, for the coincidence of the two to seem normal to contemporaries. People, that is, groups, which perceived themselves as communities of custom and descent, were perceived everywhere, at every level, interlocking and overlapping. Whenever a king maintained or increased his authority over legislation and law enforcement his subjects would tend to feel themselves to be a people: being under a single law meant being a people. The elements of descent myths, political and legal ideas, the prestige of kingship, and the practice of law and government, were gaining in force from their association with the others (Reynolds 1984: 260–1).

The English presence in Ireland was a result of military conquests. The legal authority of both the Irish executive and legislature was therefore based on powers delegated to them by the English crown. Sovereignty was not invested in an Irish crown in parliament but in the English crown as established by the Irish parliament in the 1541 act, which made Henry VIII King of Ireland (MacMillan 1993: 52).

The main constitutional struggles in Ireland, from the fifteenth century until the Act of Union, centred on whether or not the authority of the Anglo Irish executive, legislature and judiciary was independent of the English king in council, later of the King in parliament (Macmillan 1993: 28–30). The original source of legal authority exercised by the English Crown in Ireland derived from the papal bull Laudabiliter, in which the papacy granted Ireland to the English king, Henry II.

The creation of the title King of Ireland emphasized that the constitutional ties between the Crown and Ireland were sovereign in nature, that by making Ireland into a Kingdom, Henry VIII, and his successors, would be kings of all its inhabitants, and not just overlords of the English living in Ireland. The contract between ruler and people extended to all the individuals in Ireland, and enunciated the idea of a single Irish political community. The declaration also meant that the King was no longer merely overlord, with its implication that his title was subordinate and limited to the papacy on the basis of the twelfth-century grant (MacMillan 1993: 32–5).

When Irish Parliaments were established they too pledged their loyalty to the King of Ireland. Even, when following the Glorious Revolution in England and the deposing of King James II, of England, Scotland and Ireland, loyalism remained central to the Irish constitutional mind. Tory churchmen were reluctant to concede that resistance had occurred, and alleged by the behaviour of James, that James had released his subjects from their Oath of Allegiance. By assaulting life, property and the established religion, by disarming Protestants, by subjecting his crown to a foreign power, and by repealing the oath in the Jacobite Parliament of 1689, he had made it impossible, physically or morally, for his Irish subjects to discharge their obligations to him. He had thereby '*Unking'd* himself', according to Edward Wetenhall, Bishop of Cork, in a pamphlet endorsing submission to King William and Queen Mary.

As to the charge that they were rebels by guilt of association with their '*Bretheran in England*', Wetenhall had two answers. The first was that the doctrine of non-resistance could be disregarded by a nation, though not by private persons, and that James's flight had left Parliament with no option but to make provision for the regulation of the state, though he was unclear as to whether the English had actually engaged in rebellion in securing William's accession. The second answer was that in accepting William's protection both English and Irish Protestants had submitted to the victor in a just war. Irish Protestants were responsible neither for the cessation of allegiance to James nor for their rescue from tyranny by a foreign sovereign; the '*Prince of Orange* was no Subject, and therefore could not be *a rebel*', providently guided to wield the sword in 'a most just' cause. And in submitting to their deliverer they were in conformity with traditional Christian doctrine (Eccleshall 1993: 52–3).

The period, during the Protestant (Anglican) Ascendency, when the Irish Parliament gained legislative independence from the British Parliament, in 1782, was when the triumph of the Protestant Patriots reached its zenith. Protestant patriotism has been seen as representative of colonial *nationalism*. But it remained *loyalist* and was a form of *loyalist nationalism*. The Irish Parliament and its Irish subjects in the Irish Protestant nation remained a loyal part of the British Empire. The threat posed by their volunteer militia that forced a Britain, whose army was engaged in the war against the American rebels, to grant legislative independence, was not for separation from Britain but a demand for equal treatment with the sister kingdom.

As an address from the Volunteer Committees of Ulster and Connaught declared, the 'magnanimity of Britain, forgetting all ancient prejudices, has obliterated every source of jealousy, by an act of ample and unequivocal justice ... let us embrace our sister kingdom with renovated affection, and evince, that freedom is the strongest cement of union and liberality is the firmest basis of power'. The address went on to insist that the 'distinction between Englishmen and Irishmen is no more; we are now one people; we have but one interest, one cause, one enemy, one friend, and we trust that the same spirit which grasps at liberty and spurns at usurpation, is equally alive to the impressions of friendship, of kindness, and of generosity'.

The Volunteer Committees viewed with 'wonder and exultation' the tide of good fortune which had poured in upon the Irish nation and the empire at large, and called upon the Volunteers not to relax their military discipline for 'we now have a Constitution as well as property to defend against the common enemy' – France. The change in His Majesty's measures and ministers in Ireland seemed the 'harbinger of prosperity and indissoluble union to both kingdoms; and ... the people of this country will ... assure his Majesty, that while England adheres to the principle manifested in her present conduct, no constitutional question between the two nations will any longer exist, which can interrupt their harmony' (Seward 1801, 1: 261–5).

Following the French Revolution and, once more, war with France, Protestant dissenters – more often than not identified with the 1798 rebellion– pledged their loyalty 'humbly', trusted that their conduct would 'on every occasion' demonstrate 'our affectionate and steady attachment to the person, family, and government of our most gracious Sovereign' (Seward 1801, 3:125–6).

Unionism

In the aftermath of the 1798 rebellion the British Government resolved on a Union of Ireland and Great Britain into one United Kingdom. Irish supporters of the Union, such as Lord Castlereagh, rejected the argument that Union would reduce Ireland to the status of a colony. Castlereagh described a colony as something resembling the present state of Ireland, in 1800, enjoying a local legislature, but without any power entrusted to that legislature – for although the Irish Parliament had *legislative* power it did not have *executive* power – having no authority with respect to regulating the secession of the Crown, having an executive administered by the minister of another country, and not in any way responsible to the colony for his acts or his advice.

Nor, Castlereagh pointed out, could an act of the Irish Lords or Commons pass into a law unless the Great Seal of England be affixed to it. And Castlereagh warned that the Protestant interest, without Union, would face 'the Catholic, relying on the argument of physical force, who would Endeavour to assert his claims against the establishment of a minority, and there appeared to be no hope of a termination to distrust, jealously and alarm'.

But, according to Castlereagh, the Union would allow the Protestant to feel secure on the broad basis of an Imperial establishment, where his property would have due weight and the mass of the Protestant population would include him. The cause of distrust being removed, the claims of the Catholic might be temperately heard and calmly discussed before an impartial tribunal, the Imperial Parliament, which would decide on the question divested of the local circumstances which served to irritate and inflame (*Parliamentary Register* 5/6 February 1800: 26).

The sectarian attacks on Protestants by Catholics, in southern parts of the Kingdom, made Union with Britain more appealing to members of the Church of Ireland than ever before. Despite the controversy over how reluctant Irish MPs were persuaded, or bribed, to vote for the Union, in ideological terms it was possible for Irish Protestants to adopt, psychologically, to incorporation within the United Kingdom of Great Britain and Ireland because, apart from the loss of their Parliament, the building blocks of the Union remained similar to those that constituted the Kingdom of Ireland: allegiance to the Crown; a willing membership of the British Empire; and protection of the Protestant interest. Just as in previous British wars, the Protestant Irish had taken their part.

In 1797, James McCay, a Church of Ireland clergyman who had witnessed the horrors of the Rebellion, realized that the security of Protestant Ireland rested upon the power of Great Britain:

> But now, by dropping all national distinction, on both sides, we have obtained our purpose indeed – one of the greatest, and most independent countries in the world, has been made still greater, and more independent – and we have been raised with her into the same – dignified condition.
>
> We were low and inconsiderable, as a distinct nation; and could have no possible honour as such, that we did not derive from our great friend and protectrix; but now we may be truly said to be our own protector; the Armies of Great Britain are now our Armies – her Nay – is our Navy – and her Glory is directly ours. (McCay 1803: 13–15)

In his *Address to the People of Ireland*, the Reverend James Gordon, author of *The Rebellion in Ireland*, warned his readers that while France was endeavouring to subdue all Europe under her power, and while Ireland's government was engaged in war to prevent this conquest, many among the people had entered into a conspiracy with the French to make them masters of the country: 'I can see no reason why you should not be more attached in national affection to the English than the French, for the history of your country informs you that you are mostly of the same blood as the English' (Gordon 1803: 3–13).

On St Patrick's Day 1803, the year of a further rebellion, in a speech to the Benevolent Society of St Patrick, the Earl of Moria called on the people of

Ireland to embrace the new national sentiment which should spring from the Union: 'Only one sentiment ought now to prevail throughout the whole Empire, that of forgetting and forgiving all past quarrels, of dropping all distinctions, except those of English, Welch, Scotch, and Irish, which ought always to exist, not as grounds of jealously, but as the division of an army into different regiments tends to excite emulation, affords opportunities of distinguishing different kinds of merit, and marking more distinctly to whom just rewards belong' (Earl of Moria 1803: 20–2).

And the new unionists had their own heroes in the war against the French, witness the poem, by J. Bertridge Clarke, in 1817, commemorating the death of the Right Hononrable John Hilpot Curran, who had fought with his fellow Irishman in the decisive battle of the Napoleonic War:

And shall I pass without the tribute due, the pride of Earth, the Lord of Waterloo?

Green Erin's eagle, Freedom's strongest shield, Champion of Truth, and star of each red field;

Valour's proud boast, and Glory's brightest sun, Th' illustrious, high, unconquer'd Wellington! Whose honors, earth's too bounded to contain;

Who, from the green sea to the western main, Made Britain's lion of monarch of each plain;

Who tore the vulture-eagle from his height, And broke his bloody beak, and smote him in his flight;

For the proud bird his noble nature lost, When his wide wing led on Gauls impious host. (Clarke 1817: 20–1)

Ireland was now an integral part of the British imperial and military experience. Yet, for Protestants, the reality of being a minority in a Catholic populated country was never far away. This was particularly acute as Daniel O'Connell led his campaign, based upon the Roman Catholic Church mobilizing its peasantry, behind his campaign to repeal the Union. This led, in October 1843, *The Northern Whig* to report the contents of a rough draft of a petition which it received from a 'very influential quarter', to be submitted for signature in the North if the repeal agitation proceeded much further.

The *Whig* further noted that Northerners 'are far more intimately connected, in their various interests, with the people of the neighbouring shores of England and Scotland, than they are with the South and South-West of Ireland'. The North, or Ulster, should either, in the event of Repeal taking place, be erected into a separate kingdom, having a separate legislature; or it should be continued in connection with England and Scotland, though the rest of Ireland were to have its own parliament; the Whig preferred the latter of the two plans.

This petition is probably the first claim to partition the island of Ireland, by Irish Protestants not British politicians, in the event of self-government being granted to the Catholic majority:

Outline of a Petition the Queen.

That your petitioners are not, nor ever have been, advocates of the Repeal of the Union, which they deprecate, as destructive to both countries.

They do no anticipate it as likely to take place.

Nevertheless, if any circumstances do induce your Majesty and Parliament to grant such a measure, we earnestly entreat that Ireland may be constituted not one, but two distinct kingdoms, with Belfast as the capital of the Northern division of the island.

Besides, we observe that the advocates of Repeal urge the distinction of the Saxon and Celtic races, as reason for disunion.

We are a people in a great measure of a Saxon race, or largely inter-mixed with that race; and we, therefore, humbly submit, that those who advocate on such grounds, a separation from Great Britain, cannot wish, or, at least, fairly demand, that the new kingdom they propose to form should contain subjects of a race which they profess to regard with hos-tile jealously.

We ourselves, indeed, disavow and deprecate any such hostile feelings, as characteristic of barbarians and heathens, rather civilized and Christian nations. We believe, that both Great Britain and Ireland are inhabited by a mixed race, descended from Saxons, Danes, Normans, Milesans, and others, mingled with the descendants of various Celtic tribes, as hostile to each other, in former days as to any foreign invaders.

We wish to see the difference of race, and former contests, thence aris-ing, to be practically buried in oblivion;

And we desire to continue as fellow subjects with all the inhabitants of the British Isles.

But we deprecate being formed into a distinct kingdom of Ireland, when a large proportion of the inhabitants of this island have been trained to regard us with unfriendly feelings as aliens and intruders.

Whether these, and other reasons for our wish, appear to anyone sat-isfactory or not, we humbly submit that, if a separate Legislature be con-ceded to a certain portion of the subjects of the United Empire, on the sole ground that such is their earnest wish, it would be unreasonable not to concede the same, on the same ground, to another portion.

We beg leave again to declare our aversion to any dissolution of the Union, and our sincere hope that it may never take place.

We petition for the erection of the kingdom of the North of Ireland (or Ulster), merely as the less of two evils, on the supposition (we trust most improbable), of the impossibility of maintaining the existing Union. (*Northern Whig* 17 October 1843)

Nationalist loyalism

At this point it well to consider that loyalty to the Crown and Ireland's place within an imperial system was not solely the preserve of unionists: nationalists too saw self-government in Ireland within loyalist terms and within an imperial system. Republicanism within nationalism was the dream of a minority. Daniel O'Connell, who campaigned to repeal the Union, wanted the restoration of the Kingdom of Ireland not an Irish Republic.

Charles Stewart Parnell , despite saying one thing to his Irish American financers and another to the House of Commons, seems to have settled for the *realpolitik* of Home Rule in his later career. He certainly became the leader of a movement that, after his death, was true to the dream of a self-governing Ireland not merely within the Empire but *within* the Union with Britain. By the eve of the First World War, the leadership of the Home Rule movement realized that they had to appease not only British unionists but also Irish unionists too to secure Home Rule and a united Ireland – under the Crown.

John Redmond, the leader of the Home Rule movement, described the Irish Unionist Party's charge that nationalists were inherently disloyal to the Crown and Empire as the 'most dishonest and ridiculous of all cries'. Redmond defined loyalty as loyalty to one's motherland; to a free constitution; to a government, which protected industry, property, lives and liberty; to a monarchy, which was the guarantee of such a constitution and government; and to a sovereign who, in his person, was its head and representative.

Redmond also asked if Englishmen remembered Ireland's past suffering through its loyalty to British sovereigns. Under King James I, the Catholic Irish fully submitted to the 'Gaelic King' who came to the English throne; they were rewarded by 'persecution, proscription, and whole-sale plunder'. When his son, King Charles I, came to the throne, English and Scottish disaffection drove the King from the throne and saw him beheaded; Catholic Irishmen did not rebel, but took to the field for him, and as a result, suffered slaughter and plunder. When King James II succeeded to the throne, again it was the English who rebelled and the Catholic Irish who stood loyal, once more suffering the penalty of confiscation and persecution (Redmond 1912a: 33–4).

Replying to the unionist inquiry as to why Irish patriotism had not developed in the same manner within the Union as Scotland's had, Redmond answered that Scotland, in contrast to Ireland, had been dealt with in a spirit of reasoned consideration. When the Scottish and English Crowns were united under the Stuarts, Scotland provided the monarch; in Ireland, Britain was engaging in an attempt to extirpate all traces of the old kingly houses, and even of the people themselves (Redmond 1912b).

Redmond had summed up the aspirational loyalty which home rulers sought to embrace, in August 1902, on the occasion of the coronation of

King Edward VII. Then he had stated that, in Ireland, Edward VII 'was not a Constitutional Monarch'. No English monarch had been a Constitutional Monarch of Ireland since the Union; the Irish Constitution was suspended (*Nationality* 19 May 1917). Redmond pointed out that when Queen Victoria ascended the throne Canadians were in armed rebellion against England; but fifty years on, the grant of Canadian home rule made Englishmen hardly believe that Canada was ever disaffected.

In Canada, as Ireland, Redmond accepted there were two races and religions; but the concession of freedom produced complete loyalty, and Canada, divided only by an imaginary line from the greatest republic in the world, had not moved towards separation from Britain because of the tie of free imperial association (Irish Press Agency, n.d.) Thus, Irish Catholics and nationalists were not inherently disloyal; they merely wanted to take their just place in the Empire argued Redmond.

This aspirational and conditional nationalist loyalism even extended to the founder of Sinn Féin, Arthur Griffith. He wished to see the dissolution of the United Kingdom of Great Britain and Ireland, and the restoration of the Kingdom of Ireland and a separate Kingdom of Great Britain. Dual Monarchy, as this policy was called, accepted that it had been a feature of Irish society that Irishmen had yielded allegiance to kings even when these monarchs had little claim to their respect and affection; therefore, republican ideals were not indigenous to Ireland but had been imported from France and America.

Two sovereign states might, he argued, be subject to the same prince without any dependence of the one on the other and each retaining its free sovereign right as a nation. The King of England might be 'elected' as King of Ireland by the free will of the Irish people who would yield him loyalty as King of Ireland not as King of England. This did not admit the 'preposterous' position advocated by some nationalists that the King of England under the Union was *de facto* and *de jure* King of Ireland (*Sinn Féin* 20 April 2007).

The Kingdom of Ireland had been a separate kingdom from that of the Kingdom of Great Britain, and its establishment would have ended the Empire's status as a single realm. The First Article of the Act of Union had declared that the 'said Kingdoms of Great Britain and Ireland, shall ... be ... for ever after, be united into one Kingdom, by the name of the United Kingdom of Great Britain and Ireland'.

The restoration of the Kingdom of Ireland would create a situation where there would be *two* crowns in the Empire, rather than one common Crown. Therefore the British King could, as he had been before the Anglo-Irish Union, be the King of Great Britain, and the King of Ireland *separately*, although the same person. This would create the separate status of British subject and Irish subject within a 'Brito-Hibernian' Empire.

The Irish would therefore be a separate nationality from Britons, Canadians, New Zealanders, Australians and South Africans, who would continue to constitute British subjects owing allegiance to the British King. For Griffith, a Briton was a native of England, Scotland or Wales. Thus, there were 4 million British subjects in Ireland and 400 million British subjects in India, but there were no Britons in either country outside the governors and speculative immigrants.

Griffith was distinguishing between the legal sense of Britishness and the emotional or nationalistic definition of Britishness. He claimed that the phrase *Civis Britannicus sum* could not be *Anglicanus* without excluding Scotland and Wales, nor could it be *Britannicus* without excluding Ireland. Griffith marked in this phrase the recognition of English, Scots and Welsh people as British citizens and the relegation of 'that part of the United Kingdom called Ireland' to the status of British subjects.

For Griffith, the phrase implied that the British Empire was Britain's possession and that Britain and Ireland were distinct entities, the one imperial ruler, the other subject nation. The kingdom was the United Kingdom of Great Britain and Ireland, but the empire was not the Empire of Great Britain and Ireland but the British Empire. Turning to his analysis of Dual Monarchy, Griffith considered the title of 'Austrian Empire' to have been a denial of Hungary, and the title British Empire to be a denial of Ireland. He noted that there was no longer an Austrian Empire but an 'Austro-Hungarian' Empire while there remained a British Empire, not a 'Brito-Hibernian Empire'.

Griffith argued that in the nineteenth century there had been no 'Hungarian Imperialists' to boast that they were citizens of the Austrian Empire, and that while the British Empire existed the majority of Irishmen would not boast that they were citizens of it; their instinct, if not their reason, would inform them that such a boast was a denial of their country's right and dignity. Many might be charmed by the idea of equal partnership with Britain in the Empire, but none, he believed, would swap the name of Irishman for that of British subject. An acceptance of the British Empire was an acceptance of English ascendancy (*Irish Review* August 1911: 269–70).

Griffith further insisted that until those in Ireland who cherished the imperial idea translated it into 'Hiberno-British' instead of 'British', they would find no audience outside the ranks of those who had consistently identified the Empire with Irish nationalist suppression. When imperialists were prepared to so translate their vision Griffith predicted that they would find nationalist Ireland willing to discuss their views (*Irish Review* August 1911: 272).

Partition

The basic difference, and a wide one, was that Irish unionists already possessed an unconditional loyalty to the Crown and the British national/imperial identity. They threatened loyalist rebellion not against the Crown itself but officers of the Crown in Parliament: in 1912 this was the Liberal

Government that, they believed, sought to expel them from the British national/imperial community. Unionists perceived their membership within the United Kingdom as an inalienable and inherited right, which no *government* had the authority to cast away. The *Belfast News Letter* explained how:

> Unionists held ... that their claim to remain under ... the Imperial Parliament is an inalienable right of their citizenship which no Government of any time has the right to deprive them of. There need be no mistake about this, it is the position which Ulster has taken up all along; it is the heart and the essence of what has come to be called the Ulster Question. It goes deeper and further than any question of what Party is in power ... It is indeed fundamental, for it goes right down to the principle of nationhood.
>
> In other words, Ulster's resistance to Home Rule is founded upon recognition of and loyalty to the nationhood of the United Kingdom. Our loyalty to that nationhood we hold in common with people of England ... Scotland and Wales, and it cannot be denied that Ulster has given the best of her sons to its service. It makes us none the less patriotic Irishmen any more than it does Englishmen and Scotsmen to their countries.
>
> Can the same be said for Irish nationalists? Most certainly it cannot. Their conception of nationality is opposed to ours both in object and in spirit; it is confined to Ireland alone, and it is hostile to the unity of the Kingdom, therefore it is hostile to the conception of nationhood to which we are loyal. Therein lies the right of Ulster to resist ... since it would be a severance against their will of a loyal people from their nationhood, which no Government has the right to do. (*Belfast News Letter* 19 September 1912)

There was no clearer articulation of how, by the eve of the Great War, unionist loyalism encompassed both allegiance to the Crown and allegiance to idea of Britishness in the form of a British national/imperial identity. In contrast, one of the consequences of the Easter Rising and the revamped Sinn Féin that emerged from it was the ending of the centuries-old association of nationalism with loyalty to the Crown.

In its place came republicanism, and with it, the end of any understanding that unionists and nationalists could reach an ambiguous compromise in their Britishness and Irishness, through subjectship and allegiance to the Crown. Republicanism meant that there could only be Irish citizens in the emerging Irish republic (certainly from the 1930s onwards). And so, in the partitioned North, Ulster unionists could triumphantly proclaim that nationalists were disloyal all along; as the former already knew.

As Sir James Craig, the first Prime Minister of Northern Ireland, told his devolved Parliament, the

> South have decided that they can do better separated from the great Mother of the Empire, that they can do better by isolating themselves and becoming what they call a Free State. We, on the other hand, say, No. We can do better for ourselves and for the Empire by maintaining the closest connection between Great Britain and ourselves – a connection which has served us in the past and has also served our colonies in the past, that has served the whole of the vast Dominions over which His Majesty rules ... and I pray God as long as I have anything to do with it we shall remain steadfast in the true faith. (*Northern Ireland House of Commons Debates*, 2: 1149)

The sectarian conflict that accompanied the birth of Northern Ireland led Sir Edward Carson to deny that the intercommunal violence was motivated on the Protestant side by anti-Catholicism, but was directed against: 'Sinn Féiners, who are engaged in a conspiracy in Ireland to overthrow the authority of the King and bring about secession from the British Government' (*Weekly Northern Weekly*, 30 October 1920). However, the Ulster Unionist MP, Major O'Neill, while accepting that Sinn Féin was not a religious organization, recognized that a less-sophisticated definition of what constituted a 'rebel' was used by many ordinary unionists, when he argued that the 'ordinary working class Protestant' could not be blamed for thinking that Sinn Féin was a largely Roman Catholic movement.

The reason why this perception was so strong among many Ulster Protestants was the belief that 'in so far as the Sinn Féiners profess any religion at all they are essentially people of the Roman Catholic faith', and 'never on one occasion have the leaders of the Roman Catholic Church taken any steps to denounce the outrages and murders which the Sinn Féin organization is carrying on' (*House of Commons Debates*, 132: 1111, 26 December 1920).

The republicanism that dominated nationalism made it easier for Ulster Protestants to equate disloyalty with Roman Catholicism. Sir Basil Brooke urged 'loyalists' therefore, wherever possible, to employ good Protestant lads and lassies' on the basis that there was 'a Catholic political party' whose 'one plank in their platform' was 'the destruction of Ulster as a unit and as a constitution'. Brooke defined a 'disloyal man' as a man who was scheming and plotting to destroy the country in which he lived; 'political Roman Catholics' (*Northern Ireland House of Commons Debates*, XVI, 1114–1120, 24 April 1934). As Craig declared on the outbreak of war in September 1939, the Irish Republican Army 'are the King's enemies' adding 'Can any punishment be too great for them?' (*Northern Ireland House of Commons Debates*, XXII: 1907, 4 September 1939).

The Troubles

In the contemporary political sense, 'loyalism' refers to those linked with Protestant paramilitaries. As early as 1971 this was spelt out quite clearly, as the Ulster Defence Association (UDA) sought to redefine the term 'loyalist', as opposed to 'unionist', because a loyalist was now seen as someone who was determined to do their 'utmost' to ensure the continued existence of the state, to safeguard his heritage and his way of life (*UDA News* 11: 6). Hence, the UDA initially chose the motto *Cedanta Arma Togae*, 'Law Before Violence', for the reason that:

> every UDA member considers that LAW properly functioning in a stable community is at all times preferable to a situation whereby LAW is subservient to the machinations of church or ... party'; [but the law was now] in disrepute in Northern Ireland because it does not exist in every rook and cranny of our land. (*UDA News* 11: 2)

To preserve law in Northern Ireland meant killing if necessary.

Beyond the simple, contemporary, classification of loyalism there is a deeper debate about its nature. Todd (1987) identifies two traditions within unionism in terms of their different ideological structures: the Ulster loyalist and Ulster British traditions. Ulster loyalism is defined in terms of its imagined community of northern Protestants while its secondary identification with Britain involves only a conditional loyalty. The Ulster British ideology, on the other hand, has a 'radically different' structure from Ulster loyalist ideology. The Ulster British imagined community is Greater Britain although there is a secondary regional identification with Northern Ireland.

Hennessey (2009: 359–60) on the other hand, suggests that Ulster Protestant identities are more complex than Todd's schema. Thus, an individual might possess a British and an Ulster identity: the emphasis, in terms of primary regional/national patriotism/identity, will vary according to the individual. Similarly, this will apply to an 'Irish British' or 'British Irish' identity; or indeed a 'British Northern Irish' identity and its inverse. From this one can argue that there are not, in fact, one, two, three, or no nations within the Ulster Protestant community, but clusters of regional and national identities; therefore one might say that, among Ulster Protestants there are three national consciousness, Irish, Ulster and British, alongside an Irish territorial patriotism, an Ulster/Northern Irish regional patriotism and a British state patriotism.

The commonality is Britishness. Thus, while loyalism, in its historic sense of loyalty to the Crown remains a potent expression of identity for unionists, it both complements and competes with Britishness. There are, indeed, different definitions of what is means to be British (such as loyalty to a Protestant Crown or loyalty to a British nation) among Ulster Protestants, but it is this Britishness that divides them from nationalists, a residual Irish national consciousness though no nationalism may be detectable among a minority of unionists. And this Britishness and unionism is an organic growth of centuries based upon loyalism to the Crown.

Chapter 2
Loyalism in Transition: Southern Loyalists and the Irish Free State, 1921–37

Leigh-Ann Coffey

In 1995 the former moderator of the Presbyterian Church in Ireland wrote a book entitled *A Precarious Belonging: Presbyterians and the Conflict in Ireland*. John Dunlop's primary intention was to provide information on the history and the culture of the Presbyterian Church in Ireland, in order that the church's current position on the situation in Northern Ireland and the political views of its members might be better understood. Attempting to explain why Ulster Presbyterians, and northern Protestants in general, are so resistant to the idea of a united Ireland, Dunlop examines Protestant fears that they would be 'overwhelmed' in a society where the majority of the population subscribed to a Gaelic, Catholic culture.

As Dunlop demonstrates, these fears are not entirely without foundation. In the chapter which provides the book with its title, Dunlop details the decline of the Protestant minority in the South of Ireland, a 'steady hemorrhaging' of the population that began following the partitioning of the country and the subsequent establishment of an independent Irish Free State under the terms of the 1921 Anglo-Irish Treaty (Dunlop 1995: 63–72). Emigration and pressure to convert to Catholicism are identified as two key factors that contributed to the rapid fall in Protestant numbers. Although Dunlop concludes that conditions for Southern Presbyterians have lately improved, his description of their recent situation, as isolated congregations cut off from the wider Presbyterian community in Ireland, small numbers of Presbyterian families worshipping in churches which once held hundreds, a minority reluctant to become involved in public affairs for fear of drawing attention to itself, inspires little confidence for the future.

That the fate of the Southern Protestants would have profound implications for relations between northern and Southern Irish states was recognized almost immediately after partition. For Free State politicians such as Arthur Griffith and Kevin O'Higgins, it was imperative that Southern Protestants were welcomed into the new Irish state to demonstrate that nationalists could govern fairly and overcome many of the long-standing divisions within Irish society (White 1975: 86, 91).

These divisions were rooted not only in religious differences but also political loyalties and cultural identities. Protestants had long been associated with British rule in Ireland and following the Irish revolution those in the South struggled to reconcile their British loyalties with their citizenship in the Irish Free State. It was hoped by some nationalists that the successful integration of Southern loyalists might convince the northern unionist population that loyalism was compatible with the treaty settlement, helping to bring about an end to partition. Yet the loyalist population did not flourish in the Free State, and as Dunlop has suggested, Ulster unionists have since used the decline of Southern loyalism as a cautionary tale, one that justifies their unwillingness to accept a united Ireland.

With both contemporaries and later scholars inclined to concentrate on the wider implications of the decline of Southern loyalism, the Southern loyalist community has rarely been considered on its own terms. For example, recent scholarship regarding the experiences of Southern loyalists during the revolution has been primarily concerned as to whether or not republican violence of this period can be classed as sectarian, with the focus on IRA motives and the nature of British counter insurgency tactics (Borgonovo 2007; Hart 1999; Howe 2006).

As a result Southern loyalists are generally portrayed as either passive victims of events beyond their control or agents of the British regime, and the assumption remains that the decline of Southern loyalism following the establishment of the Free State was inevitable. Yet sources originating from loyalists themselves suggest that they were in fact actively committed to ensuring the survival of both their community and their loyalty to the British connection in the years after 1921. A better understanding of how the Southern loyalist community reacted to a period of profound political and social change is required before it can be determined if their experiences have any relevance for the current situation in Ireland.

What follows is a brief examination of the Southern loyalist community in the first two decades after partition, a consideration of how Southern loyalists attempted to redefine their identity, community and beliefs in order to accommodate the realities of the treaty settlement.

The Southern loyalist community

Community is central to loyalty. With the emergence of nation states, governments began to rely on a sense of community to generate and validate loyalty to the state; one's political allegiance was reinforced through a sense of belonging to a national community, which shared a constructed history and culture. Southern loyalism as it existed in 1921 was a complex affair, reflecting both the local and transnational loyalties of Southern loyalists.

As Southern loyalism did not correspond with a political state per se and was therefore not supported by any form of government, the loyalist community assumed a greater role in determining its character. However, identifying members of the loyalist community in the Irish Free State can be challenging, and it is likewise difficult to analyse relations within the Southern loyalist population. Even the term 'community' is somewhat problematic when applied to loyalists in the Free State, for it implies a degree of unity between individuals that did not always exist.

Traditionally studies of Irish loyalism have focused on the north of Ireland, where loyalists formed a majority of the population and had from an early period clearly articulated their views on the nature of their loyalty and the boundaries of their community. By contrast the loyalist minority in the Southern provinces tended to be less publicly outspoken and their community appeared less cohesive. As a result of these characteristics, the Southern loyalist community came to be largely defined by the impressions of others.

Throughout the late nineteenth and early twentieth centuries, nationalists portrayed Southern loyalists as overwhelmingly Protestant, conservative and members of the landed upper classes. The loyalist community was generally described as a 'foreign garrison' whose presence in Ireland was intended to bolster the British regime; as such, loyalists supposedly felt little connection with Ireland or 'the Irish people', and it was assumed that they supported British rule largely because their privileged positions in Ireland were dependent on the continuation of the Union (Brown 1985: 106).

Such views are not entirely inaccurate. The overwhelming majority of loyalists were Protestants and the Protestant population had long controlled Irish politics and society. Even after the revolution, Protestants generally retained a pronounced economic advantage. Protestant farmers, for example, continued to hold on average larger farms than did their Catholic counterparts, and Protestants were also disproportionately represented among the professions (Bowen 1983: 79).

In contrast with Ulster, where loyalism was equally represented at all levels of society, Southern loyalism at the time of the revolution was dominated by the landed gentry (Buckland 1972: xiv–xv). Status was carefully observed within loyalist society, and it is clear that the gentry assumed paternalistic leadership roles both during and after the revolution; Lord Midleton, for example, was instrumental in representing loyalists' interests during the negotiations which led to the AngloIrish Treaty and the establishment of the Irish Free State, while the *Irish Times* made much of the fact that among those representing the 'ex-unionist' community in the first Free State Senate were: 'seven peers; a dowager countess; five baronets and knights' (Buckland 1972: 223–71; *Irish Times*, 7 December 1922).

Former Irish landlords were strong supporters of the relief associations created after the revolution to aid loyalists in the Free State, and they also provided guidance for those seeking employment or making arrangements to emigrate (*Church of Ireland Gazette,* 10 July 1936). The gentry were highly valued within the loyalist community largely because of their connections with Britain and the empire; many owned British estates and had been educated in British schools, while Irish peers were admired for their involvement in British and Imperial political affairs.

The tendency of both contemporaries and scholars to focus on the role of the landed gentry within Southern loyalism, however, has resulted in a distorted impression of the loyalist community in the Free State. While it cannot be denied that Southern loyalism was closely tied to the upper classes, sources from the loyalist community suggest that the gentry's dominance of Southern loyalism was declining in the post-independent period. Their connections with Britain were valued and respected by other loyalists, but these same ties also generated considerable resentment.

It was acknowledged, for example, that the gentry's education, familial connections and 'special capabilities' meant that they were more likely to find opportunities abroad, but Southern loyalists who left Ireland after the revolution were open to criticism for not contributing to their community or their country (*Church of Ireland Gazette,* 24 October 1920; 9 May 1924; 17 April 1925). As were all those who had traditionally relied on land or connections with Britain for their livelihoods, the Southern gentry were preoccupied in the years following the establishment of the Free State with their own economic survival.

While the landed elite would always maintain a special position within the Southern loyalist community, evidence suggests that as early as the late 1920s other elements within the community were gaining greater prominence. The professional and middle classes in particular emerged from the shadow of the gentry to provide more energetic, pragmatic leadership. An article in the *Church of Ireland Gazette* in February 1925 noted the disappearance of the landlord from Free State economic and social life, and concluded that the Church and its community would become increasingly dependent upon the substantial farmer, the businessman, the merchant and those with professional training (*Church of Ireland Gazette,* 13 February 1925).

Lawyers, physicians and clergymen worked alongside the gentry to provide support for loyalists who had suffered during the revolution, and were frequently responsible for bringing cases of hardship to the notice of loyalist relief associations. The growing importance of the business and professional classes had political ramifications for the Southern loyalist community. It has been suggested that individuals with business interests were more likely to co-operate with the new Irish regime in the hopes that it would establish a degree of stability, and prominent businessmen and professionals also urged their fellow loyalists to support *Cumann na nGaedheal* during Free State elections, arguing that a party which was concerned with business interests was best for the loyalist community (Brown 1985: 109; *Church of Ireland Gazette*, 3 August 1923).

Other groups within the Southern loyalist community also came to play significant roles in maintaining Southern loyalism after independence, although they have received little attention from scholars. Lower class loyalists, for example, were not numerous and left few records of their existence, and yet the loyalism of small farmers and urban labourers was a source of inspiration and encouragement for others in the community. Even prior to the revolution, wealth was not a precondition for loyalism; the loyalty of lower middle-class Protestants in early twentieth-century Dublin has been described by Jack White, who concluded that 'patriotism ... was the common – indeed the obligatory – attitude of their religious and social group' (White 1975: 57).

It is unlikely that such loyalty died away immediately after the creation of the Free State, despite the numerous pressures faced by the lower classes to conform to the views of their nationalist neighbours. The plight of its most vulnerable members provided a cause around which the entire loyalist population could rally. The loyalist press made much of the social pressures and financial hardships faced by small rural loyalists, who were praised for upholding the British connection in less civilized regions of Ireland (*Church of Ireland Gazette*, 21 September 1928).

Loyalists from different backgrounds and from different regions of Ireland joined together to provide support for those who had suffered losses during the revolution or who found themselves ostracized in a nationalist Irish state. Neighbours helped to replace property that had been stolen or destroyed, and offered shelter and support to fellow loyalists who found themselves homeless or boycotted. Members of the Church of Ireland were encouraged to make donations to support poor rural Protestant parishes. Relief associations, such as the 'Southern Irish Loyalist Relief Association' and the 'Irish Claims Compensation Association', were organized and maintained by loyalists in London and Dublin. These organizations were heavily involved in publicizing cases of hardship that existed in the Free State and were instrumental in arranging for compensation to be paid to Irish loyalists.

The Southern Irish loyalist community was not limited to those living within the Free State. Although reliable figures are not available, it is clear that large numbers of loyalists left Southern Ireland during the revolution and its aftermath. Some fled to escape the violence, some left out of principle, and many chose to emigrate in order to avoid the economic and social problems that beset the new state. Loyalist migration is generally mentioned only in passing to support the argument that Southern loyalism declined rapidly with the establishment of the Free State, and few attempts have been made to learn more about the destinations or experiences of loyalists abroad.

Sources originating from the community, however, suggest that loyalists outside of the Free State continued to play a role in the development of post-independence Southern loyalism. Loyalists living outside of the Free State supported the various campaigns to alleviate the suffering of distressed loyalists and pressured the British government to provide relief, both financial and otherwise, for those who had suffered during the revolution. The Irish Loyalist Imperial Federation, formed in 1934 to 'safeguard the constitutional rights and liberties of South Irish born loyalists', boasted of members in Canada, Australia, India, France, Belgium and throughout the African continent (*Notes from Ireland*, November 1934). Many Southern loyalist emigrants settled in England and the various Dominions, and thus represented for Free State loyalists a very tangible link with the rest of the British Empire.

The extent to which issues such as class, religion and geography threatened the survival of the Southern loyalist community needs to be acknowledged. These issues had long been a real danger to the unity of the community, and remained heavily influential in determining individual experiences in the Free State (Brown 1985: 109). Although similar divisions existed within Ulster unionism during the same period, the Southern community was more vulnerable due to the lack of strong leadership and its minority status within the Free State. However, it appears that Southern loyalists were largely able to overcome the effects of such divisive factors immediately following the revolution in their efforts to provide support for the more vulnerable members of their community.

Loyalists felt it was their duty to assist one another, which led to the establishment of numerous support networks, varying from informal ties between neighbours to organized relief associations such as the 'Southern Irish Loyalist Relief Association'. During this period many Southern loyalists also became more willing to question the traditional structure of the loyalist community; individuals from outside of the landed gentry began to play a more active role in the community, and there were many who felt that loyalty to the British connection was more important than shared cultural or religious identities.

Loyalism in the Free State

In the period immediately following the revolution, most loyalists who remained in the Free State struggled to express their acceptance of the treaty settlement without betraying their loyalty to Britain or downplaying their sense of British identity. Recognizing that there were few viable alternatives to the treaty, prominent figures such as the Earl of Midleton encouraged the loyalist community to support the settlement and to shift the principle focus of their allegiance from Britain to the Free State (*Irish Times*, 16 December 1921).

This was presented as a duty, with loyalists ' bound by their Christian vows' to support 'a lawfully constituted government', even if they could not bring themselves to 'love' the new state (*Church of Ireland*, 23 November 1923). In countless articles, letters and sermons, loyalty as an abstract concept was explored with reference to political theories and religious doctrines. After loyalty to God, it was argued that allegiance to one's country was the greatest loyalty of all (*Church of Ireland Gazette*, 21 September 1923). Although under the terms of the treaty they remained subjects of the British king and members of the British Commonwealth of Nations, loyalists were reminded that they were first and foremost Irish citizens and that their fate was now tied to that of the new state. Most loyalists could appreciate the logic behind such statements, but were initially reluctant to offer up more than token declarations of loyalty for the Free State in petitions and motions addressed to the government (*Irish Times*, 12 December 1921).

For many this was a period of reflection, in which they carefully examined their loyalty to Britain and considered whether Southern loyalism could be successfully adapted to meet the realities of the new Free State. 'It is all very well to say that this loyalty can be transferred' wrote one columnist, but:

> Loyalty is an affair of the heart, and it is not possible to force the heart to follow the head. Behind the old loyalty was a clear and definite scheme of things – an ideal – which does not lie within the new … There was the British ideal of justice, toleration, fair dealing, and the institutions which embodied that ideal – the sanity, sense of fact, and stability which informed them. (*Church of Ireland Gazette*, 21 September 1923)

As this statement from the *Gazette* suggests, loyalists in the Free State began to place more emphasis on values and principles that were seen as inherently 'British'. 'Loyalty' was the topic of a sermon preached on Armistice Day in 1923 by the Rev. G. A. Chamberlain, who asked: 'Now, when we speak of our loyalty to the Crown, or to England or to the Empire, what do we mean? Do we not mean loyalty to certain great principles in life for which these stand – justice, liberty, order, toleration? It is loyalty to an ideal and pride in the memories of a fine tradition. Well, can we not still be loyal to these high things?' (*Church of Ireland Gazette*, 23 November 1923).

The connection between 'Britishness' and these values was not always made so explicit, but terms such as 'democracy', 'freedom', 'fairness' and 'law and order' were consistently used in discussions regarding the legacy of British rule in Ireland and the more recent treatment of the Free State by Britain. Such British traits were frequently contrasted with the characteristics that loyalists associated with Irish republicanism. During the revolution the loyalist press accused *Dáil Éireann* of being undemocratic and its members of ignoring the will of the Irish people (*Irish Times*, 12 December 1921; 29 December 1921; 17 April 1922).

Loyalists believed that the violence of the civil war period was an inevitable outcome of the republican's rejection of all things British; while praising

Kevin O'Higgins for his tough stance on crime, the *Church of Ireland Gazette* added: 'Of recent years these two words, law and order, have come to be of little account in the Irish vocabulary', before suggesting wryly that they had been rejected by nationalists for being too closely associated with the British regime (*Church of Ireland Gazette*, 2 November 1923). By focusing on values they equated with Britishness, loyalists believed that they had found an acceptable means of maintaining their dual allegiance to the Free State and to the British connection. Such principles were respected in any civilized nation, they argued, and their adherence to these values would make them better citizens of the Free State.

The issue of religion was frequently raised in discussions regarding the values related to Britishness. As has already been established, there was a strong association between Protestantism and loyalism, with the majority of Southern loyalists belonging to the reformed faith. The Protestant churches in Ireland maintained a strong loyalist ethos and attending church services on a weekly basis became one of the few ways in which Southern Protestants could actively express their British identity in a communal setting in the years after the revolution.

The connection between Protestantism and loyalism was so firmly established that applicants to the second Irish Grants Committee, a committee appointed by the British government in 1926 to consider compensation claims from Southern Irish loyalists, frequently cited their Protestant religion when asked for their loyalist credentials (see PRO CO 762/15/163; CO 762/168/2876). Most Protestants in the Free State believed that the values they associated with Britishness were derived in part from their reformed faith, yet within the Southern Protestant population there was a surprising amount of debate regarding the exact relationship between religion and loyalism.

For some, Protestantism was a central element to loyalism. Such individuals drew heavily on an older anti-Catholic tradition that dated back to the reformation, in which it was argued that Catholics were unable to offer complete loyalty to any secular authority as their ultimate allegiance was owed to Rome (*Church of Ireland Gazette*, 13 May 1927). This tradition also suggested that values such as freedom of conscience – values strongly associated with the British state – were contrary to the teachings and hierarchical structure of the Catholic Church (*Irish Times*, 20 October 1928).

Yet it appears that others within the Southern loyalist community were uneasy with arguments that attempted to make loyalism the exclusive preserve of Protestants, or that suggested Catholics were unable to appreciate British values because of their faith. Prominent loyalists discouraged sectarian statements and presented the values associated with Britishness as having universal 'Christian' appeal, rather than pertaining to any one denomination or faith. Southern loyalism does not appear to have been rooted in any formal theological and doctrinal teachings (Bowen 1983: 110) and many loyalists were willing to overlook religious differences for those who had suffered during the revolution for their loyalty to Britain and who continued to support the remaining ties between the Free State and Britain.

The various relief associations established in the aftermath of the revolution received large numbers of claims from Catholics, and they prided themselves on providing aid to all deserving applicants regardless of their beliefs (Brennan 1994: 356). In 1926, members of the Church of Ireland began to call for the formation of a committee to investigate outrages that had occurred during the revolution in the hopes of obtaining compensation for the victims.

It was noted that not all victimized loyalists were members of the Church of Ireland or even Protestant, but the decision was made to investigate all outrages nonetheless: 'an injustice is an injustice, irrespective of the creed of the sufferer, and the Church of Ireland would be rendering a service to the State in helping any who have been oppressed to obtain freedom from oppression' (*Church of Ireland Gazette*, 24 Sept 1926). Tensions remained, however, between the loyalist ideal of a non-sectarian loyalty and the inescapable fact that this loyalty was directed towards what were commonly seen as Protestant values.

The treaty was initially accepted by much of the loyalist community because although it established an independent Irish state, it also upheld links to the king and empire, symbols that could provide a focus for a renewed Southern loyalism. The values to which loyalists attached so much importance were closely associated with British territories overseas, and the empire frequently featured in expressions of Southern loyalism.

According to the Southern loyalist interpretation, the empire was the product of Britain's historical mission to spread its values to less 'civilized' parts of the world. Loyalists took immense comfort in the idea that they were part of a worldwide community, which now shared British values and beliefs (McDowell 1997: 21). Loyalist involvement in the empire and its affairs provided a means of reaffirming their allegiance to British principles.

The war of 1914 to 1919, for example, had presented Irish loyalists with the ultimate opportunity to actively demonstrate their loyalty to British values, and later commemorations of the war dead were used to reinforce the connections between Ireland and the rest of the empire (Morris 2005: 155). At the dedication of the war memorial at St Andrews College in Dublin in 1921, the Provost of Trinity College stressed that 'the highest service of those who valued their Imperial citizenship was not inconsistent with being a good Irishman' (*Irish Times*, 1 December 1921).

Commemorations of war time service also accommodated attempts to create a more inclusive form of loyalism, as it was continually emphasized that Irishmen of all political and religious creeds had fought and died together in the service of king, country and empire. Just as the empire was seen to embody the values, which were at the core of Southern loyalism, the monarchy provided another tangible symbol of the British connection around which Southern loyalists believed they could rally without bringing their allegiance to the Free State into question.

Loyalists were fervent supporters of the royal family in the years after the revolution, with the loyalist press reporting on important royal occasions such as marriages and christenings in detail. Members of the Church of Ireland included the king in their weekly prayers, and special services were also held in times of crisis or celebration, such as the king's illness in 1928 and the Silver Jubilee in 1935. Rumours of a royal visit to the Free State persisted for years, and there was much excitement in 1932, when the first royal Christmas message was broadcasted on the radio (*Church of Ireland Gazette*, 30 December 1932).

For the loyalist community, the king was closely tied to the commonwealth. It was during this reign that the commonwealth had been established, and he quickly became a 'symbol of the Commonwealth's spiritual unity' (*Irish Times*, 6 May 1935). Through celebrations of royal occasions Southern loyalists were able to establish a sense of solidarity with the rest of the empire, and they took great comfort in knowing that they shared their loyalty to the king with others around the world. George V inspired particular affection, and was seen to embody the values associated with Britain not only in symbolic terms but also on a personal level. He was described as 'a father to his people' [and] 'among the hardest workers in the country, never sparing himself in his people's service', and he was praised for his 'simple dignity', sense of duty and 'direct and straightforward principles' (*Church of Ireland Gazette*, 30 December 1932; *Irish Times*, 2 July 1928; 1 February 1935).

It was often suggested that he had a special interest in Ireland and its people, and he was credited with doing much to end the Anglo-Irish conflict (*Irish Times*, 20 March 1925; 11 May 1935). A number of loyalists seeking compensation for losses sustained during the revolution wrote directly to the king in the belief that he would personally ensure that their applications received a fair hearing (PRO CO 762/14/131).

Many have seen the apparent willingness of Southern loyalists to support the Free State government and to redefine their loyalties as evidence that Southern loyalism disappeared quickly in the years after 1921. It is assumed that loyalists who could not adjust to the changes around them left the country, while those who remained (those with a 'stronger sense of Irishness', it is implied) abandoned their British loyalties in order to integrate into Free State society.

These assumptions reflect a misunderstanding of how Southern loyalism was reinterpreted in the post-revolutionary period. The issue of British emblems in the Irish Free State is revealing (Morris 2005). Shortly after the establishment of the Free State, the Irish government began to systematically remove all symbols associated with the former British regime. The Irish

Tricolour replaced the Union Jack, the King's head was removed from postage stamps and coins, and postage boxes were repainted green. By the late 1920s, 'A Soldier's Song' had replaced 'God Save the King' at state events, despite its lack of official status.

The government's campaign was occasionally overshadowed by unsanctioned republican activity. In the early 1930s, for example, the IRA destroyed statues of William III and George II in Dublin, removed the Royal Arms which decorated several former government buildings, and made threats against businesses and shops which displayed the Union Jack. The reaction of the loyalist community to these actions was decidedly mixed.

For some loyalists, the elimination of British symbols confirmed fears that the nationalist majority would not tolerate any remaining links between the Free State and Britain, but others became unlikely defenders of the Irish government. They argued that the government had to make some concessions to popular nationalism and pointed out that dominions within the commonwealth, such as Canada and Australia, had their own national symbols and anthems (*Church of Ireland Gazette*, 10 May 1929).

The reluctance of loyalists to unite as a community in order to publicly condemn the Free State's removal of British emblems, or later to speak out against the ongoing erosion of the treaty settlement, has allowed doubts to be cast on the strength of Southern loyalism. The loyalist discourse surrounding the Free State's growing republicanism is deserving of further consideration, however. The disappearance of British emblems in the Free State generated a variety of reactions, but the community was far more united in its denunciation of the manner in which these symbols were removed and the treaty gradually undone.

While it was possible for some to defend the new state's desire to establish its own national identity, loyalists were appalled that illegal republican activity went unpunished and that a series of Free State governments showed an utter disregard for a political settlement that had been agreed upon by both British and Irish representatives. They believed that British rule had left a legacy of good government and civil liberty, a legacy, which was to be safeguarded under the terms of the treaty.

These values now appeared to be under attack from a criminal element within Free State society, with the connivance of elected officials who were willing to use dishonest and unconstitutional means to fulfil their republican agenda. The Southern loyalist community might have rarely voiced its disapproval over government actions, but by practicing obedience to authority and general good citizenship, loyalists believed that they were in fact actively upholding Southern loyalism in a very public manner.

Interestingly, once loyalists had begun the process of reconciling their British loyalties with the existence of the Free State, their attitudes towards the new state became decidedly less hostile. Shortly after the end of the civil war loyalists were praising nationalist leaders for establishing a stable government, and they spoke optimistically of the Free State's potential to play a future role in international politics (*Church of Ireland Gazette*, 2 January 1925; 7 August 1925; *Irish Times*, 11 September 1923).

The confidence of many loyalists and loyal institutions was such that beginning in the mid-1920s they began to openly express a sense of 'Irishness'. The Church of Ireland, for example, began to emphasize its Irish origins, culminating in the year-long celebrations in 1932 to commemorate the fifteenth hundred anniversary of St. Patrick's arrival in Ireland (*Church of Ireland Gazette*, March 1932; Bowen, 1983: 109).

A flurry of family and parish histories were published, as were works on notable Protestant and loyalist figures who were portrayed first and foremost as great Irishmen. Loyalists might have been reacting to external pressures, attempting to cultivate an Irish identity in response to those who claimed they did not belong in Ireland, but evidence suggests that the community's confidence in both the Free State and in the position of their community was growing.

Loyalty to the Free State was expressed in a more willing and positive manner by the late 1920s; although it remained an 'obligation', many Southern loyalists acknowledged that for the most part the majority had not abused their powers (*Irish Times*, 11 February 1928). It should be noted, however, that loyalists tended to express loyalty to the country rather than to the political state, referring to personal, idealized versions of Ireland, and that this tendency became more pronounced as the Free State political culture became increasingly republican in nature (Dunlop 1995: 72).

Terence Brown, in a discussion of modern Ulster unionism, has warned against confusing the 'unionist sense of identity with the unionist sense of loyalty'. He goes on to suggest that 'the unionist is loyal to the British crown as the symbolic expression of the constitutional reality of the British state in whose commonwealth the citizen and subject feels his or her interests are most likely to be protected' (Brown 1991: 74–5, quoted in Dunlop 1995: 117–18).

A similar observation could likewise be made regarding Southern loyalists in the Free State. In its most basic form, Southern loyalism post-1921 consisted of an adherence to the political arrangement established under the treaty, in which the Free State gained a measure of self-government while remaining part of the empire. Southern loyalists supported the arrangement because they believed that the remaining ties with Britain would not only benefit the new state but would also safeguard the interests of the loyalist community. As symbols of both old and new ties between Ireland and Britain, the king and empire featured heavily in expressions of Southern loyalism.

Brown's observations regarding Ulster unionist identity also have relevance to the Southern loyalist situation. He describes Ulster unionist identity as a 'confused matter', one that until 1920 consisted of a broadly defined

Irishness existing within a British context. With partition, British and Irish identities began to polarize as Irishness became increasingly associated with a culture that was exclusively Catholic and Gaelic in nature. Unable and unwilling to accept such a limited definition of Irishness, Ulster unionists concentrated on cultivating a British identity for their community.

Southern loyalists likewise struggled in the aftermath of the revolution to maintain their pluralist identities. Although the Southern loyalist community has tended to be identified as both Irish and British, loyalists found it difficult to reconcile the two in a state where such identities were regarded by the rest of the population as incompatible.

It is important, however, to also recognize the differences between modern Ulster unionism and Southern loyalism in the Free State. Both are products of the conditions in which they developed. Following partition and for most of the twentieth century, Ulster unionists focused their efforts on the maintenance of the Union between Northern Ireland and the rest of Britain. This long-standing campaign has shaped both their political loyalties and their sense of identity.

The Southern loyalist community, on the other hand, lacked a definitive focus for their energies in the years after the revolution. Until 1921 the loyalist community had been primarily defined by its support for the political Union between Britain and Ireland. Once the treaty settlement had been established, loyalists were forced to redefine their loyalties and beliefs. Politically, they remained loyal to the king and empire, but the treaty settlement and conditions in the Free State prevented loyalists from fully engaging in British affairs.

As a minority, however, the loyalist community could not expect to play a significant role in the development of the Irish Free State. Recognizing that adherence to a narrowly defined loyalism would further limit their relevance in the Free State, Southern loyalists sought to create a loyalism that was less exclusive and that would prove to be adaptable to future political developments. This meant redefining the boundaries of their community and focusing on 'British' values, which were compatible with the existence of an independent Irish state.

Reassessing Southern loyalism proved to be a painful experience for loyalists in the Free State. However the transition was made easier by the fact that, unlike Brown's Ulster unionists, Southern loyalists did not always clearly distinguish between identity and loyalty. They were Irish loyalists, 'imperial Irish', law-abiding Irishmen and women who valued their 'imperial citizenship'; they identified as both British and Irish, and considered their loyalty to each state as a natural extension of their identity.

Southern loyalists readily acknowledged that their dual allegiances could prove problematic at times, but they also believed that neither the Free State nor Northern Ireland could move forward without reconciling the two dominant traditions that existed on the island of Ireland. Many loyalists hoped that their community might demonstrate that pluralist identities and allegiances were not only possible but also desirable, bringing about an end to partition.

Conclusions

Southern loyalists felt strongly about their allegiances and identities, and it was not uncommon for individuals from within the community to express personal and often contradictory opinions on contentious issues. Loyalists might be willing to act together on practical matters, such as relief efforts to support those who had suffered during the revolution, but there was less of a consensus as to how the community might best ensure the survival of Southern loyalism in the Free State.

Nevertheless, it does appear that there was support from at least a portion of the Southern loyalist community for a more inclusive and adaptable form of loyalism. This variant of Southern loyalism shifted the focus from political ties with Britain to 'Britishness', from allegiance to a political arrangement on a national scale to loyalty towards a local community. This is not to say that the Southern loyalists did not value the treaty settlement which maintained connections with Britain and the empire; many loyalists had first accepted the treaty solely because it legislated for the Free State's membership in the commonwealth and the king's continued role as head of state, and they viewed the growing republicanism of the 1930s with suspicion and fear.

By emphasizing 'British values', however, Southern loyalists were able to create a loyalism that had more relevance to their position within the Free State, allowing them to portray themselves as good citizens of both the Free State and of the empire. This was a loyalism designed to have widespread appeal, reflecting loyalist efforts to extend the boundaries of their community. It was open to personal interpretation and was therefore acceptable to most loyalists, regardless of their specific political views. The willingness of some loyalists to avoid religion as a measure of loyalty meant that the new Southern loyalism had the potential to spread beyond the traditional limits of the Southern loyalist community. In short, this was a loyalism that was designed to accommodate multiple identities and loyalties.

Loyalists in the Free State had reason to hope, at least for a brief period of time, that the decline of Southern loyalism was not inevitable. It is important to make a distinction between loyalism and unionism, as loyalists themselves stressed (*Irish Times*, 21 May 1921). Unionism had meant allegiance to the union, and with the creation of the Free State it ceased to have any role in the South, but loyalists continued to pledge their loyalty to the king and empire.

Loyalists considered this loyalty to be compatible with the terms of the treaty settlement, and some Southern loyalists believed that the rest of the

Irish community would eventually share this view as the Free State became more confident regarding its membership in the commonwealth. With the loyalist community committed to promoting the British connection, why then did Southern loyalism die out? In many ways, Southern loyalists were disadvantaged by circumstances over which they had little control. Their minority status and declining numbers, for example, made it difficult to sustain a sense of community.

There were also many problems of their own making. In their efforts to create a loyalism with broad appeal, loyalists tended to ignore differences within the community, and their emphasis on good citizenship and obedience did not encourage members of the community to challenge the growing republicanism of the Free State. Post-independence Southern loyalism placed a great deal of importance on the remaining political links with Britain as preserved by the treaty, and it could not survive once the treaty settlement had been undone.

By the late 1930s, the ' British values' that had come to characterize the loyalist community were increasingly associated with Protestantism rather than any political loyalties (Bowen 1983: 198). However, the ultimate failure of Southern loyalism should not detract from the efforts of some Southern loyalists to reconcile their multiple allegiances and identities. The decline of Southern loyalism is perhaps not as straightforward as is often assumed, and if the Southern loyalist experience is to be used as a cautionary tale for Ulster unionists, more needs to be done to understand the challenges faced by post-independence Southern loyalism and the reasons behind its ultimate demise.

Chapter 3
Post-Agreement Loyalism and the International Dimension

Roger Mac Ginty

A well-established theme in the dominant narrative of the Northern Ireland peace process has centred on the role of international actors (most notably the United States, and to a lesser extent the European Union) in encouraging the Northern Ireland parties to reach and implement a major peace accord. At different times and on different issues, the British and Irish governments, the Social Democratic and Labour Party, Sinn Féin, the Ulster unionists, and to a certain extent, the Democratic unionists all courted, and were courted by, the United States and other outside parties. Northern Ireland's loyalists, whether as a community or as represented by politico-militant groups, have largely been absent from the internationalizing of the Northern Ireland peace process.

This chapter seeks to explain the main reasons why loyalism has been resistant to the internationalizing dynamic of the peace process, and why international actors did not feel compelled to make overtures to loyalists. The main focus of the chapter is the post-GFA period. It is worth beginning with a note of caution in relation to many explanations of the Northern Ireland peace process. Farrington observes that many accounts are 'overly agential', or too readily place emphasis on a coterie of selected key players to the exclusion of more holistic and complex accounts (Farrington 2006: 277).

To the credit of the British and Irish governments, and to Northern Ireland's political parties, researchers have been given access to a mass of primary and secondary material, and many academics, journalists and political insiders have been tempted to write 'instant history'. But there has been a downside to intensive research on the Northern Ireland peace process. Many researchers have interviewed the same cast list of 'key players' in the Northern Ireland peace process (Mac Ginty and Darby 2002).

This has led to the construction of a hegemonic narrative of the peace process, and has reinforced the position of the 'key players' as guardians of the narrative. The master narrative tends to emphasize the role of certain actors, certain critical moments, certain phrases and certain sequences.

The orthodoxy of the master narrative means that critical or alternative accounts of the peace process tend to be marginalized. Yet, even with the benefit of the minimal hindsight offered by a little more than a decade, the master narrative of the peace process is beginning to look a little too neat and a little too self-contained. In short, it may be too early to piece together anything but a skeletal narrative of the Northern Ireland peace process.

For the purposes of this chapter, it is worth noting that some of the widely accepted explanations of the US role in the Northern Ireland peace process may be too gushing and prone to shifting the centre of peace process gravity significantly nearer Washington than it otherwise should be. This should not be taken as an attempt to deny the importance of the United States and other external agents in the evolution of the Northern Ireland peace process. Instead, it is a call for perspective. There can be little doubting of the significance of the external dimension to the peace process. Yet, in the master narrative of the peace process this is often broken down into sequenced 'bite-size' events. Thus, in the early 1990s a well-connected Irish-American lobby managed to persuade presidential candidate Bill Clinton to take an interest in the tantalizing possibility of a peace process in Northern Ireland.

On assuming office, Clinton did become engaged on the Northern Ireland issue, and made a number of apparently crucial interventions, such as granting Gerry Adams a US-entry visa in the run up to the 1994 IRA declaration of a ceasefire, appointing George Mitchell as chair of the multiparty talks, and engaging in a 30-hour marathon of cajoling telephone calls in the run up to Good Friday 1998. Thereafter, the Clinton administration, and less so the Bush administration, supported the two governments in encouraging the Northern Ireland parties to accommodate with each other and implement the GFA.

There is much merit in this explanation, and there can be no doubting the energies and personal commitment of Clinton, Mitchell and their colleagues. Such compartmentalized explanations though, can be too focused on an overly neat sequence of events and underestimate meta-explanations that examine the role of politico-social culture, and structural factors such as a changing international context.

Moreover, many of the accepted explanations of US involvement in the Northern Ireland peace process have an element of 'Kremlinology' about them. At times they rest on the overinterpretation of scant details. For example, much was made of how baby boomer Clinton failed to develop an early rapport with cricket-loving John Major, or how Clinton's time as a Rhodes scholar exposed him to television pictures of the early agonies of Northern Ireland's Troubles and so sparked an enduring interest. Some of this may be true, but we have no real way of knowing and so it may be prudent to be circumspect in engaging in supposition dressed as analysis.

The 'irrelevance' of loyalism to the peace process

One aspect of the master narrative of the Northern Ireland peace process is that loyalists are often portrayed as bit-part players. In many ways this is accurate. If we exclude the DUP from the definition of loyalist and despite the media presence of David Ervine, Billy Hutchinson and others, loyalist political parties during the peace process were unable to develop popular political parties. Any representation they had in the talks was largely courtesy of 'peace process gerrymandering', or the creation of an electoral system with top-up seats so that minor parties could be included.

With such a small constituency, the 'major players' in the form of the British and Irish governments, the United States, and the other main parties in Northern Ireland did not have to pay much attention to loyalism. Moreover, loyalist violence, both before and during the peace process, did not threaten the British state. Indeed, it was in part sponsored by the British state, though the extent to which this sponsorship was official or devised to complement the idea of a 'rogue' military is the subject of debate.

One alternative explanation of the peace process (shared by ousted unionist politician Robert McCartney and former republican prisoner Anthony McIntyre) was that the British government's primary strategic aim in the peace process was to stop republican violence, as it *was* a threat to the British state (McIntyre 1995: 97–122). While much republican violence was contained by the 1990s, the IRA was still capable of 'spectaculars' or violent incidents that 'mattered'. These spectaculars mattered because they directly impacted on the British state and took the form of mortar rounds in Downing Street garden, bombs on British soil that cost billions in insurance claims and even cost the City of London the chance to host the European Central Bank.

Loyalist violence, on the other hand, threatened a more 'expendable' population: republicans and young working-class Catholics. It was not a direct threat to the British state or its interests. It can be argued that loyalists, along with a number of other political and militant actors from Northern Ireland, had veto power over the peace process. Sufficient loyalist violence would have made an IRA ceasefire untenable and so collapsed the peace process.

But the loyalist ceasefire, while ragged and armed, held sufficiently well to keep republicans on board. Once on ceasefire, loyalists could be more easily ignored. A further reason for describing loyalism as largely irrelevant to the peace process and the post-Agreement implementation process is that for significant periods of the peace process it was difficult to take elements of political loyalism seriously given the activities of their more militant counterparts.

Notwithstanding the ceasefire, loyalists still engaged in a good deal of racketeering, drug dealing, feuding, rioting and stirring local-level sectarianism at Holy Cross, Harryville and elsewhere. There would always be limits to the political development of 'new loyalism' (McAuley 1996:127–53; McAuley 2002a: 106–22) if some militants seemed to be engaged in a competition to see who could become the most convincing caricature of feuding bling-laden chav druggies (Silke 2000: 107–27).

The limits to a loyalist international dimension

There are rather obvious reasons why connections between loyalism and international actors were so poorly developed in the aftermath of the GFA. First, Northern Ireland's loyalists were not among the 'top four' parties in Northern Ireland, and were not members of the power-sharing Executive. They did not have to be courted by international actors.

Even at the high point of their electoral strength, the 1996 Forum elections, the combined vote of the PUP and the UDP did not manage to gain 5 per cent of the vote between them. In the 1999 European elections, a poll geared towards personality politics, high profile David Ervine only attained a shade over 3 per cent of first preference votes. Given their electoral weakness, most peace process actors (both internal and external) probably calculated that loyalists could be ignored as long as the main loyalist militant groups remained on ceasefire.

While the UDA ceasefire was 'derecognized' by the British government in October 2001 because of the involvement of the organization in violence, this violence was mainly directed towards its own community and did not threaten a resumption of tripartite republican-loyalist-British state violence. The fact that the disarmament of loyalist groups never became such a seismic issue as IRA disarmament, was indicative of the wider truth: loyalist violence (and capacity for violence) was secondary to that of republicans from the perspective of many internal and external actors.

A second reason why connections between loyalism and international actors were so poorly developed in the aftermath of the GFA, relates to the post-Agreement dynamic of the peace process. With the conclusion of the Agreement, attention shifted towards the implementation of the Agreement by the local parties themselves. This particularly applied to Sinn Féin and the UUP between 1998 and 2005, and Sinn Féin and the DUP from 2005 onwards.

This emphasis on accommodation between the main Northern Ireland parties limited opportunities for the internationalizing of the peace process in general. Certainly, international actors were rhetorically supportive of the implementation of the Agreement, and the European Union through its Peace I and II schemes funded very significant levels of third sector peace-building. Yet the onus was on local actors to give life to the institutions they had created in the GFA and to fulfil their promises. Arguably the most significant external inputs into the peace process had occurred at the formative stages of the process.

Third, when Bill Clinton left office, White House attention to Northern Ireland declined dramatically. In a sign of the import the Bush administration attached to Northern Ireland, Ireland went without a US Ambassador for over a year (*Guardian*, 17 February 2004). The first Bush appointee, Richard J. Egan had no background in international diplomacy. Instead, he was a 'Bush Pioneer' or a major contributor and fundraiser for the Republican Party. He described his second year in post as 'very, very boring' and advised that 'anybody with aspirations for the job should think twice' (*Irish Times*, 9 September 2004). The Bush administration simply did not have the level of engagement with Northern Ireland shown by the previous administration. Indeed it is understandable that it did not have a sense of ownership of a peace process that had been closely associated with President Clinton.

Bush did visit Northern Ireland twice during his terms in office. The first was in April 2003, but the purpose of the visit was to discuss the Iraq war with Tony Blair (who could see political advantages in not hosting such discussions in London). Less than an hour of the twenty-hour visit was spent with Northern Ireland politicians, and some of that was taken up with Sinn Féin appraising Bush of the folly of Iraq invasion.

A second visit, in June 2008 when the Bush Presidency was winding down, was equally short and with no political importance (BBC News Online, 16 June 2008). Bush's engagement on Northern Ireland was minimal. They included exhortations to militant groups to disarm, exhortations to local politicians to accommodate each other, not inviting Gerry Adams to the White House St Patrick's Day reception, banning Gerry Adams from fundraising on his trips to the United States, hosting a visit by murdered Belfast man Robert McCartney's family, and hosting an annual visit by the Northern Ireland chief constable. This did not amount to sustained interest.

Despite how his Presidency turned out, it is worth remembering that Bush had little initial inclination to be an interventionist President. He came to power decrying Clinton's predilection for nation building and other open-ended foreign policy commitments, and was anxious to reassert White House dominance over the State Department on foreign policy issues. As history will record, once in power, Bush's foreign policy adventurism was disastrous. His initial distaste for open-ended foreign policy entanglements fell by the wayside after 9/11, with his defence secretary Donald Rumsfeld telling Americans to '... forget about "exit strategies"; we're looking at a sustained engagement that carries no deadlines' (cited by Bacevich 2003: 226). But beyond Afghanistan, Iraq and a laudable interest in AIDS in Africa, the Bush foreign policy was remarkably uninterested in large swathes of the planet.

Northern Ireland was one of these areas, and significantly, there was no attempt to draw Northern Ireland into one of the central organizing themes of Bush's foreign policy: the War on Terror. Northern Ireland's militant groups fitted into the US State Department's definition of 'terrorism', especially when not on ceasefire: 'premeditated, politically motivated violence perpetrated against non-combatant targets by subnational groups or clandestine agents, usually intended to influence an audience' (US State Department 2001: vi).

Despite the Bush administration's reputation for fabricating links between various overseas actors (e.g. Saddam Hussein and *Al Qaeda*) there was no attempt to link republican or loyalist groups with the apparent phenomenon of 'new' terrorism after 9/11 (Cunningham 2007). In short, Northern Ireland lay outside of the defining themes of US foreign policy, and in such circumstances, the opportunities for loyalists to make connections with the US administration were limited.

Rather than labour the post-Clinton lack of interest in Northern Ireland, this chapter will advance two further arguments that help explain the limited connections between loyalists and international actors (especially the United States). The first is that international actors, especially formal state or institutional actors, often have very limited means to connect with local actors in target states. As a consequence of this, they found it difficult to make meaningful connections with Northern Ireland's loyalists. The second argument is that local actors often have more agency than is reported to ignore, resist or subvert overtures from international actors.

'Wrong type' of actor

Many major states and international organizations have very well developed institutions and mechanisms to manage their external relations. International diplomacy, with its ritualistic presentation of credentials and legal protection offered to diplomats, is a byword for the institutionalization of relationships. States are very good at dealing with other states using formulaic devices. Conversely, many states are very poor at dealing with non-traditional political actors. In a sense, loyalists, as non-traditional political actors, have been the 'wrong type' of political actor and so many international actors have found it difficult to establish useful relationships with them.

The post-Cold War era is littered with examples in which international interventions in the name of peacebuilding or peace enforcement have failed to meaningfully engage with local political actors. Instead, international actors have either brushed aside national rulers in target countries and installed their own proxy puppets (e.g. regime change in Iraq or Afghanistan) or have made linkages with national elites to the exclusion of the general population. Critics of the 'liberal peace', or the dominant form of internationally supported peacemaking, have pointed to the multiple flaws in post-Cold War peacemaking (see Mac Ginty 2006; Mac Ginty and Richmond, eds. 2009; Richmond 2005).

This form of peacemaking is held to be unreflexive to local conditions, rolling out the same formulaic and technocratic style of peacemaking and peacebuilding regardless of context. It becomes peacebuilding from IKEA, or a 'flat pack' standardized peace. In this view, Bougainville becomes Bosnia, and the Solomon Islands become Sierra Leone as the same international technocrats from the same international organizations and supportive INGOs enact the same peacebuilding policies.

Critics charge that the liberal peace is deeply ethnocentric in terms of its ideological ambitions. Thus, it is accused of promoting a certain type of liberalism that privileges essentially western values that it believes to be universal. Western style democracy replete with western style political parties and civil society are believed to be superior to alternative forms of political and social organizations that may draw on traditional or customary practice. The free market is believed to be central to sustainable peacemaking, and is often promoted through 'aggressive social engineering' that can overlook the profound human consequences associated with the shock doctrine (Pugh 2006: 153).

The liberal peace also stands accused of using a formulaic set of instruments to promote its preferred form of peace. The chief tool in the liberal peace toolkit is state building. As a result, post-civil war societies have borne the brunt of enormous international interventions in the name of 'good governance' and 'bureaucratic reform'. All have been aimed at 'correcting' state 'dysfunctions'. Sriram (2008) has described it as 'peace by governance' or the introduction of successive governance reforms in post-civil war societies in the hope of 'programming' violent conflict out of the polity. Others have pithily likened the liberal peace enterprise to a 'getting to Denmark' process, or a generic 'any state' with a functioning bureaucracy, developed economy, and compliant foreign policy (Pritchett and Woolcock 2004:191–212).

The repeated failure of international actors to understand and engage with local norms of belief and behaviour in war-torn and post-civil war societies has been well documented. Rajiv Chandrasekaran's account of life in Baghdad's post-Saddam green zone brings into relief the physical, social, economic and cultural separation between international actors and the indigenous population (Chandrasekaran 2007).

Similar accounts of post-Dayton Bosnia-Herzegovina illustrate how international organizations (mainly NATO, the EU and OSCE operating through the Office of the High Representative) usurped local politicians to an extent that it became known as the 'European Raj' (Knaus and Martin 2003: 60–74). David Chandler noted that 'sovereignty has in effect been transferred to Brussels' (Chandler 2007: 605).

The chief point is that the key agents and mechanisms of international peacebuilding and peace support are poorly equipped to engage with political actors that are not made in their own likeness. Northern Ireland-based political actors that did make sustained and useful connections with international actors during the peace process tended to conform to the norms of 'doing politics' that were favoured by international actors.

In the main, Northern Ireland's loyalists did not 'play the game' as assiduously as some of the other parties. In the case of dealings with the United States, both the British and Irish governments had well-trodden diplomatic paths that enabled high level access. The Social Democratic and Labour Party had well-established links with scions of the Democratic Party. The new Irish American lobby, influential in drawing Clinton's attention to the opportunities presented by the peace process, knew how to 'work the system'.

This lobby was not cut from the same clerical and tweed cloth of the more established Irish-American lobby. Instead, it was media savvy and seemed able to catch the spirit of the first term Clinton Democratic administration. They were determined to make things easy for the administration and alert them to the potential for a low cost, but high kudos return foreign policy initiative. To a certain extent, the Irish-American lobby prepared the ground for other Northern Ireland based actors, 'translating' messages into a language that could be understood in Washington.

There was no Ulster loyalist lobby in the United States that Northern Ireland's loyalists could turn to for 'translation' services. Although there was a significant Ulster-Scots diaspora in North America, this had not materialized into a cohesive or effective political machine capable of advocating the loyalist or unionist cause. Added to this was an inward-looking tendency among many loyalists. Loyalism, as a political or cultural project, was not geared towards attracting or cooperating with external patrons and confederates.

While Sinn Féin could forge links with liberationist or revolutionary groups (especially during the Cold War), loyalists could not replicate this. The true strength of republican links with its international 'brotherhood' is open to debate, and doubtless it was useful for internal housekeeping purposes to be seen to be 'revolutionary' when the peace process actually meant reform and conformity.

Some loyalists sought solace in defensively aggressive overseas political projects (Zionism and apartheid South Africa), but such links were shallow and instrumentalist. A post-GFA fad of flying of Israeli flags in loyalist areas of Belfast, for example, seemed solely geared towards annoying those Catholic republicans flying Palestinian flags in nearby ghettos, rather than any meaningful connection with the Zionist state (Hill and White 2008: 31–50). Post-GFA loyalism seemed all too ready to accept (even wallow in) the 'cold place for Protestants' narrative rather than put together an active and outward-facing political project.

It is worth stressing that this is not an essential argument. It is not the case that somehow loyalists 'introverted' or 'lack confidence'. Instead, a combination of structural factors connected to political, economic and social trends produced a political culture in the late twentieth and early twenty-first centuries that meant that Ulster loyalism was not in a position to be outward oriented at that period in time. In a generation things may be very different.

By opening a Washington office in 1995, Sinn Féin illustrated that it understood the importance of bringing the message to Washington and communicating it in a way that was relevant to Washington. Northern Ireland's loyalists failed to take a similar step. In many ways, they did not see it as 'their peace process' (particularly in the early years of the peace process when the phrase 'pan-nationalist front' was in use) and so did not feel motivated to lobby for the process to be advanced.

Nor, with energies divided between at least two political parties, could they match Sinn Féin's organizational and financial strength. The PUP and the UDP did make visits to Washington and elsewhere, and they were kept in the loop of consultations, important visits and draft documents that made the stuff of the peace process. But, this did not occur to the same extent as with other parties.

Crucially, loyalist political culture was not particularly easy for external actors to access, especially with the limited political antennae of many international actors. The loyalist story and loyalist political organizations did not easily fit the narratives that many external actors came to expect from the Northern Ireland peace process: Catholic versus Protestant, nationalist versus unionist, pro-united Ireland versus pro-United Kingdom, pro-violence versus anti-violence and, eventually, pro-Agreement versus anti-Agreement.

Reality, of course, was more complex than the simplistic dyads designed to aid easy comprehension, and the loyalist story was complex indeed. It involved some very strange juxtapositions, which may have left many overseas audiences perplexed. Thus, initial suspicion of the peace process resulted in eventual hopeful embrace of the Agreement (by some loyalists). A fair proportion of foot in mouth knuckleheads joined wonderfully articulate loyalist spokespersons, while violent feuding, murderous spoiler groups, drug dealing, extortion and other forms of criminality punctuated the loyalist ceasefire.

In short, the loyalist story did not fit the preferred peace process template that many international observers favoured. Of course, the stories of many other peace process actors were no less riddled with complication and contradiction, but many other actors, and especially Sinn Féin, were adept at promoting a coherent narrative for external consumption. Howe cautions against regarding loyalist political subculture as being static and somehow left behind (Howe 2005a, 2005b). Instead, it was fluid and vibrant, capable of adopting elements from multiple sources and forging its own very specific political identity. The foreign policy apparatus of large states was poorly equipped to connect with this highly localized political subculture.

Local agency

The United States is unrivalled in its position as the world's only superpower. While it may have bouts of introspection and isolationism, or may feel threatened by the rising or resurgent giants of China, India, Russia or the European Union, the US ability to project hard and soft power is formidable. US strategic doctrine means that the state must be capable of fighting two and a half wars simultaneously. In 2008, the United States spent $607bn on its military, or 41 per cent of total world military spending. This figure amounted to seven times that of Chinese military spending and over ten times that of Russian spending (SIPRI 2008).

To put American military might into perspective the US Marine Corps alone has more attack aircraft than the Royal Air Force, and more personnel than the entire British Army (Bacevich 2005: 16). Suspicious that its own autonomy may be limited, the United States has been wary of unfettered multilateralism, and has proved adept at thwarting or opting out of international activism on climate change, arms reduction and an international criminal court. The global economic crisis notwithstanding, Reports of US decline have been greatly exaggerated. It is still the engine of the world economy, with a 2007 GDP of $13.8 trillion; significantly ahead of its nearest rivals, Japan and China at $4.4tn and $3.5tn respectively (*Guardian*, 14 January 2009).

The United States also wields enormous cultural power; whether through Hannah Montana or Microsoft, its cultural reach is unrivalled. Yet, despite this enormous ability to project power, it is also worth noting that there are also limits on its ability to secure the outcomes it wants. The world's remaining superpower was unable to influence Northern Ireland's loyalists (a few hundred aging hoods, their 'mini-me' acolytes, and a few dozen more politically minded colleagues) to disarm and 'get with the programme'.

Part of the reason for this was that Northern Ireland was not high on the list of US priorities and there are limits to the amount of coercive power that the United States would be willing to direct towards a community situated in part of one of its chief allies. But there are two other reasons: limits on the power of external actors, and the agency of local actors to resist, ignore, subvert and adapt the ministrations of powerful external actors. While the liberal peace (or the dominant form of peacemaking favoured by leading states, leading international organizations, and international financial institutions) can be portrayed as being hegemonic and all powerful, closer examination reveals that the agents of the liberal peace are prone to fallibility and distraction.

The liberal peace is not applied uniformly in all places. Some locations are regarded as being strategically or economically vital (Iraq), while others are regarded as marginal (Horn of Africa). Moreover, power projection by leading states is prone to funding shortfalls, and changes in leadership and political priorities at home. So rather than being Leviathan agents of change, leading states may not be as capable of projecting their power as some may argue.

Often, local actors are portrayed in two caricature modes: as truculent opponents of peace (who can therefore be coerced or 'neutralized') or as passive victims or beneficiaries who can be patronized. Yet closer examination of local situations in societies emerging from violent conflict is likely to reveal a much more complex picture. Some local actors may be amenable to being co-opted by external actors (and so become local agents of the liberal peace). Others may adopt courses of resistance, by either actively resisting external interventions or more passive forms of resistance such as 'waiting and seeing' in the hope that international actors will lose interest and turn their attention to other areas.

The loyalist attitude towards the United States during the peace process was largely one of benign disengagement. This in itself was a form of agency. If it were minded to coerce loyalists into a particular stance, the United States and other external actors would have found that they had little or no leverage over political or militant loyalism. While republicans and other political parties from Northern Ireland actively courted external support and attention, loyalists did not.

To a certain extent, republicans and the mainstream political parties became path dependent on attention from London, Dublin and Washington. As a result, to be cut off from high profile attention from Downing Street or the White House amounted to a cost, even in the form of embarrassment. Loyalists did not succumb to such a situation of path dependency. Roy Garland highlighted a certain independence of mind in loyalist political thinking: 'Loyalists don't need phone calls from George Bush or anyone else to realise we had to say yes to something' (*Irish News,* 29 November 2004).

Conclusions

In many ways the international dimension to loyalism in the post-Agreement period is a non-story: loyalists were not important enough to be courted by major international actors and the high point of an internationalized peace process had passed when the GFA was reached. Certainly individual loyalists have been involved in 'lesson learning' visits abroad, and from time to time loyalist politicians have met with international leaders.

International monitors who had eventually gained the trust of the paramilitary leaderships oversaw loyalist disarmament in June 2009 and January 2010. This does not, however, reflect an internationalized community or a political stance that has been heavily influenced by external pressure. Yet, the non-story of international influences on loyalism in the post-Agreement era is revealing in a number of ways. First, it suggests that the dominant narrative of the Northern Ireland process may have too readily accepted the importance of international actors in the course and outcome of the peace process. The dominant narrative is a little too neat and sequential.

Second, it points to the lack of leverage held by the world's remaining superpower on loyalism. The United States had nothing that the loyalists wanted. This is revealing about the limits to power (both hard and soft) in the twenty-first century.

Third, by largely maintaining a stance of disengagement from the internationalized aspects of the peace process, Northern Ireland's loyalism was displaying a form of agency. This did not amount to outright resistance to the peace process, or an ability to derail it, but it suggested a distinctive path, one that has been overlooked in the dominant narratives of the peace process.

Note

The author is grateful to Kris Brown and Cathy Gormley-Heenan, both from the University of Ulster, for their comments on a draft of this chapter.

Chapter 4
The Politics of Fear?
Provisionalism, Loyalism and the
'New Politics' of Northern Ireland

Kevin Bean

In the summer of 2009 following racist intimidation from loyalist gangs which resulted in more than one hundred Roma immigrants fleeing their homes in South Belfast, the condition of the Protestant working class and the nature of contemporary loyalism once again became the focus of widespread media and political concern. Provoking unanimous condemnation from Northern Ireland's political class, the attacks sparked further debate about what many perceive as a culture of intolerance and the crisis in the loyalist ghettoes. It was frequently said that, as the national conflict subsides, racism is becoming the new sectarianism in some loyalist communities (Cadwallader 2009).

Amidst fears that the BNP and Combat 18 were winning support among young loyalists who would previously have devoted their energies to attacking Catholics, these narratives portray racist violence not simply as an expression of endemic bigotry, but rather the latest symptom of the disintegration of the loyalist working class (BBC News 2009a). Drawing on the language of anti-racism, employed in recent debates about the rise of the Far Right and the future of the 'white working class' in Britain, loyalists are simultaneously perceived as racist thugs and victims of a deepening sense of alienation and disillusion at finding themselves on the margins of society (McGurk 2009; Sveinsson 2009).

One of the loudest voices expressing outrage was that of Deputy First Minister, Sinn Féin's Martin McGuinness, who, condemning the attacks as a 'totally shameful episode', called for 'strong, clear and decisive leadership *standing together* against [racism] (Clancy 2009a; emphasis mine). In adding his voice to British prime minister Gordon Brown and DUP junior minister Jeffrey Donaldson's calls for a clear, collective response from police, public authorities and local communities to 'face down' the racists, the response of this leading Sinn Féin politician demonstrated how firmly embedded within Northern Ireland's political mainstream, both he and his party had become (Finn 2009; McDonald 2009).

In distinguishing between Sinn Féin's position, 'standing together' with political and civic leaders within the dominant consensus, in contrast to the racists, 'isolated within the community', who 'need to be brought to book', McGuinness was not just locating the Provisionals at the heart of the new dispensation; implicit in his criticism was the idea that sections of the Protestant working class were now beyond the pale of civilized society (BBC News 2009b).

Underpinning this (republican) analysis of loyalism as a thoroughly reactionary political and social force lies a series of rarely articulated but powerful binary oppositions between a disorientated, crisis-ridden loyalist community and a confident, advancing nationalism. This view of the marginalization of loyalism in republican discourse expresses no mere triumphalism or infantile point scoring: rather it has become an intrinsic element in Northern Ireland's communalized politics and, as such, enjoys a clearly defined function within Provisional strategy as it has developed since the GFA.

This chapter explores the development of that strategy since 1998 by considering its aims and significance in relation to the wider goals of the Provisional movement. It considers how republicans define loyalism as an ideology, the importance they place on its historical and contemporary relationships with unionism and the British state, and the perspectives they hold about its future political trajectory. What emerges not only helps us to understand the nature of contemporary Provisionalism, but also indicates some of the underlying patterns and key features of what has been called the 'new Northern Irish politics' (Tonge 2005).

Compelling dialogue

Throughout the 1990s one of the most striking features of Sinn Féin's journey into the political mainstream was the seeming shift in the party's attitude towards unionism and loyalism: in particular, the adoption of a new posture of reconciliation towards the Protestant population, which was frequently cited as evidence that a much wider revision of republican politics was underway (Bean 1994). In calling for dialogue with unionists, leading Provisionals increasingly used the language of consent and conflict resolution. Thus from the beginning of the peace process leading Sinn Féin politician Mitchel McLaughlin argued that:

> We cannot and should not ever try to coerce the Protestant people...We understand why there is conflict in our society...not only do we understand the IRA's use of armed struggle; we also understand why loyalists use violence and we understand why Britain uses violence. (Wilson 1992)

This new discourse linked the language of reconciliation to a narrative of transformation and political advance through the medium of the peace process. Thus, Martin McGuinness saw the GFA as part of a transitional process: 'an historic compromise between Irish nationalism and Irish Unionism... [in which] [c]herished positions have been reworked and remoulded to facilitate changed political realities'.

Similarly, post-1998, Gerry Adams argued that the only sustainable way forward was through 'genuine enlightened dialogue between all of us who share this island' (Sinn Féin 2003). For Sinn Féin, the May 2007 formation of a power sharing government, involving the party and the DUP, confirmed Northern Ireland's entry into what McGuinness defined as a 'new political era based on peace and reconciliation' (Bowcott 2007).

Sinn Féin's new found interest in the politics of reconciliation extended beyond power sharing initiatives within the political elite, towards an embrace of grassroots unionism and loyalism. This self-conscious and much vaunted strategy of 'unionist outreach' and 'conflict resolution' claimed that republicans were genuinely committed to 'establishing a consensus for a shared future based on a respect for each other's differences'. Building on 'many years of quiet engagement' with churches, trade unions, and voluntary and community groups, Sinn Féin expressed the hope that this dialogue would be 'inclusive and open, without limits, a dialogue that would dispel fears, cast away myths and misconceptions and establish trust' (Friel 2007a).

As one east Belfast republican activist involved in dialogue with loyalists observed: 'our republicanism compels us to engage with those of opposing political viewpoints... [especially] the most diehard' (Ó Donnghaile 2009). At local government level, Belfast Sinn Féin councillors Alex Maskey and Tom Hartley were very public exponents of reaching out to unionist communities and 'working for all the citizens of the city', during their time in office as Lord Mayor (Clancy 2009b; Mitchell, C. 2002).

This strategy of engagement was very much in tune with the widely expressed hope among local politicians and national governments that the GFA would provide a framework for new forms of political reconciliation between nationalists and unionists (Elliott 2007; FitzGerald 1998; McKittrick 2007; Powell 2008). Both in official discourse and academic literature, great emphasis was placed on the role of civil society and 'grassroots dialogue' in the business of promoting conflict transformation (Buchanan 2008; Cochrane and Dunn 2002; Power 2005).

Those with a more radical perspective even suggested in the period leading up to the GFA that new forms of cross-community class politics might emerge, as republican and loyalist activists encountered one another in the new political dispensation in Northern Ireland. These 'transformational' expectations arose, on the one hand, from an accurate appreciation of the grievances of republican and loyalist communities and, on the other, from an unduly optimistic assessment of the transformative potential of post-conflict politics. Thus one commentator could plausibly suggest that:

> If Sinn Féin and the loyalist parties begin to work in tandem they have the potential to create the most dynamic and exciting source of people power in the North (there is) a real opportunity to maximise their political strength and bring their experiences to bear upon the shaping of the future. (Regan 1996: 31–2)

Some loyalists, most notably David Ervine of the PUP joined in these calls for a 'new vision', arguing for 'a class politics … a crossing of the divide, the politics of commonality' (Ervine 1996). After the GFA as 'once sworn enemies talk(ed) to each other on first name terms', Ervine's emphasis on the importance of 'face to face' dialogue as a prelude to building class solidarity, seemed to strike a chord with many former combatants. Former prisoners, in particular, played a key role in developing an active, if somewhat limited, cross-community civil society (Hall 2000, 2003; Shirlow and McEvoy 2008). As one loyalist leader put it, republicans 'extended the hand of friendship [to loyalists] more than the unionist parties' (Rowan 2009a).

As a result, a range of cross-community organizations involving republicans and loyalists have worked together on matters of common interest such as joint educational and welfare projects for ex-prisoners, suicide prevention campaigns, contact networks to contain interface violence and formalized social entrepreneurial partnerships encouraged by the funding streams of the PEACE II and PEACE III programmes (Community Foundation for Northern Ireland 2006; Hall 2007b; McCaffery 2008; Mitchell 2008; Upper Springfield Development Trust 2004).

However, in spite of hopes that cross-community activism could form the basis for common political action between republicans and loyalists, the overall balance sheet has been far from positive in post-GFA Northern Ireland. The proliferation of 'peace walls' alongside entrenched sectarian patterns of living and voting provides evidence of the failure of David Ervine's hoped for 'politics of commonality'. The links that have developed between republicans and loyalists have been largely pragmatic and sporadic, for example the formation of cross-community partnerships in pursuit of funding opportunities or the set-piece debates organized by the West Belfast Festival (O'Connor 2009; Ó Donnghaile 2009).

Disconnected from wider political projects or grassroots *political* engagement between specifically *loyalist* groups and Sinn Féin, the *political* dialogue that has occurred between Sinn Féin and loyalist groups such as the PUP, and the UPRG has been rather far from fruitful (Clancy 2009b; Sinn Féin 2002). A much heralded joint initiative in 2006 between Sinn Féin and the PUP in Derry, promising 'sustained dialogue' and a 'genuine process of reconciliation', has produced very little of long-term or lasting value (Young 2006).

Most tellingly of all, there have been no examples of political co-operation between republicans and loyalists on matters of common interest in the Legislative Assembly. The PUP's Dawn Purvis, addressing a republican audience in an interview with *An Phoblacht*, agreed that Sinn Féin's 'unionist engagement strategy was a good idea', but wondered what had happened to it or what it had achieved since its launch in 2006 (Purvis 2008). As one experienced observer of Northern Ireland's community politics concluded in 2004, the initial flush of progressive thinking evidenced by loyalist and republican ex-prisoners going into each other's communities and publicly debating new perspectives had passed; instead these grassroots contacts, alongside the potential for new forms of politics have been '... effectively sidelined by the "political process" (and) now seem to have been shunted into the sidings' (Hall 2004:1).

Uniting Irishmen?

Understanding the nature of Northern Ireland's new dispensation and the political process from which it has emerged is the key to understanding the true meaning behind Sinn Féin's language of inclusiveness, diversity and engagement. Unfolding on a qualitatively new terrain and in radically altered local and global political contexts, contemporary Provisionalism's aims, ideology and political strategy, have undergone a profoundly radical shift.

Since its founding moment, the central underlying assumption of Provisionalism has been its belief in its own subjective agency and in the potential of transformative politics. Above all, the Provisionals' project drew its meaning from a long-established universalist strand in republican politics, informed by a belief in the potential to transform the political consciousness of unionists and 'substitute the common name of Irishman in place of the denominations of Protestant, Catholic and Dissenter...' (Tone 1998: 46).

Arguing that unionism was a false consciousness manipulated by British Imperialism throughout the twentieth century, to maintain a policy of divide and rule, republicans remained utterly resolved to embrace Protestants and unionists as an integral and valued part of the Irish nation, whether they liked it or not (Cronin 1980; Sinn Féin 1958). The product of historically determined colonial structures of power, which promoted division, loyalism/ unionism had, from the republican viewpoint, fuelled a sectarianized consciousness among large sections of the Protestant population.

For republican socialists in particular, winning over the Protestant working class to the cause of the socialist republic was the only way of breaking both the connection with Britain and the connection with capitalism (Connolly 1988; English 2006; Gilmore 1974). This analysis was influenced by Marxist arguments that:

> the Protestant working class has no political existence as a class and fights as part of the Loyalist community ... [Material and economic benefits] ensure that Loyalist workers have a direct stake in the British connection and the oppression of the nationalist community. (Irish Freedom Movement 1987: 108)

In these readings of loyalist/unionist consciousness, the relationship to Britain remained pivotal. As one republican argued: 'breaking the union with Britain [through revolutionary armed struggle] will be a necessary step to breaking them from their supremacism, their loyalism', even if this entailed significant unionist resistance and a possible civil war between nationalists and unionists following British withdrawal (Brownie 1980; Dowling 1981).

Rejecting the idea that loyalism/ unionism enjoyed any form of democratic legitimacy or cultural authenticity, republicans dismissed, as lacking 'any sense of engagement with political reality', attempts to characterize it as a valid identity and heritage. Defining unionism as a 'racist and imperialist ideology', republicans warned against feeding the insatiable appetite of loyalism, which sat 'like a hungry fat cuckoo in a nest ... the more it gets the more it wants' (Sinn Féin 1980, 1983).

Perforce, the Provisional movement had little choice but to define unionism in these *political* terms, for to use the language of cultural identity would not only have conferred essentialist legitimacy on unionism and taken republicans on to the terrain of constitutional nationalism, but it would also have undermined the fundamental justification for the armed struggle as an anti-imperialist campaign and reduced Provisionalism to mere sectarian defenderism (Bean 2007: 223–7; Daly 2008).

As *political ideologies* there were fundamental contradictions between republicanism and unionism that could not be resolved on the cultural plane: to republicans, compromise over issues of self-determination and the constitutional status of Northern Ireland was clearly impossible (McKearney 1998). The Provisionals saw the transformation of unionist consciousness purely in terms of confrontation. As Gerry Adams argued in 1981: 'we cannot and we should not ever tolerate, or compromise with (by government structures or any other means), loyalism. Loyalism is a major obstacle to democracy in Ireland and to Irish independence' (Sinn Féin 1981).

By the late 1980s, however, a new Provisional politics of engagement was emerging in response to a shifting and often unstable political and ideological environment. Internationally, the changing geopolitical context of the post-Cold War world and the ideological retreat of radical and national liberation movements were to have a profound impact. As long-established ideological forms and political projects were turned on their axes, the discursive framework and political space within which Sinn Féin operated underwent a fundamental transformation (Ryan 1994).

As one Provisional activist has described it:

> The general retreat of the left had an impact on republicanism when republicanism was becoming increasingly isolated anyway...A whole array of ideological positions no longer seemed applicable...it was a period of flux and change when there was a sense of crisis and a lack of ideological certainty. (Ó Broin 2005)

This ideological crisis within republicanism occurred at a time when the dominant discourse in Western societies was becoming increasingly coloured by the essentialist politics of difference.

Forms of identity politics adopted by previously marginalized or 'oppressed' groups became vehicles for seeking recognition through appeals for parity of esteem, positive discrimination and the acknowledgement of collective rights in the public sphere (Barry 2001; Taylor 1994). The state's response frequently took the form of an official multiculturalism, which recognized cultural differences as a political category, and allocated resources accordingly.

Multiculturalism as a political project reinforced the view that identity and its parent framework, tradition, now acted as the central organizing principles of contemporary politics (Furedi 1991). These new particularistic forms of politics were diametrically opposed to the universalist ideologies which had constituted modernist politics since the Enlightenment: in particular, they ran counter to the transformative ideologies of the left which had historically identified themselves as assertive, culturally blind and designed to mobilize individual and collective subjects such as the working class or the self-determining nation to implement their historical project (Heartfield 2002).

These new ideological currents were to impact significantly on the framework of politics and public life in Northern Ireland. The GFA, itself a product of new particularist forms, conjoined with the essentialism of local political forces to institutionalize the politics of difference across the region (section 75 of the Northern Ireland Act 1998 as an expression of the framing of equality and respect for categories of difference within public life: First Minister and Deputy First Minister 1998). Bestowing formal recognition and equal legitimacy upon the antithetical aspirations of unionism and nationalism, the Agreement transformed them from opposing political projects to irreconcilable cultural differences.

Although conducted in the dynamic language of process and movement, this repudiation of universalism and embrace of particularism has given rise to a culture of stasis and stabilization, informed by a key assumption of the new political dispensation, that existing 'identities' and communal allegiances cannot be transformed, just as *political* conflict in the North cannot be resolved, but only managed and regulated by the state (O'Neill 2001). The contending parties have narrowed their focus from a conflict rooted in universalist concepts of self-determination and democracy to one focused around rival expectations and demands from opposing cultural identities and communities (O'Neill 2007).

Whatever the rhetoric of pluralism within the new Northern Irish politics, there can be no real hope of transcending these divisions while 'the key unifying factor in Northern Irish politics is nothing more than the mutual respect of both parties for the politics of difference' (Hadaway 2009).

The continuation of war by other means?

In adapting to this new political and ideological environment, the Provisional movement was undertaking more than a tactical readjustment as they entered Northern Ireland's political mainstream. Increasingly challenged by the consociational assumptions and institutional structures of the GFA, the Provisional leadership was forced to radically revise many of the fundamental premises of its historical project (Bean and Hayes 2009).

As a result the new politics of Sinn Féin was increasingly characterized by a substantially diminished sense of political agency and historical subjectivity, combined with a more general loss of faith in the transformative potential of politics. Operating in a polity designed to manage rather than transform the conflict between the newly designated *ethnic* blocs of nationalism and unionism, Sinn Féin was compelled to scale down its ambition from national self-determination to representation of the nationalist community: advancing nationalist interests *within* the state rather than overthrowing it (Ó Ruairc 2007).

Increasingly focused on the business of securing immediate goals, post-agreement Provisional strategy soon became driven less by an ambition to transform unionism than a desire to gain advantage over it (Shirlow 2007). The parameters of Sinn Féin's 'new' response to loyalism were in a sense already pre-determined by earlier republican characterizations of the unionist bloc and the nature of its relationship to Britain.

Paradoxically, while Northern Ireland's new political dispensation with its sectarianized dynamic of interethnic competition demanded that Sinn Féin radically rethink its responses to unionism/ loyalism, Sinn Féin's strategy towards unionism often demonstrated very little surface change. Indeed, much republican rhetoric remained comfortably familiar to its supporters, dangerously or duplicitously so to its detractors (Frampton 2009: 79). The notion that republicans might advance their project through exploitation of unionist divisions had been an important theme in the Provisionals' peace process strategy before 1998.

A key strategy in this earlier period had been to neutralize unionist opposition through a combination of diplomatic manoeuvre (notably involving the United States government), the construction of a pan-nationalist alliance, and the exploitation of the political and social divisions within unionism. In 1994 an internal republican briefing paper, the Totally Unarmed Strategy (TUAS) document, argued that Provisional strategy should aim, *inter alia*, to 'create a dynamic which ... [could] ... expose the ... Unionists as the intransigent parties [and] ... heighten the contradictions between British unionism and "Ulster Loyalism"' (Moloney 2002: 498–9).

Likewise, after 1998, it was suggested that republicanism might be advanced through careful manoeuvring within the structural dynamics of the GFA alongside exploitation of external factors such as a favourable international conjuncture and a positive combination of economic and demographic forces (Anderson 2003; de Bréadún 2008; Harrison 2008). These conjectures reflected an on going republican narrative of long-term nationalist advance in the context of unionist economic decline, leading to the steady erosion of unionism's self-confidence and political power.

For the loyalist working class in particular the collapse of the old certainties would, it was argued, increase their sense of political alienation and intensify the unionist community's collective identity crisis (Bean 2007: 204). Some republicans argued that unionism's economic crisis would mean that increasing numbers of 'middle- and higher-class Protestants will see their economic interests lying in an all-Ireland environment' (O'Hamill 2005). Drawing on the South African model of transition and echoing Stalinist conceptions of the 'progressive anti-imperialist bourgeoisie', Sinn Féin leaders argued that a 'progressive unionism' willing to cooperate with the republican project in its own political and economic self-interest could emerge from within the unionist social elite (Adams 1993).

In what might be characterized as the high politics of the peace process, Sinn Féin's tactics of political gamesmanship appeared to be almost entirely designed to intensify and exploit unionist divisions. The protracted, tactical nature of decommissioning, the ambiguities within IRA pronouncements of a commitment to exclusively peaceful and political means, and the final bargaining around republican recognition of the policing and justice systems, all acted to increase unionist uncertainty and suspicion (Frampton 2009: 103).

From a Provisional perspective the tortuous negotiations and long drawn out crises that followed the GFA were brilliantly successful in closing down all the options available to unionists other than that of including Sinn Féin in government. The emergence of the DUP at the expense of the UUP in 2003 was the final product of Sinn Féin's strategy of 'divide and rule', ultimately permitting Sinn Féin to achieve its aims of going into government with a party that was not only the dominant electoral representative of the unionist community, but also had no viable rivals on its right flank.

In the continuation of war by other means, loyalism played an important role in Provisional strategizing, although often a very different role from that suggested in the language of peace and reconciliation. Instead, Sinn Féin focused on the contradictions implicit within loyalism's historical and contemporary meaning within the unionist bloc, in particular the troubled relationship between constitutional unionism and loyalist paramiltarism. Exploiting the tensions that surfaced within unionism during the Drumcree protests and pointing out the strong electoral support for Ian Paisley and the DUP in militant loyalist areas, guilt by association often proved a useful rejoinder to unionist charges that Sinn Féin was inextricably linked to the IRA.

On these occasions Sinn Féin used loyalism to attack 'rejectionist and reactionary unionism' by arguing that '[s]ectarian anti-Catholicism ... [was] at the heart of historical and contemporary unionist politics' and that, as such, there was considerable common ground between mainstream unionism and loyalism (O'Leary 2000). In particular, republicans argued there were a shared set of ideological assumptions between the 'shaven lout who throws the pipe bomb' or the 'drug fuelled hood who jumps on his victim's head', and unionist politicians and Protestant fundamentalists who 'identify nationalists as the enemy within' and who by viewing 'Catholic as unacceptable ... in the eyes of God ... create a context within which attacks on Catholics are inevitable' (Friel 2006a; McCloskey 2006).

This was especially the case among the 'fragmented rump of UUPs, PUPs, DUPs, UDAs, and UVF and all manner of fundamentalist alphabet men' [who were competing] 'to be the legitimate heirs to a brand of [traditional] unionism still engulfed in the centuries old swamp of bigotry and sectarianism' (Nellis 2009). However, the resonance of this narrative for many nationalists meant that its usefulness for republicans went beyond a mere debating point. The identification of loyalism with unionism had a long history among nationalists: even before the outbreak of the Troubles 'loyalist' had been used as a blanket term to describe all unionists, not just those associated with paramiltarism (Adams 1986: 113–26).

Although the Provisionals maintained a keen appreciation of the different tendencies within unionism and how such differences might be exploited militarily and politically, their working assumption was that the unionist bloc remained essentially intact. Unionist politicians, for obvious reasons, had long been keen to distance themselves from a loyalism, which they defined as a deviant paramilitarist form fundamentally distinct and opposed to their own constitutional unionism (Bruce 2007; Farrington 2008; Moloney 2008; Walker 2004).

However, Sinn Féin propaganda acknowledged no such nice distinction: to republicans any differences were of degree rather than fundamental character; loyalists were simply and would always remain '*unionist* paramili-taries' (Friel 2005a). Moreover, in describing groups such as the UVF and the UDA in this way the Provisionals argued they were simply echoing loyal-ism's own self-definition as an integral part of the unionist family (David Ervine, quoted in Spencer 2008: 44).

'Barking mad on the edge of Europe'

Despite periods of crisis and hiatus the underlying character of Northern Irish politics has settled into a recognizable and apparently immutable shape in the ten years following the signing of the GFA. Structurally the pattern is one of communal competition for power and resources, while ideologically the contending parties define themselves through the politics of identity. The two conflicting 'traditions' of unionism and nationalism are embedded into the Agreement's institutional structure while 'normal' politics focuses on gaining both symbolic and actual advantage over one's communal opponents (Friel 2008).

For example, proposed British government funding for projects in loyalist areas may be described as the 'UDA's payoff money' (Nellis 2006; 2007) or the consequence of a strategy that 'sectarianised the issue of poverty ... while elevating special pleading above empirical analysis' (Sinn Féin councillor Chrissie McAuley, quoted in Friel 2006b). Tensions in interface areas and disputes over housing policy are routinely framed in this way, as loyalist claims that Catholic encroachment into 'Protestant areas' provokes conflict are countered by Sinn Féin arguments that sectarian tensions are main-tained and manipulated by unionist politicians and loyalist paramilitaries (de Rosa 2001; Sinn Féin 2001).

Other long-running disputes over discrimination in employment and sectarian violence have also proved to be politically expedient for the Provisionals, allowing them to seize the moral high ground and stake a claim to victimhood on behalf of the nationalist community (Anderson 2007; Gillespie 2006). This is increasingly important as Northern Irish poli-tics have become a bidding war for funding and resources conducted by unionist and nationalist politicians on behalf of their respective communi-ties. It is this type of competition, combined with frequent appeals to the British state as an external arbiter in disputes, that now defines the terms of trade and the rules of engagement between unionism and nationalism in the new dispensation; the protracted debates over the devolution of justice and policing (BBC News 2009c).

One of the paradoxes of Northern Ireland society is that beneath the sur-face of sectarian conflict lies a curiously stable, highly regulated and man-aged political environment, where party politics are often played out in the form of a stylized theatrical performance in which communal politicians play to their respective galleries, never completely returning to open war yet unable to reach a satisfactory conclusion (Dixon 2002). As Richard English has perceptively observed, after 1998 the new Northern Ireland was 'facing a culture war and a political struggle between two antagonistic communities, rather than any harmony between them' (English 2005).

The most obvious effect of this political stalemate has been the expansion of both the DUP and Sinn Féin beyond their traditional constituencies to become the acknowledged champions of their respective ethnic blocs (Evans and Tonge 2009). The PUP's Dawn Purvis describes Northern Ireland's political stasis as a consequence of 'the politics of fear', an environment in which the DUP and Sinn Féin 'seek to maintain division through fear in order to serve... [their] own interests' and reproduce a sectarianized politics based on 'separate but equal' nationalist and unionist communities (Moriarty 2009).

Significantly these divisions at the political level both reflect and reinforce the deepening segregation and communalization of public life in the region in the wake of the GFA (Coulter and Murray 2008; Shirlow 2001: 67–74; Shirlow and Murtagh 2006). Sinn Féin expresses this political stalemate through two distinct, but conjoined narratives of the nationalist and loyalist communities. The nationalist population is the new 'risen people', former victims of loyalism borne along towards victory on the tides of history and demography.

Loyalism, in contrast, is characterized as being in disarray, stagnating in isolation far away from the currents of modern life (Friel 2005b). The belief that the loyalist community faces a profound social and economic crisis has become quite commonplace across Northern Irish politics, as commentators frequently point to 'the irreversible decline within the Protestant working class', while loyalists themselves highlight problems of social deprivation and alienation in their communities, contrasting their collective disadvantage with the perceived onward march of the nationalist community (Howe 2005).

Beyond social exclusion, poverty and joblessness, many republicans understand the crisis of loyalism as an existential problem, whose characteristics were historically determined by the formation of the unionist bloc and its privileged relationship to Britain. For Gerry Adams: 'Unionists are the human face of this very negative connection with Britain. At times my heart goes out to them. I know working class loyalist areas are leaderless. They were able to live too long in the shadow of the empire and the shadow of the Orange Hall' (quoted in Bean 1994: 19).

Loyalists were an 'outpost people', the frontier guards of a dead empire and as a 'manifestation of British rule in Ireland' republicans believed that 'the moral responsibility for all loyalism's crimes lies with the British state who had sanctioned and armed them' (Derrig 1999; Sinn Féin 2000a). Loyalism's contemporary sense of alienation, it was argued, was a product of the unionist obsolescence for British interests:

Unionism's problem is that it is on permanent Sentry Duty and its services are no longer required. Barking mad on the edge of Europe – the unionists have no place left to go. Everything that defined who was on what side of the Orange Maginot line has melted away, or is in terminal decline. (Sinn Féin 1999)

In post-conflict Northern Ireland, loyalism appears to face a collective psychological and political crisis exacerbated by the advance of a self-assertive nationalist community. Gerry Adams' therapeutic language of conflict resolution was frequently extended into the metaphors of madness: republicans portrayed loyalists as sociopaths unable to come to terms with the contemporary world or even like King Lear, reduced to raging 'ever more impotently against ... [their] inability to continue to exert their absolute power' (Lane 2001).

Lacking an autonomous political project, philosophy or raison d'être beyond sectarianism and racism, the 'resident psychotics' of loyalist paramilitarism behaved like a 'wounded animal, cornered by history and lashing out in blind rage' (Lane 1999; Sinn Féin 2000b). Theirs was 'a hateful and degenerate sub-culture' that could not come to terms with change; to republicans, loyalism was 'nothing but a by-word for [an] irrational hatred of republicans in particular and Catholics in general' (Sinn Féin 2000c). Loyalist paramilitary groups, such as the UDA, were not 'politically driven', instead they had a history of 'bloody sectarian murder that has degenerated into a quagmire of criminality and drug dealing' (Whelan 2007).

In the context of the profound political disengagement of the poorest unionist communities, republicans believed that the history of loyalism posed insurmountable problems for the development of a coherent political movement. For example, it was suggested that the PUP would not long outlive David Ervine because most loyalists continued 'to view the world in crude orange and green terms' (Friel 2007b).

Even radical republicans with established links to their loyalist counterparts were sceptical of the future potential of 'progressive' unionism as the voice of the Protestant working class, contrasting the IRA's relationship to the republican community with the authoritarian and elitist character of loyalist paramilitaries: 'the UVF, like loyalist organisations in general ... seemed to have little support within its own community. The mains that kept its bulb glowing had to be located extraneously, for the most part within the security apparatuses of the British state' (McIntyre 2007: 7).

Although clearly rooted in older republican positions, which characterized unionism as a false consciousness and servant of British imperialism, notions of an existential crisis within loyalism represented a new turn in republican thinking, serving as key framing mechanism for the new politics of Sinn Féin on two distinct, but intimately related levels.

On the one hand, the nationalist community's supposed political and economic expansion could be contrasted with the terminal decline and blinkered insularity of loyalism. On the other hand, having established the trope of a crisis ridden, reactionary loyalism, this narrative could be counterposed to an account of a progressive, cosmopolitan nationalism to produce a self-congratulatory triumphalism which both flattered the republican base and reassured them that Sinn Féin's strategy was indeed working (Campbell 1998). In a revealing turnaround these derogatory narratives about loyalism appear to bolster the republican ascendancy in the same way that themes of Catholic backwardness and inferiority had acted historically to legitimate the dominance and maintain the unity of unionism (Elliott 2009: 182–99).

Part of who we are?

While the supposed binary opposition between the nature of republicanism and loyalism is most clearly expressed in disputes between the political parties, it has remained one of the Provisionals most fundamental, if unspoken assumptions: from the culture wars surrounding the authenticity of Ulster Scots and discrimination against the Irish language through to funding disputes between the West Belfast and the Maiden City Festivals, St Patrick's Day and 'Orangefest' parades, the richness and inclusiveness of nationalist culture is continually played off against the thin gruel and mediocrity of loyalist traditions (Friel 2001a; 2005c).

The discourse of cultural superiority became increasingly important to the Provisionals as Sinn Féin's revolutionary project diminished in the 1990s and its focus narrowed to securing its position within representational politics in Northern Ireland. In the context of political retreat, these narratives of cultural superiority may be understood as an attempt to restore a sense of meaning and purpose to a republican movement, which increasingly finds it acting at variance with historical republican aims.

By constantly rehearsing the catechism of binary opposition between republicanism and the loyalist Other, the republican leadership sought to reconnect with its constituency by stressing how much the nationalist community had gained from the new dispensation at the expense of loyalism. The choreographed sectarianism of Drumcree and Holy Cross was only one such example that served to reinforce nationalist prejudice as loyalists dutifully played out the role allotted to them by Provisional strategists (Friel 2001b).

Although Gerry Adams' definition of the Orange Order as a legitimate expression of unionist identity and 'part of who we are as a nation' seems far removed from these negative stereotypes, both narratives actually share a deep pessimism (Adams 2009; Walsh 2009). In contrast to Tone's objective of a *political* transformation rooted in universalist ideas of democracy, the contemporary Provisional project rests instead on particularist concepts of *cultural* identity.

Consequently, despite the language of engagement and transition, Sinn Féin's adoption of the politics of recognition actively precludes the possibility of any fundamental change in loyalist consciousness. Indeed, their strategy seems not only to require the existence of the loyalist Other, but is actually designed to reproduce it as a permanent feature of political and social life.

For some this managed stalemate is 'the best that can be done for a while' (Noam Chomsky, quoted in Graham 2009). Others hope that the identity politics and the communal supplication for resources that have come to define public life may be challenged by the economic recession and the impact of cuts in British government expenditure in the region (Clarke 2009; Socialist Party 2009). However, the opposite is more likely to be true.

Despite the increasing sense of political ennui and disengagement revealed in complaints that '[t]he gap between the politicians and working class communities is getting wider all the time', the economic crisis is likely to produce *more* rather than *less* division as ethnic political entrepreneurs, like Sinn Féin, attempt to pull up the drawbridge and secure both real and symbolic advantage for their constituency at the expense of their communal opponents (McCaffery 2008).

Thus, while it may seem perversely quixotic to discuss the future of an Ulster Scots Academy or agitate for an Irish Language Act during a period of financial stringency what these debates clearly reveal is that it is neither 'bread and butter issues' or even the constitutional status of the state, but rather the politics of difference that will continue to define both Sinn Féin's strategy and what passes for 'real' politics in Northern Ireland (BBC News 2009d).

Chapter 5
From Politics to Community Development: In Discussion with Billy Hutchinson

Graham Spencer

Billy Hutchinson, a former UVF prisoner and political representative of the PUP, gained a seat at the Northern Ireland Assembly along with his political colleague David Ervine after the GFA in 1998. Engaged in dialogue and negotiations with both British and Irish governments throughout the peace process, Hutchinson played an important part in facilitating the political transition, which was to draw the UVF away from violence.

The culmination of this transition was the decommissioning of paramilitary weapons in 2009 where Hutchinson acted as interlocutor between the UVF and the IICD on the path to the removal of weapons which took place in July 2009. Hutchinson continues to play a central role in the internal debates about community activism and change, which now occupy UVF attention. Having lost his seat as a PUP representative at the 2003 Assembly elections Hutchinson subsequently became a community development worker and is now based in north Belfast.

This chapter, set in the form of an interview, explores with Hutchinson the process of change, which shifted UVF consciousness from an adherence to political violence towards the realization that such violence was counter productive given changed political and social circumstances. Acknowledgement that republican transformation away from the violent to the political demanded a reciprocal response from loyalism obviously posed greater difficulties for loyalists given the absence of a coherent political project or foothold in any specific political constituency. In that instance, the argument about ending violence and resolving the weapons issue was made on the grounds that loyalist reaction would be best expressed as a gesture of support for democratic development and post-conflict 'normalization' and that the GFA had delegitimized violence as a response to social and political difference.

In this chapter Hutchinson provides explanation of areas such as the PUP's early experiences negotiating with British and Irish governments, the party's strategy during the early phases of the peace process, the shift towards internal transformation within the UVF during the period of the GFA and after, how decommissioning was achieved, the development of community-based politics and the problems which lay ahead for loyalism.

Hutchinson's comments provide an important insight into not just the chronology of events, which the PUP and UVF were involved in, but how one community of loyalism has reacted to recent history and how it might continue to try and deal with future pressures, changes and concerns.

In discussion with Billy Hutchinson

GS: Can you explain how you saw the PUP's role in the peace process and what it actually achieved?

BH: The governments wanted us on board and the reason they wanted us on board was because they realized that we were trying to influence the UVF and Red Hand and they were comfortable with that as long as each was not engaged in any violent activity. The Irish Government was quite happy for us to be involved because what they didn't need was some sort of loyalist activity around the Irish Republic. I suppose what we achieved was a progressive loyalism, or a progressive unionism, and I don't mean in the party political sense but in the sense of people. We actually broke the ground for others to walk on and the Agreement would not have been signed, if we hadn't been involved in the talks.

GS: What do you mean when you say that the PUP broke the ground for others to walk on?

BH: We were the people who said that we should be talking to republicans. We were the people who actually said that negotiations were good. We were the people who were saying that we shouldn't be worried about how the Agreement would turn out between the two governments and the Northern Ireland community. And we were arguing that the Agreement was based on a three-legged stool, where if one of the legs collapsed then obviously the whole stool collapsed. We were also arguing for Articles 2 and 3 of the Irish constitution to disappear and making it known that this would strengthen the Union rather than weaken it. The people who were most opposed about being in with republicans, namely the DUP, who were saying never, never, never, then went and did share power with republicans. And even though they may not acknowledge how we created that ground for them to walk on because they wouldn't want to give us any credit for it, we certainly did just that. They would never have been able to walk that ground if we hadn't actually prepared it.

GS: How much of the debate for change was influenced by the military men and how much of it was down to the political thinkers?

BH: I suppose it was somewhere around 70 per cent political and 30 per cent military. But political people were being listened to by the military people and vice versa. We knew that this would be a long road and that we needed people sharing the vision, which, of course had to come from those of a military background who believed in a political way forward. We needed people who had been there and were recognized with having military backgrounds but who could argue that the way ahead needed to be both non-violent and political.

GS: How difficult was it to influence the military people that the political way was the right way and what obstructions did you come up against?

BH: The military leadership initiated this whole thing in terms of encouraging people to have discussions and telling them how to move forward, so they were already brought into this need to move on and initiate change. The difficulty came through middle managers that may not have bought into it. So although the top level leadership was agreed we had the next level that we needed to work with and the level below that again. They were the people where we needed to build this shared vision or shared way forward and they were the people who had to be convinced. The obstructions came whenever things went wrong or things were perceived to be wrong. People got a bit jittery when we started talking about negotiations with the Irish Government.

My argument was to impress that just because other people defined something as acceptable did not mean it was acceptable to us. So when certain documents came out some got very unhappy, claiming that the documents did not reflect what we told the Irish. The doubters had built expectations and read things that weren't there so it was a question of managing this dissent and waiting for the reality to emerge so people could see it for what it was and not what they thought it was. But in many ways we were lucky because we had a forward thinking leadership who weren't going to take knee-jerk reactions. It helped greatly in that they were constant in that approach and that it was the same people all the time that we were dealing with.

GS: Republicans have the long-term vision of Irish unity, but presumably you were trying to secure and entrench what already existed?

BH: We weren't trying to secure and entrench all that existed, what we were trying to secure and entrench was the Union and as part of that we wanted the Irish Government to give up Articles 2 and 3. We wanted the Irish Government to give them up, so that they didn't have a claim. We wanted them to say that they had no longer had a strategic selfish interest.

GS: The same as the British had said to republicans?

BH: We wanted them to acknowledge that there were British citizens living in this island and they needed to be protected under British jurisdiction. And we achieved that, because if you look at the GFA you will see that agreement on how to move forward wasn't a short stepping-stone to united Ireland. The Irish Government, along with the British Government, were trying to convince loyalists that they didn't have a selfish interest in a united Ireland either, that they wanted peace first and foremost and if the people of Ireland as a whole decided they wanted a united Ireland, then that was a different thing.

GS: Were you responding to events as you went along or did you have a long-term goal of how you were going to achieve security for the Union?

BH: Our role was about trying to convince people that we had a long-term goal of achieving the Union but it was about arguing that case. But what we really were doing was firefighting. In terms of being able to take each issue as it came up during the whole period from probably 1994 to 1998 we were fighting it on a weekly or daily basis. The issues changed as we moved from one thing to the other and we decided what we needed to do within that environment. It was a question of taking a very positive stance but at the same time, being able to articulate to the leadership of the UVF and the others, that this was the way forward and to support it.

GS: Do you think that your ability and skills as negotiators were better in 1998 than they were in 1994?

BH: I can remember in December 1994, going to meet the civil servants for the very first time and the civil servants knew who the team was because the people I had negotiated with in prison were put in to renegotiate with us again on exploratory dialogue. Because we had already been at the table and negotiated with them before – they knew how we operated, so that team was set up to try to counter us or at least to understand us and tackle the questions they knew we were going to ask. The reason I led the delegation was because of my experience of negotiating with these people before in the prison, so although they knew about me I also knew a bit about them.

GS: Did you see the civil servants as just out to stifle you?

BH: I think what they were there to do was to prolong things. They would have long protracted talks about issues and obviously decommissioning was one of them but it was my job to steer them away from talking about it in the first instance. We kept putting loyalist things on the table and we kept saying we're here to negotiate and we have to agree on terms of the agenda and here is what we need on that agenda. It came to the point where they actually used a tactic of divide and conquer. They went to the UDP and they talked to people in the UDP negotiation team who would agree with us about prisoners and guns but who were then encouraged to not let this happen. I went to a meeting and this guy started talking about prisoners and guns on the same sort of agenda and I said we're not talking about prisoners and guns. I said those are separate issues and they're not inextricably linked. That was I suppose a continued thorn in our side. Some of the UDP, particularly the people who were perceived as the senior people of the delegation, even though they weren't down in name, wanted to talk about guns and prisoners and they knew that we were quite vehemently opposed to it, so this did create problems which the civil servants tried to develop.

GS: So do you think you would have made quicker progress operating alone, without the UDP?

BH: No, because I think that our strength was together. We did not make quicker progress at that time because we weren't together in terms of our voice. This was not helped by other people with other agendas, whether that was coming from the UDA or whoever. From our point of view we were trying to focus on how to move forward and we didn't want it to be all about paramilitary issues. We also needed to look at socio-economic issues and wanted to talk that through completely separate from all the other issues. We didn't want all points of conversation to be about paramilitary affairs, which would have been what civil servants were after. We also had to have our own agenda recognized and addressed. The civil servants wanted to keep people on board and they wanted to be able to manage loyalism. They obviously knew that people were working together to keep ceasefires intact and they probably wanted to be careful how they handled the agenda, but at the same time, they were rushing to get to the end, before we'd even got to the beginning and that was the difficulty.

GS: Looking back would you like to have seen exploratory dialogue taking place with both Irish and British teams rather than just the British?

BH: I suppose in many ways it would have been better, because the Irish were always more receptive to what we were saying, because they could see that we were sort of rooted in grass roots and talking from that point of view. Obviously they were also concerned about the damage that people could do with the weapons that they had and a particular interest to keep everybody on board because of that, so they would be more sympathetic in that sense. They probably would have wanted to deal more with the issues that we wanted to deal with and then get to the weapons issue towards the end.

GS: After the Good Friday Agreement was reached how did you see yourselves moving ahead?

BH: I suppose after the referendum my concern was that the British Government at that particular stage wanted to bolster the two largest parties and weren't really interested in people who were on the periphery. But their difficulty was that a number had been elected to the Assembly, such as the PUP and Women's Coalition and they couldn't ignore us. They couldn't have talks with the Ulster unionists and not have talks with the rest of us. But I think that when David Trimble took the position of no guns and no government it made it impossible for us because it increased anti-Agreement feeling in unionist areas. He handled it badly, but we paid for it as well.

GS: So weapons really did become the dominant issue for you?

BH: Well the weapons did become the dominant issue and particularly for republicans, but it also broke any sort of notion of conflict resolution between republicans and loyalists, in the sense that the weapons would come at the end, after all of the institutions were up and running. This was an agreement that was held, not by the UVF and the IRA, but certainly between the political representatives of Sinn Fein and the PUP. That was removed and it was removed because what we then had was rather than the weapons being given up because we were living in a democratic society, the weapons were given up to keep two Sinn Fein ministers in government.

GS: If republicans at that point had given up weapons would the UVF have followed instantly?

BH: No and that wasn't the case. Any discussions we had with republicans, particularly through Sinn Fein, were based on the position that decommissioning was certainly an issue for people in our society, but it was an issue after we had the institutions up and running and not before. What we got, rather than a conflict resolution process or transformation process, was republicans moving out of synch to actually save their own skins and for me, that made a mess of the whole decommissioning problem because the test in terms of decommissioning was about whether this was a project or whether it was reality. Republicans kept talking about it as a project and the unionists kept arguing that is was not a project but what needed to happen because of signing up to the GFA. So we had all of those arguments and decommissioning was a test for both loyalists and republicans. It was a recognition that we had reached that stage to nail the frame around democracy and acknowledge that we were all inside it.

GS: Were you talking quite closely with republicans at that time about all these points?

BH: Oh, we were talking regularly to them. We had talks in Hillsborough when Blair made his speech about 'the hand of history' and we had discussions when the Irish and British were talking about everybody handing in weapons and from that we build a statue to the future. It was all that kind of stuff. At that particular time I had met with senior republicans about what was going on and they said that nothing was going on because there would be no decommissioning. They went on about how they were moving forward but they were forced into that position by Trimble. In many ways, they saw the relationship with

Trimble as a piece of interdependency but for me that was where we started to see the cracks. That situation started to make it hard for us because it made it more difficult for us to work in the political arena and to actually do things.

GS: Did you find that you were continually being dragged back to the decommissioning issue?

BH: Not only were we being dragged back to the decommissioning issue, we were being dragged back to the lowest common denominator all the time, in terms of the people on the streets who didn't want any movement and wanted to continually create problems, whether it was Drumcree, or any other protest. That is what was happening, and it was on both sides. We had to deal with people who wanted to mess everything up and we had to deal with that as well as this notion of no guns no government, which Trimble created.

GS: The loyalist tendency has been towards reaction whereas republicans have a political strategy. Was that not part of the problem?

BH: We also had the problem with republicans where, for the first time, they were also learning how to negotiate with governments. But, they were trying to manage that process and change from a politics of protest to a politics of delivery, which was a big issue for them that they had to learn. Because they continually talked about having a project, so they also cultivated this vision about where they were going. The difficulty with that is that you lose sight of the obstacles and how to get round obstacles. They just felt they could give up guns have two ministers back in place and everything would be rosy in the garden, but it was far from that.

GS: How did the UVF of 2009 differ from the UVF of 1998?

BH: I think what happened was that society changed a great deal, circumstances changed, opportunities to do things in 1998 weren't as good as they are in 2009 and paramilitaries sit in a different context in 2009 than they did in 2008. It's a growing opportunity and circumstances are right for change now, which weren't right in 1998. I suppose in many ways whenever you want to do something you have to create the circumstances for it to happen, and from 2007 circumstances started to change. The UVF started to work to actually make sure that they could meet those circumstances and gained a sense of purpose and conviction from that.

Q: At what point did you think decommissioning was going to happen?

BH: Probably from about 2007 and the reason for that was because we'd lost an opportunity when the republicans did it. When republicans decommissioned it wasn't a surprise but we didn't expect them to do it because we thought they would have held to their principles. The reality was that politics shifted their principles because they needed to get people into government and that's why they did it.

GS: When republicans decommissioned did you feel pressure to follow?

BH: No, there was never a pressure in terms of doing it and the reason was because there was nothing in it politically. The people who were trying to bring us under pressure, weren't trying to pressure for the UVF to decommission but to discredit us. My argument was that this needed to be done at some stage, but the time had to be right. The UVF leadership thought about it more from 2007 and felt that they needed to seize an opportunity to start working towards this end and that's what they did. They sold the whole thing themselves so they need to take the credit for it.

GS: There must have been tremendous resistance though?

BH: In many ways the debate had been about where loyalism was going and there were some hard questions the leadership had to answer. It was a long process, which probably lasted a couple of years and consisted of leaders deciding how they were going to do it. They called a very small cabal around them and decided that this needed to be done in a very contained way and then work it out and out through the organization. They decided they didn't want to tell everybody at the start what they were doing, so they went with a small group. From there they came up with the idea of how it had to be done, and then they started to sell it to the others, until they had every unit in agreement.

GS: What was the argument for doing it?

BH: The bigger argument was that the UVF needed to reinvent itself and volunteers within the UVF should have a different role to play given the changed circumstances. The case was made that they still have a battle and a war to fight, but not necessarily against the same people. Rather efforts should now be directed against poverty or community. So there was a notion that battlegrounds had moved and that tactics had moved as well. And all this change had to be done in a non-violent way. The issue of not needing the weapons any longer was built into that discussion.

GS: So it was very important to keep confidential when decommissioning was going to happen?

BH: That was because we didn't want people running all over the countryside with cameras and police looking for people moving stuff about. The other issue was that people were in talks with the UDA who weren't working at the same speed and there had been a discussion around when we would announce. It wasn't the question of a date because dates have been avoided like the plague, but more a question of when the two organizations could release a statement. Even though the UVF had already complained, they held back for the UDA and what happened then was that some of the things going on within the UDA discussions had been leaked to media people. So, the thing was filled with problems right from the very start and for a number of reasons we weren't making it public because we were right bang in the middle of the marching season. We had all of those problems and the thing was fraught with danger, because people in the print media were just interested in stories and how they could make the whole thing negative, rather than look at the positive side. We wanted to try and control the media but then they started printing nonsense about this person not agreeing with and that person, people who weren't even involved.

GS: Was it a process or was it more a case of dealing with one area at a time?

BH: It was a process. We'd sit down, because I was the interlocutor and I sat down with people and we worked out the logistics of how we were going to do it and then we put some stuff in place for it to happen and looked at what was going wrong, or how things could go wrong. We carried out dry runs and worked on how we could improve. We were running these things by the IICD and most of it was in code, giving them scenarios about what could happen and what couldn't happen and that's how it took place. Setting it up from start to finish probably took us about three months. I think our concern was that once it was done, the British Government or everybody else was just going to say okay they've done that now we can forget about loyalist communities, but our argument was that we weren't going to allow that to happen. So we had a number of meetings where we actually decided that once this was done we would need to talk about what needed to be addressed in loyalist communities and in particular, investment. What we didn't want to do was to have a connection between the socioeconomic stuff that needed to happen and the decommissioning, so that's why we didn't do it at the same time.

We're now arguing that both governments and the political parties need to be dealing with these communities. Nobody can say well, you know, we're not going to decommission if you don't do x, y and z, because the decommissioning is nothing to do with that. The decommissioning was based solely on the fact that society had moved on in 2009, that we are living in a democratic society, that we needed to show an act of faith and the act of faith had to be decommissioning because there was nothing else to do. When you make decisions like that you know that they're not always popular decisions and that there will always be people who will ask what did you do that for? This would be not so much people who are in positions of power, but those who are not in positions of power and it's very easy to criticize decisions when you're not in that position.

GS: Was the UDA supposed to go ahead with decommissioning at the same time as the UVF?

BH: The plan was to have discussions about what was happening and people would fill that in for whatever reason, but the particular issue of timing with the UDA was not worked out. I also think that they had bad advice from others. I can't actually prove who gave them the advice, but that advice seemed to suggest they had a negotiating position, which was wrong. It was rumoured that they wanted five workers and £10 million invested in projects. The rumour was they wanted £5 million from the Irish Government and £5 million from the British Government for socio-economic issues and projects. But the NIO [Northern Ireland Office] who you might have been negotiating with did not have responsibility for those sorts of issues, which falls to the First and Deputy First Minister.

On the point about a negotiation stance; the first thing you do is don't put yourself in a position you can't get out of. So for instance, if you ask for that sort of money and it's not forthcoming, what do you do? Do you just keep your guns and go on with it? Particularly whenever you're in an untenable position this is not a good move and bear in mind this occurred alongside the UVF who went ahead with it. We followed the decommissioning legislation, which the IRA would have had to do as well.

GS: Did you have verifiers there?

BH: Yes. The verifiers for us also acted as verifiers for each government and there were three from each jurisdiction. None of them were clergy and we didn't identify them. We chose those who we saw as 'critical friends'. They were brought in and briefed and they agreed that they didn't want their names identified, because they didn't want to go through that whole process of people vilifying them.

GS: Why did you select critical people?

BH: We needed to have people who we felt had a sense of independence and understood what was going on. We also needed people we could trust, who had some sort of proven track record as trustworthy. The leadership has to have a say in the people chosen and they knew the verifiers through having previously come into contact with them within a UVF constituency.

GS: What is the UVF now?

BH: From 2007 to now there's been a metamorphosis where the organization has changed and continues to change. I suppose the UVF are offering their people the opportunity to get involved in political activity, community activity, ex-prisoners associations and so on. They're encouraging people to get involved in those areas and that's how they will probably continue to exist in the future. And of course, because of a dissident republican presence they'll still be there.

GS: Are dissident republicans a real fear?

BH: It would be foolish to underestimate them but the dissident republicans in my view are not a worry. They're very capable of destabilizing the whole process, but I'm not sure that they want to destabilize because if that were the strategy then all they need do is to kill a senior loyalist, or a senior republican. Of course, having said that, they have the potential to do that quite easily. But the other thing is that quite a lot of the political voices that come up from dissident republicans are not from the military part of those republicans. It's coming from people who are not interested in being involved in a military campaign, but are interested in taking on Sinn Fein's position of stopping short of a united Ireland.

GS: You have used the term 'progressive loyalism' but what do you mean by progressive?

BH: I'm talking about bringing loyalists to a point where they recognize the political change that is happening and understand their part in that and actively seeking to influence it rather than actually waiting for it to be done to them. That they are now proactively making decisions about what a new Northern Ireland looks like and should be whether that's about being in the council, or being in the Assembly, or being in a room and talking about what needs to happen in nationalist and loyalist communities and getting some sort of agreement, it doesn't really matter. So it's about how people get leadership, how they allow people on these estates to speak for themselves and to work with them to actually develop that.

GS: Is there a sense of relaxation in the community starting to emerge or are people still fearful?

BH: There are still a lot of issues to be dealt with. There's the whole problem of sectarianism and there's living with the past. Those two things need to be dealt with. But I also think there is a curiosity about what's happening which is coming through that takes the form of people talking to each other about what they're doing and what they're not doing and working together on projects. And then you've got another sort of layer where you have people in the unionist community who feel totally sold out, disgruntled and disconnected with the political and social change. Alongside this you have people in the republican community who are in that same position, but you've got others who are more relaxed because they feel that they've won the war and that Sinn Fein will deliver everything they want them to deliver. Republicans and nationalists are finding it harder to actually get people to get engaged in some of this community work and they're turning up the same people all the time, whereas in loyalism more people are coming forward to get involved and find out about what's going on. I also think that more people see the constitutional question as constructively dealt with and the movement is towards it being resolved. But for me personally, sectarianism and being able to share space with nationalism is now the primary concern.

Chapter 6
The Ulster Volunteer Force and the Path to Decommissioning

Chris Hudson

When attempting to fully understand loyalism and its journey since the GFA it is first necessary to take a step back and observe the transition since the loyalist ceasefire in 1994. This has been a journey of incremental change based on a new paradigm, which developed within loyalist thinking long before the ceasefire. I speak in particular with reference to the UVF because that is the organization I have engaged with throughout the peace process.

My first encounter was in early 1993 in Dublin, which led to an arranged meeting in Belfast during early 1994. The Belfast 'face to face' was not a meeting of minds and there were harsh words and some issuing of threats to the people of the South (Irish Republic). In that discussion, one of the participants (later given the codename 'Craftsman') even suggested to me that there was no reason why loyalists should not carry out a bombing campaign in Dublin. His contention was that this strategy had delivered for the Provisional IRA in London. Yet this man went on to be one of the main players in taking loyalist paramilitaries from a violent reactive position to one of positive engagement with all parties on the ceasefire and eventual decommissioning.

Naturally when the 'Craftsman' issued his threat I expressed my disagreement on the bombing of Dublin, but I could see why he might believe in such an idea. There was a perception among loyalists that the British governments were capable of submitting to IRA violence aimed at the 'mainland' and in particular the financial centre of London. Just how much of a pressure tactic this suggestion was is difficult to tell, but quite soon we moved from a sustained bombing campaign in Dublin to the possibility of a loyalist ceasefire and eventually to the ceasefire itself.

Strategies along the road to peace

It is my contention that the will to bring hostilities to an end had firmly taken hold in the thinking of senior UVF personnel at that time, but the logistics had not been put in place. My role along with many others was to help the strategy along the road to peace. The UVF had worked this through to its logical conclusion but needed people to map the way.

In 1993, I informed Fergus Finlay, political advisor to the then *Tánaiste* (Irish Deputy Prime Minister) Dick Spring, TD of the intention of the UVF to take the war to the Irish Republic if there was any attempt at introducing joint authority. One horrific proposal from the UVF was that they would 'take out' (shoot) the occasional tourist on the streets of Dublin; preferably an American tourist with sympathies to the IRA armed struggle (as they saw it). This, they thought, would avoid the logistical difficulties of a bombing campaign in the Republic, which could kill innocent Dubliners, who would in all likelihood be indifferent to the conflict in Northern Ireland. Such a bombing campaign was not ruled out, even as both republicans and loyalists inched towards their respective ceasefires.

I was always convinced from my early meetings with UVF leaders that the trajectory they were embarked on would also eventually reach a positive conclusion regarding weaponry. My feeling on this difficult and convoluted transition was always based on a position that one does not have to be an admirer of loyalist paramilitarism in order to see the significance in their cautious steps on the peace road. It was also possible through my involvement to sense that all potential obstructions would have to be overcome if a final and peaceful conclusion was to be reached.

In an interview with Peter Taylor of the BBC I once stated that I thought the PUP leader and former loyalist paramilitary David Ervine had made a firm commitment to try and bring the Northern Ireland conflict to a close. What impressed me about David was that he decided to do this by remaining within the loyalist UVF in order to drive the debate internally. He had not decided to move to the sideline and bark at his former colleagues with moral indignation.

Throughout 1993 I met with David Ervine many times. On most occasions a 'military man', whom as I stated, was given the codename the 'Craftsman', accompanied him. I quickly came to the conclusion that the 'Craftsman' was also sincere about where he hoped to take this process. If David gave the analysis, then the 'Craftsman' was the engineer driving the process that would lead to the loyalist ceasefire, support for the GFA and finally the journey towards decommissioning. My task as a conduit between the UVF and the Dublin government was not to negotiate, but nuance what the UVF were saying and make it clear that Dublin understood their position. I was always nervous that something could get lost in the telling, so I listened very carefully to what I was told. I made sure never to spin anything or put an over optimistic tone on interpretation.

My background as a Dubliner of Catholic nationalist background would not make me a fan or flag waver for loyalism, yet those that I communicated with never led me to believe one thing while they were doing another. I was probably an unlikely candidate to act as a go-between and it was to the credit of the UVF leadership that they found no issue with my background. It showed a level of political maturity that their main aim was to make sure that I was clearly relating their concerns and thinking in order to help move their own internal process of change. As David Ervine said, I could help with the 'mood music'.

Talking with the UVF leadership

Initially I was surprised that the UVF leadership did not match the comical stereotyping portrayed in much media reporting and I became increasingly convinced that their attempt to develop a peace process, which would run parallel to the Sinn Féin/ IRA process, was serious. The return to violence by the PIRA in 1996 after ending its ceasefire with the Canary Wharf bomb was a real test of will for the loyalists. However, they held the line and maintained their ceasefire with some help from certain quarters. I had been approached at that time to get the Dublin Government to make a statement, which could help the UVF leadership to restrain their volunteers, who were voicing the need for revenge.

The then *Taoiseach* was John Burton TD, Leader of Fine Gael, which was in government with the Irish Labour Party and Democratic Left. The Leader of Democratic Left, *Prionsias De Rossa* TD, who was also Minister for Social Welfare, met with me and agreed that John Bruton would reiterate sentiments in a speech suggested to me by the UVF. The purpose of this would help them maintain their ceasefire. John Bruton included a short text by me in his address to the joint houses in the United States, which proved extremely helpful, along with a number of well-attended rallies throughout Ireland calling on the PIRA to 'give us back our peace'.

In one Dublin rally, which was attended by some seventy thousand people, I made an address congratulating the loyalists for maintaining their ceasefire. This remark received sustained applause from the crowd. I had told the UVF that I was going to do this and hopefully it would encourage them to hold firm to the peace process. In seeking reassurance from both governments that no concessions would be granted to republicans without return to a sustained and credible ceasefire before reacting, loyalists showed a level of sophisticated thinking for which they rarely receive credit. Despite the best efforts they were not going to be provoked back into retaliatory action against the nationalist community, which would have led to the loss of innocent Catholic lives.

But if there was an incident that nearly derailed the loyalist ceasefire it was the Omagh bombing of 1998, which was carried out by the Real IRA and killed 29 people along with a pregnant mother carrying twins. I was contacted by the UVF and asked to travel to Belfast. Unfortunately I was not in a position to travel as I had suffered a mild heart attack and was recuperating at home in Dublin. Later my wife, Isabella, received a call from a senior member of the UVF insisting they needed to talk to me. Isabella stated I could not leave the house and there would be concern if I attempted to travel, but the UVF were empathic they needed to see me. Immediately a senior UVF member would travel to Dublin in order to deliver an important message, which I was to relay to the Dublin government.

The message consisted of two questions: 'What are you going to do about the Real IRA and are you going to crack down?' I knew this man was deeply concerned that there would be a loyalist revenge attack, maybe even in the Republic. He explained that a definite and clear response from the Dublin Government was needed in order to lower the temperature in the loyalist community. This message was subsequently passed on to *Taoiseach* Bertie Ahern by a senior government advisor.

A combination of national and international condemnations about the Omagh bomb helped to defuse pressure for loyalist retaliation. This was a real test of nerves and there were serious concerns at the time that loyalists would react violently, but again statements and decisive actions against dissident republicans in both jurisdictions proved extremely helpful in averting this prospect.

Years later, the Irish editor of the *Observer*, Henry McDonald, was to write: 'PUP leader and East Belfast MLA, David Ervine, confirmed that Hudson had played a key role in calming loyalist paramilitary anger in the aftermath of Omagh. Speaking before the PUP's annual conference, he said: "Chris Hudson's contribution to saving lives on this island cannot be underestimated. He played a massive part in calming fears and passing on assurance" ' (*The Observer* 10 October 2004).

Holding the line after Omagh was a key moment in terms of showing the intent of loyalist leaders to avert a return to cyclical response and counter response violence. And although the UVF and UDA engaged in interorganizational feuds after the GFA, the transition towards peace remained generally steady and cohesive. But there were of course still a number of problems to be overcome.

For example, after the GFA loyalists continued to insist that joint authority was never a runner. Any threat of joint authority, they threatened, would lead to civil strife and a situation where loyalists would make it unworkable. They would seek allies within the United Kingdom, they stated, to assist in disrupting and troubling the British government's efforts to implement joint authority.

One bizarre possibility outlined to me by a prominent member of the UVF was that thousands of loyalist volunteers would descend on Dublin and attempt a march from O'Connell Street to the *Dáil Éireann* (Irish parliament). They would be prepared to take casualties, even volunteers killed, he suggested in order to inflict serious disruption on the Republic's capital. They would also be willing to face any onslaught by Dublin republican groups and the *Gardaí Síochána* (Irish police). The plan would be that only experienced volunteers and young fit men would take part on such a march. Fortunately, the Dublin Government saw that the electorate would never have forgiven them for putting the citizenry of the Republic in the front line of the Northern Ireland Conflict if this were to happen.

Decommissioning and the UVF

In May of 2007 the UVF announced that they were standing down as a military organization. This was another step along their incremental journey and progress towards the final act, which was to be decommissioning. I welcomed the news stating that the Dublin Government was informed. I explained in an interview that my perception was that the UVF was 'standing down' and putting its weapons ' beyond reach'.

I also said: 'Nothing I can say could ever make up for the hurt felt by someone who has lost a loved one in the Troubles, but we, as a community, have to move forward. I would have loved for the UVF to have said this week that it had decommissioned all its weapons. But the UVF is like other organisations, it doesn't take kindly to being told what to do. It's a shame that the weapons weren't decommissioned 15 years ago, but I believe it is an issue which will be sorted out sooner rather than later' (*Irish News* 5 May 2007).

I well remember David Ervine telling me all those years before that there would be setbacks and terrible things would happen which we would have no control over, but he went on to say no matter what happened neither of us could walk away. David looked straight at me one time and stated categorically that Sinn Féin and the DUP would be in government one day at Stormont and on that day me and him could go and have a few pints because our work would be done. So much has been achieved, but one of my deepest regrets is David did not live to see it.

When we reflect on the beginning of the peace process let us remember that there were two ceasefires, one on behalf of the PIRA and the second announced by the CLMC. It is the latter of these two ceasefires, which sometimes disappears in the dominant narrative of Northern Ireland's path to peace. During this period I also wrote a piece in *The Observer* challenging the UVF to consult ordinary unionists about their views on decommissioning. I stated that I was very disappointed that the UVF had not started to decommission and encouraged the organization to engage in a consultative process with the Protestant community to gauge their views on disarmament. Most unionists wanted the UVF to decommission some weapons and I felt it was important for the organization to respond to this desire. I did not believe that unionist politicians would get the UVF to decommission, but they could not turn their backs or a deaf ear to their own people.

I also said in the article that loyalist paramilitaries have an obligation to the greater loyalist and unionist community, in particular those who voted 'Yes' to the Agreement, but not excluding those who voted 'No'. They should listen to that community and seek direction from them. I would be surprised if there are any people who voted PUP who did not think it was time to turn the key in order to lock up the arms. I suggested the establishment of alternative decommissioning schemes such as the possibility of logging paramilitary weapons involving a third party to confirm they are out of use, as was the case at the end of the El Salvador conflict.

Leading journalist Henry McDonald reported on my proposal stating that such comments were significant given that I was still in contact with the UVF leadership and regularly conveyed their views to officials in Dublin. In response to wider media interest to my comments I was interviewed on RTE's 'Morning Ireland' and invited to develop this view further.

The UVF and the IMC

When UVF leaders first participated in direct 'face to face' meetings with the IMC they insisted that decommissioning was not on the table. They argued that the organization was not in a position to negotiate the giving up or destruction of loyalist weapons. The weapons were the property of 'the people' ever since gun running at Larne in 1913. The position clearly stated at those initial meetings was that the UVF were in total opposition to decommissioning on a point of principle. Representatives were adamant that the UVF would not decommission weapons because the weapons belonged to 'the people', on whose behalf they operated. They maintained that the UVF had never given up weapons before and had no intention of doing so now.

But these representatives also knew that decommissioning was an essential part of the peace process as stipulated by the GFA and that this apparent opposition was more a holding position strategy, as leaders worked out the dialectics of preventing weapons on principle, to recognizing the liability of keeping guns, to how the practicalities of decommissioning might be worked out. This initial opposition was therefore only one in a series of possible incremental stages. Interestingly, the cacophony of so-called 'respectable' people calling on loyalists to decommission more often than not came from those who would be the last to positively respond to the decommissioning act.

From 2007 the UVF leadership was particularly pleased with relations on the ground, which had been significantly helped by interface meetings with republicans. This in turn underscored the changing mood and a more positive if tentative intent was emerging for concrete action on decommissioning. By late 2007, UVF representatives related to the IMC their concerns with a number of issues. The two most pertinent being conspiracy theories (which in their opinion could be embellished by informants) and, to use their language, 'agent provocateurs' whom they believed could be involved in derailing any discussion around decommissioning. Still, however, there was no intimation that decommissioning was going to happen. Words were mentioned that things were 'going according to plan', but no attempt to spell out what that meant.

The UVF appreciated the view of the IMC that there would be difficulties as long as decommissioning did not happen, but from the leadership point of view weapons had been 'put beyond reach' and this was the best that could be hoped for. This, they believed, rather than verifiable decommissioning provided closure. At this point, it was difficult to ascertain from the language of the UVF as to whether it was impossible to deliver decommissioning because of opposition within the ranks, or, because it was still a point of principle. They made the point on a number of occasions that they never looked for the PIRA to decommission and could not believe it when that organization did decommission.

A particularly interesting comment was made at a meeting in late 2007, which sounded like a key turning in the lock that might open the door to decommissioning. This was that retaining weapons could only lead to people ending up in jail. I understood this to be a clear indication that UVF thinking about decommissioning had significantly progressed. This comment was not part of a hidden UVF narrative and it is difficult to accuse the UVF of not telling the whole story when the story was still being written.

Internal debates

The rationale of their internal debate was still in progress and difficult issues were continually being confronted. Representatives were necessarily cautious and evasive when dealing with questions about decommissioning and there was the added problem of the logistical difficulties associated with the whereabouts of all weaponry. This problem was further compounded by the need to account for every weapon since in many cases weapons had been purchased autonomously to avoid the possibility of infiltration by the security forces.

The threat of dissident republican activity further compounded difficulties in terms of obstructing the pro-decommissioning debate, presenting very real external threats and dangers. But even against this background there was emerging a clear desire to confront the decommissioning issue and convince the rank and file that they were now living in a new paradigm where matters of defence had to be left to the security forces. The UVF also believed that mainstream republicans understood the problems they were up against and were not seeking to exert pressure on them to decommission, which would have made the transition even more difficult.

In relation to issues of criminality, the UVF expressed the same dilemma which had been expressed by the PIRA leadership, namely that the organization could not be held responsible for every bar room brawl. They indicated that anyone could use the flag of convenience of a paramilitary organization to demand, intimidate or bully. They also recognized the problem that loyalism did not speak with one voice as with mainstream republicanism and this meant less control and a greater incoherence, particularly with regard to finding agreed positions and consensus on the way ahead.

Nevertheless, taking these issues into account, there seemed to be a growing sense that the UVF was moving along a deliberate if incremental trajectory, as defined by their previous commitments to the peace process. At a meeting later in 2008 the UVF were satisfied with the discipline within their ranks but continued to state the view that it was better to decommission mindsets instead of guns. They also stressed that the peace process should not be taken for granted, that it was important to protect the gains made and allow people to get on with their lives. But even though a reference was made to guns being around for seventy years, representatives also made it known that they would not stand in the way of decommissioning if it were a possibility.

This suggested that although some way down the track, decommissioning was now a central consideration and there appeared to be a recognition that the decommissioning issue had to be resolved. The UVF were always clear that they were only speaking for themselves and not any other paramilitary organization. They recognized that the UDA had serious problems making progress or taking a cohesive line because of an inability to act coherently through its segregated leadership. It seemed to be agreed wisdom that those who spoke for the UDA had no mandate to agree on anything and everything had to be referred back for more discussion through the various areas, sometimes creating analysis to the extent of paralysis.

Clearly too much democracy is not the best ingredient to reach agreement. From my own experience as a former trade union official, those who did the negotiations always had to be clearly mandated to make some agreement, even if it did go to the membership with a recommendation for acceptance. However, this was not the world of industrial relations. This was the world of 'terror groups' and managing the endgame of conflict.

The UVF are well aware that the PIRA decommissioned to get into government and that no such scenario existed for loyalists. No argument could be made within the loyalist organizations about decommissioning being a strategic move, which would lead to greater political influence. The argument for decommissioning could only be made on the basis that it is the right thing to do for the benefit of peace and social stability.

But, I still get the sense from loyalist paramilitaries that the conflict is not resolved. They have stated this to the IMC and I am sure they have repeated it in many other quarters. They know there will always be a section of republicanism that will be in permanent revolt against the very existence of Northern Ireland. This today is clearly manifested in Republican Sinn Féin (RSF), *Eirigi* (meaning 'rise') and the 32 County Sovereignty Movement;

groups which can be compared to religious fundamentalist groups. Their nearest comparison is most likely Islamist *Jihadi* in Palestine, who will never accept the state of Israel. Israel will always have to be on alert against such Islamo fascists irrespective of whether there is a democratic Palestinian state up and running.

The threat from republicanism?

Similarly, loyalists believe that there will always be a threat from Irish republican fundamentalist groups, even if Sinn Féin fills the First Minister and the Minister for Justice positions. Nor do loyalists trust the British Government to defend them, believing that ultimately they will always have to look to themselves to protect Northern Ireland which is not only their homeland, but their redoubt.

When I spoke to the 'Craftsman' within days of the murder of the two young soldiers, Sappers Quinsey and Azimkar, outside Masserene Barracks, and PC Stephen Carroll in March 2009, he reassured me that this would not have a negative impact on debate within the UVF. He admitted that at a recent meeting there were some young men there who were very angry and who wanted something 'to be done'. But their viewpoint, while listened to, was not to be acted on.

Of particular importance here was the statement from Sinn Féin's Martin McGuinness, in which he labelled the killers of the soldiers and policeman as 'traitors', condemning the murders outright. This was seen as a crossing of the rubicon for republicans. The consensus at the UVF meeting was that given the progress made since the signing of the GFA in 1998 there was no longer an enemy community.

After the recent murders, it became apparent that there was a broad cross-community consensus, which united against the killers and full-scale violence returning to Northern Ireland. When I asked the 'Craftsman' at the end of the meeting if there were grounds to be cautiously optimistic, I was told to drop the 'cautious' and to be optimistic. There was no sense of the UVF wanting a return to violence. The prevailing view was that it is now the responsibility of the police to deal with dissident republican groups.

Even now, it is important to recognize that the UVF were not going to do things according to the schedules of others. In October 2005 loyalist terrorists rejected calls for them to follow the PIRA and decommission their weapons. A UVF spokesperson confirmed that the organization would not be disarming. He stated that decommissioning was not on their 'radar screen' and was unlikely to be in the future. The UVF commander added that the organization had not spoken to the IICD for almost four years (*The Observer*, 2 October 2005) even though at the same time the Irish Foreign Minister, Dermot Ahern had said there had been discussions with the loyalists about disarmament, a claim rejected by the UVF leadership (a UVF spokesperson confirmed there had been no contact with Dublin for the previous eighteen months at that time).

The spokesman also went on to explain that the UVF has made clear there is only one link they will use between themselves and the Irish government and that is the Dublin trade unionist Chris Hudson, reinforcing that without use of that envoy there would be no dialogue. The UVF at this time were explicit in their resistance to decommissioning and especially so in order to facilitate Sinn Féin's entry into government in Northern Ireland without comparable gains to working-class loyalists.

The UVF had made it clear that they would not dance to the IRA's tune (*The Observer*, 2 October 2005). Some four years later in July 2009 the picture was quite different, but a refusal to be pressured into change still endured. The UVF did decommission and not because they were reacting to others, but because at that stage they had determined it was the right thing to do. This is an important point, which should not be ignored. Their journey had come to a logical conclusion based on their own thinking and working through their own internal structures.

Reflecting on the situation now and any danger of a return to loyalist violence it is important to acknowledge the discipline of the UVF after the murder of Constable Carroll and Sappers Quinsey and Azimkar. The deciding factor was the sense of outrage, which emerged from the whole community. Against this reaction the UVF questioned the logic of retaliation and decided that any counter violence would be futile; a gesture of defiance against the development of peace which Northern Ireland had so comprehensively embraced.

But it should also be known that loyalists expressed some anger at the critical onslaught from the media about decommissioning, which carried next to no supportive comments from unionist politicians and failed to acknowledge the difficulty of reaching this outcome without the 'carrot' of political gains. While senior people in the UVF said to me that they were not looking for celebration for what they did, they were also certainly not expecting condemnation and cynicism. This perhaps reflects the perception among many journalists that loyalism is essentially a negative entity, without legitimacy or credibility and so therefore not worthy of careful analysis or consideration.

Dangerously, there is reason to suspect a threat to loyalism from dissident republicans, which is likely to manifest as threats to kill loyalists or unionists. Members of the unionist community are vigilant against dissident republican attempts to stir up the loyalist community and many believe this to be the logical and strategic next step by dissident republicans who seek to destabilize Northern Ireland and make the political option appear unworkable against a resurgent tradition of violent resistance.

In relation to this objective many loyalists are angry about what they see as the inability of republicans to allow unionists and loyalists to develop and entrench their own cultural interests and sense of identity. They believe that republicans are all too intent to try and dispel the legitimacy of both culture and identity. Because of this there is a sense in the unionist/loyalist community that they are constantly being pursued by republicans who cannot look beyond their passion for an Ireland that never existed.

Unionists and loyalists hope that this perception can be moderated to allow full recognition of the Irish identity (including the Irish Language) but within the context of Northern Ireland. In response, however, this requires unionists and loyalists to desist from insisting that Britishness in Northern Ireland is best manifested by the enduring and least moderate aspects of Protestantism and Orangeism.

Threats issued against loyalist and unionist leaders are now being treated seriously by the security forces. In speculation, one might reasonably assume that dissident republican aims are devised to damage the roll of Sinn Féin in the Northern Ireland Executive, who the dissidents see as arch traitors to the sacred republican holy grail. Presumably the dissidents would hope to see the violent 'Balkanization' of Northern Ireland as part of a strategy to be rid of Northern Ireland by stealth. Surely, we can only wish them the worst and hope they fail miserably in their nihilist plans against the wishes of the Irish People.

'Standing down' the UVF

It is against this problematic background that the UVF have taken the step to decommission and stand down their organization to the greater extent. They believe that this is a major contribution to the continuing peace process, as well as a serious confidence building measure. It is also a risk for democratic politics and civil society since dissident attempts to reignite conflict are more likely to be resisted without recourse to armed violence.

Decommissioning is a gesture of intent, which signalled a turning away from violence as a response to political opponents, and this was achieved while serious nervous tension prevailed within UVF ranks. In that sense, loyalists have taken an enlightened approach to the violence of dissident republicans by realizing that any violent response will only give dissidents the credibility they crave. Better to let the security forces of North and South deal with the dissidents, but firmly and swiftly. If this becomes the reality then this can only auger well for the normality of political and social life in Northern Ireland.

The UVF now exists only as a commemorative organization, celebrating the Battle of the Somme and other conflicts where Ulstermen participated. I have stayed on this journey since 1993 because I believed that it was possible. These people were serious about bringing this conflict to an end and to reach a definitive conclusion. But they were adamant that it would be done in their own time. In the words of the great American poet Walt Whitman they were 'listening to a different drummer'.

Conclusions

When David Ervine spoke to me on the Shankill Road (after my first meeting with UVF senior commanders) and argued the significance of my meeting with the UVF it was clear to me that David believed the link, I was about to establish, would be a contributory factor in the peace process. Should I have listened and agreed with the voices of the cynics and gone on cursing the darkness and the paramilitaries, refusing to get my hands dirty in the muddy waters of the conflict?

It would have been easy to go on singing about 'tunnels of peace' and allowing the bodies to continue to stack up, but that would have been immoral. Surely it is more important for us all to try and entrench the structures of peace and stability. Do we not all have an obligation to maintain the peace and consolidate the gains? I feel privileged that David Ervine put his trust in me and allowed me to try and build on that trust by pursuing efforts to stop the killing and bring the conflict to a close. I thank God for that opportunity.

Chapter 7
Quis Separabit?
Loyalist Transformation and the Strategic Environment

Lyndsey Harris

Drawing upon empirical research[1] this chapter examines interactions between the leaders of the UDA and the UVF with their grassroots members. Furthermore, it will also highlight how the UDA and UVF have interacted with each other. Therefore, the central focus of this chapter is on the strategic environment, which loyalists understand as encompassing the paramilitary world. This might sound preposterous to suggest that there are two 'worlds'; nevertheless, it is evident from the empirical data gathered that loyalist paramilitaries do disaggregate the strategic environment in which they operate.

It is apparent, for example, that political negotiations and military tactics, which are employed to defend their 'Britishness' or achieve their preferences, are separated from internal organizational discipline. We will discuss the military means and political 'voice' that has been employed by the leadership of both organizations in an attempt to control grassroots members and move the organizations towards a process of exiting the political environment in Northern Ireland.

The strategic approach and loyalist paramilitaries

It is necessary to stress that the strategic tradition within academic analysis assumes that behaviour is rational. Everyday understanding of 'rational strategy' equates to the implementation of a preconceived and premeditated plan that is systematically followed through. The end is identified and the means are selected according to their efficacy in obtaining that end. The assumption that can be found in much of the prevailing literature on the Northern Ireland conflict is that republicans had such an end and the means were rationally proportionate.

Loyalists are often portrayed as having no such end and so their means were incommensurate and hence irrational (Anderson 2004; Lister and

Jordan 2003; McDowell 2001). By complementing the work conducted by M. L. R. Smith (1997) on the strategic tradition of the republican movement, it is believed that a similar method of enquiry can be employed to examine loyalist paramilitaries and this will add to our understanding of the, so far inadequately documented, military dimension of the Troubles. The essence of the strategic approach is 'simply to trace the line of thinking of a particular political entity in order to comprehend how it proposes to achieve its objectives; and also look at the ideological assumptions and values that underlie that entity's thinking and how this informs the way it formulates its strategy' (Smith 1997: 4)

Value systems of loyalist paramilitaries

In previous publications the author has sought to demonstrate how using a strategic theory approach has revealed that the value systems of the two main loyalist paramilitary organizations differ (Harris 2006; 2008a; 2008b). It is important that we consider these differences briefly here to enable understanding of the motivations and interactions within the strategic environment.

In essence, it has been established that the UVF's value system can be identified as informed by notions of Britishness, which translated into a paramilitary mindset requiring the defeat of the IRA to maintain their ultimate value of loyalty to the Crown and preserving Northern Ireland as a part of the United Kingdom. Conversely, the UDA's value system was said to contain notions of Britishness, which includes the desire to maintain cultural practices and the need to defeat the IRA to ensure the ultimate core value of the defence of 'their' communities (McAuley 2008).

These differences have meant that at key moments in Ulster's past both organizations differed in their response to a number of political situations; for example, the UDA had very little issue with presenting an idea of an independent Ulster in 1979, which maintained links to the Britain through Commonwealth membership (McAuley 1991, 1995; NUPRG 1979). The UVF, on the other hand, would not have considered this a viable option given their core value of wishing to maintain the Union between Great Britain and Northern Ireland. It can be argued that these differences in values have influenced organizational approaches in considering how, when, and if they should cease to exist.

In 2004, Neumann argued that the idea that loyalist paramilitaries were in decline was a fallacy because during the post-1998 period violence continued in an attempt to assert themselves as leaders or the only people capable of protecting/defending the Protestant community and associated cultures. What the author's study revealed is that while the UVF leadership may have demonstrated an expressed wish for the organization to enter into decline, they were also faced with internal matters and engagement with other actors in the strategic environment, such as the LVF, which they felt had to be dealt with before any exit could be considered.

In comparison, the UDA leadership, which has been identified as possessing a central value system of defending 'their' communities and culture, has been less inclined to focus on exiting the strategic environment while enclaves of interface violence has continued. This is highlighted in CTI discussions concerning the future of the organization and links to the lack of an effective political representation for the organization (Hall 2006; 2007a). Therefore, the UDA continue in their wish to be seen as defenders of their own communities.

The importance of leadership

Crenshaw (1987) uses the organizational approach and Hirschman's (1970) *Exit, Voice and Loyalty* framework to explain how organizations act when in decline. According to organizational process theory leadership is elevated to be a key variable, which is said to transcend mere organization survival; leaders are said to wish to enhance and promote the organization and their personal ambitions are tied to the organization's visibility and political position.

A key principle of this theory is that the incentives an organization provides for its members are critical to its survival (1987:19). With this approach in mind, and the application of the strategic theory, it is important to remember that individual members of a terrorist organization will also have varying degrees of loyalty to the UDA or UVF 'brand'. This latter aspect was certainly evident when respondents were asked about the nature of leadership within loyalist terrorist organizations and whether they could identify any differences, operationally or ideologically, between the UDA and UVF or even between their adversaries, the republican paramilitaries.

UVF leadership

A response in regards to the latter, recorded in 2004, from a Senior Brigade Staff Officer of the UVF indicates an acknowledgement that offering incentives and the varying degrees of trust in a terrorist organization leadership were important factors in understanding UVF activity. In response to the question: 'is this same lack of confidence [as identified in senior command levels of the organization] evident in volunteers?', the respondent replied:

> Even more so because... I sit here 4 or 5 days a week having 20 or 30 different conversations with different people at different levels – they are going out and doing a day's work, maybe having a meeting once a week or even once a month and they depend totally on what they are told at that meeting – the only other information [they receive] is sound bites

on the news or what they read in the papers. They don't have in depth conversations the way I would do, so I have to assume their confidence is even less than mine...

It probably goes back to our background and where we come from – the difference with the Provos is that there would almost be a religious blind faith in leadership, where[as] that does not apply [with]in loyalism and never has; it wouldn't matter in loyalism how good a leader you are, or who you are, you are only as good as your last decision. The first mistake you make and they jump all over you. Its different in the Provos, it's about control as well for them. I have asked Republicans about this and yes there was a lot of disillusionment in their movement [during the peace process, signing of the Belfast Agreement and decommissioning] but they did not make a public fuss about it. I asked what they did – did they join the Continuity [IRA]? The answer was, 'No, they went home and cried into their beer'. No fuss with a few notable exceptions like Anthony McIntyre' (A14, 2004).

While this response does demonstrate the need for the leadership to provide incentives to the grassroots members, the concluding part of the quotation indicates an underwritten belief among the leaders of the UVF that the preferences of the PIRA, centred around securing a united Ireland (as understood by the UVF leadership) has not been realized.

It is clear that the respondent is inferring a lack of impetus among the PIRA in the post-Agreement period to continue representing their grassroots members. We could also deduce from his response that this senior member of the UVF's Brigade Staff is asserting that the options available to the PIRA regarding the representation of its volunteer's views are much lower down their preference list. In comparison, he is suggesting that this is a central facet of leadership in the UVF, which requires them to listen and represent grassroots members.

Respondents were also asked to identify whether the leadership of their organizations had remained constant. A unanimous answer was recorded from UVF respondents in which they described that their overall command, the Chief of Staff and the Brigade Staff of Belfast of the UVF, has remained constant: 'I think it has been within the central leadership the last 25–30 years as stayed the same. I think that in the Brigade Staff in Belfast there haven't been very many shake ups' (interview with author). Confirming the longevity of the UVF's Chief of Staff, Respondent Y added:

It has, yes [leadership remained constant]. You have to remember too that that is an ageing leadership, which doesn't particularly bode well for the future because these honourable or principled men are a dying breed and these are the last that are left who have walked the walk; whilst there would be some left in middle management, for want of a better term, the next tier below is all young people who were young babies when the ceasefires were called so they have no notion of what fighting the war was like. (County Antrim, 2005)

However, members from the Londonderry and Mid-Ulster regions identified more recent changes in their Brigade Staff for differing reasons: in Londonderry there was a coup which deposed the local commander following allegations of drug dealing, extortion and heavy-handed tactics in 2003. Respondent I described:

The same leadership has now been in control for two years, as I say over the past two years there has been a remarkable change in Londonderry itself... the previous leader was expelled and they needed to replace him – this was not done through violence. This leader is now more approachable and if anything needs sorting out he would do it by talking without bringing out bats and sticks rather than if you went back to what it was in the later 1980s to early 1990s. Definitely there is a big change in Londonderry. There have been five or six local leaders that I remember since growing up around here. (Respondent I, 2005, Londonderry)

Specifically for the UVF in Armagh and the general mid-Ulster region, Respondent R stated that there had been:

... a change in leadership two or three times because younger more militant members have taken up more recently and not been prepared to take on this stuff ['constructive, community activity']. Within mid-Ulster there has been a change since Richard Jamieson's death. [10th January 2000] (2005)

Given that the Progressive Unionist Party have been credited by other respondents for their restraining influence upon the UVF by providing political analysis it was important to identify how the UVF continued to be, on the whole, a unified organization given the very little influence the PUP had in the County Armagh region. When asked, does that mean that they [UVF] do not really have any restraint then – what is keeping them together, is it the leadership? Respondent R offered the following interpretation:

I think it is to a certain extent, and some of the older members or former members will have a respected voice of reason. I suppose they will listen to them at the minute and that is what has helped and if we hadn't had that I dread to think [what may have happened]. If we hadn't have had the ex-prisoners here working away in the background I think you would have a totally different situation than what we have at the moment because a lot of them don't see Belfast with loyalty because they are not living in this area – what might apply down there won't apply up here and each area needs to be looked at differently. (County Armagh, 2005)

Leadership of the UDA

From a UVF perspective, Respondent A suggested, '... probably the UDA leadership has not been as stable and there has been a far greater turnover of men in the UDA in senior positions, which has not helped [the peace process]'. This view was shared by former PSNI Chief Constable Sir Hugh Orde, whose impression of the UDA leadership was that the main aim of loyalist paramilitaries was 'self interest'. However, Orde did make a distinction that there were some Brigadiers who were trying to mould the organizations away from self-interest pursuits:

> If you were to summarise the brigadiers' activities... [Jackie] McDonald [South Belfast Brigadier], I think is different a bit – I think what we might be seeing is (and I'm on record somewhere in the media saying this) a split within loyalism at the brigadier level. I think that is a possibility and I think that the McDonalds of this world may, or are committed to get something for his community rather than something for himself.
>
> [Jim] Gray [Former East Belfast Brigadier] – incapable of making that distinction; the man is into it for himself. The frustration is we cannot catch him: I think there may be something there that suggests there may be a glimmer of hope but I think that if that is the case then they need huge support. They just don't know how to do it. They are not that sophisticated. If you look at when they have stood for election, when they stand, no one votes for them and when they have put people up, they have lost their deposits, which is very different to the other side of the divide. (Sir Hugh Orde, Knock, 2005)

There was a clear identification among respondents associated with the UDA that the membership now felt that the 'fear factor' in sharing opinions about the direction of the organization had disappeared along with the removal of rogue 'Brigadiers' such as Adair. This was summarized by a member involved in the CTI discussions who stated: 'I'm just happy that the fear has gone. You know it is going well when you don't get slapped for talking' (Hall 2006: 18). Clearly, in facilitating the airing of grassroots members' views to the leadership, this has highlighted a change in leadership methods employed by the Inner Council.

One UDA Brigadier interviewed recognized that the type of leadership required in a post-ceasefire political climate of Northern Ireland differed from what was expected during the height of the 'troubles'. Speaking in 2005, he stated that, unlike the above respondents, he would not agree that the leadership of the UDA was less stable than UVF leadership but he acknowledged the changing nature of leadership that was required for post-1998 loyalist paramilitary organizations:

It is very hard for the leadership of any organisation at the minute because there is so much of a change in the climate and in the situation [in Northern Ireland]. If you could just imagine being a member of any of the Inner Council or of the UVF structure; going back, the history of the organisation structure and from their infancy was a defence mechanism from attack: how do we stop them bombing us? How do we stop them shooting us? How do we stop an incursion? What way are we going to do this? That doesn't exist anymore; the threat doesn't exist anymore, it is not the same threat from the Republican side and the thing is, how do we deal with the subtleness of Sinn Féin? How do we deal with the criminality within the organisation or accusations of criminality? How do we remain a part of our own community? How do we move on and what direction do we go? It would be very hard now because there is so much change and how do you keep people motivated? We are talking of at least 10,000 members of the UDA. (Respondent D, Co. Antrim 2004)

Returning to Crenshaw's (1987) identification that incentives for membership need to remain to ensure members' wish to sustain loyalty towards the brand of the organization, Respondent D, highlights an acute awareness of this when he discussed the decisions facing the UDA Inner Council. He noted:

I know it may sound daft but it may have been easier for the leadership a few years ago; when they woke up in the morning thinking about how they might kill somebody or how to stop somebody killing somebody, or how to defend the area, or how to procure something: that was all straight forward. Now, most of these things are on the backburner and they have to have an organisation prepared to defend but prepared to move on and move into an area where nobody really wants an enemy. As far as the UDA go they would need serious input from the UPRG; they need serious input from their own community to tell them that, 'we don't want you doing that anymore; you have to stop this'. (Belfast 2005)

Note the emphasis in the concluding comments of this statement regarding the need of the community to tell the UDA to stop their activities; as far as Respondent D is concerned, until this occurs the UDA will continue to act in a 'defensive manner' in the name of defence because this is a central part of their values and objectives. Crenshaw (1987) analyses that only when there is no possibility of exit can the organization's leaders resist the demand of members for change.

Therefore, we can argue that this depends on the organization's stated value system. For example, we find that for the UVF with a core value of maintaining the status quo in terms of the constitutional position of Northern Ireland 'exit' is not as much of a problem with core members of the UVF happy to follow the road of politics as a means of 'exit', while the general perception from the empirical data gathered suggests that rural members in areas such as County Armagh were content to 'exit' into 'nothingness' and return to a civilian life.

The UDA on the other hand, with a core value and organizational origins of 'defending' their communities means the possibility of exit is perhaps thwarted because of issues such as interface violence and tensions surrounding parading issues arising from the wish to uphold Protestant cultural values. Crenshaw, however, observes from Hirschman's (1970) analysis that leaders of an organization can avoid disastrous extremes of exit and voice by soliciting the loyalty of its members. This does seem to have been realized and attempted by the Inner Council of the UDA with the UPRG's assistance through the CTI scheme in which members were invited to discuss issues facing loyalism in a number of workshops across Northern Ireland.

The 'John Gregg Initiative' (named after the North Belfast Brigadier who was murdered during loyalist feuding) set the background for the CTI discussions:

> Their [UDA Inner Council] intent was to: (a) work towards the day when there would no longer be a need for the UDA and UFF [Ulster Freedom Fighters]; (b) desist from all military activity; (c) develop a strategy for the organisation which would be one of community development, job creation, social inclusion and community politics; and (d) work diligently with other political parties and the two governments to create an environment which would secure a lasting peace.
>
> Realising that this was a major change for the organisation, it was felt important to engage with the rank and file membership of the UDA, for the first time, in genuine dialogue. The consultation process which was then initiated was aimed at 'establishing a baseline' setting out how ordinary members felt about the current political situation, the social needs of their communities, and whether they believed the conflict itself was over. It was also to canvas views on how to move into the future, the UPRG hoping that the membership would support the UDA leadership's preferred aim of engaging in a genuine conflict transformation process. (Hall 2006: 7)

However, the soliciting of views through the CTI only went as far as discussing matters such as criminality within the organization; possibilities of community development work; and responses to the Belfast Agreement (1998). The Inner Council prevented any talks regarding the consideration of decommissioning during the first two phases. However, the subsequent withdrawal of the politically controversial £1.2m CTI funded scheme in October 2007 resulted in a large gap in the process of grassroots consultation. It was clear in follow-up interviews that respondents felt, particularly those in leadership positions, that this demonstrated the failure of politicians in Northern Ireland to appreciate the tentativeness needed in a move to ensure grassroots members and all Brigadiers of the Inner Council of the UDA could move forward together in search of an appropriate decline of the organization.

Differences between the UDA and UVF

The fears outlined above regarding the possibility of younger members rising to leadership positions appears to have been reflected in the impetus of the paramilitary organizations to look for exit strategies, particularly the UVF. Respondent B suggested that there are further issues that have also led to the UVF being able to consider the disbandment of the organization, which are linked to the UVF's belief that in their objectives in defeating the PIRA and maintaining the constitutional status quo: 'the UDA were very much pro-Good Friday Agreement at first but when they seen [sic] what way the thing was swaying they quickly jumped to the other side and I don't see that as having a great deal of integrity'.

Perhaps, this statement is better linked to the capabilities of the UVF leadership to bring the rank and file members of its organization along with their desires to disband, whereas the UDA have been faced with a membership who do not wholly subscribe to the view that the PIRA are genuine in their decommissioning and rejection of armed conflict, or, at the very least, felt that republicans still posed a threat to loyalist objectives. During the recorded CTI discussions the mistrust of PIRA objectives was apparent:

> When a show of hands was called for (in each area) on the question, 'was the war over?' a majority of participants stated that the war was *not* [emphasis in original] over. However, when this was probed further it was apparent that most members thought that while the IRA's *military* [emphasis in original] *might* [emphasis my own] be over, their *political* [emphasis in original] war was certainly not. For the IRA it was a change in tactics, but their goal remained the same – a united Ireland. (Hall 2006: 10–11)

Other participants pointed to the fact that interface violence still continued and it was viewed as a concerted campaign by republicans and also the dangers of dissident republican attacks on their communities:

> If it is over why are there still attacks on Protestants of the Fountain Estate [Londonderry]? ... The problem is that Republican dissidents are increasing in number, and they are quite prepared to continue the war.

If we were to disarm, our communities would be left defenceless. (Hall 2006: 8)

The discussions over the intent of republicans also mirrors the difference highlighted by UDA members in their approach to conflict transformation. A UDA Brigadier stated that the UVF were much more inclined to enter into dialogue with republicans and 'their form of loyalism [socialism]' whereas the UDA were reported to have said:

No, we were in combat with those people and we were not prepared to sit down and have dialogue with them in terms of bringing them into our community... We don't want them to understand us, we just want to be left alone, thank you very much. We have no wish to form friendships with them or cups of tea or go down the pub for a drink with them and the vast majority of Unionism and our community feels the same way. (Respondent F, 2005)

Further distinctions were offered by UVF respondents in the differences between the two main loyalist organizations centring on the belief that the UVF was a better disciplined force. Respondent C discussed the historical roots of the UVF and that the 'UVF certainly see themselves as a more disciplined force', which was due to the UDA's vigilante origins and lack of a central command structure. Dawn Purvis, who since 2007 is leader of the Progressive Unionist Party, also highlighted a belief that the 'UVF are looking for reasons to justify their inexistence, the UDA are probably trying to justify their existence' (County Antrim, 2005).

The analysis contained in this quotation does have some credence when we compare the CTI discussions held by the UDA and the reluctance of the leadership to allow discussions on decommissioning and the UVF's conflict transformation forums, which had a stated desire from the beginning to move towards the disbandment of the organization. However, what Purvis' comment also supports is the feeling among many UDA respondents that the UVF consider themselves to be a superior force in comparison with the UDA, and that elitism operates within the organization.

Feuding and internal discipline

In a similar vein to the discussion above, Crenshaw asserts that '[c]ircumstances may alter incentive structures. If an organisation is forced into inactivity, substitute incentives must be found; some groups might shift towards dealing drugs for example' (1987: 20). The implications of Hirschman's (1970) theory of organizational imperatives are that organizations behave differently in competitive and non-competitive environments.

It is useful to remember this when considering the feuding that has occurred among loyalists. The strategic approach, however, delves deeper in the analysis of the feuding situation as it provides an explanation as to upon what the competition centres. When examining the internecine feuds that have occurred within loyalism academics and the media have suggested the following reasons: territorialism (Gallagher and Shirlow 2006); power and megalomania (Bruce 2004); and, criminality (McDowell 2001).

In mapping the strategic approach over this period of loyalist history we can identify that a combination of all of these explanations can be used to account for the reasons behind the loyalist feuding; all of which centre on the desire to be the organization that fulfils its preferences and value systems. Particularly, in the case of the UDA it is a quest to establish who rightfully represents the best interests and 'defence' of their communities. Drawing upon empirical data gathered and mapping the strategic approach over academic literature of the loyalist feuding, this section will analyse whether the inter- and intra- organizational feuding had any ideological basis and the implications for loyalist transformation. Gallagher and Shirlow suggest that: '[s]ince 1994, loyalism has witnessed a divide between those who wish to reposition Loyalism and those who have been unable to shift into a non-violent and non-criminal role' (2006:150).

Formation of the LVF

The Loyalist Volunteer Force was created following a series of events: in 1996 the leader of the UVF's mid-Ulster Brigade, Billy Wright, was ordered to attend a meeting with the Brigade Staff following his alleged involvement in drug dealing and of being a police informer, following the loss of a large number of weapons from his unit and 'an unusually large number of its people arrested' (Bruce 2004: 510). Wright, however, failed to attend and continued flouting Brigade Staff orders by involving himself in the Drumcree parade protests and ordering the killing of a Catholic taxi driver, Michael McGoldrick. He was expelled from the organization, and with the help of Alan Kerr (an ex-UDA brigadier who had also been expelled) established the LVF.

A statement of objectives and organizational aims created by the LVF demonstrated a commitment to:

> To use the Ulster conflict as a crucible for far-reaching, fundamental and decisive change in the United Kingdom constitution. To restore Ulster's right to self-determination. To end Irish nationalist aggression against Ulster in whatever form. To end all forms of Irish interference in Ulster's internal affairs. To thwart the creation and/or implementation of any All-Ireland/All-Island political super-structure regardless of the powers vested in such institutions. To defeat the campaign of de-Britishisation

and Gaelicaisation of Ulster's daily life. (Document held in the Linen Hall Library, no date)

However following the death of its leader, Billy Wright, in December 1997, the organization showed no signs of continuing with any political initiatives outlined in their publication, *Leading the Way*. The publication itself became sporadic and eventually non-existent. It was increasingly reported in the media that the LVF were involved in anti-social behaviour, sectarian attacks and drug dealing.

The first violent feud between the UDA and the UVF in the summer of 2000 originated because a LVF colour guard was allowed to participate in a parade organized by the UDA's C Company on the Shankill, which proceeded to march into UVF territory, and violence escalated. In the previous weeks leading up to C Company's parade, the LVF had been involved in the killing of Richard Jamieson, a prominent UVF member.

As Gallagher and Shirlow explain: although the UDA was officially supporting the Belfast Agreement, the federal structure of the organization meant that Johnny Adair, leader of C Company, was able to 'flout the organisation's stance regarding criminality and sectarian violence' and he began to formalize links with the LVF (Gallagher and Shirlow 2006: 150). According to Johnny Adair, however:

> The causes of the feuds went back a long way. Both factions of the Loyalist paramilitaries had always held grudges against each other but forgot them and united against a common enemy of the Republican movement. Now though, the IRA guns were silent and it was far easier for the old jealousies to return. (2007: 208–9)

Nevertheless, between August and December 2000, seven people were killed because of the feud and over 500 loyalists left homeless (Gallagher and Shirlow 2006: 150). Gallagher and Shirlow provide a convincing analysis of the 2000 feud in which they highlight that:

> While there is no denying that paramilitaries are involved in criminality, the feud was also a battle about the legitimacy of transitional Loyalism and the anti-transformation actions of C Company. It was a battle fought on highly symbolic terrain in Ulster Loyalism – the Shankill Road, which is viewed as a Protestant heartland in Northern Ireland. (Gallagher and Shirlow 2006: 150)

Gallagher and Shirlow produce an analysis that is distinct from the media's interpretation of criminality being at the heart of the feud (in which members were said to be fighting over territory to sell drugs and facilitate racketeering). They suggest that C Company:

...engaged in a politics of resistance...based on a politic that situated C Company as the true defenders of Ulster and the province's Protestant people and complete segregation between the two groups is espoused. The war is incomplete because Irish Republicanism has yet to be defeated. (Gallagher and Shirlow 2006: 153)

Listing two key arguments surrounding this assertion, Gallagher and Shirlow, maintain that this 'casting of difference'... has also led C Company to attack pro-peace loyalists and consequently 'C Company's resistance was as much about internal discipline, against what it regards the cancer growing within Loyalist ranks, as it is about defeating traditional enemies' (Gallagher and Shirlow 2006: 153). Importantly, they note that this may not mean that they were trying to derail the peace process but they were more interested in trying to maintain control within the loyalist ranks. The second argument espoused by the authors maintains that the resistance of C Company is territorial.

Internal tensions within loyalism did resurface, although this time it occurred within the UDA following the killing of LVF man Stephen Warnock (Adair 2007: 211–50), which according to Adair was sanctioned by Brigadier of East Belfast, Jim Gray. In 'tit for tat' style, Gray was targeted by the LVF and Adair infuriated the Inner Council by attending Warnock's funeral against their orders. As a result Adair was stripped of his title as Brigadier of West Belfast and expelled from the organization.

Shortly after Adair's attendance at Warnock's funeral the UDA released a statement saying: 'As a result of ongoing investigations the present Brigadier of West Belfast is no longer accepted in our organisation.' Adair defied orders, however, and he describes how: '[w]ithin hours, a banner went up on the Shankill declaring, "West Belfast Brigade – business as usual, no change"' (Adair 2007: 208–10). A series of expulsions and violence ensued. However, Adair's re-incarceration for breaking the terms of his early release scheme aided the UDA in regaining control of the Lower Shankill but there were still signs of splits within the organization, which re-emerged more recently with the expulsion of the South East Antrim Brigade.

Bruce (2004) suggests that it was egotistical characters that have caused the feuding within and between the loyalist paramilitaries. It would be true to say this has certainly played a role; nevertheless, if we wish to find an explanation that accounts for the entire feuding period, the analysis of Gallagher and Shirlow (2006) is much more convincing. Mapping strategic theory over these events we can see that there is a clear tension that exists, emphasized by divisions within the UDA, which suggest differing interpretations of whether the organization has fulfilled its stated objectives as set out in their value system to defend the Protestant community.

Personalities have been able to seize upon this insecurity in a similar fashion to encapsulation of the traditional siege mentality (Aughey 1989;

Longley 2005) and model themselves as the righteous leaders of loyalism. This is exactly what Crenshaw refers to when maintaining that in situations surrounding exit:

> Organisations may have to devote their efforts into distinguishing themselves from other groups in order to prevent defection to successful rivals. Competition may inspire escalation, as each group tries to outdo the other in violence in order not only to retain existing members but to attract new recruits. (Crenshaw 1987: 24)

In 2004 the UVF were criticized for getting involved in a further feud situation that led to increased violence and a 'stand off' around the Garnerville Estate and the UVF ceasefire was again discredited by the British Government. It is clear from UVF respondents how they viewed the LVF:

> The current feud, what I think it is, is that certain elements within loyalism (the LVF) want to portray themselves to a certain degree to the people in their communities as loyalists but they are really just masquerading as loyalists to cover their ass to be selling drugs. I would say that it is just a gang of people. What reason do they have to exist when its founding member is dead and most of the other ones are serving time and have no real connection? ... For example, in the Garnerville Estate there are pensioners and it has been highlighted in the media to a degree but perhaps not to the extent that it should have been, you won't get a taxi service to the estate; so if you're not getting a taxi service you are maybe getting pensioners who cannot walk to go to the shops and has to get a relative that is may connected to another group [UVF] to come in and the [LVF] members that were living in the Garnerville Estate didn't want those people coming...
>
> It goes back to what loyalists see themselves as loyal to. We would say that we are loyal to the community. Now, if the community are coming to you and you can only hear pleas for so long before having to act...I think that it suits the government and media to portray it as gang warfare or feud over areas, money etc...I think that the LVF may have thought that the UVF leadership had become complacent [following the end of the previous feud in 2000] or led politically but I think you will find that now it's like a wound; if you leave it, it will fester and I think that wound has just festered and now it is a case of just cut it out. (Respondent L, County Antrim, 2005)

This insight confirms that although they were perceived as breaking their ceasefire, members of the UVF did not consider this contrary to the peace process and they were 'getting their house in order' before they could commit to any disbandment. Mervyn Gibson also supported this assertion in his analysis of the feuding:

> The UVF are actually trying to transform communities and are involved with the PUP, other elements of their movements in trying to transform loyalist communities and get away from criminality and drug dealing and to get communities built up and empowered. So, I think there are ideological reasons and I also think that and hope that this may be the last 'clean out' because when organisations do transform or change into something else they often tend to have a last blow out before they do. I think the UVF are thinking: "we are transforming ourselves, moving away from militaristic goals into political representative or community-based organisations or a commemorative organisation, we are moving away from all that is military and we cannot have something there that is keeping drawing us back to the military. So, we need to sort this out once and for all."(Gibson in an interview with the author, 2005)

What is evident when applying strategic theory to this period of loyalist paramilitary history is that there is a combination of factors, which have led to the continued use of violence to achieve a specific end. The identification by respondents of personality-led feuding and the wish to extend criminal empires certainly accounts for the violence. For example, Respondents M and N observe that:

> I would say that some of it is personality; some of it would be due to criminality. I would say that the UVF does not like to be labelled as drug dealers because the LVF do it and you know yourself how easy it can be to be tarred with the one brush. (M, County Down, 2005)
> The feuding in this area (Bangor) is two organisations clashing some-times over personality clashes but it is also about issues too. As far as the LVF is concerned it's just a drug issue. (N, County Down, 2005)

Nevertheless, it is also possible to identify that these 'deviants' such as the LVF, Adair and Wright, have been credited with trying to achieve some-thing (albeit criminal rackets, and/or anti-agreement policies, and/or overall command of the organization) that is at odds with what the mainstream leadership of both the UDA and UVF wish to achieve. Hence, the import-ance of understanding the value systems of both of these organizations and an analysis of the strategic environment enables the strategic analyst to syn-thesize the material available to examine the feuding.

It is clear that a lack of centralized leadership within the UDA enabled members to assert their 'voice', which was aimed at the leadership of the UDA. In a sense, Adair was making the claim that he could do a better job for the loyalist community: 'I am the stronger, more determined leader who can defend you better'; and also to the republican movement: ' I am not going away'. The UVF on the other hand, had a clear aim of conflict transformation established from the 1994 ceasefires and the LVF were viewed as an obstacle to achieving this. As respondent O highlighted in response to the question, 'what do you see as the reason for the loyalist feuds?':

> I think going back in time feuds with the UDA; I think basically it was putting the house in order. I know from a UVF point of view they couldn't accept the criminality that existed within certain organisations, which was basically encroaching into areas that were controlled by the UVF and they weren't accepting it. The current situation that exists with the LVF is basically eradicating drugs and the UVF will not accept that there are scum within our society that are supplying drugs to our young people. I think that you can now see a cooperation between the UDA and UVF in eradicating that ... I am a fan of restorative justice but there are times when that just doesn't work and sadly this time with the feuding [between the UVF and LVF] it doesn't fit there because it is not something that can be dealt with by peaceful means. (County Tyrone, 2005)

In various ways the leadership of the UVF had to assert their authority and ensure that a similar situation to what occurred within the UDA leadership did not happen to their organization and also they were not drawn back into the use of military means in the future, once they had set a firm commitment to exclusively political voice. Furthermore, they were under increased pressure from their own rank and file members who witnessed events such as what happened in the Garnerville Estate to act. Finally, it was viewed as an internal issue, which following the disaster of the 2000 feud the UDA stayed out of: Billy McKeown (UPRG) was asked whether the UDA was involved in the 2004 LVF–UVF feud and replied:

> They have made a policy from not getting involved ... because it is internal you see the LVF is ex-UVF and that is up to them to deal with ... there are ministers on the Loyalist Commission who would step in and mediate tomorrow but the UVF won't recognise the LVF as an organisation; they class them as a bunch of drug dealers. (County Down, 2005)

All of the feuding between 2000 and 2004 involved violent means. However, during most recent feuding in 2006–07 within the UDA, we have witnessed a move by the Inner Council to avoid the use of violence to deal with the South East Antrim Brigade and the Shoukiris. Both of these parties were viewed by the Inner Council to be acting against the objectives of the UDA and particularly their attempts to formulize a conflict transformation scheme. As a result the two factions were expelled from the organization without the use of violence.

It appears we have witnessed a realization within the UDA that violent means will not help achieve this objective: This is reinforced when we consider that during 2009 it was apparent that splits still existed within the Inner Council regarding the realistic possibility of full decommissioning with conflicting Reports regarding North Antrim and Londonderry's Brigadier, Billy McFarland's commitment to decommissioning appearing in a number of local newspapers (Rowan 2009b). Nevertheless, it seems the Inner Council was capable of negotiating the continued move towards conflict transformation at the leadership level and on 6th January 2010 decommissioning was delivered by the UDA and verified by the IICD.

Conclusions

This chapter has revealed that, just as organizational process theory indicates, leadership is a key variable in the ability of loyalist paramilitaries to consider and conduct exit strategies. Nevertheless, the strategic approach reveals that this is because it is the leadership of the loyalist terrorist organizations who decide whether military means should be employed to achieve an objective. Thus, incentives based on violent methods should no longer be applied in a peace process but as we have witnessed until 2006 there was a continued use of violent means employed in punishment and feuding situations.

What the strategic approach reveals is that the use of military means in a post-ceasefire scenario has been conducted with an aim of enforcing internal discipline or 'policing' their communities and as an expression of their continuation in wishing to uphold their values and meet their stated organizational preferences, all of which can be heightened in a competitive post-conflict strategic environment.

The announcement in June 2009 by the UVF that they would engage fully with decommissioning is unsurprising given an examination of their values and attempts to ensure consultation with its members. However, given the lack of grassroots consultation on decommissioning UDA weaponry; the fractured nature of its leadership; and the 'nervousness' of the UDA regarding recent increases in dissident republican activity, it is unsurprising the UDA took longer to decommission. Furthermore, it was significant that when decommissioning did occur, the IICD accepted that the breakaway group of the South East Antrim Brigade had no standing connections with UDA Inner Council as they had yet to fully decommission.

Chapter 8
Transforming Loyalist Communities: A Participatory Peace Research Approach

Aaron Edwards and Stephen Bloomer

The part of Mr Verloc in revolutionary politics having been to observe, he could not all at once, either in his own home or in larger assemblies, take the initiative of action. He had to be cautious.

Joseph Conrad, *The Secret Agent* (1907): 38–9

Introduction

This chapter analyses the conflict transformation process whereby the UVF brought an end to its campaign of terror in May 2007 and finally decommissioned its weapons and explosives in June 2009. Both authors worked closely with the UVF and its political partners in the PUP on peacebuilding initiatives aimed at transforming loyalist communities, and actively contributed to the strategic debate during the former's so-called internal consultation process. Working alongside the late Billy Mitchell[1] (1941–2006), one of the key architects of the UVF's eventual transformation beyond terrorism, they aided him in promoting the benefits of the peace process to grassroots loyalists, to knit together the various levels of the unionist community in a co-ordinated effort to build peace, and in providing leadership and assistance to a number of localized projects in the East Antrim area and further afield. They were 'critical friends' of the progressive loyalist[2] movement, whose 'job' it was 'to keep a watching brief on the principles and practice being developed during the process' (EACTF 2003).

Both authors would approach their involvement in the conflict transformation process from an 'insider-partial' perspective (Wehr and Lederach 1991) by provoking debate, chairing discussion and offering advice on how to make the EACTF initiative more relevant to the local community and external audiences. This assistance was provided at a time when the local and national media seemed preoccupied with venerating the 'celebrity gangster' (see Chrisafis 2005; Hain 2005; Haydon 2005; Magee 2003), which had infected the subculture of loyalist paramilitarism, particularly since the 1994 ceasefires (see Spencer 2008).

Nevertheless, the authors remained adamant that the progressive elements within loyalism were entitled to empower themselves and transform their communities beyond violence. In turn they were granted unprecedented access to the UVF organization, and worked in partnership with strategists in the PUP and local community leaders to encourage militant loyalists to abandon their strategy of 'armed resistance' (see Bloomer 2008; Bloomer and Edwards 2009; Edwards 2007; Edwards 2009; Edwards and Bloomer 2004; 2005; 2006).

This chapter has three interrelated aims. First, it explores the methodological parameters within which we worked and how this relates to the broader interrelated research area of peace and conflict studies. We pay particular attention to the action-orientated work of academic-practitioners who have chosen to intervene in the real world for the somewhat altruistic cause of eradicating violence from human relationships: we refer to this approach as 'participatory peace research'.[3] Second, it details the specific case of UVF terrorism in Northern Ireland, with particular emphasis on explaining how the organization's own internal logic finally brought its armed campaign to an end. Finally, it makes several observations from the first-hand experiences of two academic-practitioners closely involved in post-conflict peacebuilding activities and suggests broader lessons that this may have for other divided societies emerging from violence.

Inside the 'Ethnographer's Tent'

Empirical research is the cornerstone of erudite scholarship, yet it can have wider utility and applicability beyond the seminar rooms and lecture theatres of universities and other educational institutions. The rise of action research and its variants has been emblematic of the drive among some social science researchers to make interventions in the social and political world they study. The aim of what one scholar calls 'participatory research', in particular, is to democratize the knowledge process while instigating social change (Stoeker 1999).

The authors adopted what Wehr and Lederach (1991: 97) call an 'insider-partial' approach to their research and conflict mediation activities:

> The insider-partial is the 'mediator from within the conflict', whose acceptability to the conflictants is rooted not in distance from the conflict or objectivity regarding the issues, but rather in connectedness and trusted relationships with the conflict parties. The trust comes partly from the fact that the mediators do not leave the postnegotiation situation. They are part of it and must live with the consequences of their

work. They must continue to relate to conflictants who have trusted their commitment to a just and durable settlement.

Working in partnership with Billy Mitchell our intention was to provoke debate and discussion within the progressive loyalist community and ultimately to hasten movement by the UVF and RHC towards abandoning the strategy of terrorism (see Edwards 2009).

We were conscious of the work of other scholars who had become immersed in their study of republicanism (Burton 1978; Lundy and McGovern 2006) and loyalism (Bruce 1992; Nelson 1984). However, with the possible exception of McAuley (1994) these had been largely temporary assignments. Where we differed was that we lived and worked among the people we studied. In practical terms this necessitated an ongoing debate between the authors on the appropriate balance to be struck between what Pike (1993) terms 'emic' and 'etic' research approaches. In Pike's view language operates differently from an insider's or emic perspective than it does from an outsider's or etic perspective 'and consists of a system of hierarchies', each of which can be examined from alternative points of view by the observer, and all which help a person to relate to the "physical, social, aesthetic, and philosophical environment" (1993: 78). In a bid to provide an accurate picture of the state of play within progressive loyalism in terms that our research partners would understand we operated primarily from an emic point of view. Moreover, because we sought to collaborate closely with progressive loyalists in peacebuilding initiatives, we were also conscious of the much broader philosophical and ethical parameters within which other peace researchers had carried out their work in the past and it is those to which we now turn.

From Peace Research to *Participatory Peace Research*

Johan Galtung (1988: 1) once wrote that 'The basic concern of peace research is the pursuit of peace with peaceful means, if possible in a wholistic [sic] and global manner'. Galtung was the founder of the Oslo Peace Research Institute and an uncompromising advocate of the normative leanings of peace research. He vigorously articulated the need for independence in research and recommended that peace researchers should adopt 'a resolutely global and more sociological focus', and that, like health professionals, would maintain 'a Hippocratic-like professional commitment to look beyond personal preferences and biases' (Lawler 2008: 81). Like advocates of participatory research Galtung also recognized that there is a certain point when academics cross the threshold and become agents of change, thereby impacting on the socio-political world they study.

Successful participatory researchers who wish to 'pursue peace with peaceful means' and thereby have a positive effect on the social world around them are able to draw on their professional academic experience as well as the rich, detailed insider intuition of their research partners (Stoeker 1999: 842). Yet, this is more than just academic good practice; it is fundamental to those working within the sub-field of participatory peace research. We consider participatory peace research to have its intellectual roots in the broad field of peace studies. As a field of scholarly inquiry peace studies can be traced to the 1950s, when many of its key figures were drawn more from the disciplinary boundaries of natural sciences, economics, psychology, anthropology, education and sociology than political science and International relations. And it was the diverse backgrounds of its principal proponents which 'helped arguably to stymie their original goal of establishing a methodologically distinctive and theoretically robust field of social scientific enquiry' (Lawler 2008: 74).

In many respects this multidisciplinary intellectual heritage quarantined peace studies from the sterile debates raging throughout the social sciences over positivism. It also made peace researchers more sensitive to the experiences of those they studied. Looking back over half a century of peace studies research, Galtung (2009) revealed how his own methodology was based on the obsession:

> to search, again and again...adding to Western empiricist research critical and constructive peace insights from all corners of the world. And letting theory and practice grow hand in hand, not stopping at diagnosis-prognosis in the name of Weberian value neutrality, [nor] leaving practice to foreign office amateurs who jump from one disastrous failure to the next, like from Middle East to Sri Lanka to whatever.

Yet even in the most empirically-rich research projects it is useful to have some sort of methodology in mind. In the words of the pre-eminent sociologist C. Wright Mills researchers should:

> Avoid the fetishism of method and technique. Urge the rehabilitation of the unpretentious intellectual craftsman, and try to become such a craftsman yourself. Let every man be his own methodologist; let every man be his own theorist; let theory and method again become part of the practice of a craft. (Mills 2000: 224)

Perhaps one of Mills' most important contributions to the social sciences was the challenge he issued to other social scientists to think reflexively about their research. Like Mills, but unlike leading voices in peace studies such as Galtung and Lederach, both authors approached their research from an agnostic/atheist, left-leaning standpoint.

Turning to Galtung's (1988) three rules about managing oneself in relation to commissioned work for states and other powerful entities, he argues that peace researchers ought to have (1) total freedom of expression, before, during and after the contact, (2) to make the interaction public, and (3) to be careful about institutionalized links. Although written in the context of the Cold War and addressing the dilemma facing researchers who may want to work with state powers, the rules translate to many modern contexts and merit consideration. Above all, Galtung (ibid: 4) writes, those who wish to serve the cause of peace must adhere to the overriding principle of research autonomy.

Building on Galtung's broad parameters of peace research Lederach has offered a clear conceptual framework for successful conflict mediation, which the authors sought to emulate in the Northern Ireland setting:

> First, these natural helpers, or mediators, emerge from within the set-ting. Their knowledge of the context and their relationships with people are seen as a resource, not an obstacle. Second, they are connected on a long-term basis, and are not "in and out" of the setting. Third, they are chosen not for their expertise or profession, but for who they are in the network. Their value lies not in a service to be performed but rather in a relationship in which they are involved. (Lederach 1997: 96).

Here we chose the methodological framework of ethnography to collect our data, while exploiting the anthropologist's tendency to empathize with local cultures and, thereby, ultimately, understand their point of view.

Of particular importance for our efforts here was the writing of the Polish ethnographer Bronislaw Malinowski, who famously remarked that it was essential in socio-cultural research 'to grasp the native's point of view, his relation to life, to realize *his* vision of *his* world' (1932: 25). In Malinowski's view (ibid: 25) the goal of accurate, successful ethnographic fieldwork must adhere to the following three-pronged directives:

1. The organisation of the tribe, and the anatomy of its culture must be recorded in firm, clear outline. The method of concrete, statistical docu-mentation is the means through which such an outline has to be given.
2. Within this frame, the imponderabilia of actual life, and the type of behaviour have to be filled in. They have to be collected through minute, detailed observations, in the form of some sort of ethnographic diary, made possible by close contact with native life.
3. A collection of ethnographic statements, characteristic narratives, typical utterances, items of folk-lore and magical formulae has to be given as a corpus inscriptionum, as documents of native mentality.

In all of our work, we adhered to the principles of both peace research and the rigorous methods tried and tested by successive generations of ethnographers. We now turn to explain how we applied the principles of participatory peace research to the transformation of loyalist communities.

Transforming loyalist communities

It was considered unthinkable that organizations like the UVF and UDA should continue their violence long after the Provisional IRA halted its 'armed struggle'. Yet, from a strategic perspective, it was completely rational for the UVF to end its terrorism on its own terms because it had begun and sustained its armed campaign on its own terms (see Edwards 2009: 155; and Harris 2006). So how and why did UVF terrorism come to an end? What were the internal and external stimuli which led the organization to declare an end to its campaign of terror in May 2007 and finally decommission its huge arsenal of guns and explosives over two years later in June 2009? To answer these important questions it is necessary – briefly – to describe the origins, nature and trajectory of the UVF terrorism.

The UVF was formed in late 1965 as a preventive measure to guard against the potential of a resurgent IRA threat, which many unionists anticipated would rear its head upon the occasion of the 50th anniversary of the Easter Rising in April 1966. The UVF was both a product of union-ist anxieties and an instrument to be used by those hostile to the liberal unionist regime of Prime Minister Captain Terence O'Neill. Originally founded in the borderlands of rural Ulster, its first recruits were drawn from West Belfast and East Antrim. The UVF's early commander was the shipyard worker and former soldier Gusty Spence.[4] Following attacks mainly on Catholic civilians, members of Spence's group were impris-oned. Meanwhile the undercurrent of street violence between Catholics and Protestants had reached boiling point and spilled over into violence. A round of tit-for-tat violence gripped Northern Ireland as loyalist and republican paramilitaries emerged as respective defenders of their com-munities after 1969.

Throughout the conflict the UVF won a reputation as a deadly and ruth-less organization, killing almost 542 people between 1966 and 2002. Out of the total number of deaths attributable to the UVF during the 'Troubles' (427 in all) a startling 84 per cent were civilians, 10 per cent were other loy-alists, 5 per cent were republican paramilitaries, and 1 per cent were security forces personnel (Edwards 2009: 152). A range of factors contributed to the UVF's decision to call a ceasefire in 1994, among those an internal dialogue between the UVF and PUP centred round the so-called 'kitchen cabinet', the efforts of Protestant community workers, the behind-the-scenes work of members of local clergy, and the war weariness palpable in both communi-ties (Edwards and Bloomer 2004: 8–10, 12–14).

Having served as the UVF's figurehead throughout the conflict, in August 2008, Spence called on the organization to completely decommission, stating:

> If you are the leader, you lead from the front – perhaps maybe after consultation – you have to have the confidence in yourself, the confidence in your men (to say), "I'm making a direct order here that UVF arms will be dispensed with – decommissioned, call it what you want. I expect every man to obey that". (*Belfast Telegraph*, 18 August 2008)

Spence was echoing the words and actions of others, such as Billy Mitchell, Billy McCaughey, David Ervine and Jim McDonald, who had worked to influence the UVF to transform beyond violence (Purvis 2009). Working in partnership with these individuals the authors also challenged the UVF-RHC to loosen their grip on loyalist communities, arguing strongly that armed force had long since lost its utility (see Edwards 2009).

This was a difficult argument to make. As we soon discovered, one of the most significant challenges faced by conflict transformation practitioners working within the Protestant working-class community is the difficulty in overcoming internal scepticism, suspicion and subversion. Not everyone remained overjoyed at the prospect of engaging in intense circumspection about their role in the conflict. Many had suffered profound hardships, losing family members to early graves or prison, and most were increasingly reticent about engaging in dialogue amidst internal strife and recurrent loyalist internecine feuding. Perhaps the best illustration of this was the scepticism generated from those in paramilitary circles who had been passed over for promotion by the new leadership in the local area of East Antrim, in which we primarily worked. In many respects this scepticism boiled over into a suspicion of the actions of those who had bought into the transformation process and openly challenged the authors and other activists on several occasions by the spreading of rumour and counter-rumour.

Once scepticism and suspicion were exposed as unfounded, the inevitable acts of subversion occurred at opportune moments, particularly when the PUP sought an electoral mandate for their conflict transformation activities or when the EACTF project reached a critical juncture in attempting to secure funding. David Ervine and other PUP politicians recognized this as symptomatic of a failure by the British government to provide a 'peace dividend' in loyalist areas. Yet it was also the product of the changing nature of the UVF's membership. As Ervine admitted in an interview with the authors:

> There are three sets of UVF personnel: (1) the guy that says, "its over, I'm away home"; (2) the guy prepared to work for his country, e.g. in community development or politics – [there are] not many of these; (3) then

[there are] the ones who worry me, [who consider] "patriotism the last refuge of the scoundrel". (Interview with David Ervine, 21 September 2004)

Despite the PUP's altruistic ambition to transform loyalist communities it has suffered huge political losses in recent years, especially since Ervine's untimely death in January 2007. While Dawn Purvis held Ervine's seat in the March 2007 Assembly election the party has failed to check the forward march of the DUP and remains only really effective at local-level politics. The PUP's continuing association with the UVF/RHC remains a political liability for many unionists who cannot bring themselves to vote for a party wedded to terrorist groups soaked in the blood of innocent civilians. Like Sinn Fein the PUP will always be caught in the shadow of political violence.

It is worth mentioning here that unlike Sinn Fein, the PUP does not hold Executive office in the locally devolved administration at Stormont, nor has it won many plaudits in Ireland, Britain, the United States or internationally, for its role in stabilizing the peace process. Additionally, the PUP's cavalier attitude towards seeing the conflict transformation process through to the end, risks making the party irrelevant as loyalists give up their guns and exit the political stage. In essence conflict transformation work within progressive loyalism remained a constant dialogue between the militarists and the politicos over the means, rather than the ends, of transforming loyalist communities. Unfortunately, the schism between militarist and politico attitudes has also seriously hampered the development of loyalist politics. Just as importantly ongoing tension and violence has had an ostensible detrimental effect on peacebuilding efforts by politicos (Bloomer 2008; Edwards and Bloomer 2005).

While the nature of the relationships between politico and militarist within the PUP-UVF axis remains skewed in militarist eyes, the result is that the conflict transformation initiatives undertaken by the 'politicos' remain tentative and weak. A key factor ensuring this continued weakness remains the state's steadfast refusal to support (not just financially) any meaningful conflict transformation initiatives in the community sector. Working-class communities are effectively punished while paramilitarism continues to exert a malign influence. Additionally, there has also been an absence of clear and unambiguous grassroots leadership, which has permitted paramilitarism to degenerate into organized crime. Through providing illicit opportunities for the new breed of 'cease fire soldier' it has seriously destabilized the already weak community infrastructure in Protestant working-class areas.

By 2008 progressive loyalism faced another challenge, this time in the guise of a community and voluntary sector increasingly colonized by paramilitary organizations: a continuation of the struggle by other means. The key aspect to this new phase is that the cadre of politicos and community development workers who oversaw the early development stages of transformation initiatives have become ever more marginalized. Effectively, the community workers at the helm of EACTF (including the authors) were, proverbially speaking, to 'lose the battle and yet win the war'. The UVF leadership and other key players in loyalist paramilitary circles effectively bought fully into the EACTF initiative, repositioning themselves as 'gate-keepers' in order to work closely with funding bodies and government agencies (Bloomer and Edwards 2009). Anecdotal evidence from other initiatives indicates that this is not an isolated occurrence but rather part of an overall strategy of colonization in the community and voluntary sector.

Evidence from the community and voluntary sector suggests that David Ervine's 'Type 2' (the individual prepared to work for his country, in terms of community development or politics) has metamorphosed. These individuals remained close enough to conflict transformation and community development initiatives to learn (or give the impression of learning) the language and the modalities of the politico and then use the art of the militarist to gain control. The result is that the grand scheme, conflict transformation, has been replaced with the mundane and a host of funder requirements. And yet in the grand scheme of things, at least there is an absence of overt violence within progressive loyalism and the overall direction of movement remains away from violence to politics, from militarist to politico.

From lofty ideals founded in the process of conflict transformation, these initiatives have since become run-of-the-mill community development initiatives wherein honest endeavour became focussed on skills development, capacity building, training initiatives and job creation. Success is now defined in terms of attracting new funding, rather than transforming militarists to politicos; this sort of pseudo-DDR work has been sapped of all of its creative energy and has ensured that successes are redefined simply as an absence of violence.

This may well have been the inevitable outcome of a flawed process wherein the power dynamics between politico and militarist would always ensure politico gains were short term and partial at best. At the very least the politicos can be satisfied in the knowledge that the militarists rarely, if ever, became 'spoilers' (Steadman 1997). It should be noted, however, that the costs in personal and professional terms for a number of the politicos has been substantial and remains ongoing – unwanted and unnecessary coercive pressure from militarist 'partners' continues to remain a problem, as the murder of Bobby Moffett in May 2010 starkly illustrated.

Ending terrorism: Lessons learned

Few commentators have written about the internal dynamics responsible for bringing terrorism to an end. Even fewer have analysed terrorism in relation to the two key variables which explain its persistence: 'the nature of the goals they seek and their relationship to the community they claim to represent' (see Richardson 2006: 29). The UVF case demonstrates how terrorists, once they judge the mood of their traditional supporters to be at a low ebb or indifferent to their cause, can be persuaded to end their armed campaigns. The observations made here may prove useful for those who wish to engage in participatory peace research. They are not designed to be exhaustive and there is a recognition that a researcher's own unique background and expertise may be of more relevance in identifying the nuances of the surrounding research environment. If nothing else, this chapter has outlined one methodology by which researchers can choose to 'pursue peace with peaceful means'. In any case, as Ramsbotham *et al.* have correctly observed, the emphasis of conflict resolution work in recent years has moved 'from an outsider neutral approach towards a partnership with local actors, and it is this relationship which is one of the key characteristics of peacebuilding from below' (Ramsbotham *et al.* 2008: 217).

On an interrelated matter ethno-centric models of peacebuilding rarely have positive effects on communities, especially those where ethnic exclusivism runs parallel with an undercurrent of intra-communal tension. Yet one could argue that it is just not the applicability of Western models of conflict resolution that can aid in the transformation of conflict. When both authors visited the Wi'am[5] Palestinian Conflict Resolution Center in Bethlehem in 2008 they heard first hand how a synergy of Western and Middle Eastern models of conflict resolution was effectively applied in this complex social, political and cultural setting. The Wi'am Centre describes their unique blend approach towards conflict resolution in the following manner:

> Although conflict is a human universal, the nature of disputes and the methods of resolving conflict differ from one socio-cultural context to another. For instance, in the Western-tradition, conflict is commonly perceived to occur between two or more individuals (interpersonal); while in the Middle Eastern tradition, conflict exceeds the individual to reach the collective or the wider family. (Wi'am 2009)

By blending together Western and indigenous conflict resolution practices the Wi'am Center has proven itself to be culturally sensitive and acceptable to local communities. In many ways our own experience of the progressive loyalist transformation process was sympathetic to local concerns, working with abstract concepts of peacebuilding but in ways understandable to the communities themselves.

As we discovered, it is advisable to read up as much as possible on the intended research environment before, during and after embarking on research in divided societies. Just as practitioners of military force must train and prepare for their deployment in hostile operational theatres (Kilcullen

2006) so peace researchers must make every effort to prepare for peaceful intervention in conflict zones. In an increasingly globalized world, where there is often too great a tendency for commentators to graft liberal peace 'solutions' onto the 'problems' facing marginalized groups, the progressive loyalist case study detailed above may offer an alternative approach.

Conclusion

Those engaged in participatory peace research should endeavour to remain resilient and vigilant, as well as sympathetic and non-condemnatory, in their approach. Adopting the moral high ground and speaking in platitudes only serves to reinforce the stereotypes that genuine peace activists in Northern Ireland and elsewhere serve to challenge, especially in those areas where violence is most acute. Often decisions that they make can have far-reaching consequences. The ambient dangers experienced during our research into loyalist paramilitarism took place when these groups seemed to be locked in an endless cycle of bloody feuds. To be useful good empirical research must be based on immersion in the subject matter, high quality interviews and participant observation. As we discovered, it should adhere to a reflexive research approach and a commitment to 'peace with peaceful means'.

Studying a complex social, cultural and political phenomenon like progressive loyalism presents a unique set of challenges. Indeed there are inter-related problems of access, managing community expectations, and an almost insatiable tendency in the media to promote negative stereotypes. Added to these challenges are ambient dangers which still exist for researchers who wish to explore loyalist paramilitary groupings, their local interest groups, and the political parties associated with them, at close quarters. This has led some scholars to suggest that the study of difficult subject-matter ought to be left to others, such as journalists, who are more willing to venture off the beaten track (Farrington 2006: 279). Relying disproportionately on secondary source material, of a frequently sensationalized nature, is not an ideal method for any serious analyst to adopt, even in societies where political violence still underpins the relationships within and between the two communities.

Nevertheless, the lack of access – particularly in terms of Ulster loyalism – is something which continues to seriously hamper informed discussion. It has led to the tendency among some commentators to study the phenomenon of loyalist paramilitarism from a detached journalistic position and in a way that accepts – without question – that the goals of such groups are simply criminal and devoid of a rational political or strategic dimension (see Spencer 2008 for a counter-argument). This chapter has sought to challenge this simplistic narrative of Ulster loyalism.

Notes

Acknowledgement: The authors would like to thank those progressive loyalists named in the chapter for facilitating their ongoing participatory peace research. Thanks also to Gusty Spence for taking the time to read and discuss our work with Aaron Edwards. We dedicate this chapter to the memories of G.H. and J.C.G. for their sound advice when we needed it most.

1. Billy Mitchell acted as a gatekeeper into the community we sought to research. He was a former senior member of the UVF, and its one-time purported leader in the 1970s, and had served 14 years in prison for UVF activities. Upon his release he worked tirelessly to build peace within and between the divided communities in Northern Ireland. His death, in July 2006, robbed the EACTF initiative of its most vocal and energetic strategist.
2. 'Progressive loyalism' is a term that has gained considerable currency since 2003 among those loyalists who associate themselves with the UVF, RHC and PUP 'constituency'. Although the term is used to differentiate the UVF-RHC-PUP brand of loyalism from the fundamentalist and deeply conservative elements within mainstream unionism (such as the DUP), it was born out of the bloody, internecine feuding of 2000 and 2004.
3. The authors prefer to employ the term 'participatory peace research' to denote the conscious and deliberate actions of researchers to intervene in a conflict environment to empower those traditionally seen as 'research subjects' and where the outcome is achieving 'peace with peaceful means'.
4. It was largely through *ad hoc* discussions between Aaron Edwards and Gusty Spence that we gained the necessary impetus to continue to challenge the malign influence of paramilitarism and transform loyalist communities.
5. Wi'am translates into 'cordial relationships' in Arabic.

Chapter 9
Loyalism, Orangeism and Britishness: Contemporary Synergies and Tensions[1]

Andrew Mycock, James W. McAuley and Jonathan Tonge

Perhaps the most visible expression of loyalism in Northern Ireland can be found in the Orange Order, especially through its set piece commemorations and in particular its parading tradition. Such parades give open and very public expression to notions of loyalty and identity (Bryan 2000). Within this, several writers have drawn attention to the key role of the Order (correctly titled the Loyal Orange Institution) in defining popular constructions of Britishness for many Northern Irish Protestant unionists (Kaufman 2007; Kinealy 2004; McAuley and Tonge 2008). Central to this is the linking of core themes of past and present within the Protestant unionist tradition (McAuley and Tonge 2007). Through this the Orange Order provides not just a teleological link that connects current generations to those who are seen to have defended the Union, but also provides a crucial institution shaping a historical narrative that celebrates a particular view of 'Britishness' and the British national past.

Moreover, it is an institution that seeks an active role in articulating and propagating a view of history whereby ties with the rest of the United Kingdom are seen as organic, founded on a common ascription to the British Crown and the Protestant faith. Within such narratives, events such as the siege of Derry in 1689 and the victory of Crown forces led by King William III at the Battle of the Boyne, together with the sacrifices of Ulstermen at the Battle of Somme in 1916, are seen as pivotal moments both in British constitutional history and as symbol of the legitimacy of Northern Ireland as part of the Union.

Orangeism and political change

Since the signing of the GFA in 1998, the political and social framework of Northern Ireland has undergone radical change. For example, few would have predicted a collation government comprised of Sinn Féin and the Democratic

Unionist Party or indeed the apparently genuine *bon homie* between former First Minister, Ian Paisley, and his Deputy, Martin McGuinness. Political parties in Northern Ireland have also expressed a greater sensitivity, in the public realm at least, to the complex and interrelated factors that define the politics of citizenship and identity in the United Kingdom and the Republic of Ireland.

This would appear, in part, to be in response to stated intent of the GFA for Northern Irish citizens to recognize: 'the birthright of all the people of Northern Ireland to identify themselves and be accepted as Irish or British', promoting: 'full respect for, and equality of, civil, political, social and cultural rights ... and of parity of esteem and of just and equal treatment for the identity, ethos and aspirations of both communities' (HMSO 1998).

Indicative of this shift, according to McAuley and Tonge (2009), has been a greater preparedness of Irish republicans to acknowledge the legitimacy of bi-nationalism, while also continuing to actively agitate for a united Ireland. Thus, Sinn Féin party leader, Gerry Adams (2009), has argued republicans should re-evaluate their perceptions of unionists, as 'in a United Ireland the agencies, management, symbols and emblems need to reflect the diversity of our society'. In so doing, Adams highlighted a more sophisticated approach to identity politics, formally acknowledging a positive role of the Orange Order in a post-reunification Ireland. He suggested: 'Orange marches, albeit on the basis of respect and cooperation, will continue in a United Ireland', though he mischievously noted only if its members wished to. This suggests a significant shift from earlier comments on the Orange Order, whom Adams described as neo-fascists with, a 'bigoted and irrational hatred of Catholics' (Adams 1995: 113).

But although there is a considerable shift in the tone of rhetoric of the leadership of Sinn Féin, McAuley and Tonge (2009) also note that republicans and nationalists have continued to reinforce a sense of distinctive Irishness while also reacting critically to some Orange Order marches. Some persist in taking more direct and aggressive action such as attacking Orange halls or throwing missiles at Orange parades. Clearly tensions remain as to the perceived cultural, religious and, indirectly, political legitimacy of Orangeism in Northern Ireland.

This would suggest, for some, the culture and identity of the Orange Order and its membership continue to be associated with a fixed and belligerent oppositional Britishness as a form of colonial identity adopted by Ireland's 'misguided' Protestant minority. For Orange members, however, their British identity is one that is continually under threat and must therefore be defended. Whereas the challenge of James and Irish Home Rulers has been seen off, contemporary threats are seen to come from two contradictory directions.

First, Irish republicans and nationalists are perceived to be deliberately attempting to undermine key facets of Britishness in Northern Ireland.

This is seen as both a political and cultural threat, raising questions as to the motives for Sinn Féin's participation in government and the continued opposition to 'Orange culture'. Attempts to project a sense of Irishness are seen as premeditated in denying Protestants freedom to express their Britishness. Second, the British state's preparedness to deal with Sinn Féin draws attention to the conditionality of the Union and also raises questions regarding the extent to which loyalty to the Union is reciprocal. While the Orange leadership has always unequivocally condemned loyalist paramilitary violence (rather urging its members to join the security forces to combat militant republicanism), they appear deeply engaged in a 'culture war' which Orangeism forms a Maginot line for 'Protestant-Britishness'.

Orangeism, Protestantism and Britishness

The remainder of this chapter, therefore, seeks to explore the extent to which the Orange Order continues to project a coherent collective political identity founded on a common ethno-religious 'Protestant-Britishness' (McAuley and Tonge 2007: 35). First, we consider the relationship between citizenship and nationality in understanding competing constructions of Britishness, of which the Orange variant is but one. Second, we look at how recent developments concerning the politics of identity in the United Kingdom have impacted on constructions of Orange Britishness. Finally, the chapter explores how leading figures within the Orange Order view their identity(ies) and the extent to which transnational dimensions of Orangeism continue to draw on a common sense of Britishness.

The signing of the GFA and the subsequent devolution of governmental responsibility in a range of policy areas to the Northern Ireland Assembly would appear to suggest some recognition of distinct Northern Irish political nationality and citizenship. However, the GFA also formalized a unique solution to Ireland's recent Troubles; one that reflected persisting ambiguity of responses to the complex legacy of the British Empire.

The Agreement confirmed the right of citizens to hold both British and Irish citizenships and the recognition of the birthright of all the people of Northern Ireland to identify themselves and be accepted as Irish or British – or both. Such moves raise a number of questions as to the existence and relevance of a British nationality and its relationship to the citizenship conferred by the UK state; something of course that is of major concern to Orangeism.

Empire, state and Orangeism

This needs some further exploration. Citizenship and nationality are frequently viewed as being synonymous, thus indicating that nationality confers rights and responsibilities on citizens, and that every citizen is a national of a particular state. Such a view is erroneous. Though citizenship is interconnected with nationality, they are not interchangeable. Nationality denotes legal membership of a state from which citizenship develops conditional rights and obligations that involves an active element.

These political rights are distinct from more passive forms of nationality, which often draw on shared cultural or ethnic dynamics (Mycock 2010). Within a single state there is potential for two differing but overlapping forms of identity to emerge. One is based on civic constructions founded on a common citizenship, which can differ from those based on a national ethnic community that is not necessarily congruent with a particular state. Within states such as the United Kingdom the relationship between nationality and citizenship is further complicated by a multinational framework, which encourages layered identities that can overlap in complementary or conflictual terms. Citizenship and nationality can therefore be understood at state *and* sub-state national levels, encouraging divergence within and across the multinational state.

The relationship between citizenship and nationality is made more complex by the legacy of empire. Empire gave rise to a British national-imperial consciousness that drew together a disparate range of national groups within the United Kingdom and beyond, or their elites at least, extending the political and cultural borders of the British nation and state within imperial contexts, meaning ethnic and civic identities persistently overlapped while remaining necessarily ill-defined to negate messianistic projections of Englishness or Britishness.

The centrality of war, Protestantism and the monarchy in defining a uniform, if not universal, British identity is well documented (Colley 1992). The engagement of 'otherness' in the expansion of Empire and extensive plantation in some imperial territories further emphasized the core attributes of an ethnicized and racialized national-imperial Anglo-British identity (including the spread of Orangeism, often through Army regiments). This encouraged a transnational Britishness, which drew strongly on its Anglo-centric political and cultural core founded on common institutions, symbols, cultural practice and 'invented traditions'.

The British imperial experience was one where political, social or cultural interchange was not bounded within a discrete national, or indeed multinational state, framework. This meant that the boundaries between metropole and imperial periphery were ill-defined. For example, debate continues as to whether Ireland can best be understood as a British colony, or one of the colonizing nations that established and ran the British Empire (Howe 2008).

David Fitzpatrick (2001) suggests that Ireland's status oscillated between periphery and metropole; formally integrated into the United Kingdom but often considered 'akin to a colony'. Here the role of religion and ethnicity were important, with Protestant settlers in the North of Ireland often viewing relations differently to their Catholic counterparts. Though both groups contributed to the expansion and maintenance of empire, their view of the position of Ireland vis-à-vis the rest of the imperial metropole differed considerably.

Union in 1801 did not stimulate a similar process of incorporation as with Scotland or Wales, and the growth of Irish counter state nationalism during the nineteenth century, together with the failure to devolve political power through Home Rule, led to insurrection and the eventual partition of Ireland. These 'degrees of coloniality' (Howe 2008: 138) highlight that Britishness was a plural identity that could therefore be understood in both national and imperial terms, though many of the central tenets were common.

This was particularly true of the Orange Order's understanding of Britishness. The Order's allegiance to the British state has its origins in the fear of the Catholic threat to the political order established in the wake of the Glorious Revolution of 1688. It was best represented in belief in the legitimacy of the Protestant Ascendancy and the continued exclusion of Catholics from most high-ranking positions in politics, society and the monarchy. Its origins were national, multinational and transnational, being in part a reaction to the rise of Irish nationalism in the late eighteenth century, but also located in broader concerns about the threat of Catholicism in the United Kingdom and across Europe.

The Union and empire therefore, provided the best defence against perceived and actual threats of Catholic expansionism. The economic benefits of imperial trade became increasingly apparent during the nineteenth century, thus deepening ties with the rest of the United Kingdom where Orange lodges also formed, particularly in industrial cities such as Liverpool and Glasgow where Protestants with no Irish connections also joined (Day 2008). As Kinealy (2004: 226) notes, by the end of the nineteenth century 'the Orange Order has firmly established itself within British society'.

Empire however also provided opportunities to develop Orange networks in new settled lands and undertake missionary work to civilize indigenous peoples across the globe (Etherington 1999). The development of Orangeism in Australia, Canada and the United States drew on common constructions of Britishness and was rooted in a British-Protestant ethnicity, which reproduced hierarchies of power evident in Ulster and the rest of the imperial metropole (Kaufman 2007: 3). But Orange lodges in settler societies proved less accommodating of formal expressions of sectarianism, reflecting both their more overtly multi-faith composition and the comparative lack of political sensitivity about the constitutional status of Ireland (Dudley-Edwards 1999; Kennaway 2006: 10).

Though monarchy and Protestant faith were central to transnational constructions of Orange Britishness, such sentiments declined in salience during the twentieth century, as members of lodges outside of the United

Kingdom shifted political loyalties towards their host states. The erosion of the Protestant hegemony of political and economic power in Northern Ireland, combined with shifts in the composition of Northern Irish society and its attitudes, provided significant challenges to the Orange Order. This elicited contradictory responses from Northern Irish Protestants whereby, membership of the Orange Order fell, but the intensity of its activities grew. Orangeism increasingly found expression as a common religious and cultural identity but not one focused on the defence of the Union or a particular understanding of Britishness.

Orangeism and the peace process

In particular, the Orange Order became increasingly active in response to the peace process, which in part was viewed as part of an ongoing dilution of Britishness (McAuley and Tonge 2007: 41). The signing of the Anglo-Irish Agreement in 1985 stimulated an increase in the numbers of marches, the routes of some proving controversial. This, in turn, stimulated intense debate about equality of civil rights and the freedoms to express 'cultural traditions' founded on allegiance, history and identity. Central to such displays was the importance of Protestant and British identity though claims that marches were not sectarian or political conveniently overlooked the interplay between civic and ethnic nationalism.

The demise of empire and decline in salience of key identifiers that shaped nation-imperial Britishness, such as ongoing secularization of British politics and society and crisis of the monarchy, raised important questions as to the loyalty of those in Northern Ireland who continue to support the Union. Disillusionment with the British state, particularly with regards to the preparedness to introduce power sharing with Irish nationalists and republicans, encouraged the partial replacement of British identity with one allied to Ulster Unionism.

Though steadfastly committed to the maintenance of the Union, the coherence and cohesion of Orangeism in relation to Britishness began to fragment, thus revealing the inherent complexities of an identity shaped by national, multinational and transnational signifiers. Orange Order concerns regarding the peace process have highlighted the conditionality of Ulster loyalty to UK citizenship. As loyalty to the Crown and Protestant faith is not necessarily founded on a common UK citizenship, many saw the Orange Order's understanding of Britishness as one founded on an increasingly outdated, defensive and reactive ideology (Kinealy 2004: 218).

Last-gasp Britons?

As we shall see though, the Orange Order's allegiance to Britishness highlights the tensions between citizenship and nationality in a post-empire state. Identities in Northern Ireland, as elsewhere in the United Kingdom, have proven open to significant shifts in response to changes in the political, socio-economic and cultural environments. Since the late 1960s, unionists in Northern Ireland have rejected 'Irish' dimensions of identity in favour of a more diverse framework of British, Northern Irish, Ulster and Protestant identities. But such shifts belie a pervading lack of agreement in understanding or expressing a unionist British identity (McAuley 2010; McAuley and Tonge 2009).

For some, such as Tom Nairn, the promotion of a British identity by unionists is representative of 'last-gasp Britons', who appear deliberately blind to shifts in attitudes in the rest of the United Kingdom. He suggests that unionists seek the 'customary ethos of Britishness to stay in place ... to maintain the Kingdom's last resort Sovereignty over Northern Ireland' (Nairn 2002: 116). Broadly, however, Nairn's thesis conveniently overlooks divisions within the unionist community in Northern Ireland; he seeks to deride all forms of British identity in pursuit of Scottish independence.

Orange Order ascription to their distinct understanding of Britishness highlights the plurality of unionist identities both within Northern Ireland and also across the rest of the United Kingdom. As Todd (1987) has shown, unionist identity is multiple, differentiated between 'Ulster loyalist' and 'Ulster British' traditions, which Porter (1996) suggests is reflective of multiple ethnic and civic constructions of Britishness (see also Aughey 1999).

Within this framework, the Orange Order has maintained an ascription to a form of national-imperial Britishness whose origins remain strongly associated by many with a bygone age. This encourages a view that Orangeism is increasingly out of step with perceptions of British identity in the rest of the United Kingdom. This is highlighted if we consider the centrality of parading to Orangeism. While there is some resistance from modernizers within the Order, the dominant view remains an insistence upon unfettered ability to march throughout Northern Ireland. Indeed, this 'right' is perceived as a core plank in Orangeism's opposition to the dilution of Protestant rights. This view again finds the Order disjointed from more everyday narratives and behaviour. Whereas, once Orange parades and other public forms of community and identity were commonplace across the United Kingdom, they for many now appear 'immodest, intolerant and therefore un-British form of patriotism' (Weight 2002: 532).

As Kaufman (2007: 2) explains the ethno-cultural associations of the Orange Order remain crucial in presenting a politicized Protestant identity that is central to their understanding of Britishness. More recently, however, the Orange Order has increasingly focused on civic constructions of identity framed within British and Northern Irish frameworks. This is in part due to shifts in how citizenship and nationality are understood both within the United Kingdom and across the former Empire.

During the nineteenth and early twentieth centuries, the extension of political, economic and social rights in the United Kingdom began a process, which has led to the nationalizing of citizenship. This process was accelerated by the demise of much of the British Empire and the introduction of legislation to restrict immigration from the Commonwealth (Mycock 2009). More recently, politicians and others have engaged in deliberations in an attempt to articulate a post-empire twenty-first-century Britishness.

Key to such deliberations have been a number of pervasive themes linked to the modernization of the British state and constitution, and the promotion of a discrete framework of values which have been defined by and have also shaped a range of national institutions. Gordon Brown has emerged as the most influential exponent, seeking the 'rediscovery' of 'long-standing British values', such as tolerance, liberty, decency, fair play, responsibility, openness, internationalism and civic duty which are reflective of the 'British genius'.

This understanding of Britishness has been historically substantiated through the establishment of a repetitive discourse, which stresses a 'golden thread' of British constitutional progression (Brown 1999, 2006). Brown has further suggested that a unique combination of values gave rise to a range of 'great public institutions admired around the world' such as the National Health Service, the Armed Forces, museums, universities and the BBC (Brown 2004).

British identity and Northern Ireland

Such moves would indicate that the parameters of debates about UK citizenship and British nationality are increasingly projected as national and synonymous. But the resulting debate about British identity has been characterized by the general absence of Northern Irish voices. A lack of clarity persists though as to whether such debates focus on 'Britain' or the United Kingdom, or if the government is promoting Britishness or United Kingdom-'ness' (Mycock and Tonge 2008). For example, government Reports such as the Ministry of Justice green paper on constitutional reform focus on the *Governance of Britain* even though the remit of the Report covers the whole of the United Kingdom.

Raising this issue is not merely constitutional pedantry; especially when as indicated above, the 1998 GFA affords the right of all people in Northern Ireland to identify themselves as 'Irish' or 'British', and that any person born on the island of Ireland is entitled to Irish citizenship. The lack of certainty as to whether policy affects Britain or the United Kingdom, not only raises questions as to the place of Northern Ireland within the Union, it also suggests that debates about Britishness do not necessarily include it. The solution to this complex dilemma has been for politicians to avoid reference to Ireland. For example, in an article defending the Union, Gordon Brown noted, 'I am Scottish and proud of it, but I am no less proud to be British – just as there are millions who are proud to be Welsh and British and English and British too (Brown 2008).

This oversight was not unique and politicians from across the political spectrum have found it easier to discuss Britishness or other national identities without reference to Northern Ireland. However Brown's oversight provoked a swift response, with DUP Deputy Leader Nigel Dodds describing the omission as a 'major error'. He noted that if Brown was 'serious about promoting Britishness, he has to encompass all its component parts' (Dawar 2008). The intervention is indicative of growing preparedness of unionist parties of all hues to contribute to debates about Britishness. Indeed, in recent times the DUP has found itself under further criticism from the unionist right, Jim Allister of Traditional Unionist Voice (TUV) recently claiming that the agreement of the DUP to enter government with Sinn Féin had further eroded Britishness (Allister 2008).

Such concerns are not new; many of the themes have their origins in the Troubles (McAuley 2007) and draw attention to what is considered an ideologically driven Irish republican and nationalist agenda to undermine Britishness. Thus, in response to what is seen as a sustained attack on the right to celebrate their British and Ulster identities, the DUP announced in June 2008 the creation of an 'Academy for Britishness'. The think tank would both undertake research on themes related to British identity and provide an 'educational vehicle' to 'engage with community groups, of all types, specific interest groups and the general public'. Peter Robinson, leader of the DUP and First Minister, has been unequivocal in his assertion that unionists 'are British and intend to stay that way' (*Belfast Telegraph* 25 June 2008).

Here issues linked to the role of banal indicators of community and national identity have proven most contentious (Billig 1995). The UUP have accused Sinn Féin of being 'intent on gutting civic buildings of any reference to Britishness' (UUP 2008). Sinn Féin requests for the Union flag not to be flown on 'neutral' public buildings are interpreted by the DUP as evidence of broader campaign of 'anti-British bigotry' (Dodds 2008). There are many examples of this perspective. Shirlow *et al.* (2005) note that many Protestants felt that the proposal to remove 'London' from 'Londonderry' was part of an attempt to deny their British identity. Further, Southern (2009) suggests such concerns are part of a broader suspicion that Catholics are attempting some form of ethnic colonization. Protestants feel that Catholics/nationalists are given preferential rights and resources to promote their ethno-cultural tradition, though this is part of a broader political agenda for reunification.

The Orange Order is recognized by many across unionism as at the core of cultural opposition to Irish unity. Nigel Dodds drew attention in a DUP party conference speech in 2008 to what he saw as politically inspired sectarian attacks on Orange Order halls and limits placed on Orange marches.

He argued that the Orange Order was integral 'to promote true cultural equality' (Dodds 2008). While such interventions by mainstream politicians highlight the competitive and fragmented nature of Northern Irish Unionism, (and the preparedness of the DUP to explicitly court the Orange Order vote), they are also reflective of the extent to which the Orange Order has emerged as a key institution to defend Britishness in Northern Ireland.

Orangeism, loyalty and Britishness

As part of this defence of Britishness, the Orange Order has over the last decade engaged in an extensive revision and rebranding of its image, activities and place within Northern Irish civil society. They have broadened their activities and have attempted to tap into debates allied to the ongoing 'culture wars' across the United Kingdom as a whole. Sustained efforts have been made to develop the role of the Orange Order as an educational facilitator. They increased outreach programmes into schools, offering their view of the role of the Orange Order in modern Northern Irish society and how its heritage continues to shape understanding of Protestant and unionist identities.

In particular, the Orange Order has welcomed the introduction of statutory citizenship education in Northern Irish schools, arguing that they offer opportunity for them to address 'the myths and misconceptions people have' (Orange Order 2008). They have also tapped into narratives allied to the promotion of equality and diversity, arguing that they are a key institution in both explaining the history of the Protestant community and also a defender of their contemporary cultural rights. Though Protestantism remains a foundational element that shapes policy and practice, Orange Order has been the greater emphasis on its role as cultural as well as a religious institution.

Central to this deliberate refocusing of the modern-day Orangeism has been the rebranding of 'The Twelfth' as 'Orangefest'. In seeking to address direct accusations of sectarianism, the Orange Order has projected the event as 'one of Europe's largest cultural festivals with music, marching and street pageantry' and a 'kaleidoscope of culture and colour' that offers opportunity for all communities to come together and celebrate the cultural richness of the Orange tradition (*The Independent* 8 July 2007). So far, this has had limited success, with Orange parades still blighted by accusations of sectarianism and drunkenness, with tensions exploding into violence in some areas where marches continue to prove contentious (Rooney 2008; Canning 2009).

Moreover, not all leading members of the Order see the promotion of Orangefest as promoting 'cultural neutrality' in Northern Ireland as positive or worthwhile. Ex-Orange Order deputy grand master, Reverend Stephen Dickinson, argued: 'this is about Protestantism, this is about

Britishness – it's not about cultural tourism' (BBC 2008). While not neces-sarily opposing Orangefest, Dr David Hume, the Director of Services of the Grand Lodge of Ireland suggests 'The Twelfth' should still provide Northern Ireland's unionist community with the opportunity to 'take a stand for their Britishness...'to help strengthen the Union' (*Londonderry Sentinel* 12 July 2008). Underpinning this, he believes the main roles of the Orange Order must remain 'in standing up for being British' and to provide 'the common thread in the fabric of the Protestant community' (Hume 2009a).

It is clear, however, that the Order has repositioned claims for their under-standing of Britishness within a broader framework of calls for 'cultural revival' and diversity across the United Kingdom. The 'truth is that being British is not about race, or creed or culture. Being British is about plural-ism not uniformity, it is about respect for difference and about difference itself' (Hume 2009b). The right of the Orange Order to promote their view of British and Protestant identity is thus construed within a narrative whereby they contribute to enrichment of civil society in Northern Ireland. Attacks on Orange Halls, restrictions on Orange marches and other moves by Sinn Féin and others are seen not only as an attack on such cultural pluralism, but also as contributing to a politically correct form of ethnic cleansing (Hume 2009a).

Moreover, the Orange Order has engaged in a sustained campaign against the Equality Commission for Northern Ireland who they accuse of 'a long term strategy to wipe the face of Britishness from Northern Ireland'. As with the main unionist political parties, the role of banal indicators of British national identity such as the Union flag and emblems of government insti-tutions has proven central to this narrative. Leading figures within the Orange Order have described the role of the Equality Commission as a 'con-tinuous partial attack on the symbols of Britishness in Northern Ireland' (*Belfast Telegraph* 22 January 2008).

Hume's (2008) views the Union and Orangeism as similar, both are regarded as being pluralist institutions with a diverse range of views con-nected to a common ascription to key values. Hence, the Orange Order defence of the Protestant faith and support for the Union is now founded on the promotion of distinct values such as the support for 'civil and religious liberty'. As such, the Orange Order's Britishness draws on a similar value-laden approach as many leading British politicians and indeed recognizes that people have multiple and layered identities. This means that Ulster identity and British identity are not seen in opposition.

However, focus on the religious dimensions of identity highlight differ-ences in content that suggest the Orange Order is out of step with main-stream public opinion across the United Kingdom when defining Britishness (see Yougov 2005). For Hume (2008), the United Kingdom is 'a majority Protestant nation and the ethos of the Protestant faith'. Political support for the Union has emerged as an important theme in light of the threat of secessionist nationalism across the United Kingdom, and 'Orangemen must take a lead in speaking out for the Union' (*Orange Standard* June 2008). The Orange Order has continually stressed that '(w)e support the Union. We want the Union. We are, and we remain, United by the Kingdom' (Hume 2008). This suggests that their variant of British nationalism is not devoid of political content.

The key dynamic that shapes loyalty to the Union thus remains the Protestant Crown rather than Westminster. The Order has argued the UK government should not 'tinker' with the unwritten constitution and the principle of the 'head of state being of the majority religion' (*Orange Standard* November 2008). Moreover, concerns have also drawn attention to the lack of resonance of Northern Ireland in debates about the constitutional future of the United Kingdom. The Orange Order has encouraged members 'to remind our fellow countrymen and women across the narrow strip of water that we are at least as British as they are' (*Orange Standard* June 2008).

But by linking the Protestant faith with loyalty to the Crown and military service, the Orange Order distinguishes itself from most other groups who promote the Union. The County Grand Secretary of Fermanagh, Robert Dane, noted that 'Protestant culture is different. It is often based around service to the crown in the uniform of the country' (Orange Order 2009c). According to Southern (2007: 84–5) this draws attention to the extent that the Troubles have encouraged the persistence of a form of Britishness shaped by war that has endured in the post-conflict period. This was reflected in an interview with the current Grand Master of the Orange Order, Robert Saulters, where he claimed the recent conflict in Iraq again played a part in defining contemporary Britishness.

The Orange Order has also been active in the memorialization of the 'sacrifice' of those 335 members of the Order who were killed during the Northern Ireland conflict including those within the Security Forces. History and sacrifice are central to the reproduction of community memories, with the First World War and the Battle of the Somme contributing to an identity founded on loss, durability and loyalty in the face of the challenge on others. In 2007, the Order also marked the 25th anniversary of the liberation of the Falklands by passing a loyalty resolution (McAuley and Tonge 2008). Such sacrifices mean that to many Orangemen, the Union 'is more than a mere concept' (Hume 2008) suggesting war continues to play a part in defining and celebrating British identity.

Britishness beyond Orangeism

The Orange Order has not simply focused on identity issues within Northern Ireland and has invested considerable effort in promoting a common Ulster-Scots community. This has involved the promotion of the parades as an integral part of Ulster-Scots heritage but has also seen greater emphasis placed on common cultural and linguistic attributes (Stapleton and Wilson 2004). However, attempts to re-imagine Ulster Protestantism as part of a broader Ulster-Scots community should be seen in part as a response to the growing threat of Irish nationalism. It is therefore not devoid of political content and has involved calls for a united stand of 'the Grand Orange Lodges of England and Scotland in calling for the positive promotion of the benefits of the Union for our peoples' (*Orange Standard* July 2008).

The threat of Scottish secessionist nationalism is seen as the most pressing threat to this bi-national community. Drew Nelson, Grand Secretary of the Grand Orange Lodge of Ireland, noted 'We believe that the people in Scotland who are calling for independence are misguided' (*Orange Standard* December 2008). Such analysis has chimed with a preparedness of the Grand Lodge of Scotland to 'mobilise to defend the Union'. Grand Master, Ian Wilson, argued the Orange Order need to 'get real' about the threat of Scottish nationalism and has even gone as far as to encourage members in Scotland to vote Labour in an attempt to nullify the threat of the Scottish National Party (*The Scotsman* 19th October 2009). This marks a shift from earlier calls by Jack Ramsey, former Grand Secretary in Scotland, who suggested Orangemen would turn to paramilitarism if independence was enacted (*Sunday Herald* 8th July 2001).

Emphasis on the common threats to the Union and Britishness for Orangeism across the United Kingdom is instructive, indicating that their focus has also become increasingly national and multinational rather than transnational in its focus. However, as Bridge and Fedorowich (2003: 8) note: 'Britishness outside Britain persists well beyond the demise of the British Empire'. For a significant though dwindling number of people, particularly those who fought in the Second World War or who were educated under an imperial school system, the notion of an 'ethnic Britishness' persists which is founded on common, shared ethno-cultural rituals, symbols and other ties (McGregor 2006).

Even if, as Stuart Ward (2001) suggests, a common Britishness has been strongly diluted by the 'mother country's' actions in nationalizing citizenship and pursuing a European integrationalist agenda, the political and cultural legacy of former colonial ties continue to flag enduring notions of a shared (predominantly white) British past. Moreover, Britishness remains central to post-colonial debates about citizenship and identity across the Commonwealth and beyond. Britishness remains core to debates in the former 'White Dominons', particularly in Australia and New Zealand (Meaney 2003; Pearson 2000).

The Orange Order has been keen to emphasize such ties in Canada, the United States and elsewhere, drawing attention to shared Ulster-Scots heritage and the potential for their 'fellow brethren' to come to Northern Ireland to take part in the Orangefest. Indeed, Robert Saulters (2009) expresses this directly, when he suggests the 'Orange Order has 100,000 members throughout the United Kingdom, Republic of Ireland, the United States, Canada, Australia, New Zealand, Togo and Ghana. We are a world-wide fraternity'. But claims that those in 'Canada, Australia, New Zealand and other nations will know just how proud the peoples of these great countries are of their British ancestry and heritage' (*Orange Standard* September 2008) are not always borne out.

While the meeting of the Imperial Orange Council in Belfast in July 2009 suggested the 'sense of friendship is strong', the central place of the Christian message overrode any enduring expression of common Britishness. Although the Council drew attention to opposition to Orangeism in other countries, its internationalism was strongly shaped by a shared religiosity (*Orange Standard* August 2009).

While official pronouncements from the meeting made no reference to a common British identity either in historical or contemporary contexts, the Orange Order in Northern Ireland has drawn attention to continued transnational ties, and the role of empire and the Commonwealth, both in their shared sacrifices in past conflicts and their continued constitutional ties to the Crown. Concerns have been expressed as to the preferential status of Europe and the European Union in relation to the Commonwealth with which ties are seen to be weakening, reflecting a 'growing ignorance and indifference on the part of many British institutions towards the Commonwealth ethos' (*Orange Standard* September 2008).

Grand Lodges in England and Scotland differ in their aims considerably from other non-British Orders. Both state explicitly on their websites that their respective institutions seek to 'maintain intact the Protestant Constitution and Christian heritage of the United Kingdom', whose principles 'have made the United Kingdom the greatest nation, under God, in the world'.[2] Non-British Grand Lodges make no reference to contemporary British links, preferring instead to state their civic loyalty to their host states.

Conclusions

The extent to which contemporary UK citizenship supports a discrete British nationality is questionable. The curtailment of citizenship rights for Commonwealth and other citizens outside the United Kingdom has not been absolute. However contemporary unionism and Orangeism understand British nationality in the post-GFA period as central, both in expressing loyalty to the Union, and in sustaining a distinct Northern Irish cultural identity. This would suggest that they view Britishness as civic and ethno-cultural both within national and multinational contexts, somewhat undermining recent claims about the role of the Orange Order as an institution whose interests are primarily cultural and tied to education and tourism.

The Orange Order continues to draw on many facets of Britishness (first identified by Linda Colley) that highlight the politicized nature of debates about citizenship, identity and the constitutional future of the United Kingdom. Together with other groups who identify with key facets of a nineteenth-century Britishness, particularly those in Gibraltar, the Orange Order continues to profess loyalty to a set of institutions and British values that are considered to be exclusory or non-essential and therefore overlooked by most British politicians.

They see attempts to renegotiate the unwritten constitutional order that has supported an Orange identity as part of a broader programme to dilute or even eradicate Britishness. While such concerns are certainly overstated, they do not differ significantly from other British nationalist groups. The resonance of monarchy, war and Protestantism, suggesting an enduring sense of anti-Catholicism, in defining Britishness raises fascinating questions as to the enduring legacy of a national-imperial identity that many commentators have long since confined to history.

Interestingly though, proponents of 'new' Britishness (such as Gordon Brown) and those within the Orange Order share a common myopia when considering the considerable and rich transnational dimensions. Both fail to acknowledge continued links with the Commonwealth or other places where the legacy of empire remains or where large of numbers of Britons have migrated when outlining their divergent views on Britishness. Though the monarchy continues to provide strong constitutional links that extend the borders of UK citizenship and Britishness, the Orange Order have consistently explained their understanding of identity within Ulster and United Kingdom contexts. This would suggest that the more generous dimensions of Britishness that continue to flourish between Orders across a number of other countries is not one which influences unionists or Order members in Northern Ireland.

Analysis of the pronouncements and views of leading figures within the Orange Order and various unionist political parties reveals a strong synonymy in the key areas of concern regarding the perceived attacks on Britishness in Northern Ireland. Structurally, both the Orange Order and the main political parties agree on many of the central tenets of twenty-first-century Ulster Britishness. What is less developed is a broader picture of how citizenship, Britishness and Orangeism is understood within the mainstream Orange Order membership. Moreover, though strong links among the various Orange movements outside of the United Kingdom persist, it would appear that common loyalty to faith and culture does not extend to a shared Britishness.

Notes

1. The authors are grateful to the Economic and Social Research Council, for the provision of a grant (RES-000-23-1614 'The Social and Political Bases of the Orange Order in Northern Ireland').
2. See www.orangeorderscotland.com and www.gole.org.uk

Chapter 10
Auxiliaries in the Cause? Loyalist Women in Conflict and Post Conflict

Catherine McGlynn and James W. McAuley

> Northern Ireland's 'politicians, almost all male, display the worst in masculine combativeness towards each other and disdain towards women'.
>
> Cockburn 2003: 78

One of the more memorable of the many loyalist murals that appeared during the Troubles was painted at Spier's Place on the Shankill Road. Its imagery addressed the roles of women within loyalism and sought to display continuity over some 90 years of unionism. One side of the mural was a reproduction of a postcard originally issued during the Home Rule crisis, showing a raven haired woman holding aloft a rifle and a Union flag in defence of Ulster, declaring: 'Deserted! Well I can Stand Alone'. The other part of the mural showed what was seen as a modern equivalent, a masked woman holding a shotgun, while standing on guard, as a man behind her works a field by tractor, underpinned by the text: 'A Protestant farmer's wife guards her husband against sectarian attack [from] across the border'.

The mural marked a rare public display of women within loyalism, the iconography of which remains largely obscured, especially when compared to Irish republican street art, where images of female paramilitaries and women in active political roles are much more commonplace, and the female 'freedom fighter' has been clearly represented in a number of street murals (Sales 1997a: 144). In comparison the iconography of loyalist political murals and its other public images are almost entirely masculine (Coulter 1999: 240–1), reflecting a strong emphasis on masculine/warrior symbolism in most expressions of loyalist identity that leaves virtually no form for the feminine (Meyer 2000).

What do we know of those women who identify as loyalist? To begin it is important to recognize that loyalism as a political and social movement has as a whole been marginal to the public face of politics in Northern Ireland, subsumed by the politics of unionism. Women in this arena have often found themselves subject to double marginalization, both as women and as loyalists. This sidelining is reflected elsewhere; Rooney (2007) for example, points to a clear absence of gender awareness in the vast literature surrounding the conflict.

Given that there is greater academic focus on republicanism and Irish nationalism and that there has been a marginalization of gender within the accounts of loyalism and Ulster unionism that do exist loyalist women again find themselves obscured. With very few exceptions, writings on the structural position and politics of women from loyalist and unionist backgrounds have been all but absent.

In examining the dynamics of gender relations within loyalism it is apparent that the marginalization of women from both communities from the sphere of formal politics during the years of violent conflict was exacerbated by the risks associated with high profile political activity in the midst of a violent conflict and because Northern Irish society has retained a stronger commitment to traditional gender roles and sexual morality than the United Kingdom as a whole (Cochrane 2001).

In this chapter we will assess the impact of these constraints on women's political participation in party politics, grassroots community action and paramilitary activity and ask whether the situation has changed in the period of political transformation following the GFA. We will argue that in the formal sphere of electoral politics there has been significant progress in terms of an increase in the number of unionist and loyalist female politicians.

However, parity with men is nowhere near being achieved and the dominant unionists parties have not embraced a mode of politics that increases the profile of women's rights as an issue. In the more informal community sphere activism within the loyalist community and beyond it shows how women have played a crucial role in strengthening Northern Irish civil society, although this has not been an unproblematic process and the need to channel former paramilitaries' energies into this sphere has presented fresh challenges.

Unionism and gender in historical perspective

The long history of the absence of women from the leadership and organizational structures across all political parties and formal political groupings in Northern Ireland has been widely observed (see McCoy 2000; Roulston 1996). Following partition the development of politics in both states in Ireland were best characterized by the promotion of conservative values (Mulholland 2005: 167), reflected directly in the composition of its political and administrative élites. What followed was the construction of a predominantly male polity across the island resting on gendered discourses and roles, reinforcing the primacy of men as decision makers and major political actors, and women's roles as located in the family and community (O'Dowd 1987).

Hence, in Northern Ireland, throughout the period of the Stormont government (1920–72) as few as twenty women in total were selected as parliamentary candidates and only nine were ever elected (Brown *et al.* 2002: 76; Rynder 2002: 44). At any time there were never more than four women holding seats in any one parliamentary session, and only one ever held the post of minister (McCoy 2000: 5) and before the evolution of the contemporary devolved administration there had never been a woman in the position of leader or deputy leader of any major party in Northern Ireland.

In the first eighty years of Northern Ireland's existence only three women were elected to Westminster and women's representation at the local level never exceeded 15 per cent (Wilford and Galligan 1999). It was only after the imposition of direct rule and the reintroduction of the single transferable vote, that the number of female councillors increased, the number of women in local government seats doubling between 1977 and 1997 (Cowell-Meyers 2001). Women from both communities also found positions of political influence in the voluntary sector and the extensive network of QUANGOs that flourished in the era of direct rule (Cochrane 2001).

Across Northern Ireland's polity the restricted representation of women in the party political arena reflected the reproduction of essentially conservative social values (Jacobson 1997), while a complex weave of sectarian and patriarchal relations reinforced their socially subordinate position (Morgan 1995a 1995b; Walker 1997). These factors combined to reinforce the ideological positioning of women (Condren 1989; Morgan 2003) and the structural exclusion of women across political party organizations and local political structures (Morgan 1992).

Within unionism the dominant social, gender and political relations were framed by fears over the security of the state, often underpinned by fundamentalist readings and interpretations of 'the Calvinistic nature of Protestantism' (McWilliams 1993a) influencing 'organizations operating at the interface of politics and religion' (Fairweather *et al.* 1984: 266). All this led to a highly gendered construction of 'formal politics in Northern Ireland', an arena 'dominated by men' (Sales 1997a: 202).

That is not to say that the history of women within unionist politics is entirely void. Several unionist women were prominent in politics during the early twentieth century, particularly in opposition to Home Rule. On 28 September 1912, some 228,991 women (alongside 218,206 men) signed a *Solemn League and Covenant,* with its pledge to use 'all means which may be found necessary to defeat the present conspiracy to set up a home rule parliament in Ireland' (reproduced in Carlton 1977: 65). Although it has been claimed that it merely reinforced the 'auxiliary status' of women and that they displayed a 'specifically gendered understanding of unionist women' (Urquhart 1996), there was also formal representation in the unionist political leadership through the existence of the Ulster Women's Unionist Council (PRONI 2007). Others actively lobbied for the unionist position through Church-based organizations (Morgan 2003: 248).

Following partition the emerging 'cold war' between the two states (Hennessey 1996) institutionalized sectarian, political, social and economic relations across the Island. In Northern Ireland, unionist hegemony constructed and strengthened, developing a series of discourses prioritizing the perceived need to protect the very existence of the state and marginalizing the 'enemy within', primarily defined as its Catholic population.

As the 'imperative of containing internal divisions shaped the dynamics of Ulster unionism' (Reid 2008), the unionist administration increasingly branded as 'untrustworthy' all those who sought to offer alternative discourses and politics (McAuley 2010). Those falling within this category included unionist liberals and all those who sought to promote class and gender-focused oppositional politics. Unionist national identity and politics continued to be gendered through participation and structure of the organizations central to unionism (Racioppi and O'Sullivan See 2001). Combined, these factors reinforced the marginal position of women in the public arena and the increased unionist understandings of the roles of women as being confined to the support of politically active men (Racioppi and O'Sullivan See 2000; Ward 2002).

Sometimes, however, that support proved a crucial resource to the unionist cause (Rooney 2000). In the contemporary period for example, Potter and MacMillan (no date: 20) suggest that the 'level and impact of this support cannot be underestimated [and that] (t)he notion that men in the community could pursue a paramilitary campaign without the acquiescence of a significant proportion of the women in the community is unrealistic'.

Despite the centrality of such support and the evidence provided by Ward (2004) that pro-Union women were engaged at many different levels across political parties and community organizations, such involvement has almost always remained obscured from the wider gaze. While some of the activities are often seen as an extension of the traditional domestic and career roles (such as providing refreshments at meetings), as Rachel Ward (2002; 2006) makes clear it is a vast over-simplification to seek to simply dismiss the activities of all unionist women merely as 'tea-makers'.

Peace and politics:
loyalism, women and community activism

Despite the abysmal record of involvement by women in formal politics in the years prior to the signing of the GFA, there was clear engagement in other political arenas, particularly community-based organizations where women had a significant presence 'in local networks and beyond' (Brown *et al.* 2002: 76). Indeed, women in Northern Ireland have a long and positive record of engagement in community politics and a strong history of involvement in those areas of civil society operating in a context 'of activism in communities' (in the) 'absence from formal political structures' (Porter 1997: 83).

There is now considerable evidence to support both the quantity and quality of women's contribution to voluntary and community-based organizations, whether in 'single community' work (Sales 1997a) or in cross-community projects (Cockburn 1999). The involvement of women at the community level in loyalist areas, and women's activity in community issues, such as housing, has been a consistent feature of working-class loyalist communities (McAuley 1994). Such involvement has made extremely positive contributions towards social life, welfare support and in beneficial social organization within many unionist communities (Galligan and Wilford 1999; Hill 2003). As McCoy explains:

> Hundreds of women contribute positively, and with enormous energy, to the social and political fabric of Northern Ireland at every level. For the most part, they are to be found in the hundreds of voluntary and community organisations through which the citizens of Northern Ireland attempt to compensate for the deficiencies of democratic politics and government in their region. (McCoy 2000: 3)

One consequence is that women have often been most directly associated with 'peacemaking'. In part this is justified. Through a variety of non-violent interventions, and their deep involvement in cross-community initiatives, women have often been seen to be at the forefront of peacemaking initiatives (Jacobson 1997). As Cockburn (1999: 13) puts it:

> Well ahead of peace moves between the (masculinist) paramilitary forces and the (male dominated) political institutions involved, women were establishing working links across community boundaries.... In stepping across communal boundaries, they were at risk of violence from both their own and the other side (though less at risk than men would have been).

The existence of voluntary groupings and organizations 'organized by and for women' throughout the Troubles, many of which were driven and organized by working-class women (McWilliams 1995: 17) often operating across the sectarian divide (Wilford 1996: 49) is undeniable, although we must bear in mind the tendency identified by Ashe (2008) and Sales (1997b) to accept essentialist portrayals of women as inherent peacemakers who are often morally superior to the 'men of violence'. This idea, that women necessarily seek peace more actively than men has been directly questioned through community-level case studies (Alison 2004; Aretxaga 1997). The parallel notion that women who are politically involved are necessarily more politically progressive than men must also be challenged.

Given the dominant unionist constructs of politics outlined above, grass-roots community work presented women with an arena in which they could be active and influential but in a divided society this work also had the potential to brand anyone involved as a 'Lundy'; a traitor to the unionist cause. Moreover, attempts to foster cross-community feminist action often foundered because of the perception within unionism that feminism was a smokescreen for republicanism (Miller *et al.* 1996; Morgan and Fraser 1995).

An example of this is the Northern Ireland Women's Rights Movement in the 1970s, which was beset by division over how to deal with conflict-related issues such as women prisoners and support for those non-state combatants who had been gaoled. The movement finally split over conflicting visions of how to respond to the republican hunger strikes of the early 1980s (Racioppi and O'Sullivan See 2001).

The reasons behind this perceived connection are multilayered, but two factors stand out. Feminism transgresses the social conservatism of established unionist groupings in Northern Ireland and Bell (2004) suggests that this creates difficulties because feminism itself is seen as partisan. In addition, women's activism has faced restrictions caused by the same attitudes, endemic across unionism and loyalism that have caused obstacles for all grassroots campaigns. Criticism of existing social and economic conditions or decisions taken by mainstream unionist politics has been taken to be an open questioning of the very existence and validity of state. This limited the necessary political opposition that would allow loyalists to make greater demands for welfare and other resources from the state (Community Relations Information Centre 1992; Inter Action Belfast 2006).

The Catholic nationalist republican bloc had a long tradition of community-based politics of opposition and state resistance (Nelson 1984; Sales 1997a) and this augmented the idea that such activity (and those involved in it) was innately suspect and dangerous. Such concerns persist across loyalism and as Dawn Purvis explains: 'I think feminism within unionism has become equated with socialism and they are not regarded as "unionism friendly"' (Purvis, cited in *An Phoblacht*, 18 November 2008).

To conclude this section, it is clear that to project women only as 'peace-makers' in Northern Ireland says little of value (Morgan 1995a). While at times some women have made powerful contributions to limiting violence, the actions of others have merely reproduced social, cultural and even physical violence. Hence, it would be more precise to claim women have been both peacemakers and peace preventers, mirroring the spectrum of political attitudes, responses and beliefs across Northern Ireland.

In the years when the conflict was at its height women in the loyalist community found themselves restricted by the fear of being disloyal twice over.

Grassroots political action in general, and feminist campaigns in particular, were perceived as forces that could undermine the precarious position of unionism, something that could only be shored up through uncritical unity in the face of 'the enemies' of republicanism and progressive politics.

War and politics: loyalist women and the paramilitaries

As the conflict saw the rapid militarization of largely working-class areas of Northern Ireland and the creation and growth of paramilitary groups and organizations that grew up within identifiable neighbourhoods and socially bounded communities (Burton 1978; Darby 1986; McAuley 1994, 2004a) it manifested what Lysaght (2002: 51) identifies as a 'plethora of male-only fraternal organisations and male dominated military and paramilitary' groupings.

Women largely remained peripheral to loyalist paramilitary groups (Buckley and Lonergan 1983), the development of which were bound by identifiable political, social and economic parameters that drew directly on local cultures, traditions and values, including established gender divisions. Initially those few women who had become active gained their status from being either the wives or girlfriends of loyalist prisoners, rather than holding an individual membership of the paramilitary organization itself (McAuley 1994). Alison (2004) confirms a pattern whereby women were introduced to paramilitary organizations through male contacts (most often husbands or partners, and sometimes by other family members).

While women have been known to be militarily active in republican groups (Ward 1989: 258–9) less is known about the activities (and even less about the motivation) of female loyalist paramilitary members. Recent evidence and analysis concerning female activism within loyalist organizations is both groundbreaking and tentative, and at times contradictory (see Alison 2005; McEvoy 2007; Potter and MacMillan: no date). Broadly, within paramilitary quarters women have long established primary roles in 'support roles', such as in the movement or concealment of weaponry, and in the realms of 'welfare work' (support for male prisoners and their families, first aid, and so on).

Sometimes such roles were formalized, as with Women's Rights Department of the UDA as it existed throughout the 1980s (and specifically constructed to 'support' men); but often such functions were provided much more informally, or by women who were only on the fringes of loyalist paramilitarism. Some women may have pushed their involvement beyond 'welfare and first aid', but Alison (2004) summarizes the broad pattern of involvement correctly when she says within loyalism women's activities 'have primarily been in the realms of "welfare work" (support for male prisoners and their families), first aid, and cleaning, moving and hiding weapons. A minority of women have been involved in more directly combative roles' (Alison 2004: 452).

She further suggests that part of the reason for this was that loyalist paramilitaries organized along a clear sexual division of labour and stereotypical gender lines (as did republican groupings). Further, at times they utilized strategies drawing on wider gendered constructs, for example, the belief that security forces were more reluctant to perform body searches on women than men because of the negative publicity that such actions might attract (Alison 2004).

Only a tiny minority of women were ever involved directly in combative roles within loyalist paramilitarism and there is little or no evidence of women's direct involvement in 'high end' paramilitary activities such as bombings and shootings (McEvoy 2009; Potter and MacMillan, no date: 20). Consequently, only a tiny number of women were imprisoned for paramilitary activity (see Table 10.1). In the context of around 50,000 gaoled for paramilitary offences throughout the Troubles (Shirlow *et al.* 2010), the numbers imprisoned are minute, although clearly the notion that women were entirely absent from involvement in political violence is false.

Central to the political and individual developmental of many politically motivated prisoners in Northern Ireland was the period of imprisonment itself (Shirlow *et al.* 2010). Common to the male prison experience was a growing stress on the legitimacy of the prisoners as political actors and for many a deepening sense of political understanding, which in turn was to provide a guide to future actions (Shirlow *et al.* 2010). Personal accounts and biographical recalling and explaining the experiences for non-state combatants gaoled throughout the Troubles, while not plentiful are increasingly commonplace (Crawford 1999, 2003; Whalen 2007).

There appear to be few equivalent histories of female political imprisonment in Northern Ireland. While this may simply represent just another

Table 10.1 Female imprisonments in Northern Ireland 1969–2007 by paramilitary affiliation

Organization	Number	%
Continuity Army Council	4	3
Irish National Liberation Army	4	3
Provisional IRA	88	69
Real IRA	6	5
Loyalist Volunteer Force	1	1
Red Hand Commandos	1	1
Ulster Defence Association	6	5
Ulster Freedom Fighters	7	6
Ulster Volunteer Force	11	9

Source: Adapted from Northern Ireland Prison Service, Freedom of Information Request, cited in Potter and MacMillan, no date.

example of gender blind academia, it may reflect the 'defensive and intro-spective organisational style' (Corcoran 2006) that women loyalists felt forced to adopt. In part at least this was because of limitations imposed by wider socio-cultural values across loyalism and unionism (see above), and the challenge offered to established views of public and private, by the rec-ognition of women taking such roles (McEvoy 2009).

Despite a focus by McEvoy (2009) on the autonomy of women joining paramilitary organizations, their motivations for joining were broadly in line with those for men (Shirlow *et al.* 2010). Like male combatants, women became engaged for political, cultural, and economic motivations and most seek to explain and justify their actions in the context of defence of their communities, families and political beliefs (Alison 2004). Work concerning the motivations of female paramilitaries is in its infancy, and our under-standing of the reasons for women's involvement in political violence in Northern Ireland is not aided by the broad tendency within the media to focus upon their appearance and sexual behaviour of such women, rather than what they regard as rational and political reasons for their involve-ment (Taylor 2000).

There are other areas worthy of further investigation. Alison (2004), for example, points to the 'sexualisation of violence' and a gun subculture as a significant area for further research. While there are some noteworthy exceptions (Bairner 1999a, 1999b; Lysaght 2002; Youth Action Northern Ireland 2002), it is also with some justification that Ashe (2004) argues that mainstream social science research on Northern Ireland politics has shown little attention to the concept of masculinity.

Of the material that is available, Harland's (1997) work in inner city Belfast provides clear evidence that the dominant construction of mascu-linity among young men still rests upon 'traditional' values, such as being 'strong, brave, intelligent, sexy', and in control of every aspect of their lives. Further, 'real men' are seen, as 'unemotional' and Harland's samples were derisory towards any traits among men that they perceived as fem-inine. The centrality, and consequences, of this in 'the hyper-masculine world of loyalist paramilitary organizations' (Alison 2004:456) needs fuller exploration.

Women in loyalism and unionism in the post-conflict era

The ceasefires of 1994 and the subsequent political process paved the way for the diminution of large-scale structured violence and created the possibil-ity for a political settlement and new democratic institutions, albeit within a framework that has proved to be extremely fragile. Following the sign-ing of the GFA and the emphasis on wider participation throughout civil society in Northern Ireland, there was a growing momentum in support of the increased participation of women in all aspects of public life, including electoral politics (Galligan 1998; Wilford 1999a, 1999b). There are several indications of this, for example, in the development of the Women into Politics (WiP) project (drawing initially on a large informal network of community women's centres), creating as it did a broader social space for women from different communities to meet to further political dialogue and debate (*Women's News*, No. 100: 10–11) and to develop and support political leadership roles by women (Cockburn 2003: 78).

The most obvious result of this emphasis on participation has been the increasing visibility of women in party politics. The 2001 General Election marked the election of three women, Michelle Gildernew (Sinn Féin) Sylvia Hermon (UUP) and Iris Robinson (DUP) who all held their seats in the election of 2005. Female representation also increased at the local level and by the time of the 2001 local elections their presence increased to 19 per cent (see Table 10.2), while in the May 2005 elections women took 125 seats, 21.5 per cent of the total (Ward, M. 2006). That said, following the 2005 elections, of the 26 district councils, only 3 had a female mayor or chair, while 6 had women in the deputy mayor/ chair role (Northern Ireland Statistics and Research Agency 2006: 23).

In January 2010 Arlene Foster took on the leadership of the DUP on a caretaker basis as the First Minister Peter Robinson took time out to deal with an investigation into a financial and personal scandal involving his wife, the MP Iris Robinson. The appointment of Foster was a remarkable achievement for a party where high profile female candidates for election had usually had connections by marriage or family to established male DUP politicians, but even more astonishing considering the treatment meted out by the DUP's negotiating team to the NIWC during the peace talks of the 1990s.

The NIWC drew on the existing network of women's groups, such as the Derry Women's Centre and Shankill Women's Forum (Wilford 1999a: 89) to

Table 10.2 Northern Ireland local election results 2001 by gender and party

Party	Women	Men	% women
UUP	27	127	18
DUP	19	112	15
SDLP	31	86	26
Sinn Féin	17	91	16
APNI	11	17	40
Other	0.3	41	7
Total	108	474	19

Source: Fearon and Rebouche (2006: 287).

develop a manifesto promoting inclusive reconciliation, promoting human rights and as 'a non-sectarian, broad-based coalition of women of all political hues and religions' (NIWC, 1996). Their election to the forum created to negotiate a peace agreement resulted from a campaign conducted from a standing start immediately before the close of nominations (Cochrane 2001).

In one notable incident when the NIWC representative Monica McWilliams was making an important speech concerning the contentious issues of Orange parades and the parades commission, she was forced to do so against a soundtrack of barracking and 'mooing' noises from Ian Paisley and fellow members of the DUP. In another widely reported clash Willie McCrea of the DUP openly declared: 'as long as I live I will have a mission, which is to teach these women to stand behind the loyal men of Ulster' (cited in Sengupta 1998).

The appointment of Arlene Foster and the success of other women candidates in recent years could signify that unionist and loyalist politics has progressed from the contempt displayed for the NIWC. However, although the number of women in electoral positions has increased this is does not mean that the parties have rethought the gender dynamics of their party agendas. For example, although the UUP has overtly encouraged women's participation in unionist politics Brown *et al.* (2002: 82) indicate that it 'developed no gender-specific policies to promote women members to the Assembly'. Indeed, among all of the main political parties in Northern Ireland they have consistently selected the fewest number of women candidates, to the point where none of the UUP's elected representatives to the Assembly were women (see Table 10.3).

Even when women are elected as public representatives there are divisions surrounding institutional opportunities. As Cowell-Meyers (2003) points out women are often confined, and certainly over represented, on those Assembly committees seen to engage with areas, such as social services and care, deemed to be of traditional concern to women.

Table 10.3   Northern Ireland Assembly, by gender and party, March 2007

Party	Number of Women	Number of Men	Percentage of Women (%)
Alliance	2	5	28.6
DUP	3	33	8.3
SDLP	4	12	25
Sinn Féin	8	20	28.6
UUP	0	18	0
Other	1	2	N/a
Total	18	90	16.7

Source: Adapted from WiP website, 2009.

Across unionism the promotion of women's involvement within the existing political structures has remained a difficult task. It was only on the margins, within for example, the confines of 'new loyalism' (McAuley 2002a, 2002b) that established social relations, including those around gender, were challenged. Thus, for example, as the PUP came to prominence it began increasingly clear that the party were prepared to openly debate the politics of reproductive rights (Jennings 1999:11). Dawn Purvis, the PUP's leader and the first female leader of a major Northern Irish political party identifies this engagement with issues of gender and sexuality as one of the most important divisions between the PUP and the DUP:

> The key areas of difference would be policy issues and probably a lot of the time round Section 75 [a statutory obligation for public authorities in Northern Ireland to promote equality of opportunity for all]. So for example we oppose discrimination against people just because they are lesbian, gay or bisexual. I think the DUP would avoid having a written policy on that. We're pro-choice. We believe that women should have a right to choose whether or not they terminate a pregnancy or not. The DUP would be totally opposed to abortion under any circumstances. (interview with the authors, 2007)

The PUP along with the (now defunct) UDP found common cause on the issue of women's rights with the NIWC and also Sinn Féin during the forum negotiations. However, the DUP and UUP have not moved to accommodate this gender-aware style of politics and the difficulties Sinn Féin and the PUP have encountered in forging cross-community consensus on social and economic issues (Shirlow *et al.* 2010) have set further limits on the emergence of such a style of politics.

The continued instability of formal political arrangements and continued anxiety about the way forward means that the space created by the peace process of the 1990s for exploring non-constitutional issues has to some extent closed up and there is less pressure on established unionist politicians to re-appraise their approach to women.

As has already been discussed, community politics empowered women who had been marginalized (or banished) from political involvement to become active and involved and they often sought to create and fulfil new opportunities to discuss the gendered and social relations of unionism. The rapidly changing social circumstances created by the ceasefires of 1994, precipitated by the greatly reduced levels of overt paramilitary violence, opened up social space for the expression of the more community-based political culture created by women in coping with decades of sectarian violence and 'the destruction of normal family life' (McWilliams 1997: 79–92).

Sales (1997a, 1997b) suggests that this period marked a spike in community activity representing a distinct growth in campaign groups and organizations based on promoting women's involvement at and beyond the local level. Linking with the more formalized political positioning of the PUP this was, in part at least, harnessed at the time to revitalized local loyalist politics (McAuley 1997; McAuley and Hislop 2000). In the post-Agreement period the PUP sought to project a restatement of loyalism within a broad framework of social democratic values and to highlight a clearer social and economic focus within unionism.

Increasingly, women found new or revitalized outlets through groupings based in community centres and other local meeting points, public meetings and day conferences (Morgan 1995). Women have also been engaged in 'single identity work' through community projects designed to define and protect their identity as unionists and loyalists. Thus, for example, throughout the mid-1990s within loyalist communities a grouping calling itself, 'Women Raising Unionist Concerns' (WRUC), with the declared aim of 'saving loyalist traditions' engaged in a whole series of direct peaceful actions designed to bring to the public attention the perceived marginalization of working-class Protestant culture.

Within loyalist communities, social connections and bonding remains strong (Cairns *et al.* 2003), but as Ashe (2009) notes, in the post-conflict period women have increasingly become framed as passive actors, (e.g. by being understood as receiving male former prisoners back into the family). This mirrors wider gendered constructions such as those observed by Cockburn and Zarkov (2002: 13) who note how following conflict 'the traditional militarized gender regime endows men with the power in politics and locates women's importance in the family'. As with the world of electoral politics the continued instability and division between communities has closed up some of the space that allowed women to explore different roles and experiences at the grassroots level.

The increased importance of community activism for those previously (or currently) associated with paramilitary activity also carries with it the potential to marginalize women in an arena where they have traditionally been strongest. Loyalist paramilitary groupings such as the UDA and UVF have long seen grassroots politics as a means of augmenting the legitimacy of their status as community defenders (McAuley 1991; Nelson 1984) and have at times received state support to pursue this agenda (McCready 2001). Ironically when the UDA moved into activism on issues such as housing they were taking over tasks that had previously been dismissed as women's work (Weiner 1980).

In the post-ceasefire era those associated with paramilitary groupings have focused on grassroots activism as a means of providing direction to members and leadership to the community (Hall 2000, 2003, 2004). As this has been a particularly important role for former prisoners who are overwhelmingly male, and as community-based politics becomes even more important following loyalist paramilitary decommissioning, there is a potential for women to be 'crowded out' of this arena, although this is mitigated in part by the connection of the UVF to the PUP, which as discussed is a party that has persisted in its commitment to a nuanced gender politics.

Conclusions

There are various and complex reasons for the level of women's political involvement in Northern Ireland. These include individual and structural factors and patterns and trends that stretch far beyond the particularities of Northern Ireland or the dynamics of the conflict. Although such voices have grown slightly louder following the ceasefires of 1994 and increased engagement with processes of conflict transformation, women still remain notably absent from politics and other public arenas.

In the formal political arena Cowell-Meyers (2003) concludes that in the new Assembly the major concerns for both men and women are more similar than different. While our understanding of the roles played by women in paramilitary groupings is far from complete, it is apparent that most women who became involved were recruited through connections with male paramilitary members. Across unionism any evidence of a drive towards gender equality remains distant, while 'the patriarchal nature of Protestant working-class society seems to impact on all aspects of life' (Potter and MacMillan, no date: 20).

For significant change to occur in electoral politics the dominant unionist parties will have to embrace change. For the DUP at least the higher profile of women at Westminster and the Assembly suggests some willingness to make progress. However, where the DUP has been most consistently challenged in its still novel position as the biggest unionist party has been in the area of the constitution, with Jim Allister and the Traditional Unionist Voice taking on the role finessed by Paisley as the force that harries unionists who seek any form of rapprochement with Irish republicanism. This continued pressure marginalizes the prominence of other modes of political dialogue and change.

At the grassroots level, women have consistently carved out roles as activists, although this too is an area where uncertainty about constitutional politics has limited partnership between women of different communities. The crossover with paramilitarism in this arena has also been problematic. The overwhelmingly masculine structures of the UVF and UDA have sometimes reinforced the idea that women are passive maintainers of the home front, or that they are the gender that will search for peace while men go to war.

In addition, the need for former paramilitaries to entrench their post-ceasefire leadership through grassroots politics can obscure the strong and ongoing contribution made by women to developing civil society organizations in loyalist areas. However, as the history of loyalist and unionist women shows, in spite of the persistence of obstacles that have impeded their progress in Northern Irish politics, they have exhibited sufficient agency to organize and agitate for social and political change. Popular and academic coverage of loyalism have obscured loyalist women but examination of party politics, grassroots campaigns and paramilitary organizations reveals the complexity and vitality of their experiences and contributions.

Chapter 11
Reflections on the Relationships Between Loyalism and Church
Phillip Orr

Despite their self-identification as Protestants, working-class, loyalists often possess very limited connection to the church. This chapter will describe the ways in which ecclesiastical institutions and working-class loyalism have drifted apart and it will suggest reasons for the drift. There will be an attempt to show the social need in working-class communities, to which many Protestant churches have either been oblivious or unable to effectively respond. However there will be some discussion of those faith-based projects that have started to address this need. The chapter will focus especially on the loyalist ex-prisoner and social activist, the late Billy Mitchell. There will also be a short examination of role models for local Protestant community workers within England and the United States.

The chapter draws on research undertaken in 2007 when the Centre for Contemporary Christianity in Ireland commissioned the author to create a short study of religious faith and loyalism. The work involved interviews conducted in 2007–08, complementary visits to churches and para church projects and analysis of sociological and economic data. It may be assumed for the purposes of this chapter that the term 'working class' indicates a social group who are unlikely to occupy 'professional' jobs and more likely to rent rather than own their own homes. 'Loyalists' may be regarded throughout this text as citizens who embrace the culture of the Loyal Orders or a particular paramilitary heritage and who possess a deep pride in the British Ulster identity. 'Loyalist working class' is a term, which applies where these two social categories overlap.

Loyalism and church

The churchgoing figures for Northern Ireland are impressive; 34 per cent of the Protestant population attended church at least once a week in 2005, even though this figure indicates decline from 46 per cent in 1968. However the reality is that most working-class loyalist communities present a less impressive picture, even though areas where loyalists live may contain a range of church buildings or mission halls (Orr 2008: 16–17).

A survey conducted in the Lower Ravenhill area of East Belfast during the mid-1990s produced interesting statistics. There were ten churches in the vicinity but only 28 per cent of the churchgoers lived in the neighbourhood. Some 31 per cent of the Lower Ravenhill's churchgoers *used* to live in the area but had moved to suburban or rural locations and returned on Sundays to attend their place of worship. A study of the leaders of these churches generated the information that out of 32 individuals, only 3 resided in the area.

The disconnection between the lives of worshippers and the local people was thus considerable. One per cent of church members were unemployed whereas the figure for the Lower Ravenhill was 34 per cent. During 42 interviews conducted with local residents, 22 people claimed it was only 'old folk' or children who went regularly to church. A similar number suggested the area's greatest need was a local supermarket but nobody mentioned anything to do with church (Orr 2008: 17–18).

An investigation in the dominantly Protestant town of Newtownards was conducted during 2003 and revealed evidence of disconnection between the Protestant churches and other civic groups. Most of the town's 28 churches had little or no contact with community, voluntary or statutory workers who operated in disadvantaged loyalist areas. This 'disconnect' was a source of dissatisfaction to these secular agents. Interviewees felt that churches 'only get involved with vulnerable people to convert them' and lamented how faith-based groups did 'evangelistic commando raids' on loyalist estates rather than put down proper roots.

In their own defence, church leaders claimed they were suspicious of involvement with 'community groups', given that many had paramilitary colouring. Some churches said they had their fingers burned in the past, engaging with such organizations. And indeed, as a community audit conducted by the same researchers during 2005 pointed out: 'Paramilitary organisations are often perceived as policing the estates rather than the Police Service of Northern Ireland' (Orr 2008: 20–1).

Surveys conducted by Derek Bacon in and around the largely Protestant town of Coleraine in the late 1990s showed interesting findings, which confirm ecclesiastical isolationism. Contacting over 80 churches, he found that they rarely made their premises available to any group from outside their congregation or denomination. Some 72 per cent of respondents indicated that they had little contact with voluntary, statutory and community workers and yet many thousands of hours of voluntary service *were* actually being given in Coleraine, but *inside* a church context, organizing church youth groups and visiting the house bound or elderly members. Bacon's verdict was that, by and large, the church did not feel it owed a duty of fraternity to a wider civic society (Orr 2008: 18–20).

A widely attended conference, held in Belfast as long ago as 1991, discussed the topic of community work in Protestant areas. It flagged up negative verdicts on the nature of the Protestant church. Ecclesiastical individualism was a perceived cause of community problems within loyalist areas. Delegates felt that fragmentation of church culture into independent mission halls and manifold denominational mutations over the decades was responsible for the lack of social cohesion in loyalist working-class areas because it initiated a paradigm of dogged disunity. This mentality seeped through into the rest of society and prevented progress with shared community initiatives and it actually gave a 'role model' to loyalist paramilitary groups, which so often tend to splinter and feud (Orr 2008: 18).

Derek Bacon has pointed out some of the insecurities that may have made the Protestant church wary of 'reaching out' or adapting to the world around it. He explains how in Northern Ireland, 'until the 1970s the religious world was stable. Church leadership was trained in a familiar task in a system undisturbed for generations. There was strength in this way and little call for experimentation or specialist ministries of the kind taken for granted elsewhere on these islands'. Several decades later, 'with the traditional model no longer working as it once did and their central bodies under equipped to offer incisive support' many local churches are 'struggling to meet the demands of a world conditioned by realities they were unable or unwilling to foresee' (cited in Orr 2008: 17).

The growth of un-churched working-class culture is difficult for the church to take, given the vibrancy of evangelism and concern for the 'urban poor' in a bygone era. Within an area such as Protestant West Belfast, with a strong memory of an era of social hierarchy and pre-NHS charity, institutions like the Presbyterian Church's Shankill Road Mission took children on holidays, provided clothes and food parcels to the needy and gave support to troubled families. Almost every street had its mission hall, in which the 'old fashioned gospel' of personal change and uplift was preached, unsullied by theological compromise or experimentation.

Now the population of the Shankill has been reduced because of urban redevelopment, the tensions of the Troubles and more recent paramilitary feuds. What is also lost is a Shankill church culture that once gloried in its charitable role and conservative theology. Many church-going citizens on the Shankill joined the exodus from the area. Arguably, they experienced the upward mobility that often accompanies an aspirational religious life, a syndrome known as 'redemption lift' (Orr 2008: 15–16).

A youth worker employed by a local council in County Antrim offered the author several negative opinions on the churches' relationship with loyalist communities:

> In my experience the churches...pay lip service to getting involved with loyalists...if you ask me the churches live in a great big white ivory

tower ... perhaps they feel they will lose control if they open their doors more widely...they need to see that the halls and real estate that they have could be of service to the whole community and not just be used for the church members themselves...open your doors. Get to know the faces of the local people who don't go near your church. Build rapport. Reach out!'. (Orr 2008: 20–1)

Loyalism and Orangeism

Another problematic issue for the relationship between loyalism and churches is that many Protestant clergy have difficulties in acting as chaplains to the local lodge of the Loyal Orders. The advance of ecumenism and the community relations agenda within society have made it harder for clerics to associate themselves with Orange culture.

The debacle of Drumcree was not the final chapter in the story of civic disruption brought about by thwarted parading rights. Rioting accompanied the alteration of parade routes in the Whiterock area in 2005, and it involved loyalist gunmen firing at security forces. Commercial premises were burnt out, vehicles hijacked and citizens attacked while going about their daily lives.

The inarticulacy of the Orange leadership, when trying to distance themselves from the violence, only added to a sense that the Loyal Orders were volatile and ill led. That inarticulacy owes something to the fact that talented and confident professionals have walked away from the Orange Order. Many able Protestant clerics have kept their distance, thus robbing the organization of some of its most eloquent and sagacious leadership material (Orr 2008: 27–9).

Some clergy have tried to reframe the relationship. One church leader, who despite being interviewed by the author did not want his identity revealed in print, has made attempts to reconnect with the band culture, which dominates 'The Twelfth' and can present some of the festival's most aggressive elements. A band has been asked into this cleric's church hall to give concerts, so as to help bridge the gap between the church and local loyalism. However, the church, which is involved in this enterprise, has also attempted to build a relationship with neighbouring Catholic priests, to indicate to them that the hospitality being shown to loyalists is not a 'hand in glove' relationship or an attempt to rebuild an old pro-Union coalition.

But problems may arise from situations such as this and they need to be carefully negotiated. An Orange Lodge, which is fraternally connected to this band, may desire to have a service in the church. To refuse may cause offence but to agree may mean the carrying of flags and regalia into the sanctuary, which will offend church members who wish to see the gospel kept separate from political affiliation within a divided society.

The problems posed by connecting with paramilitary culture may be even greater, given the image of this culture in the media, which has focused on gangsterism, as epitomized by the UDA's infamous Johnny Adair, rather than the effective community work undertaken by numerous loyalist ex-prisoners, in initiatives such as the Alternatives Project, which seeks to implement restorative justice in Protestant areas, or the interface monitoring work that involves loyalist leaders in arduous management of community tensions at difficult times in Northern Ireland's calendar (Orr 2008: 29–33).

Church and paramilitarism

To reach out to communities where the UVF or UDA are held in esteem is hard for Protestant churches which contain policemen, former members of the UDR/RIR and prison officers, who were charged with watching, arresting and incarcerating members of these organizations. The tensions are increased because at various stages, loyalists mounted attacks on Crown forces and prison staff and often perceived them in a negative light, as mercenary-minded traitors to the 'Protestant' cause.

Despite the conversion experience of numerous loyalist prisoners while in gaol, any widespread and successful church initiative to achieve reconciliation with militant loyalism is probably far off. The church would have to respond with self-investigative rigour to the accusation by high ranking ex-UVF men that inflammatory and inhumane rhetoric by evangelical clerics enticed them to commit violence and that those same clerics then walked away from them when they responded to the rhetoric by engaging in violence.

One figure in UVF culture has suggested to the author that the Protestant church has a retributive rather than a restorative approach to justice, in which ex-paramilitaries always live on the social and moral margins because of what they did. He believes that his colleagues need to be accepted back into the community and understood as participants in a war that hit the working class with terrible ferocity and led to grim deeds on every side, as all wars do.

Many citizens of loyalist communities also perceive the church as operating a rarified middle-class agenda, in which working-class culture is taboo. The average church service, with its wordy liturgy, acquired etiquette and communal singing, would be disorienting to many working-class loyalists, even though they may have a family heritage of church going. The popular evangelical initiative known as the Alpha course, which is beloved of Ulster churches, would seem very off putting to many working-class people, with its emphasis on a carefully modulated and discursively studious encounter with faith. And in the eyes of the old school fundamentalists who are often found in loyalist areas, alcohol consumption and smoking are forbidden and a visit to the bookmakers, the cinema or a dance is illegal, making a commitment to faith dependent on many lifestyle curtailments.

The ruthless nature of the loyalist paramilitary campaign during the Troubles made it hard for churches to handle the task of connecting positively with communities on whose gable ends gunmen in balaclavas were celebrated. The style of the loyalist campaign made it difficult for the uninvolved to endorse it. The IRA had a set of visible targets: the Crown Forces, members of the judiciary, politicians and prison officers. Commercial and civic targets represented the infrastructure of the state and could be dismantled by means of a bombing campaign, albeit one that could kill civilians in the process.

However, loyalist targets, such as IRA members, were harder to identify as they did not wear a uniform and seemed to 'hide away' in Catholic communities. Bombing the infrastructure was not a popular option, for those who sought to uphold the state. As a result, the ordinary Catholic civilian was often the only 'available' target. It is also clear that loyalists could not justify their pro-state violence by means of arguments from the sophisticated global gospel of 'national liberation'.

Thus, loyalist combatants were left relying on ideologically unmediated physical force, which looked therefore like atavistic and indiscriminate revenge, sometimes involving murders, which were not only callous but also sadistic, as in the case of the so-called Shankill Butchers. Such killings still appal Protestant ecclesiastical sensibility, which prefers to think of war as something which can be embraced each Remembrance Day as a tragic panoply of heroic deeds that upstanding young Ulstermen once performed, in a noble cause, conducted 'over there' in Europe, without too much personal barbarism, against the irredeemably barbaric force of German militarism.

Church and community

There is much for the church to do if it wishes to 'bite the bullet' and interact fully with the loyalist working class. Their communities are often in poor shape. The Department of Social Development's Task Force Survey, called 'Renewing Communities', reported in 2004 and focused largely on inner city zones of Belfast, such as Sandy Row, Shankill and The Village. The Report diagnosed 'low educational achievement, low aspirations, physical and mental problems...apparent acceptance of economic inactivity [and] fragmentation within the community'.

Of concern to the Report's authors was the way that children in loyalist communities seem predisposed to fail at education: 'By the time they get to primary school, many people have already established poor behaviour patterns and demonstrate a low level capacity to engage positively with purposeful and structured learning'.

A range of statistics was used to indicate the under achievement. In recent studies of local government wards where high numbers of school leavers obtained no qualifications, 13 of the 15 worst examples were wards denominated as Protestant and working class. The DSD Report also noted an adult incapacity for engagement with the knowledge economy. In the Crumlin, Shankill and Woodvale wards of Belfast, 82 per cent, 79 per cent and 74 per cent respectively of all 25- to 74-year-olds had no educational qualifications of note. The Report noticed early teenage pregnancy, alcohol consumption and drug abuse, obesity, poor diet, stress and lack of exercise, as well as paramilitary turf wars and control over the social composition of loyalist areas, even though these organizations have officially 'stood down'.

The Report noted the long-term impact of the contraction of employment due to loss of heavy industry and security force related jobs. Another crucial factor, already alluded to in this chapter, has been a drift to the suburbs of the able, the devout and the fortunate, leaving many working-class communities feeling stranded, without a reservoir of skills, social capital and benign leadership (Orr 2008: 5–6).

Not surprisingly, comparisons have been made between loyalist areas and other more prosperous localities, situated not far away. The 2001 Census revealed that the Shankill ward, with a population of just under 4000, fared badly when compared with Malone, a ward containing over 5500 inhabitants. Shankill had 451 lone parent households and Malone had 112. Shankill had 467 single pensioner households and Malone had 295.

The consequences are considerable, given that these types of household are usually economically worse off and more socially vulnerable. The Shankill had 1821 people with no qualifications while only 441 people in Malone were in that position. Also in Shankill, 36 per cent of the population were suffering from long-term illness or disability while the figure in Malone was 12 per cent (Orr 2008: 6–7).

It is not just in Belfast that disadvantage can be seen. An examination of the 36 zones designated as Neighbourhood Renewal Areas, under the Northern Ireland Government's 'People and Place' strategy, revealed distress in towns where a casual observer might assume that prosperity was the order of the day. In the Sunnylands ward of Carrickfergus, 31 per cent of the population have a long-term health problem, compared with 19 per cent for the borough as a whole. Only 25 per cent of this dominantly working-class area got five or more 'good' GCSE passes in recent examinations, as compared to 65 per cent throughout Carrickfergus as a whole (Orr 2008: 7).

Research on working-class alienation was undertaken in 2003 for the Office of the First Minster and Deputy First Minister. The Report emphasized that community organization has been underdeveloped in Protestant areas, noting that the inhabitants proclaim loyalty to the state and are thus reluctant to tackle the state for any of its failures. And there is the matter of the famed 'Protestant Work Ethic'. As one loyalist respondent said during the survey: 'The Protestant ethos is that community stuff is like charity, it's like handouts and it is somehow a slur on their working ethos' (Orr 2008: 7–9).

A report for the 'Shankill 21' focus group in the previous year highlighted another issue; disaffiliation from the police. Many locals felt that the police were 'a foreign body' due to the reluctance of PSNI members to live in volatile loyalist areas. There was anger at a perceived bias towards recruitment of young nationalists, in the ongoing attempt to make the police acceptable to 'both sides' (Orr 2008: 9–10).

The experience of the elderly is also dark. As a Report by the LINC resource Centre indicated in 2007, the elderly within working-class areas feel that: 'we've lost the sense of community. We would have helped one another, now it's all closed doors... you are more isolated because you keep your door locked and be wary opening it... law and order disappeared... respect is gone' (Orr 2008: 9–10).

The problems faced at the other end of the age range are serious. A youth worker who deals with teenagers who are mainly from loyalist estates in Portadown, has revealed a key issue: 'Now that many of the paramilitary units who controlled the drugs trade are being dismantled, there is an increased danger of young lads setting up their own drug selling empires to make money and gain self-esteem'.

This youth worker has discovered widespread substance abuse: 'we have found socks, which the lads spray with deodorant so as to inhale the fumes. We have found canisters of Ronson lighter gas, which the lads also inhale. Substances such as... furniture polish and nail varnish are so readily available... under age drinking has got worse and the age at which it starts has fallen... attitudes to booze have changed, partly due to the change in the licensing laws... many have started drinking at an early age in the presence of their families... many of these parents probably developed alcohol dependency during the Troubles in order to cope and then they tolerate alcohol use in their children' (Orr 2008: 69–71).

And problems exist for loyalist communities that live in proximity to interfaces where trouble flares. Loyalists who exist as a minority within nationalist parts of Northern Ireland also struggle with isolation, fear and low morale. No community is more affected than the Protestant population of Derry, a city that has seen loyalist numbers shrink dramatically, west of the Foyle. Even in the more 'mixed' Waterside, to the east of the river, there is a sense of being cut off from the life of a city pervaded by a nationalist ethos.

Of course there are numerous loyalists living in working-class communities who possess a decent standard of living and enjoy a calm environment. There are housing estates such as Seymour Hill, in Dunmurry, with waiting lists of would be residents. Even within the most difficult areas, people can sometimes live very productive lives. However the evidence presented in this section of the chapter indicates a lot of human need and a very tangible distress.

Billy Mitchell and the politics of peace

At his funeral in 2006, Billy Mitchell was mourned by a number of republicans as well as hundreds of UVF men. This was a testimony to someone whose career in the upper echelons of the UVF was followed in later years by exemplary community work and commitment to the peace process. Billy experienced Christian conversion in 1979, while in gaol. On his release he began a campaign to encourage local churches to 'show selfless, sacrificial solidarity' with loyalist working-class communities whom he believed to be the 'victims of structural injustice', having been banished to the margins, with poor job opportunities and inadequate health care as well as a pariah status as a so-called sectarian underclass (Orr 2008: 37).

Billy had absorbed the sectarian sermons of hardline clerics as a young loyalist and he later said that they had enticed him into militancy. However during his time behind bars he began to develop an understanding of the harsh working-class conditions of his youth and it would inform a very different practice of faith: 'the home where I spent the bulk of my childhood was a wooden hut that has long since been demolished...there was no running water...a large bucket served as a toilet...for entertainment we had a wireless...for pets we had field mice...I was supposed to be one of the privileged Prods [but] when I was in Long Kesh I encountered dozens upon dozens of loyalists...whose experiences of growing up were similar to my own...we know from personal experience what it is like to live below the poverty line. Our upbringing made us practical social activists' (Orr 2008: 37).

In gaol, he read widely and learnt about famous Christian practitioners of a socially engaged faith. He admired such figures from Britain's past as the early Labour activist, Keir Hardie and numerous heroes of the church overseas, such as the martyred Central American bishop, Arnulfo Romero. He studied the life of Dietrich Bonhoeffer, who was executed for plotting to kill Hitler (Orr 2008: 38).

Released in 1990, Billy founded the LINC initiative, a project of the Church of the Nazarene, geared towards assisting needy loyalist communities and, in particular, helping ex-prisoners and their families. With the arrival of the loyalist ceasefires in 1994, he assisted the newly formed Progressive Unionist Party to articulate a class-based critique of traditional unionism. He began work on conflict transformation projects in areas where the UVF had held sway, helping to engender new thinking that turned on resolving conflict through dialogue and community development, assisted at times by the American Mennonite activist and writer, Jean Paul Lederach.

Billy co-founded, *The Other View*, a magazine dedicated to shared nation-alist and unionist perspectives. He contributed to peacebuilding in loyalist communities through the instigation of restorative justice projects, centring on an attempt to bring perpetrator, victim and community together, to effect reparation and reform, rather than resorting to punishment beatings or expulsion from the host community. As Billy told an interviewer: 'Peace-building is about seeking a commitment to developing creative alternatives to violence through dialogue with the enemy [and] current and former par-ticipants in the conflict are a key resource in the peace-building process' (Orr 2008: 39).

In his *Conflict Resolution Papers*, Billy Mitchell focused on 'the cross of Christ'; an emblem, which spoke to him of God's selfless love for human-ity and his power to reach the condemned, the trapped and the lost. Billy wrote about the church's obligation to manifest the same sacrificial love and to rescue those who are ill treated by society. He insisted that: 'the world of injustice, where prejudice, intolerance, exploitation and violence hold their prey in a vice-like grip...that is where Christians ought to be' (Orr 2008: 40).

Billy noted that traditional church members in Northern Ireland had 'been locked away in their holy huddles and spiritual bunkers' and had 'lost the significance of the incarnational theology described in St Paul's letter to the Philippians', where Christ is said to have 'emptied himself, taking the form of a slave, being born in human likeness'. Rather than repenting of its own failure to 'build a bridge between a world of hurting humanity and the love and compassion of a healing Saviour', the middle-class church had held up paramilitaries and their host communities for condemnation as public scapegoats and this has led to ecclesiastical self-righteousness for 'so long as we can point to the scapegoat we have no need to look at ourselves'.

For Billy it was crucial that 'respectable' Protestant churches recognize that loyalists are 'flesh of our flesh and bone of our bone. They are the mani-festation of our failure to resolve our difficulties' (Orr 2008: 41). So Billy insisted that local Protestant denominations needed a leadership that under-stood the importance of both evangelistic and social gospels. He lamented that, until recently at least, community development was not 'a concept that is taught at theological seminary or that is included in the curriculum of Christian training colleges'. It was important in Billy's eyes that thinking Christians, including theologians, speak up about issues of justice, in light of Noam Chomsky's dictum that it is 'the responsibility of intellectuals to speak the truth and expose lies' (Orr 2008: 41–2).

But Billy stressed that loyalism would also have to change. It would have to find a more aspirational and pluralist ideology, a task made all the harder by political sterility in traditional unionist ranks and the unabashed crim-inality of all too many self-proclaimed loyalists. In an article in *The Other*

View, he argued that connecting up one's faith with one's politics was not about creating a fresh version of the Protestant ascendancy or a 'Protestant state for a Protestant People' but rather letting the Christian desire for widespread justice, freedom and charity permeate one's thinking.

In that regard 'Unionists must accept the multi-faith and multi-cultural nature of the UK...we must reject...any reliance upon political parties to legislate in defence of our faith'. So loyalists ought to be committed to 'a classless society where all citizens are afforded equality in terms of race, religion, gender, sexual orientation, age and ability'. For Billy Mitchell, this was a loyalism that would be 'true to the legacy of the Reformation'. It would be loyalism as a contemporary out-working of the democratic values of the Solemn Oath and Covenant, which holds such iconic status in loyalist popular history (Orr 2008: 42–3).

Faith, loyalism and political change

In some quarters, positive change is now underway to connect faith and loyalism in new and positive ways. The Church of Ireland and Elim clerics in Maghera have made efforts to help the loyalist community preserve its parading traditions in a way that takes account of republican sensibilities. They have initiated a 'Forum for Accountable Community Engagement' and are ready to talk to anyone in order to resolve territorial disputes. When interviewed, Reverend Robert Miller was expecting up to 40 meetings in the summer of 2008, to work out a solution to the problem of that year's parade routes. He prays with the Orangemen and offers advice but says he is not their 'chaplain' but rather a friend who is prepared to offer counsel or critique where required (Orr 2008: 74–5).

The Reverend Mervyn Gibson *does* occupy the role of chaplain within the Order and sees that as a positive function. He also sees himself as a 'critical friend' of the paramilitaries in East Belfast, whom he meets as he works in Westbourne Presbyterian Church. He has been a mediator between individuals in the loyalist community and between feuding groups. He has gained stays of punishment for unpaid loans. He has dedicated loyalist murals, provided the ceremonies and images are peaceful and the art truly belongs to the local community (Orr 2008: 72–4).

The Baptist pastor, Alan Hoey, has been operating within the Monkstown housing estate in Newtownabbey. He has built relationships with loyalist leaders and has held outreach meetings, which have been well attended by men and women who would not normally go to church. He has gone into a local loyalist club and has brought his church choir to sing on the premises. The church has organized 'fun days' for the estate's children. Monkstown church takes a warm approach to the local people, among whom many of the church members live. These members believe in an evangelical message of transformative conversion (Orr 2008: 77–8).

Meanwhile the Eglinton Presbyterian Church in Derry has brought in loyalist prisoners and offered them employment, redecorating church premises as part of their rehabilitation. In County Down, the Baptist Church in Downpatrick often opens its doors and spills out into the street, while enjoying its communal Sunday lunch. The locals from the small loyalist housing estate nearby are welcome to join in. In Coleraine and Newtownards, which received 'bad press' earlier in this chapter, positive faith-based community work is now under way. The chairman of the community forum in the latter town is currently a local clergyman.

On Belfast's Shankill Road, the Presbyterian cleric, Noel Agnew has made a practice of visiting the pubs and chatting to men and women whom he describes as his 'friends'. Tom Wilson, pastoring a church in Dunmurry involves himself and his congregation in various community initiatives within the Seymour Hill estate (Orr 2008: 57–78).

A number of projects are underway with women from loyalist working-class communities. Courses on self-esteem, health and creativity have been attempted at venues such as East Belfast Mission and Ballynahinch Baptist church. High quality youth work with at risk teenagers is undertaken at several venues, such as the O-Zone in Portadown, where expertise is brought to bear on drug, alcohol and substance abuse and the issue of sectarianism is confronted. At a Community Church which exists in the Sunnylands estate within Carrickfergus, church members make a special practice of 'getting alongside' young people at vulnerable times of the year such as the 'Twelfth' celebrations (Orr 2008: 60–71).

For many Christian projects, moving towards co-ownership with the local community has been the goal, and it is an objective that groups such as the 'Bridge' centre in Ravenhill have already achieved. Some Christian projects have begun to recognize the great importance of celebrating the local community. Pictures of local people and places adorn the walls of the Vine Centre on the Crumlin Road in inner city North Belfast and rooms are named after local people who have earned respect.

One Church of Ireland congregation elsewhere in North Belfast is contemplating the creation of a 'well being centre' that offers therapies, exercise and nutritional advice to locals. Already the church provides a regular community breakfast to everyone who comes along. The Hard Gospel Project in the Church of Ireland has, among other things, attempted to get churches involved in celebrating their community through researching and presenting stories of local lives and local achievements (Orr 2008: 67–72).

Some individuals, motivated in large degree by radical Christian convictions, have involved themselves in what they perceive to be a positive brand of party politics. John Kyle, a doctor with a general practice in East Belfast, has become a representative of the PUP on the City Council (Orr 2008: 75–7). But a cautionary note must be sounded. Undoubtedly, funding restrictions will apply in a new era of widespread spending cuts and personal and corporate debt. This will make it difficult for ambitious projects to be initiated and then properly maintained.

Learning from others

A number of projects undertaken outside Northern Ireland are proving helpful as local faith-based workers try to take their relationship with loyalist communities more seriously. Outreach work in inner city London by the Baptist denomination is one such instance. At one stage 'redemption lift' had taken many of the brightest and best Baptist church members away from the inner city to the suburbs. Not a single inner city Baptist clergyman lived close to his 'flock'.

During the past twenty years the denomination has responded to this challenge through the work of pastors such as Colin Marchant, who has worked in various inner city environments and now lives in Newham in the East End. His philosophy was summed up in a recent interview with the author:

> Speak simply to people, love them deeply and be there in the district for them. Unlock your area, walk into it, read the local papers and see the local problems. Do things *with* people not *for* them. There must be no attempt simply to "get them into church". Share the task with people who burn like you... The church leaders... must live with the people... I have taken as my creed the need for three types of change – conversion to Jesus as Lord, conversion of the local church and conversion of society. I have seen whole communities that need transformed, in particular our large, run-down housing estates. We need an "estates theology" and an "estates ministry". Our kind of mission has to be about the incarnation.... (quoted in Orr 2008: 49–50)

Colin Marchant came to Belfast to help the team who were planning the faith-based community centre in East Belfast known as 'The Bridge', which has been mentioned above. Marchant offered insights about how an inner city community might participate in, and take ultimate control of, a project, which was dedicated to social renewal and wished to radiate a Christian ethos. Colin is a member of the Bonny Downs church, which participates in the 'Transform Newham' enterprise, which has brought local congregations together to engage in innovative community work in that part of London.

Recently one of the key personnel in the Irish Presbyterian Church visited Bonny Downs to see what could be learnt from the work there. Bonny Downs was founded in 1908 and has seen many changes since Edwardian times. In 1998, its members established Bonny Downs Community Association, which is located close to the church in a formerly disused community centre. It is connected to the church but has a separate constitution, which includes the promise 'never to impose our Christian faith and belief on others' and a vow to 'serve and respect all people, regardless of their gender, marital status, race, ethnic origin, religion, age, sexual orientation or physical and mental capacity'.

At the community centre there is a cafe. There is also an attached sports project. Educational facilities are available and counselling is given to those who might benefit. Special activities are offered to the young and the elderly. The centre is staffed by a mix of volunteers and paid workers; it has 1000 users a week and it contributes to the social capital of this deprived and multi-cultural area in a way that does not deny the orthodox evangelical inheritance of Bonny Downs church yet feels wholly non-threatening for the 'non believers' who use the facilities. It offers a model for Protestant churches, which wish to respond to social need on their doorsteps. How skilfully Bonny Downs handles its multi-cultural client base may be especially instructive for Ulster churches, which are based in those loyalist areas, which are experiencing the arrival of migrants (Orr 2008: 48–52).

In Atlanta Georgia, the work of Bob Lupton has become a model of progressive community work within troubled urban environments. He has visited Northern Ireland to share his experiences. He has addressed conferences held by the Centre for Contemporary Christianity in Ireland and has influenced the thinking which goes on at the East Belfast Mission, which aims to build an 'urban village' rooted in Christian values, situated on the Lower Newtownards Road. This village is to be tailored to the needs of locals who feel threatened by adjacent upmarket regeneration projects that portend mass gentrification. Staff from the mission have been in Atlanta and witnessed Luton's work, at the heart of which lies the principle he calls 're-neighbouring'.

This is a process whereby committed Christians make a decision to live in or near a troubled community and build relationships of a truly reciprocal kind that break down class barriers and augment the social capital of the neighbourhood. Lupton refers to 'people of faith' as 'the greatest resource of hope and vision within any community' and calls for Christian professionals in particular to repopulate social environments, which at first sight appear alien. He suggests that the imperative for re-neighbouring ought to be taught from the pulpit and, prior to that, within the seminary (Orr 2008: 52–4).

However, the obligation to re-neighbour is *not* generally taught in Ulster's Protestant churches or seminaries. Some radical Christians are already trying to practise it, as in the instance of the small Carrickfergus Community church which was mentioned earlier, many of whose members have come to live in the estate, but most Northern Irish clergy rarely talk about a Christian's choice of home as a theologically informed or missiologically attuned act.

Property acquisition continues to be seen as a God blessed step away from the rented accommodation of the housing estate, the tower block and the red brick terrace. An acquaintance of the author has pointed out that in her part of suburban Belfast, the houses were built with front doors facing the surrounding hills, as if demonstrating that the owners were turning their backs on the inner city from which they came. It should be borne in mind that many loyalist working-class communities live in sprawling housing estates in peripheral semi-urban environments such as Rathcoole in County Antrim and Ballybeen in County Down.

For a mission-minded Christian who is not familiar with this kind of terrain, 'moving in' would be a more daunting and less chic option than setting up home in London's Shoreditch or other 'down at heel' metropolitan locales which readily lose their reputation for inner city poverty and gain a whole new image as a 'cool' bohemia, with the mere addition of a few cafes and night clubs, a spate of property renovations and the arrival of the first young professionals who are ready to live next door to the refugee families and aged Cockneys.

Re-neighbouring in Rathcoole or Ballybeen would be nothing like this. To happen at all, it would have to be motivated not by inventive urban vanity but by a genuine and quiet desire to help repair some of the social fractures in Northern Ireland. It would have little attraction for those who wished to be part of a bright new wave of transformative post-terror gentrification. Successful re-neighbouring in these parts of Ulster would have to involve a genuine willingness to seek out and share the good things within a working-class culture that is often despised by others but also a readiness to handle some features that would clearly intimidate or disappoint new citizens – such as the ongoing legacy of paramilitary turf wars, the insistent summer street culture of flag and bonfires and the often grey council house architecture of 'redevelopment'.

Conclusions

It should be clear from this chapter that the church can be a resource for loyalist working-class communities. But not just as a 'first aid unit' for social casualties. It could be a place for thought. It could be a place for Protestant self-criticism and self-affirmation and a space for speculation about economic policy and political decision making. It might be a space for considering ideology and for asking questions about how a particular template of Britishness disempowered the very working-class communities that were the most devoted to waving the Union Jack.

Local Christian thinkers could develop new theological insights, based on the experience of fighting for the rights of, and attempting to reanimate, demonized or struggling communities. Theology as dilettante speculation about God and his rules, undertaken in the lecture rooms of academia, on behalf of affluent believers, could come to be seen as of little value to working-class loyalists. Churches could start to emerge which celebrate those things in the loyalist heritage that are truly benign and yet which offer critical friendship, based on a daily interaction between Christian principles and a set of social and economic realities that have for far too long been condemned or ignored.

Chapter 12
Loyalist Former Prisoners and Community Development: In Discussion with Tom Roberts

Graham Spencer

The issue of how ex-prisoners should be factored into debates and policy that shape how Northern Ireland moves from conflict to peace remains contentious for those who became victims through the actions of ex-prisoners. For such victims it is perhaps understandable why there remains a refusal to acknowledge the important role that ex-prisoners can play in the conflict transformation process. However, recent studies highlight the significance of ex-prisoners in the transformative work, which has moved Northern Ireland to a relatively stable, if early, peace (McAuley *et al*. 2010; Shirlow and McEvoy 2008).

These studies point towards leadership being shown by former prisoners in trying to address conflict tensions and seeking to confront and defuse communal antagonisms. This action has resulted in dynamics of change, which 'have utilised the organizational capacity of paramilitary groups in reformulating skills, ideas, knowledge and abilities into various channels of conflict transformation and positive community roles' (McAuley *et al*. 2010: 35). Notably, ex-prisoners have played a key part in 'preventing a drift back towards conflict and in developing confidence in political futures, both within their ethnic block and in formulating and securing the new relations between unionism and nationalism' (McAuley *et al*. 2010: 36).

These efforts though have taken place against a backdrop of political apathy by the dominant political parties, who continue to ignore the problems faced by ex-prisoner groups (presumably among other reasons because of fears about how associating with such groups could hamper attempts to cultivate an image of political respectability). This chapter seeks to highlight some of the problems faced by former prisoners by drawing on the work of EPIC (Ex-Prisoners Interpretative Centre) and the experiences of its Director, Tom Roberts. A former UVF prisoner, Roberts is well aware of the problems faced on a daily basis by former prisoners and his comments here serve as a useful reminder that in the 'new' Northern Ireland issues remain which are rooted in the discordant relations that continue to exist between the past, present and future.

The history and role of EPIC

EPIC has been operational since 1995, although its origins go back considerably longer. Initially, its primary objective was to address the problems surrounding the reintegration of politically motivated prisoners into the community and in particular those prisoners from a UVF or RHC background. Through the study of other conflicts throughout the world, it has recognized the importance of successfully reintegrating former combatants in terms of consolidating the peace.

While successful reintegration of ex-combatants in itself makes a significant contribution to peacebuilding, EPIC have, through a wide range of activities made a much wider contribution to peacebuilding in Northern Ireland. Examples of these activities are as follows:

- Creating opportunities for ex-combatants and others to engage in dialogue with adversaries (humanizing and de-stereotyping).
- Youth intervention (using the experience of former prisoners/combatants to influence youth to channel energies towards non-violent methods of resolving conflict).
- Assisting former UVF/RHC activists to contribute positively and non-violently to their communities.
- Resolution of interface violence by lines of communication with republican activists.
- International study visits to other regions in post conflict and building of relationships with academic institutions in the field of conflict resolution.
- Assisting UVF/RHC in the process of transformation.
- Provision of Welfare Rights Advice service to both ex-prisoners and the wider community.
- Community Transport Service.

The concept of EPIC originated in the late 1980s when significant numbers of politically motivated prisoners began to be released. These were people who had been incarcerated at the height of the conflict in the early to mid-seventies. It soon became apparent that there were no suitable agencies to cater for problems surrounding their reintegration. Through the Quakers, who realized in the course of their prison work that both loyalists and republicans were experiencing similar difficulties, a series of joint exploratory meetings were convened.

The significance of these meetings cannot be overestimated bearing in mind that they took place five or more years before the IRA and loyalist ceasefires of 1994. It took considerable courage and foresight to engage in those early encounters and it is testament to their value that many relationships built then endure to the present day. EPIC has continued from those early days to create opportunities for ex-combatants and others to engage in dialogue with all sections of Northern Ireland society and beyond. What are particularly important are the relationships between ex-combatants from across the political spectrum.

Using the experience of former prisoners EPIC has attempted to influence and persuade youth of the value of non-violent methods of conflict resolution. It has been accepted that young people are receptive to being influenced by those who have had the experience of involvement in the violent component of our conflict. The romanticism associated with political violence and armed struggle can be more readily demystified by those who have lived the experience.

EPIC has endeavoured to provide former UVF/RHC activists with the skills necessary to pursue their objectives through non-violent methods and to contribute positively to peacebuilding in Northern Ireland. Initially skills such as negotiation and mediation were acquired by bringing in the expertise from recognized agencies and organizations. However, the emphasis was always on empowerment and through a 'training for trainers' approach there is now a skill base established within the ex-prisoner community. Political Education has enabled activists to show leadership to both their former paramilitary groupings and their wider community

Relationships built with republicans have enabled staff and volunteers from EPIC to contribute positively to resolving tensions and violence on the interfaces. The trust that has been established has enabled communication to be maintained at times of high tension. The mobile phone network is an example of this, where activists are on constant call to dispel rumours and diffuse tensions during high risk periods such as contentious parades.

Through EPIC, joint delegations of loyalists and republicans have participated in international exchange visits to other conflict zones throughout the world with the emphasis on mutual learning. Areas visited include Nicaragua, the Basque country and south Africa. This has enabled shared experiences both between the various regions to identify common themes and construct models of best practice in peacebuilding. Relationships have also been developed with local universities and research conducted in relation to conflict. EPIC have completed a research project involving a collaborative partnership between University of Ulster, Queen's University, *Tar Isteach* (a republican ex-prisoner grouping). This examined the roles played by ex-prisoners in the development of the peace process and the barriers that prevent them resuming full citizenship. Further relationships have been developed with academic institutions throughout the world and EPIC have contributed to conflict resolution studies at both Harvard and Stanford.

EPIC is committed to assisting in the process of transition and has consistently worked on addressing the issues that prevent politically motivated ex-prisoners resuming full citizenship. This work is extremely important in a post-conflict situation because there are examples from other conflict zones of ex-prisoners/combatants resorting to criminality if they are unable to resume full citizenship and pursue legitimate occupations. There is evidence that this is already occurring in Northern Ireland and it is imperative that those unscrupulous elements of paramilitary groupings are given no excuse for their nefarious activities.

Unfortunately, the major barriers requiring legislative change still remain and show no sign of being seriously addressed. Paragraph 5 of the Prisoners section in the GFA states:

> The Governments continue to recognise the importance of measures to facilitate the reintegration of prisoners into the community by providing support both prior to and after release, including assistance directed towards availing of employment opportunities, re-training and/or re-skilling, and further education.

Both the British and Irish Governments have failed to address the legislative barriers that prevent former prisoners resuming full citizenship. What is the point in 're-training and/or re-skilling' former prisoners when the present discriminatory legislation prevents the utilization of these skills? The situation has become even more absurd since the GFA. There are ex-prisoners serving the public in District Councils, the Northern Ireland Legislative Assembly and elected to Westminster. There is also an ex-prisoner considered suitable to hold the joint most powerful office in the Northern Ireland Assembly, yet other ex-prisoners are deemed, under current legislation, unsuitable to drive a taxi.

Other examples of institutional barriers preventing former prisoners resuming full citizenship exist in the following areas:

- Pension restrictions
- Ineligibility for employment in many sectors including the Civil Service. In relation to the security forces this can even be extended to include children and relatives
- Denial by the Compensation Agency of compensation in respect of criminal injuries and criminal damage claims
- Difficulties in respect of loans from banks and building societies
- Restrictions on international travel
- Accessing PSV licenses
- Ineligibility of ex-prisoners and their partners to adopt or foster children.

It is a fact that considerable numbers of paramilitary activists, most likely the majority, have served prison sentences. If these activists are to be prevented by the discriminatory practices previously outlined from resuming full citizenship then the conflict transformation process in relation to paramilitary groupings is made that much more difficult. Former paramilitary activists should be given the opportunity to play full and meaningful roles in all aspects of society, free from the prohibitive discrimination that presently exists. EPIC, since its inception in 1995, has consistently worked on addressing the issues that prevent politically motivated ex-prisoners resuming full citizenship.

Interview between Graham Spencer and Tom Roberts

GS: How have the problems that ex-prisoners face changed since the Good Friday Agreement?

TR: There was a hope, say from the ceasefires in 1994 until the GFA, that the issue around prisoners and ex-prisoners would have been addressed properly within the political developments that were taking place and indeed there was a paragraph within the GFA which said that both the British and Irish governments would pay attention to the problems that existed and do something around addressing them. But it has been a source of great disappointment for me personally, in that nothing really has changed in terms of the barriers that exist that prevent former prisoners from resuming what I would term a full citizenship.

GS: What are those barriers?

TR: The one that would have most impact would be the discrimination that exists in employment, where because you're deemed to have a criminal record, there is a whole raft of job opportunities that you can't take advantage of because of security vetting. And not only does that impact upon the ex-prisoner, but it also impacts, quite wrongly I believe, on their families as well. The offspring of ex-prisoners sometimes find themselves barred from occupations that the general public can be part of, the most obvious, of course, being the security forces. You have the situation now where children who were unborn at the time their fathers or mothers went to prison are being held responsible for what their parents have engaged in.

GS: Are you finding that employment opportunities are opening up?

TR: It's very disappointing given the energy that has been put in by ex-prisoners' groups on behalf of ex-prisoners, both republican and loyalist, where you have this much sought after concept of cross-community support and when you have republicans and loyalists agreeing that these things need to be dealt with which aren't being dealt with. And then you actually have the absurdity of a former republican prisoner holding the joint most powerful political position in the land, whereas it's quite possible he would be unable to drive a taxi.

GS: What is EPIC doing to try and address that situation?

TR: Well probably the most important part of it is lobbying those with influence to convince them of the merits of putting all these issues right in terms of the overall peace process. We obviously lobby the British and Irish government and the political parties. We've been involved for 13 years or more now with an ex-prisoners' working group, which has represented all the various ex-prisoners, republican and loyalist, but with relatively little success.

GS: How many ex-prisoners would you be representing?

TR: Really they're educated guesses but there are 30,000 that went through the prison system during the course of the conflict and maybe 10 to 12,000 of those were loyalists. When you apportion that in terms of the UDA and the UVF, it's very difficult to gain a figure, but certainly it's thousands of people from a UVF background who have been through prison.

GS: And how many ex-prisoners will try and use your facility for help?

TR: When we were first formed our ethos was solely to address the reintegration problems around ex-prisoners. It's now 9 years since the last prisoners were released, that's prisoners from pre-1998 who fell under the terms of the GFA, so there are relatively few prisoners in the prison system now. Years ago, you had a constant stream of prisoners coming out and they would have used us to help them address their immediate needs. That has by and largely gone now. Our role has changed over the years and I would view us more as a peacebuilding organization now, where we have harnessed the influence and energy of former prisoners to assist the organizations in their transition.

GS: Do the ex-prisoners help themselves as much as they perhaps could?

TR: There are quite a few ex-prisoners who are probably unaware of the barriers that exist, because there are certain terms of employment, certain occupations that it's quite easy to move back into. Small building firms, with people who are joiners or bricklayers, for instance, aren't too much concerned about background, as long as workers can do their trade in a competent manner and a lot of them are living in a sort of blissful ignorance, if you like, until they come up against an obstacle. One of those being, as an example, that you can't legally insure your own house or property, because of the clause in the insurance contract and that actually impacts on ex-prisoners' families, because an ex-prisoner's wife, if she attempts to provide an insurance cover in her own name can't get it if her husband has a criminal record.

GS: What problems do ex-prisoners face as well as reduced employment prospects?

TR: I've no doubt that long-term imprisonment does have a psychological effect, but if you take any human being in any society and tell them you can't get a job, you can't insure your house, you can't access criminal injuries if you're assaulted on the street, or, you can't access criminal damage if your house is damaged, that will present any individual with psychological problems. Clearly you would probably feel you're being excluded from resources that any other member of society takes for granted and that's going to have a psychological effect on anybody, irrespective of whether they were in prison or not. But there is also a sort of a resigned apathy among many ex-prisoners, where the 'I need not apply' type of attitude prevails, because the assumption is that the ex-prisoner has no chance of getting an interview, let alone the job.

GS: Do you set ex-prisoners up with interviews for jobs?

TR: We try to assist them in whatever way we can. We signpost them to all the organizations we can that can help with training, interview techniques and other associated skills. We don't provide the service ourselves, but we have relationships, there's no use us reinventing the wheel if there are organizations that provide those services, we just try to impress upon them the uniqueness of ex-prisoners' problems in relation to issues and then hopefully they'll tweak their systems to take that into account.

GS: So although you're called an ex-prisoners' group, your work is really much broader than that?

TR: Very much so and in terms of the loyalists, in particular the UVF, we haven't got the resources that republicans would have in being able to departmentalize various aspects. Republicans would be very much just focused on ex-prisoner issues, whereas because of the lack of resources, there's more demands made on relatively few human resources that exist within loyalism so you have to deal with a broad range of subject matter.

GS: You indicate that republicans deal with ex-prisoners differently than is the case with your community. Is this not a reflection of negative attitudes towards prisoners from the unionist/loyalist community generally?

TR: There would be a greater acceptance of ex-prisoners within the nationalist republican community than there would be in the unionist community towards loyalist former prisoners that is true and there are all sorts of reasons for that. I believe not least that the republicans have had a long history of conflict, with, in this case the British state, so the community is conditioned better to deal with imprisonment, because it's gone on for so long. It's only this phase of the conflict, that is, in the last 40 years that loyalists have gone to prison in any significant numbers. Probably the other argument within unionism is that if you wanted to combat republican violence, the state forces were there, the Army, the Ulster Defence Regiment, Royal Irish Regiment, or the RUC were there, as vehicles that you could have used to combat republican violence.

GS: What have you learnt working with republicans?

TR: The biggest thing for me is that it has broken down a lot of the mythical barriers that existed between loyalists and republicans. I've said to people if you take away the constitutional question and some cultural differences, on a human needs basis, we're not a lot different, we're the same people really and it's about how to accommodate that within those cultural and constitutional differences. The one thing about a prolonged series of engagements over the years with republicans is that a lot of us have the maturity when we can be perfectly honest with one another without wanting to resort to violence.

While there are problems that still appear intractable, at least we're working at them. I think it's important to be able to tell people when their behaviour is impacting badly on you and your community, because sometimes we can be offending each other and not even knowing we're doing it. So it's important to talk to one another, to gain a greater degree of understanding and I believe the more interaction and dialogue that you can have with your political opponent the less likely that violence will be an outcome in the future.

GS: How does that work and how do you go about assisting transition?

TR: We have worked with the UVF on an ongoing basis to use whatever resources we can to allow them to develop the process that helps them with their transition. We hold meetings, we encourage debate among people, we interact, we negotiate and dialogue with republicans around issues of common concern to both communities, the most glaring example of that would probably be the problems around interfaces.

GS: Is your peacework a series of short-term objectives and projects, or do you work to a long-term goal?

TR: What people who work in these circumstances on the ground do is, I believe, give politicians the space to be creative about the political structures that they work in. But on another level the conflict here is not being resolved. Rather it's being managed and our primary role would be to try and facilitate that conflict management.

GS: When you try and access government funding for your kind of work how do you design your projects and bids?

TR: In terms of our funding at the minute, we have targets to meet in terms of things that we said we would do, but the majority of the work that me and other staff would be engaged in is largely unquantifiable. In terms of peacebuilding, how do you count the dogs that aren't barking? This is the dilemma. And it puts extra pressure on individuals and the organization as a whole because they have to make targets that they can't devote all their time to meeting simply because the majority of their time is spent doing other things.

GS: So much of the work that you do can't be proved, it can't be written down and it can't be quantifiable?

TR: There are obvious outcomes that people can see visibly, such as say how the UVF have changed and if there's an understanding there it is that change doesn't happen by accident. It's as a result of organizations, like ourselves and others, who are helping people to move in a direction that hopefully society wants us to move in.

GS: Some people in other loyalist organizations have said that the biggest problem with loyalism is loyalism itself. Would you agree with that?

TR: In terms of contributions and the difficulties that they face, loyalists probably made the most groundbreaking, pioneering moves towards finding political solutions here. If you compare that to the mainstream unionist parties, they didn't show the inventiveness, or indeed the courage, to look for radical solutions to our political problems. So I would be hesitant to say that loyalists are their own biggest problem. There are problems within loyalism, but in the broader picture I think loyalists have punched well above their weight in terms of their contribution to an ultimate political agreement.

GS: Is class difference now starting to become an issue whereas previously it was submerged beneath the constitutional question?

TR: Obviously there's not enough emphasis being placed on the social inequality. The constant and strongest complaints you would get, say around the political establishment, the Belfast Agreement and devolved government, would tend to come from the areas that are most socially deprived and most acutely affected by the conflict. People from those areas will constantly tell you that nothing has really changed for them and you will regularly hear people talking about the peace dividend having done nothing for them. By and large, the benefactors of the peace have really been the business classes, whose businesses are now able to operate without the impact that the violence and bombing campaign had. Because those businesses are able to function more efficiently and freely now, it is really those who are representative of those businesses who are seen as having benefited most.

GS: So does that mean the underlying issues don't get addressed?

TR: All the ingredients that caused conflict here in the first place still exist, so there is a degree of fragility about all the political structures and the peace that we now have. Moreover, sectarianism is still rampant in this society. The constitutional question is not resolved at all. Indeed if anything it's been fudged. Republicans, for example, would sell the political establishment here as being little more than a transitional stage, whereas unionists view it as being permanent.

GS: Is there an enduring negativity in the Protestant psyche and the expectation that things will go wrong?

TR: There's a whole different mindset and culture within the two communities; unionism seems to need this exactness, you know, where every 'i' is dotted and 't' crossed before they're comfortable with something. In contrast the nationalist attitude tends to be we can leave that until next week, it'll be sorted then. But unionists are very precise and trust exactness.

GS: Do the unionist parties treat you with a degree of contempt? What is your relationship with the politicians like?

TR: In terms of mainstream unionism, I don't believe that they pay much attention to the issues that affect loyalism and they don't set good examples either, in terms of the way they deal with what is supposed to be a partnership government. Indeed, they barely talk to one another, so it doesn't send a good message. The impact of this image of a partnership government which is little more than point scoring or swinging handbags at each other can be far more serious on the ground, when people take their lead from that sort of behaviour.

GS: Is sectarianism the main issue that you are dealing with at the moment?

TR: It's one of the big issues. The other thing is the social and economic deprivation that is being experienced in areas most acutely affected by the conflict. Certainly there is a correlation between these problems being most strongly felt in the most socially deprived areas. There is also serious educational under attainment in those areas which is both abysmal and frightening. You therefore have a disaffected youth, who don't see any future for themselves in society, who don't see themselves in employment, getting married, having children and supporting families in the ways of conventional 'normal' society. They don't have those expectations and they don't see those opportunities for themselves, so they're susceptible to malign influences within their communities to engage in all sorts of violence. It may well be the case that, in turn, sectarianism is being used as a banner for that dislocation. You have people on either side of the peace walls who are up against these problems, with very little aspiration in terms of their future, but who use religious and political differences to attack each other and who find meaning and worth in forcefully living out those antagonisms.

GS: Is criminality on the increase here because of this?

TR: It's not just because of the social deprivation that criminality is on the increase but because there is a police service which is in transition and ill equipped to deal with criminality. Add to that that you have the paramilitaries, the UVF on this side, the IRA on the other side, who by and large are off the stage now, and who during the conflict filled a policing vacuum in the areas where they were strong and in control and you can see the potential problem. The police aren't yet equipped to adequately fill the vacuum that has been left, so criminality has risen. The criminals don't have the same fear now in terms of retribution for what they're engaged in.

GS: Are you finding that the youngsters are reverting to the idea that they missed out on the romance of the conflict and is that causing problems?

TR: That's where I see a big role for former combatants and former prisoners in demystifying all this romanticism, because there's certainly nothing romantic about lying in a prison cell for years or losing your life because of conflict. And to a considerable extent ex-prisoners have that credibility, because they have been through the conflict. They have been through imprisonment or suffered broken families and loss of loved ones and they can convey that to young people, making it clear that the romanticism around conflict is largely unfounded.

GS: It would appear that there will be some people who will need to keep the potential of a threat high, to justify their own position and their own status. How is that going to shift?

TR: We were that wrapped up in politics that we had this naïve view, which was epitomized at the time of the GFA. The Agreement was signed on a Friday and created this expectation that everything would be fine on Saturday. We have had 40 years, arguably some people would say 800 years, of conflict here to try to work through and the legacy that it has left is enormous. Paramilitaries were made a convenient scapegoat for all the ills of society here. People would often say that even if a dog crapped in the street it was the UVF's fault or the IRA's fault. Everything was blamed on them. And I've found that scapegoating to be especially acute in these past few years. You have mainstream unionists who have now moved into a supposed partnership government with Sinn Féin, absolving themselves from all responsibility for the conflict, blaming bombers and killers from various paramilitary organizations as the cause of the whole conflict when, in fact, they were only a symptom of the political environment that was created here. Recent talk about dealing with the past seems to suggest that the representatives of those organizations in civic society are absolving themselves all responsibility for the circumstances that they helped to create.

GS: Is the UVF now basically a Somme organization or a social community group?

TR: In my opinion, the UVF is largely a benign organization, but most of the UVF would have termed themselves the 'People's Army' and now a lot of the UVF volunteers are redirecting their energy into serving those same people in a different way. A number of them are engaged in community activism, highlighting problems that exist within communities and using whatever expertise there is to address those problems. The traditional attitude of the UVF was to see themselves as defenders of the community and they still see themselves as defenders of that community. The difference now is in how those objectives are being pursued and that is in a non-violent fashion.

GS: What's the plan up to 2011 for EPIC?

TR: Well the main thrust of our work would be to try to encourage more people to engage in dialogue with the other tradition to try to devise methods of dealing with the undoubted problems that exist in a non-violent fashion. That is a worthwhile activity in itself, because the only way you're going to solve problems here, is by engaging with one another in an honest and frank fashion. Through such dialogue it may be possible to impress on others that violence is never going to resolve the problems that still exist here. One thing seems quite certain and that is without such dialogue it becomes much more difficult to make the case for peace because then the tribes will merely retreat to old positions as a response to new problems and it doesn't take much imagination to work out where that could lead.

Conclusions

Official recommendations by the CGP and the IMC now recognize the importance of addressing the former prisoners issue. Referring to the work of Quigley-Hamilton working group which in 2007 set out a guide for how employers should recruit those with conflict related convictions, the CGP Report of 2009 reiterated the Quigley-Hamilton recommendations, voicing the need to overcome conflict related convictions from 'impinging on a individual's ability to play a part in society, without taking the more controversial step of fully expunging their record' (Report of the Consultative Group on the Past 2009: 82).

The Report further concluded (along with Quigley-Hamilton) that proposals to 'eliminate discrimination against those with conflict related convictions, should be incorporated into statute and made applicable to the provision of goods, facilities and services as well as recruitment' (Report of the Consultative Group on the Past 2009). This official recognition of the need to address the ex-prisoner problem was further underscored by the IMC Report of November 2009 which stipulated 'that it is right to work so as to remove obstacles to employment and to access to the full range of services so that people who have genuinely left paramilitarism behind and are not involved in crime can play a full part in their community and in the economy. We hope that this issue will be given consideration by the British Government and the Northern Ireland Assembly and Executive' (Twenty

Second Report of the Independent Monitoring Commission, 4 November 2009: 37).

It remains to be seen whether the British and Irish governments and the Northern Ireland Assembly and Executive will act on these recommendations. As the comments of Roberts highlight, former prisoners face discrimination, which impedes the ethos of inclusivity so confidently expounded by the two governments as a central plank of the peace process. Rather, what has emerged in the case of former prisoners is an exclusive approach to the problems they face which serves to reinforce perceptions and experiences of segregation and dislocation.

Recognizing as the IMC Report does that for a number of individuals who work with ex-prisoners 'their past may give them a standing which facilitates the constructive contribution they are able to make' (ibid), it should not be taken for granted that former prisoner group leaders can continue to achieve clear and positive results when the people they seek to help continue to feel let down and disregarded by the peace process and those official parties and agencies which represent it. Clearly, a fresh and open approach is needed by the political parties to confront the discrimination faced by ex-prisoners. To not do so and to continue to ignore these problems risks fermenting antagonisms and unrest within those communities which could damage the peace process and plant the seeds for a resumption of social instability and violence.

Chapter 13

Monitoring the Loyalist Paramilitaries: The Role of the Independent Monitoring Commission[1] in the Northern Ireland Peace Process, 2003–09[2]

John G. D. Grieve[3]

> The objective of the Commission is to carry out [its functions] with a view to promoting the transition to a peaceful society and stable and inclusive devolved Government in Northern Ireland.
>
> (Article 3 of the International Agreement)

The purpose of this chapter is to describe the Independent Monitoring Commission (IMC), which was set up as part of the continuing peace process in Northern Ireland following 34 years of sectarian paramilitary violence. The intention of the legislation passed in Dublin and London was that the body created would provide an objective account and recommendations that would contribute to the rule of law in a peaceful and democratic society. The series of six-monthly Reports we have delivered are cited in Parliament, the *Dail* and the Northern Ireland Assembly as well as in the press, on television and in academic studies. This chapter is intended to contribute to help understanding of our processes and the role of our Reports and concentrates on one part of our role to monitor paramilitary activity. By and large, this chapter provides an account of multi-source intelligence that has been prepared for open (public) consumption. It is also a contribution to conflict management studies.

Although the title of this chapter is 'Monitoring the Loyalist Paramilitaries' the task of the Commission included every grouping and activity of paramilitaries in Northern Ireland. The process described here is applicable and equitable to all. The IMC was created as a part of the continuing wider peace process and normalization of Northern Ireland after years of conflict and also to resolve some outstanding issues six years after the Good Friday Peace Agreement was signed. It was created by an International Agreement and then primary legislation by the two democratically elected governments in Ireland and the United Kingdom in 2003.

The IMC issued an initial written account to clarify its role and how it would seek to apply guidelines to its work on 9th March 2004. This was accompanied by a press conference at which the Commissioners answered questions, a process that has accompanied every Report (bar one article 5 Report [see below]) thereafter.

International Agreement between the Government of the United Kingdom and the Government of Ireland 2003

Following a series of political debates about whether continuing paramilitary incidents amounted to a breach of the ceasefire or 1998 peace process, the Irish and UK governments decided to hand to the IMC monitoring, analysis, recommending and reporting.

Two articles in the International Agreement of most relevance to this chapter on monitoring paramilitaries are Articles 4 and 7.[4] We had other tasks respecting the normalization of some policing activity and the military roles; also in respect of complaints about some types of conduct by ministers and parties to the Northern Ireland Assembly that I will not deal with here. There were four elements to the process – monitor, assess, report and recommend remedies.

Article 4

In relation to the remaining threat from paramilitary groups, the Commission shall:

(a) monitor any continuing activity by paramilitary groups including:
    i. attacks on the security forces, murders, sectarian attacks, involvement in riots, and other criminal offences;
    ii. training, targeting, intelligence gathering, acquisition or development of arms or weapons and other preparations for terrorist campaigns;
    iii. punishment beatings and attacks and exiling;
(b) assess:
    i. whether the leaderships of such organizations are directing such incidents or seeking to prevent them; and
    ii. trends in security incidents.
(c) report its findings in respect of paragraphs (a) and (b) of this Article to the two Governments at six monthly intervals; and, at

the joint request of the two Governments, or if the Commission sees fit to do so, produce further reports on paramilitary activity on an ad hoc basis.

Article 7

When reporting under Articles 4 and 6 of this Agreement, the Commission, or in the case of Article 6(2), the relevant members thereof shall recommend any remedial action considered necessary. The Commission may also recommend what measures, if any, it considers might appropriately be taken by the Northern Ireland Assembly, such measures being limited to those which the Northern Ireland Assembly has power to take under relevant United Kingdom law (International Agreement between the Government of UK and Government of Ireland 2003).

A third further relevant article to this chapter (Article 13) deals with confidentiality and imposes a duty to ensure the security of people who talk to us (International Agreement between the Government of UK and Government of Ireland 2003).

Those two main articles laid out what we were to deliver and one aspect of how we should go about it. We could make recommendations in our six monthly Reports and we were empowered to report more often, but neither we nor the two governments could delay the submission of a Report. Importantly, we had no executive powers.

There were no direct precedents on how to set up and run a commission with these tasks we had been given, although we asked politicians, officials, commentators, critics, academics and everyone with whom we initially came into contact for models on which we could build. There was much from which we could take ideas and synthesize our own processes. There was no complete model or process. Essentially we used the skills and experience of our officials and the four Commissioners, which were varied. This provided a useful cross fertilization from politics, diplomacy, administration, criminal justice, policing and intelligence. My own police and academic backgrounds inform my account, not least as an intelligence officer. My contributions to the IMC therefore gave more specific weight to some instruments and tools I had used in the past. We all brought with us a reference network of contacts and sources to begin our work, not least that four of us had had experience of tactical and strategic intelligence and two of us in preparing that material (see, for example, Kerr 2008a and b Grieve 2008 and 2009).

It might be helpful to set the context. There were, besides police and security services, a large number of boards, commissions and other bodies in

Northern Ireland who were also concerned with the criminal justice system, the maintenance of standards and with the transition to a peaceful society. They touched on our work in a variety of ways but never overlapped totally. They fulfil a variety of roles: executive, supervisory, monitoring and advisory. All have some form of interest in paramilitaries and their activities. Most are confined to Northern Ireland but some operate on a UK-wide basis. We were not aware of a comprehensive and publicly available list, but we believed it to be in alphabetical order: The Chief Inspector of Criminal Justice; HM Chief Inspector of Prisons; The Commissioner for Judicial Appointments; The Electoral Commission (UK); Equality Commission; Independent Assessor of Military Complaints Procedure in Northern Ireland; Independent Commissioner for Detained Terrorist Suspects; The Independent Monitoring Commission; Independent Reviewer of the Terrorism Act (Lord Carlile); Information Commissioner (UK); HM Inspector of Constabulary; The Interception of Communications Commissioner (UK); The International Independent Commission on Decommissioning (IICD); The Justice Oversight Commissioner; Northern Ireland Commissioner for Children and Young People; The Northern Ireland Human Rights Commission; The Northern Ireland Policing Board; Northern Ireland Sentence Review Commissioners; The Office of the Oversight Commissioner; The Parades Commission; The Police Ombudsman for Northern Ireland; Prisoner Ombudsman for Northern Ireland; The Probation Board for Northern Ireland; Regulation of Investigation Powers Act Commissioners. There are also individual inquiries in Ireland North and South: the Saville Inquiry and those established as a result of the Report of the Cory Inquiry.[5]

What we learnt from this wide-ranging list was that there were some broadly similar materials (e.g. published Reports) and generalized experiences (e.g. dealing with challenges) we could consider from each of these bodies, which could be applied to understanding independence, monitoring and commissions. The essence of independence became an area for our research. While using material from many sources one issue was how were we to remain distant to ensure objectivity, how could we triangulate material from multiple sources? We achieved this by discussion and refinement of our Reports. We were different, we concluded, from other bodies because of the breadth of our interest in paramilitaries, their leadership (including political representatives or affiliates) and their violent activities.

The IMC's guiding principles

Our guiding principles were set out in the public statement the IMC issued on 9 March 2004.

- **The rule of law is fundamental in a democratic society.**

- We understand that there are some strongly held views about certain aspects of the legal framework, for example the special provisions applying to terrorism, and that those holding these views will continue to seek changes. But obedience to the law is incumbent on every citizen.
- The law can be legitimately enforced only by duly appointed and accountable law enforcement officers or institutions. Any other forcible imposition of standards is unlawful and undemocratic.
- Violence and the threat of violence can have no part in democratic politics. A society in which they play some role in political or governmental affairs cannot – in the words of Article 3 – be considered either peaceful or stable.
- Political parties in a democratic and peaceful society, and all those working in them, must not in any way benefit from, or be associated with, illegal activity of any kind, whether involving violence or the threat of it, or crime of any kind, or the proceeds of crime. It is incumbent on all those engaged in democratic politics to ensure that their activities are untainted in any of these ways.
- It is not acceptable for any political party, and in particular for the leadership, to express commitment to democratic politics and the rule of law if they do not live up to those statements and do all in their power to ensure that those they are in a position to influence do the same. (IMC 09.03.04)

Methodology of the IMC

A year after we had our published our guidelines in our Fifth Report published in April 2005 we reported how our methodology had evolved:

> 1.09 We have been asked a number of times how we make our assessments and on what information we base them. Some have asked us to put more material in the public domain. Some have challenged us on grounds that we may be or appear to be biased, and we continue carefully to consider that issue. We hope it would be helpful if we say something about the way we work.

As I have already mentioned, we went on to describe the benefit of the different skills of the Commissioners.

> 1.10 We believe it is a great strength that the four Commissioners come from different backgrounds and have different perspectives. We seek to maximise the benefit this gives us by challenging each others' thinking as well as challenging those we meet. We try to develop

assessments based on more than one source. We see if there are links between what we learn from different people and we expect to be able to triangulate different perspectives before we reach conclusions. We probe the nature and logic of the information we receive. We examine whether there are any inconsistencies. We challenge any gaps there appear to be. We question whether there might be any bias either in our own approach or in that of others and take steps to ensure it does not influence our conclusions inappropriately. We ask ourselves and our interlocutors whether other conclusions might as reasonably be drawn from the same set of circumstances. We test the confidence placed in the material and in opinions associated with it. We do all this before we come to any view, and before we write our reports. The conclusions we draw are our own.

The important concept to consider here is triangulation. We had learnt the lesson of Butler (2004) not to rely on one source or even one category of source. We went on to record:

1.11 Our sources are wide ranging. They include the law enforcement and other agencies of the United Kingdom and Ireland, as well as of any other country from which we have things to learn. But they are much wider than that. In addition to government officials and police officers we have met people from the following categories in Great Britain, Ireland North and South and in the United States:

> Political parties; government officials; police; community groups; churches; charities; pressure groups and other organisations; former combatants, including ex-prisoners; representatives of businesses; lawyers; journalists; academics; victims; private citizens, individually and as families.

We urge everybody with something material to our work to contact us. We also try to take account of the work of other boards, commissions and similar bodies in Northern Ireland and elsewhere.

1.12 We are very careful what we say in our Reports. From the beginning we have adhered to one firm principle – we treat everything we hear, including the identities of those who communicate with us, in complete confidence. Only in this way can they be expected to impart information to us, and without that information we cannot do the job the two Governments have charged us with. Therefore, we will not reveal our sources, though those people are free to say what they like about their communications with the IMC. The International Agreement lays down other constraints on us, for example so that we do not prejudice legal proceedings or jeopardise anybody's safety. But the most significant restraint is self-imposed: we will not say anything, or draw any conclusion unless we have confidence in it, and we will qualify conclusions if we think it necessary. We did this, for example, in our initial attribution of certain robberies in late October 2004.

1.13 We are not infallible, but we do believe we are thorough in our methods and measured in our assessments. If we find one of our conclusions does not stand up in the light of later information we will acknowledge this in a subsequent Report.

We then went on to describe where our thinking about our role in the peace process had got us:

1.14 We have continued to refine our understanding of the activities of paramilitary groups and of the associated issues. We share the generally held aspiration that paramilitary groups will cease all illegal activity. The Belfast Agreement of 1998 marked a watershed and, although we recognise that illegal paramilitary activity will not all be suddenly brought to an end, the transition to a peaceful society and stable and inclusive devolved government which it envisaged must not continue indefinitely.

1.15 This aspiration raises two particular questions for us. First are the indications which would encourage us to assess that a paramilitary group really was making material progress towards giving up all illegal activity. Second are the areas we would look at in assessing whether it had actually done so.

1.16 In addressing the first question on making material progress towards giving up all illegal activity encouraging indications would include whether a group had taken the strategic decision to give up illegal activity; had given a clear lead to its members that they must do so; and had declared that as a group it had stopped such activity. Other indications might include: whether the group was taking steps to end its capability to undertake criminal acts; whether it was co-operating with the police; and whether it was lifting threats against people, including those it had exiled.

1.17 As far as the second question is concerned, namely assessing whether a group had actually stopped illegal activity, we would continue to monitor and report on whether or not it still:
• used violence in any form;
• committed other crimes;
• recruited or trained members;
• gathered intelligence, targeted people or procured material;
• exiled or intimidated people (IMC Fifth Report April 2005).

Paragraph 1.14 that is quoted here refers to at least four specific and focused occasions when we checked our general processes rather than the specifics of a particular Report (two meetings were in Belfast, one in Dublin, one in the United States). At these meetings I had introduced among other advice that of Lord Laming and John Fox in the Victoria Climbie Public Inquiry (this was an examination of the failed processes, not least that of the information flow between public bodies and its analysis that had contributed to the failure to prevent the murder of a young girl by her guardians) that what was needed was – 'an investigative approach, an open mind, and a healthy scepticism' (Laming 2001: 14.36).

Lessons from European Convention on Human Rights

We were concerned from the outset to explore the evidential threshold that would underpin our deliberations, Reports and recommendations. We looked around for sources of help and inspiration. Human Rights legislation has been at the heart of what we have sought to achieve, The European Convention on Human Rights (ECHR), the United Nations Code of Conduct for Law Enforcement, Council of Europe Declaration on Policing also provided a framework for our thinking as monitoring as a form of accountability through explanation and hence transparency is a function of a wider view of normalized policing (leaving aside some of our other tasks in respect of Article 5 concerning aspects of policing that I will not deal with here).

Some of the ECHR articles we considered were:

- The right to life and the right to have an effective investigation when that had been breached by another – Article 2. Besides a basic guiding, underlying, principle this gave us some guidance on the competencies and criteria that other forms of enquiry considered were important. For example our assessments and Reports would need to be:
  - Thorough and rigorous, competent and comprehensive.
  - Show we had appropriate skills and knowledge
  - Show that all appropriate levels of review, consideration and checking of the material we were using. This was particularly apposite as Lord Alderdice, Joe Brosnan and Stephen Boys-Smith had formidable drafting and review skills.
  - Show that we use the most thorough and complete documentation at every stage as was possible and available to us.

Two other ECHR Articles close to our task were:

- Rights of liberty and security – Article 5.
- Right to private and family life – Article 8.

We also ensured that when there were questions about human rights of individuals or groups that any Reports we wrote or recommendations we made fulfilled the ECHR criteria and that they should be:

- Proportionate in all the circumstances
- Legal, we took advice
- Accountable, recorded and that we took corporate responsibility
- And any action we recommended should be necessary
- We also needed to show that our Reports and Recommendations were based on best information reasonably available, that we did not accept information on its face value, we explored, examined, investigated. We considered what would be the community impact of what we wrote (see for example Neyroud and Beckley 2001).

One way of monitoring whether we were 'promoting the transition to a peaceful society and a stable and inclusive devolved government' was through background thinking from community impact assessments. These are policing tools that we adopted in a loose fashion. They helped me to fulfil the requirement that what we wrote would not put anyone at risk (Article 13). They also helped us think about another Human Rights Acts requirement, a form of risk, gap or threat analysis and the need to be:

- Ethical, transparent, inclusive, evidence and intelligence based, wide ranging
- As far as possible locally community based and using prior arrangements for the exchange of information using a variety of methods

We tested whether our treatment of different groups was balanced. A useful account of such impact analysis is one developed by Greater Manchester Police that I had used in the past where a 'starting point will be any disparities or potential disparities identified... a judgement whether these amount to adverse impact... systematically evaluating... against all the information and evidence assembled... using as a benchmark, and making a reasonable judgement whether the policy is likely to have significant negative consequences for a particular diverse group or groups' (Race Equality Scheme 2002).

In our case although we adopted this basic philosophy to ensure that it could not be argued that we were unreasonably reporting on one group compared with another, we had not the resources that the vigorous application of the police doctrine would require. Assessing impact involved for me looking at risk and thinking through the consequences of our Reports and recommendations and I used it when checking drafts of our Reports.

Legal tests of our role: confidence and fairness

It was helpful that we had done some of the thinking I have described and been exploring how we were following the guidelines we had set ourselves, because the Reports we had produced led to the Secretary of State and the IMC being taken to the High Court charged in part with a possible perception prejudice and bias. At paragraph 133/4 of the Judgement, the Court concluded:

> The IMC must nevertheless apply some defined criterion or evidential threshold for the purposes of fact-finding, since the process would otherwise be arbitrary and unfair; and where the facts relate to criminal conduct, the criterion or evidential threshold ought in our view to be a rigorous one. The letter makes clear, however, that the IMC does apply such a criterion, namely one of "confidence". The letter quotes a key passage from the Fifth Report which we have already cited in para 26 above: "we will not say anything, or draw any conclusion, unless we have confidence in it". In our judgment that criterion, if properly applied, is an appropriate one and gives rise to no procedural unfairness on the part of the IMC.
>
> Mr Larkin took us to passages in the IMC's Reports which, read in isolation, might be taken to suggest that the IMC applies a less clear-cut criterion than one of confidence. In the First Report, for example, the language repeatedly used is that of belief rather than confidence (see the passages quoted at paras 27–28 above). On the other hand, when it comes to the findings of fact in the Fourth Report about the Northern Bank robbery, in relation to which Sinn Féin is particularly critical, the language used is more emphatic. The Report states that the information available since the robbery "leads us to conclude firmly that it was planned and undertaken by the PIRA" and that some of Sinn Féin's senior members "were involved in sanctioning [it]" (see the passages quoted at paras 35–36 above). Looking at the Reports as a whole, we see no reason to reject the IMC's clear statements that the commissioners will not say anything or draw any conclusion unless they have confidence in it.

The Judgement went on at Paragraphs 135 to 136:

> The adoption of such an approach is supported by the ruling on standard of proof issued on 11 October 2004 by "The Bloody Sunday Inquiry" tribunal, chaired by Lord Saville of Newgate. Para 23 of that ruling reads:
>
> In our view, provided the Tribunal makes clear the degree of confidence or certainty with which it reaches any conclusion as to facts and matters that may imply or suggest criminality of serious misconduct of

any individual, provided that there is evidence and reasoning that logic-ally supports the conclusion to the degree of confidence or certainty expressed, and provided of course that those concerned have been given a proper opportunity to deal with allegations made against them, we see in the context of this Inquiry no unfairness to anyone nor any good reason to limit our findings in the manner suggested. Thus, to take an example, we cannot accept that we are precluded in our Report from ana-lysing and weighing the evidence and giving our reasons for concluding that in the case of a particular shooting, we are confident that it was deliberate, that there was no objective justification for it, and though we are not certain, that it seems to us more likely than not that there was no subjective justification either. Of course we would have in mind the seriousness of the matter on which we were expressing a view, but that is not because of some rule that we should apply, but rather as a matter of common sense and justice. (High Court of Justice Queens Bench Division Divisional Court Case No. CO/9939/2005 delivered 19 January 2007)

This was significant for us because we had reached our process independ-ently and had not been aware of the Bloody Sunday Inquiry ruling. The court went on to consider our confidentiality clause.

For reasons of confidentiality the IMC cannot set out the evidence on which its conclusions are based; and the question whether an oppor-tunity has been given to Sinn Féin to deal with allegations made against it is a separate issue considered below. Subject to those qualifications, however, the passage from the tribunal's ruling sets out an approach very similar to that taken by the IMC in relation to its own Reports. As we have said, it is in our view an appropriate one. We do not accept that the IMC, given the nature of its functions, is required to adopt a more legalis-tic test than that adopted for The Bloody Sunday Inquiry. (High Court of Justice Queens Bench Division Divisional Court Case No. CO/9939/2005 delivered 19 January 2007)

It can be seen from this judgement that the court considered, as we had, learning from other public inquiries was relevant to our work.

Monitoring as intelligence/ intelligent based or knowledgeable forms of policing the paramilitaries

It will be apparent that I was bringing to our discussions and processes my experiences of policing. I was bringing to our discussions a desire, despite my intelligence experiences, to recover the word 'Intelligence' for commu-nities, the exploration of a dilemma – the broader concept of policing by communication has been an agenda of mine for some decades. Monitoring is an aspect of policing even when not performed by a public police (such as PSNI). I have a general thesis to 'make intelligence non threatening to communities'. The work we had been given by the two governments seemed to epitomize a view that informed consent, communities as educated customers and perhaps intelligence were education (see Grieve 2004 for a further discussion of these issues).

Dick Kerr introduced some other parallel processes from this world (see Kerr 2008a and Juett *et al.* (2008). We also considered and aspired to another favourite of mine, a wider use of the word 'intelligence' used by Douglas Hofstadter in 1980, which I introduced to my colleagues:

- Respond to situations very flexibly
- Take advantage of fortuitous circs
- Make sense of ambiguous or contradictory information
- Recognize relative importance of different elements
- Find similarities between situations despite differing elements
- Draw distinctions despite similarities
- Synthesize new concepts from old, put together in new ways
- Come up with ideas that are novel.

Finally to go with our consideration of Butler on intelligence (see below) Dick Kerr had introduced us to models of operational, strategic and tactical failure and possible remedies. George and Bruce 2008 in a volume that Dick Kerr had contributed to had developed another helpful list of what to avoid:

- Estimative misjudgement, uncritical acceptance of established positions or assumptions.
- Analysts doing what the boss wants, absence of breadth of research, not building knowledge.
- Failing to neither confront organizational norms, political context nor culture, no competitive analysis, no challenge groups.
- Failing to understand task of predictive warning.
- Emphasis on short-term products not long-term major trends.
- Over reaction to previous errors (this is very specifically in line with Butler 2004:115).

Assessment

There is an assessment tool I have used both for intelligence analysis while Director of Intelligence for the Metropolitan Police for evaluation and also for academic discourse. It is based on a Unit Ian Grant wrote for the Open University nearly thirty years ago which I used when studying with them as a Detective Inspector. I have since added the importance of dissent from

Lord Butler's review of intelligence (Butler 2004) and the Iraq War (2004) and Miranda Fricker's (2002) thinking, originally about feminism, on how some testimony, voices, and evidence counts for more in some debates or decision making than in others (what she calls 'epistemic imbalance'). The model is:

- Present clear synopsis of thesis.
- Distinguish fact, value, empirical, interpretation, and evaluation.
- Test propositions, immunity from tests?
- Status of evidence, testimony, collection methods and records.
- Logic of argument.
- Alternative hypothesis, evidence explanations.
- Conspiracy of silence, dissent (Butler), neglect, gaps.
- Generalization checked.
- Bias, epistemic imbalance (Fricker).
- Do you identify with argument?

How did this all work in practice? We prepare a first draft based upon discussions and meetings where relevance is explored. We also use research we have conducted ourselves, or that we have commissioned on pertinent material for example: fuel laundering, tax avoidance, organized crime, or the security industry. The format is that we summarize what we had written 6 months before, then we describe the current situation, provide statistics and then move on to assessments and recommendations. We deal with paramilitary groups by category but also make general points. We consider the role of leadership whether paramilitary or associated political groups. We then moved through various iterations of drafting and amending until the final Report is submitted to the two governments and published by them. We hold a press conference and open ourselves to questions, challenges and commentary. For the purpose of loyalist paramilitary activity in this chapter I have chosen a period longer than six months to compare – five years – to illustrate both the process we have adopted and the changes that we have reported on. It records an odyssey taken by loyalist paramilitaries.

Assessment of loyalist paramilitary activity by the IMC 2004–2009

What follows is a comparison of our assessments over time as examples of what we could comment on and what the Reports contain.

In the Fifth Report (9 April 2005) covering part of 2004 into 2005 we wrote about paramilitary groups – Loyalist Volunteer Force (LVF), Ulster Volunteer Force (UVF),/Ulster Defence Association (UDA) and Red Hand Commando (RHC)

Loyalist Volunteer Force (LVF)

2.7 In our previous Report we said that the LVF was less active than it had been, with the exception of organised crime in which it was deeply involved, and that it did not appear to want to resume significant violence although it retained the capacity to do so should that intention change.

2.8 The LVF remains deeply involved in drug dealing, and in some areas it has recruited people solely for that purpose. On 14 January 2005 cannabis and ecstasy to the value of some £125,000 was discovered in Holywood along with LVF paraphernalia. In January LVF members fired shots at a taxi company with UVF connections. We conclude as we did in our previous Report that with the striking exception of organised crime, especially in the form of drugs, the LVF remains less active than it used to be, shows no inclination to return to significant levels of violence, but retains a capacity to do so should its intentions change.

We went on to assess the Ulster Defence Association (UDA) in the same Report of 09.04.05

2.16 In our previous Report we said that the UDA had planned to avoid disorder over the summer but had undertaken shootings and assaults, and was heavily involved in organised crime.

2.17 In November last year the Secretary of State announced the de-specification of the UDA following its statement that it would desist from all "military activity", focus on social and economic issues within the community, and work with the British Government towards an end to all paramilitary activity. Part of the period under review in this Report therefore fell before this statement.

2.18 In September and October 2004 the UDA were involved in both violence and targeting... As part of a dispute with the LVF in Belfast they were responsible for an arson attack... More recently, they have engaged in targeting in anticipation of a possible dispute with the LVF following the release of Johnny Adair from prison in January 2005, and have monitored dissident republicans with a view to mounting attacks if they themselves are attacked. In January 2005 UDA members forced two families from their homes. We have found nothing to suggest that the UDA has agreed to the return to Northern Ireland of people it has exiled or that it is considering doing so. The organisation was, we believe, responsible for shootings and assaults. It remains involved in organised crime, and members were responsible for two robberies in February and March 2005.

2.19 We have always recognised that transition may be a messy and difficult process for a paramilitary group. To date it is not clear if the
UDA will achieve the transition it pointed to in its statement of
November 2004. Certainly the process is still very far from complete, and the fact remains that during the period under review it
was responsible for 2 murders.

Finally we assessed the Ulster Volunteer Force (UVF) and Red Hand
Commando (RHC) in the same Report of 09.04.05.

2.20 In our previous Report we concluded that the UVF remained active
and violent and that it continued to be involved in organised
crime.
2.21 This is still the case. The UVF undertook a number of attacks over
Christmas and New Year as part of its continuing conflict with
the LVF. Members of the same UVF unit shot at LVF members
in Belfast in mid- January... It has also undertaken the targeting
of rivals. It continues to recruit members. Several of the loyalist shootings and assaults over the period covered in Section 3 of
this Report can be attributed to the UVF and RHC. The UVF is
also engaged in organised crime. Our previous conclusion thus
stands. The UVF is active, violent and ruthless, and is prepared to
use violence to promote what it sees as the interests of the organisation. We believe it would undertake greater violence than in
recent months if it judged that those interests so required. (IMC
Fifth Report April 2005).

Four years later our assessment was very different. Despite some similarities, it is possible to see the changes that had occurred although the situation was still far from satisfactory; although what was to follow reported
in our Twenty-Second Report (November 2009) was much more heartening
for normalisation. In April 2009 we wrote in what was by then our Twenty-
First Report:

Loyalist paramilitary groups

Loyalist Volunteer Force (LVF)

2.31 The assessment we made of the LVF in our Twentieth Report was
essentially unchanged from the one we had been making for some
time. We said that it was a small organisation without any political
purpose. People historically linked to it were heavily involved in
serious crime, sometimes claiming the LVF's name if they thought
it advantageous to do so. The proceeds of these crimes were for

personal gain, not that of the organisation. The assessment we made in November 2008 still stands in all its essentials.

We recorded some considerable changes in Ulster Defence Association (UDA) in the same Twenty-First Report of April 2009.

2.32 In our Twentieth Report we distinguished as clearly as we could between the mainstream of the UDA and the South East Antrim faction. On the mainstream we said that the leadership wanted to make progress in the direction set out in its November 2007 statement but that progress was hampered by a structure which made it difficult to drive through change, the opposition of some members and by the factional split. Most elements in the leadership were seeking to downsize the organisation and to reduce the incidence of criminality on the part of members (with some success), and there had been a determination to avoid inter-community conflict. But some members were nevertheless engaged in serious criminal activity and although there had been a significant reduction in loyalist assaults most of those which had occurred were in our view undertaken by UDA members.

2.33 The UDA has remained divided between the mainstream and the South East Antrim faction. In the six months under review there were fewer acts of violence between the two factions than there had been in the recent past.

2.34 We believe that the leadership of the mainstream UDA still wants to make progress along the lines set out in the statement it issued in November 2007, and some within the leadership have been able to steer their followers a little further away from paramilitary activity. People have been encouraged to support the police and to rely on them to respond to crime. But the leadership is area based and not cohesive, there are some who remain opposed to significant change, and policy often seems to be more reactive than strategic. The result is that overall progress has been patchy.

2.35 We do see some signs that the challenge of the decommissioning of weapons is now being faced as it had not been hitherto and that there has been some movement towards the point where it might be possible to act. However, because of the state of opinion in the UDA, the uncentralised nature of the leadership and their search for a quid pro quo for decommissioning, it is somewhat difficult to judge what turn events may take and when. The fact remains however that the removal of the protections of the decommissioning legislation not later than February 2010 (and potentially by autumn 2009) makes the issue an urgent one for the UDA. By that time about two years will have passed since the November 2007 statement. If decommissioning has not occurred by then, this will inevitably cast serious doubt on the significance of the statement and on the support for change which has since been voiced.

2.36 So far as paramilitary activity is concerned, parts of the UDA continued to recruit, though we think some of this may have been on an ad hoc and relatively informal basis. But this raises the question of what is the purpose of bringing new recruits into an organisation, which is supposed to be going out of business. Some members, including at a senior level, have shown an interest in acquiring weapons. We think that this has been only on an individual basis and we do not believe that it is part of any overall leadership strategy for weapons procurement. In some instances people have been targeted for attack by members, generally because they are thought to be involved in drug-related or other crimes.

2.37 Notwithstanding the continued support for change and for the diversion of effort towards the development of the communities from which the UDA gains its support, some members of the UDA remained involved in other crimes. There were some Reports of members undertaking sectarian attacks, for example in the Tigers Bay area of Belfast and in the Ardoyne. There were a number of paramilitary-style assaults during the period under review attributable to the UDA. We believe that some of these instances are likely to have been known to senior UDA figures. There was information about the continuation of exiling, claimed to be in response to community concerns about local drug dealing. More generally, and despite the steps some in the leadership have taken, some members remained involved in a range of other crimes, including drug dealing, loan sharking, extortion and the supply of contraband cigarettes. Some of these criminals were themselves senior figures.

2.38 In the six months under review the leadership in general continued to demonstrate its adherence to the notion of change and in some cases made continued progress along that path. However the desire to move ahead is not supported by demonstrable short and long term strategic objectives, and there tends to be a focus on the priorities in individual areas rather than on those for the organisation as a whole. The lack of cohesion within the leadership and across the organisation, as well as the continued opposition of some members, continued to hamper progress. In the six months to the end of August 2009 (on which we will report in October) the decommissioning of weapons will become an increasingly urgent challenge for the leadership.

We then went on to deal with the UDA – South East Antrim Group, a splinter group, in the same April 2009 Report.

2.39 In our Twentieth Report, for the first time, we looked separately at the South East Antrim group of the UDA. We noted that like the mainstream it was pursuing community development and had said that its members should not engage in crime. We believed this had had some impact but serious crime was still as prevalent as amongst members of the mainstream UDA. We thought the leadership might recognise the inevitability of decommissioning but said that we would judge this by results.

2.40 We have no significant incidents to report for the six months under review but note that serious crime continues to be prevalent amongst some of its members. We note the establishment of the South and East Antrim Community Federation, which is directing its efforts towards community development and the enhancement of skills, particularly among former combatants, and we record the declared intention to phase out the membership of the South East Antrim UDA group over the next eighteen months to two years. This is a significant commitment, albeit on a longer timescale than would be desirable. We believe that the decommissioning of weapons is firmly on the group's radar screen, notwithstanding the feelings of some members about the recent dissident republican murders. We will continue to assess progress by results.

We then dealt with the Ulster Volunteer Force (UVF) and Red Hand Commando (RHC) in the same Twenty-First Report:

2.41 In our Twentieth Report we said that the leadership of the UVF continued to pursue its statement of May 2007 by, for example, downsizing the organisation and reducing the incidence of criminality on the part of members, though some members continued to be involved without leadership sanction. We thought that as an organisation the UVF was running itself down and was not involved in either preparatory or violent terrorist activity. We believed that some elements in the UVF might be moving to recognise that it must tackle the decommissioning of weapons but we saw no grounds for believing that there would be early steps actually to do so.

2.42 We believe that the strategy set out in the May 2007 statement remained in place and that the leadership continued to pursue it. The leadership is reasonably cohesive and we do not believe that there will be any major deviation from the strategy. The process of downsizing the organisation and reducing the level of criminality on the part of members continued in a worthwhile way. There was no engagement in either violent or preparatory terrorist activity. Some individuals sought to acquire weapons but we believe that this was on an ad hoc basis and without either the sanction or co-ordination of the leadership.

2.43 Sectarian attacks associated with UVF members, were at a low level, and there were a number of paramilitary-style assaults attributable to members. There were occasional indications of members targeting those they believed were engaged in crime, such as drug dealing, and in other forms of anti-social behaviour. Notwithstanding the efforts of the leadership, some members remain involved in a range of serious crimes. We believe that generally the proceeds of these crimes were for personal rather than organisational use.

2.44 Overall, the movement of the UVF towards an end point seems managed and cohesive and internal discipline looks fairly solid. The decommissioning of weapons remains the major outstanding issue. We believe that some in the leadership increasingly recognise that the UVF must tackle decommissioning, especially since the February 2010 (or possibly autumn 2009) deadline on the continuation of the decommissioning legislation which the Secretary of State has announced. It will soon be apparent whether it has become a deliverable option. (IMC Twenty-First Report April 2009)

This series of extracts from our Twenty-First Report illustrates a number of aspects of our assessments and our confidence in them that the High Court had commented upon. Besides the overlaps with the activities of another Commission (the International Independent Decommissioning Commission – IIDC) we describe the variety of confidence measures we applied 'believe' (paragraph 2.34), 'some signs that...' (paragraph 2.35), 'somewhat difficult to judge' (also paragraph 2.35), 'we think...' (paragraph 2.36), 'we thought...' (paragraph 2.41) as well as clear statements of what we held to be the facts of the matter. In a sense we were indicating in these paragraphs that while the IIDC was concerned with weaponry, we were concerned with decommissioning the organizations and their philosophy of violence.

In our Twenty-Second Report (November 2009) the situation was better still:

2.39 In its Report of September 2009 the Independent International Commission on Decommissioning (IICD) said that it had witnessed an event in which 'a quantity of weapons' belonging to all five UDA 'brigades' had been decommissioned.[6] It also reported that UDA representatives had said it was the first of a series of events in which they would decommission the remainder of the UDA's arms before the end of the IICD's mandate in February 2010. The IICD said it was in continuing contact with the UDA to arrange further decommissioning and that it had been told there was no difference of opinion within the leadership on the issue.

2.40 The decommissioning to date is an important indication of the intention of the joint leadership to deliver on a policy embracing the organisation as a whole, about which we have expressed some doubts in the past. The decommissioning is therefore welcome. The leadership also took steps to ensure that members did not react improperly in response to dissident republican violence, especially the three murders in March. We recognise too that in some areas (though by no means all) senior figures have taken steps to reduce the level of criminality amongst the membership and in some cases have made impressive and cross-community efforts to improve the situation ... the point we make ... about the variation from area to area is particularly marked. We urge the entire leadership to demonstrate this same strategic direction. Ensuring the acceptance by the membership of the completion of the decommissioning process as soon as possible is of course of great importance.

We went on to record:

2.46 The IICD reported in September 2009 that it had overseen two events in which 'some of the UDA South East Antrim group's weapons, ammunition, explosives and explosive devices were decommissioned'.[7] The IICD said that the group's representatives had committed to decommissioning the remainder before the end of its mandate in February 2010 and urged them to do so as soon as possible'. And further that:

2.50 ... significant event in the period under review was the decommissioning of UVF and RHC arms reported by the IICD on 4 September 2009.[8] The IICD reported in June 2009 that it had overseen the decommissioning of 'substantial quantities of firearms, ammunition, explosives and explosive devices' belonging to the UVF and RHC. It reported that the UVF had said that the material comprised all that was under the control of the two organisations. The IICD concluded that it had completed the decommissioning of UVF and RHC arms.

2.51 The IICD's Report marks a very significant and positive development. We note that the UVF leadership had prepared the ground for decommissioning with its members over a considerable period and had maintained internal discipline. We see the event as clear evidence of the organisational coherence and strategic direction to which we have referred in the past. We increasingly see a picture of an organisation on its way to going out of business as a paramilitary organisation, though that might not preclude the maintenance of some form of association for past members.

2.52 Through decommissioning the UVF has passed a very major landmark. It is the most significant indication of both its adherence to the strategy set out in its May 2007 statement and its capacity to deliver. There have continued to be indications of adherence in other respects to the 2007 strategy (though we believe that progress in some of these respects has been more marked in some parts of the organisation than in others). We believe that the leadership took steps to ensure that members did not react improperly in response to dissident republican violence, especially the three murders in March. The organisation has expelled members who have acted in a way unacceptable to the leadership. Senior members have continued to take steps to reduce criminality amongst the membership. We are aware of nothing to suggest that the organisation has engaged in preparatory or other terrorist activity, that it has organised or benefited from other forms of crime, or that there has been material recruitment.

There was some evidence of continuing criminality and violence; though by no means perfect or even complete much had been achieved by all the paramilitary leadership. There was no doubt that as we had reported these events were 'a significant landmark'.

Although decommissioning was primarily of concern to the IICD, our Twenty-Second Report of November 2009 included our assessment of the relevance to our Article 4 of these activities (see, e.g. Irish Times, 05.11.2009; Belfast Telegraph 05.11.2009; and 26.08.2009 'A Report that could open doors for loyalists' and 'Loyalist guns – the final deadline' and Newsletter 26.08.2009 'Orange Volunteers urged to end atrocities' and 'Breakaway loyalists in decommissioning move' and Sunday Life 09.08.2009 'UDA arsenal destroyed'). The IICD recorded the putting beyond use of weapons by the UVF and UDA, and we noted how this illustrated a commitment to their plans for the standing down of the organizations. A considerable journey by the paramilitaries had been undertaken and thus been described by us.

Conclusions

Our philosophy was defined by the initial thinking derived from each of our backgrounds and the rationale of our opening statement issued on 9 March 2004, publicizing how we would go about our work. The early identification of human rights as core principles was important. The process by which we refined each Report specifically allowed us to test our principles and analysis. The generalized method of exploring analytic techniques and recent commentary (e.g. Butler 2004, particularly chapter 2) offered us thinking and a methodology to avoid some of the areas that had been described as intelligence failure (see, e.g. George and Bruce 2008).

The High Court judgement was particularly helpful in that it reinforced our use of levels of confidence in our material and in the methods of analysis we were using as outlined in our Fifth Report. The process of collection, analysis, preparation, assessment and reporting as compare and contrast, similarities despite differences and differences despite similarities over our six-month reporting cycles was robust enough to survive challenges. This has built up an archive and chronology for use by all who are concerned or tasked with us to effect the transition to a 'peaceful society and stable and inclusive devolved government in Northern Ireland'.

The IMC Reports have been cited in analysis not just as news in themselves and by academics (e.g. Spencer 2008: 232), politicians (e.g. Powell 2008: 239–40, 274, 276, 278); media (e.g. Godson 2004: 769, 771; *Belfast Telegraph* 26 August 2009) and even the judiciary (cited in *The Guardian*, 19 June 2009: 2 in the pleadings of Susanne Breen against her disclosing her journalistic sources.)

The two governments' decision to give the role of preparing open intelligence Reports, a trend noted by Butler 2004 in his Recommendation 37, to an independent commission has, at least, changed the debate from one about political direction or spin of material in relation to alleged breaches of the ceasefire to one about the skill and rigour of our information gathering and the objectivity of our reporting.

Finally, this chapter could be considered a contribution to a debate about when, whether and how an Independent Monitoring Commission is still required (who should monitor the paramilitaries going out of business through democratic processes?). The current make up of the IMC could be seen to be normal for abnormal times and transition, but possibly inappropriate in a time of increasing stability and normality. The legislation set us the aim of 'promoting the transition to a peaceful society and stable and inclusive devolved Government in Northern Ireland'. This looks increasingly likely for some paramilitaries if not for some dissenters from the peace process. It could be argued that monitoring should eventually become another facet of the democratic process of normal government. Further, whether the devolution of justice and policing to the Northern Ireland Assembly might become an opportunity to change the monitoring system is a current question to be considered.

Notes

1. You can contact the IMC through our website: www.independentmonitoringcommission.org; by E-mail: imc@independentmonitoringcommission.org; by post at PO Box 709, Belfast BT2 8YB or PO Box 9592, Dublin 1; and by telephone at +44 (0)28 9072 6117 in Belfast and +353 1 4752 555 in Dublin.

2. The IMC was set up in shadow form in September 2003, formally established in January 2004. and submitted its first Report in April 2004. Since then it has submitted 22 Reports. We are only required to report on events that bear upon our period of existence. The work is incomplete at the time of writing.

3. I am grateful to my three colleagues as IMC Commissioners, Lord Alderdice, Joe Brosnan and Dick Kerr who, together with the Joint Secretaries Stephen Boys Smith and Michael Mellett, did the thinking that informs my account, as well as commented on and helped in the preparation of this chapter.

4. Article 5 for example deals with normalization of the roles of the British Army and PSNI – the closure or changes at certain sites and the curtailment of some activity.

5. The Inquiry by Lord Saville is into the events of Bloody Sunday. There are seven Public Inquiries both in Northern Ireland and in Ireland as a result of Judge Cory's Inquiry. They are currently collecting evidence.

6. Report of the Independent International Commission on Decommissioning to the Secretary of State for Northern Ireland and the Minister for Justice, Equality and Law Reform, 4 September 2009.

7. Report of the Independent International Commission on Decommissioning to the Secretary of State for Northern Ireland and the Minister for Justice, Equality and Law Reform, 4 September 2009.

8. Report of the Independent International Commission on Decommissioning to the Secretary of State for Northern Ireland and the Minister for Justice, Equality and Law Reform, 4 September 2009.

Chapter 14
Loyalism: Political Violence and Decommissioning

Neil Southern

This chapter explores two aspects of loyalism, namely, political violence and the decommissioning of paramilitary weapons. It argues that the loyalist perspective on the Northern Ireland conflict has not been paid suitable attention and as a consequence debate about loyalism has been restricted. It also argues that the impact and long-lasting effect of republican violence on the unionist community, and 'frontline' loyalist communities in particular, has not been fully appreciated and therefore some of the difficulties that loyalist paramilitary organizations have encountered during the transition from conflict to post-conflict society, have been improperly understood.

Certainly, the journey that loyalism has been on since the ceasefire of 1994, and the GFA of 1998, has not been unproblematic. We should be mindful that loyalism did not embrace the peace process on a unanimous basis; most notably with the fracture within the UVF, which led to the formation of the LVF in 1996. Loyalism also experienced serious problems in 2000 when a vicious feud was fought between the UVF and the UDA. In 2002 the UDA turned on itself with destructive results. Further, the story of 2005 was that of serious discontent as loyalist areas erupted in violence in different parts of the province. Yet, despite this, it needs to be acknowledged that loyalists have remained part of Northern Ireland's peacebuilding project although at times imperfectly (Bruce 2004).

Loyalist paramilitary leadership

All considered the leadership of loyalist paramilitary organizations has kept their rank and file in line. Indeed, this is not an insignificant point if we consider the distinct propensity loyalist groups had for violence and the fact that, because the Northern Ireland conflict was a protracted affair, many members were raised in areas where some degree of violence, or at least the threat of it, was a constant factor.

Transforming violent mentalities is a slow process and one that is easily frustrated by the regular reminders that Northern Ireland is far from being a post-sectarian society. Also, the political spokespeople of loyalism, few in number as they are, have not allowed themselves to be bullied into toeing a particular line by the mainstream unionist parties which were either openly anti-Agreement or at least acrimoniously divided on the issue.

Instead, loyalist politicians maintained a pro-Agreement position. They have maintained their independence and spoken on behalf of working-class Protestant communities who traditionally have had little by way of a political voice. But, notwithstanding the many depressing moments and dismal periods that have surrounded loyalism in the post-Agreement era, there are now signs that it has become more settled and confident about the new political dispensation and the acts of decommissioning by the UVF and the UDA tell us a lot about loyalism's progressive capacity.

However, conflict transformation within loyalism has been difficult: the process of change required much more than a simple civilianized makeover not least because militarism was engrained in its organizations. It should be borne in mind that loyalist organizations existed because they believed that they had an uncomplicated *reason* to exist and that the reason was two-fold, namely. constitutional and territorial. Constitutionally, the goal was to maintain Northern Ireland's membership of the United Kingdom and in so doing safeguard the sentimentally based Britishness of its pro-Union people (Southern 2007) while the territorial need was to defend Protestant areas against republican attack.

These two reasons constitute the strategic imperatives of loyalist organizations, which Bruce (1992, 1993) argues gave rise to a form of 'pro-state terrorism'. The attempt by the IRA and other republican groups to destroy the state by using physical force and by so doing deny one million Protestants their sense of national identity was by no means a trivial issue. Given the seriousness of the issues involved and the depth of mistrust caused by a bitter conflict, it was unlikely that loyalist organizations would vanish after the acceptance of the GFA. But if we are to gain some insight into why loyalist organizations simply have not disappeared in the post-settlement period, attention needs to be paid to the loyalist experience of the Northern Ireland conflict and the uneasy period that has followed.

Generally, this experience has a number of features, some of which pre-date the GFA, others not: a frustration born from a lack of working-class Protestant political representation as well as disconnectedness from mainstream unionist parties and politicians; mistrust of the British government; concern about the durability of the GFA itself (a reasonable concern given that the actions of dissident republican groups confirm that political violence did not end with the signing of the GFA); most importantly, the serious physical and emotional damage caused by republican violence and the question of the lasting commitment of republicans to democracy (ruling out a return to violence in similar fashion to the period 1996–97 when the Provisional IRA decided to call off its ceasefire).

We should be mindful that it was not until 2005, some eleven and seven years after the ceasefire and GFA respectively, that the IRA formerly declared an end to its armed campaign but still stating: '(W)e reiterate our view that the armed struggle was entirely legitimate' (IRA statement 28 July 2005). So, if we are to gain an understanding of loyalism both during the conflict and afterwards, attention needs to be paid to the impactive nature of republican violence and the lack of certainty about the true intentions of the IRA after the GFA, because, these factors have played their part in preventing an untroubled winding down of loyalist paramilitary groups and a speedy dismantling of their organizational scaffolding. Paying attention to republican violence also enables us to create a framework within which loyalist violence can be critically explored and in this exploration we are encouraged to consider the relationship between groups' attitudes towards their own violence and the need for post-conflict reconciliation.

Political violence, terrorism and its impact

During the Troubles political violence took extreme and less extreme forms. Most dangerous was the frequent occurrence of deadly shootings and bombings, while, although harmful to inter-communal relations, street level violence associated with stone throwing, petrol bombing and rioting in general, was less severe. It was the lethality of shootings and bombings and their often indiscriminate nature that generated a real sense of terror.

The people of Northern Ireland were accustomed to the effects of terrorism long before 11 September 2001 and the increased media and scholarly attention now paid to the phenomenon. Commentators on political terrorism tell us that attacks are often characterized by indiscriminateness, lack of predictability and sheer ruthlessness (Wilkinson 1974) and that success to a terrorist is not necessarily measured through the military objectives organizations set themselves but through such psychological objectives as producing anxiety and insecurity on as large a scale as possible (Horgan 2005).

Thus, the killing of a single Protestant or Catholic in a shooting incident was capable of sending shockwaves throughout their respective local communities and farther afield. However, bombings also aroused severe levels of anxiety. By way of example, on 21 July 1972 the IRA planted twenty-six bombs in Belfast, which killed nine people, to be followed ten days later with three bombs in the town of Claudy, which killed another nine people. Terroristic attacks of this kind created a severe feeling of vulnerability.

Unfortunately, by the standards of today's terrorism, the deaths of 18 people in Belfast and Claudy might not seem that high but if Martha Crenshaw (2000: 406) is correct to argue that the 'purpose of terrorism is to intimidate a watching popular audience by harming only a few' these bombings can then be seen as a powerful tool for causing widespread fear as well as damaging public confidence in the state's ability to tackle the threat.

For the unionist community there were other bombings that had a shattering impact: the IRA's bombing of the La Mon hotel in 1978 which left 12 Protestants dead and the bomb that exploded in Enniskillen in 1987 when 11 Protestants were killed. Given that the IRA has always claimed that it does not target on a sectarian basis, there were two aspects of these bombings that were particularly unnerving to the Protestant community (and loyalist paramilitaries) and which rendered a non-sectarian interpretation of them very difficult.

First, the La Mon bombing took place in an area that was regarded as Protestant and thus there was the strong likelihood that those present in the hotel that evening would have been members of the Protestant community. Second, the Enniskillen bomb exploded at a *time* and at a *location* during which it was extremely likely that only Protestants would be in the vicinity.

In the light of this we are encouraged to consider what Alex Schmid (2005: 139) says about the nature of terrorist targeting:

> The immediate victims serve primarily as message generators. The specific identity of the individual victims are often immaterial to the perpetrators since the effect on third parties is what matters. In this sense a terrorist murder is often de-individuated.

It is important to point out that in an ethnic conflict situation the idea forwarded by Schmid that 'terrorist murder is often de-individuated', does not mean that murders are de-ethnicized.

Given the rules of territoriality, which determined the designation of areas in Northern Ireland as 'Protestant' or 'Catholic' (and still do), there is little randomness about the place chosen to plant a bomb (or in the case of Enniskillen, its moment of detonation). Hence, while terrorist attacks like the ones mentioned above can be understood to be random in the sense that the age and gender of potential victims is unknown, they were not ethnically indiscriminate.

Perhaps the event that most hardened loyalist attitudes in particular and confirmed their fears that the IRA had a sectarian capacity was the bombing of the Four Step Inn on the Protestant Shankill Road in September 1971. As a result of this attack two Protestants were killed and many more injured in what is regarded as the heartland of the loyalist community.

Regarding this bombing Peter Taylor (1999: 87) writes that it 'introduced a new and bloody dimension that was to have dreadful repercussions'. He adds that it was 'seen as nakedly sectarian, and Belfast had never witnessed anything like it before'. This attack provoked a loyalist response and it came shortly afterwards in the form of the UVF's bombing of McGurk's Bar which resulted in the death of fifteen Catholics. Before the end of 1971, the IRA again bombed the Shankill Road this time deciding to place a bomb outside a furniture shop which claimed the lives of four people including two children – an infant in a pram and a child aged two.

In 1975 and amidst a cycle of 'tit for tat' murders, the IRA struck again in the Shankill when it planted bombs at another two pubs, which caused the deaths of ten Protestants. Further, the charge of sectarianism was not so easily countered against the lethal backdrop of the IRA's murdering of five Protestants at Tullyvallen Orange Hall in 1975 and ten Protestant workmen at Kingsmill in 1976. Accordingly, Richard English (2003: 173) states that 'the mid-seventies undoubtedly did witness IRA immersion in some grubby sectarian killings (as, off the record, republicans will themselves concede).'

An admission of sectarian motivation is, of course, damaging to republicans in that it spoils their narrative and tarnishes the pure image of an 'armed struggle' waged solely against military targets. The deaths of Protestant civilians as a consequence of a bomb explosion raised questions that were sufficiently difficult for the IRA to answer, but assassination-like shootings of the kind mentioned above created even greater problems and the answers that republicans offered were simply unpersuasive to unionists.

In this vein Kirk Simpson (2008: 467) comments: 'for unionists, the PIRA's claim to have waged a non-sectarian "liberation struggle" in Northern Ireland was rendered absurd by its attacks on civilians with no connections to the state security forces'. Certainly Bruce (1992b) argues convincingly that during the conflict the IRA and other republican groups were motivated by sectarian drives and simply concludes that 'loyalists and republicans are equally sectarian' (Bruce 1997: 57).

Attacks of the kind mentioned above allowed loyalists to present the argument that the Protestant community was vulnerable and in need of defending because of a security policy that was ineffective in tackling terrorism. For sure, the brief disarming of the Royal Ulster Constabulary and the disbandment of the Ulster Special Constabulary in 1970 following the recommendations of the Hunt Report of 1969 (Ryder 2004) did not generate unionist confidence. Indeed, the birth of the UDA in 1971 was a direct consequence of the amalgamation of a number of local defence associations which felt that the protection of Protestant areas could not be entrusted to the forces of the state.

Loyalists have sought to explain their violence as being retaliatory, or if in appearance proactive, was so within the overall context of communal self-defence. Kathleen Cavanaugh (1997: 40) says: 'loyalist violence is most affected by republican violence and most likely to escalate when loyalists feel "threatened"'. She goes on to describe loyalist targeting in this way:

> Among the loyalist community as a whole the perception is that Catholics living in strongly republican enclaves give succor to republican

paramilitants and are, therefore, culpable for their acts. Blankets of legitimacy and justification are then laid which, in the name of security, allow even the most arbitrary of killings to be justified. (Cavanaugh 1997: 45)

Cavanaugh argues that the prevalence of a sense of abandonment and feeling of physical insecurity in loyalist communities created space for paramilitary groups to step in and perform the role of community protector. However, a shift in loyalist strategy occurred around 1990 and with lethal consequences. This strategic shift manifested itself in an intensification of Protestant paramilitary violence. Moreover, loyalists believe that the escalation in their violence was a contributing factor in the IRA declaring its ceasefire and moving Sinn Féin in the direction of political negotiation. From 1990 loyalist violence became more aggressive with a marked increase in the targeting of members of the IRA and Sinn Féin.

When loyalist violence was raised during interview, a senior loyalist discussed the shift in loyalist strategy accordingly:

that reactionary response never really changed until 1990 when the UFF worked out a strategy with other loyalist organisations and I call it "they loosed the dogs of war" and for the first time they created more killings than the IRA...they [nationalist community] condemned the IRA and they condemned Sinn Féin because they blamed them for bringing the UFF into their estates...it was a thought out strategy and the strategy was then implemented and executed and that strategy brought the IRA to the table. (Senior UDA loyalist, 23 November, 2009)

Although this period witnessed the deadliness of Protestant paramilitary proactivity, loyalists' actions remained ideologically driven by the conservative goal of pro-state terrorism, which is the maintenance of the constitutional status quo. The comment also encourages us to consider the rational capacity of loyalists in their use of extreme violence. The military objective was to wage war in a manner that disrupted the IRA and its wider community by increasing the costs associated with republican violence.

In a sense, this alteration in loyalist strategy made more severe a military front that the IRA was less equipped for tackling. The IRA had felt that along with a persuasive ideology that created hardline communities supportive of the republican cause, it had the manpower and weaponry to sustain the execution of a long war against the British state and its armed forces. However, loyalists set out to upset the 'comfortable' position that it considered the republican movement to be in and to compensate for what it believed to be the ineffectiveness of the state's security policy in dealing with the type of guerrilla warfare, urban and rural, practised by the IRA.

Although this upsurge in loyalist violence had, as the grim fatalities of this period testify, a brutal sectarian dimension (and Peter Taylor's *Loyalists* makes clear that loyalists do not deny this) the political side of their reasoning somewhat contests the stereotypical image of the loyalist as a crude, unsophisticated bigot, who is devoid of political intelligence.

In his historical analysis of the IRA, English (2003: 160) accepts that 'while specific acts of vengeful retaliations against Catholics were a part of the loyalist story, it would be misleading to suggest that loyalism was (or is) purely responsive or reactive to IRA actions'. But, while English is correct to emphasize the cycle of reprisal violence that caught hold in the 1970s and remained a feature of the conflict, this should not blind us to the devastation caused by republicans' regular use of extreme violence, especially in the form of bombings, and loyalists' reaction to it.

Indeed, Peter Taylor's *Loyalists* (1999) provides us with a detailed and informative account of the self-understandings of Protestant paramilitaries and how they conceived of their violence as being principally defensive. Taylor captures the uncoordinated nature of loyalism in the years 1969–71 as the IRA campaign of violence gathered injurious momentum, and gives us a sense of its strategic limitations, which did not extend much beyond providing protection for Protestant areas.

Yet there are grounds for considering that loyalists have been truthful about the sectarian dimension to their violence and are less reluctant than republicans to acknowledge and discuss it. Peter Taylor (1999) does not have to probe too deeply before being met with a response from his interviewees that recognized the sectarian nature of much loyalist targeting. Loyalist respondents admitted that Catholics would have been targeted and killed because it was believed that they belonged to a community that harboured IRA volunteers whose actions were directly responsible for the deaths of Protestants (both civilians as well as members of the local security forces).

During one of a number of frank interviews, John White of the Ulster Freedom Fighters discussed the loyalist strategy as follows:

> It was felt that the IRA gained very popular support within their communities and it was seen as a strategy that pressure could be put on the IRA by their communities then that would have an effect in that they would consider desisting from attacks on loyalist communities. (BBC documentary *Loyalists*, 1999)

For Catholics, reasoning of this kind was bereft of morality and merely functioned to conceal the sectarian hatred of the 'loyalist death squads'. But for loyalists, Protestant civilians being murdered, or the killing of an off duty, possibly unarmed, RUC or member of the Ulster Defence Regiment man (or woman) – predominately a member of the Protestant community – while at his home with his wife and children was equally as repugnant and this point does not go unexplored by Taylor in his BBC documentary *Provos* (1997). White's sense of military logic, which he anchors in the idea of communal self-defence, found violent and gruesome expression on Belfast's streets and his comment throws into sharp relief the brutal nature of the Troubles that all paramilitary groups were, in one way or another, responsible for.

In bringing this section to a close it is worth making a couple of points. First, there is substance to the claim by loyalists that their violence was reactionary, and that in the absence of a republican campaign of violence loyalist violence would cease. Stated bluntly, this is why there is peace in Northern Ireland today.

With the exception of a small number of dissidents, republicans have moved away from violence and as a consequence loyalists have done the same. But republican violence has seared loyalists emotionally and the consequences of this can be detected in the guarded behaviour of Protestant paramilitaries post-Agreement. Loyalist energies had no outlet in mainstream unionist politics. While the PUP and UDP were an important part of the negotiations leading up to the GFA (Mitchell 1999) the UDP failed to gain any seats in the new assembly while the PUP's initial two seat success later was reduced to one.

The electoral success of Sinn Féin allowed the party to argue that politics was replacing violence for the republican community and that the heart of government was its destination but at the same time loyalism was experiencing political marginalization and a unionist mainstream that was largely unsympathetic to its needs. Thus, for loyalists, high level political leadership and direction was missing, while for republicans it was present in rapidly increasing amounts.

This goes some way in explaining the differences in post-settlement confidence between republicans and loyalists; one in the centre of politics and with a powerful voice which is used on behalf of its community and the other marginalized and almost inaudible. However, secondly, we might say that a question can be asked: what is the importance of being truthful about the past in a way that loyalists have been?

In deeply divided societies where ethnic conflict has raged, the post-conflict healing process is not the same as in cases of interstate conflict. In ethnic conflict zones populations who live in close proximity and whose enmity is historical must find new and less destructive ways of relating to each other while still remaining spatially close.

At a minimum, these new ways will reflect an attitude of greater political tolerance. But political tolerance is not the same as trust (Garcia-Rivero *et al.* 2002). Trust underpins the quality of all human relationships whether interpersonal, inter-community or between nations (Kelman 2005). While reconciliation has no absolute measure and that it can take high and low forms (Ross 2004) it is difficult to conceive of meaningful reconciliatory advances being made without trust.

In a divided society the establishment of trust requires honesty and it is in this context that the truthfulness of loyalist paramilitaries about the sectarian underpinnings of some of their attacks at least amounts to openness about addressing their violence. Given Northern Ireland's need for reconciliation and not only conflict resolution, it is regrettable that the GFA did not provide a formal context for dealing with the past and grant ex-combatants the opportunity to be honest about paramilitary violence.

Decommissioning

In their discussion of decommissioning in Northern Ireland, Kirsten Schulze and M.L.R Smith (2000) come to the conclusion that, although there were historical and ideological influences at work, basically it was not in the tactical interests of paramilitary groups to decommission their weapons. Holding out as long as possible before delivering on an issue that is of major symbolic importance is a sensible way to approach maximizing group gains, even though such actions might play a part in fostering inter-communal mistrust and undermining confidence in the Agreement itself.

Dealing with the issue proved difficult at the outset and led to the compromise of parallel decommissioning as a means of securing the survival of the multiparty talks regardless of the displeasure this caused unionists and the British government (McInnes 2000). That decommissioning was allowed to plague the post-Agreement period is to be understood in terms of the weakness of the GFA not to tie down parties with links to paramilitary organizations to deliver on the issue.

Instead the GFA stated its expectation that parties would use what influence they had to encourage armed groups to decommission their weapons within two years of the Agreement being accepted in Northern Ireland and the Republic of Ireland. IRA decommissioning took until 2005 to be achieved and from 1998 the political fortunes of Sinn Féin increased at the expense of nationalism's more moderate voice, the Social Democratic and Labour Party (SDLP).

However, regarding IRA decommissioning, senior loyalists in the UDA and UVF seem somewhat sceptical about the idea that it is total (Southern 2008) and this general scepticism was conveyed in similar terms more recently: 'they've given in all the guns that they're going to give and that's different from giving all the guns in' (interview with senior loyalist, UDA, 24 November 2009). Contrary to the IICD Report of 26 September 2005 which stated that the Commission was satisfied that 'the arms decommissioned represent the totality of the IRA's arsenal', when the author interviewed senior loyalists in 2006 in relation to preparing a research paper for a conference on the future of loyalism, it was believed that the IRA had not decommissioned *all* its weapons not least because at that point all loyalist organizations – the most dangerous source of threat to republicans – remained fully armed.

Rather, for loyalists, a mature reading of IRA decommissioning was one that recognized that the organization would not leave its community defenceless, as it had once been accused of doing during the inter-communal violence, which shook Belfast in 1969. The idea that the IRA has not decommissioned its complete arsenal does not seem to cause loyalists consternation. The fact that loyalists are unruffled by this implies that there is a need for a realistic approach to decommissioning which ultimately grounds the importance of the event in its symbolism rather than the amount of weaponry made no longer physically serviceable to the ends of political violence.

Indeed, notwithstanding the increase in the violence of republican dissident groups, loyalists have remained calm. The argument against loyalist decommissioning, in part, was connected to the threat posed by dissident groups but this argument has waned in importance in the last few years. Certainly the murders of the two soldiers at Massereene army base in March 2009 followed soon afterwards by the murder of a police officer in Lurgan, was a testing time for loyalists but Martin McGuiness' strong condemnation of the killings was a significant demonstration of the commitment of mainstream republicanism to non-violence.

In the wake of the murders a similar token of commitment to non-violence was made by UDA leader, Jackie MacDonald (2009), who confirmed that it was now the sole job of the police to deal with republican terrorists: 'it's up to the police alone to deal with them... people on the loyalist side are determined not to fall into any more traps. That's what groups like the Continuity IRA and Real IRA want us to do... Loyalism has matured an awful lot in recent years.'

The reference to loyalism's maturation is preceded by an acknowledgement that it is a matter for the legal forces of the state to address, but importantly, this presupposes that the state is capable of dealing effectively with republican terrorism and this was made known during interview:

> People are back to looking to the early 70s, whenever the police and army said they could deal with this [republican terrorism] and they didn't. So as long as the police continue to deal with it, Irish nationalist and Irish republicans continue to marginalize and isolate them I think society as a whole will be able to deal with these people. (interview with senior loyalist, UDA, 24 November, 2009)

It is interesting that the political players now include Irish nationalists and republicans whose role is undoubtedly essential to ensuring that the new form of republican terrorism is given no communal protection, no hiding place, or afforded ideological legitimacy. But while loyalists have responded in a coolheaded manner about the murders of the soldiers and policeman, an attack by dissidents on the loyalist community might constitute a greater test. This was indicated by Dawn Purvis of the PUP who said:

> It is very difficult because obviously there are those within the organisa-tion [UVF] chomping at the bit because they regard themselves as pro-state paramilitaries. Now if there was an attack on the loyalist community from these dissidents, I wouldn't like to think where we'd go but I'd hope that we would be much further down the road that loyalists wouldn't want to retaliate in any way because then you'd see then the spiral of tit for tat. (Interview with Dawn Purvis, 9 November 2009)

Clearly, Northern Ireland's more peaceful environment should not be taken for granted and neither should it go unrecognized that this has been contributed to in no small part by loyalists. During the interviews the author had with senior UDA and UVF figures in 2006, there was little sign of progress on the decommissioning front. However, in May 2007, a major step was taken on the way to consolidating the peace process in Northern Ireland when the UVF and RHC announced that they were transmuting from military to civilian organizations.

The statement, which represented the position of both groups, claimed that this organizational change was possible because they were confident in two essential respects: 'that the mainstream republican offensive has ended' and 'that the constitutional question has now been firmly settled' (UVF Statement, 3 May 2007). Nine years after the GFA, the UVF and RHC decided that the causal factors in their use of political violence had even-tually receded (but concern was expressed over the activity of republican dissident groups).

Yet two years would pass before the IICD would be able to confirm to both governments that completion of UVF and RHC weaponry had been achieved and that the UDA was expected to follow suit (IICD 2009). The steps taken by the UVF/RHC to decommission their weaponry and to the satisfaction of the IICD, is an encouragement to the UDA. The UVF/ RHC's statement did not mention the internal context of Protestant paramilitiarism which nine years ago endured a feud that resulted in UVF and UDA fatalities.

This was an important indication that tension levels between the organi-zations had decreased significantly since the time of loyalism's internecine battles in 2000, when David McKittrick (2001) commented that the feud 'itself is an argument against loyalist decommissioning, since every-one knows feuding might recur. In that event, neither group wants to be unarmed and defenceless.' On this theme Dawn Purvis said:

> I think that UVF and Red Hand decommissioning makes it easier for ... the UDA, because if you look at the history of the UVF and UDA there is

rivalry there and there has been bloody feuding between those organisations, so I think one organisation giving up its weaponry frees up the other one. (interview with Dawn Purvis, 9 November 2009)

The decision by the UVF to decommission was, as Purvis suggests, helpful in paving the way for the UDA to follow suit. What is important is that there is agreement between both organizations on the decommissioning issues. It would not be in the overall interest of loyalism for disagreement to exist on such a vital topic. Yet because of organizational differences both groups could not address the topic in the same way. As a centrally controlled organization the UVF was in a less complicated position than the UDA. Ultimately, fewer people would have taken the final decision within the UVF.

In contrast, the UDA has six brigade areas, which although linked by the Inner Council, nonetheless enjoy a considerable degree of autonomy. But similar to the point made about the need for agreement between the loyalist organizations, the different brigade areas of the UDA need to agree also. If one area is unsupportive of decommissioning or in need of convincing that the time is right, then this is likely to slow matters down. The internal feud fought between Johnny Adair's 'C' Company in the lower Shankill and the rest of the UDA in 2002, the killing of the former UDA leader in East Belfast, Jim Gray, in 2005, and the problems which surrounded the Westland estate area in North Belfast in 2006 and which led to leading UDA men in the area fleeing, illustrate the need for inter-brigade unity.

A few comments are called for with regards to the idea of *total* and *complete* decommissioning, whether republican or loyalist. For total and complete decommissioning to mean what is implied by those words, there needs to be a strong and trustful relationship between an organization's leadership and local command level. Even for centrally controlled organizations like the IRA and UVF it is unlikely that the leadership will have a list, which reflects the entirety of its organization's weaponry. Factors of *space* and *time* have a part to play in this.

It is common practice for highly armed terrorist groups who have a broad territorial reach, to distribute weapons widely within the organization. The obvious benefit of this is that a single successful detection by the security forces will not strip the organization of its military capability. Additionally, during the conflict, local commanders wanted to know that their areas were sufficiently protected should an attack take place by a counter organization or, specifically in the urban borderlands of Belfast, if inter-communal street level violence escalated to the point that guns were considered necessary to defend the physical integrity of an area.

Weapons were also needed for aggressive strikes. In terms of the *time* factor: weaponry is procured over many years and large as well as small quantities gradually increase the size of an organization's arsenal. But overtime the leadership's knowledge may well lose a degree of exactness about the number of weapons its organization holds, particularly if there have been changes in leadership.

Hence, it is not unreasonable to suggest that the main paramilitary organizations do not have a single person with a precisely detailed list of weaponry acquired over the years. Instead, to compile a list of this kind – an inventory of weaponry – it is likely that many people would have to be consulted outside of the leadership.

If we accept that some individuals might not be enamoured with the idea of total decommissioning, then there can be no guarantee that what appears on locally drawn up lists of weaponry is an absolute reflection on what is actually held thus skewing overall figures regarding what the organization possesses in total. While the leadership can guarantee a response from subordinate levels of command, it cannot ensure that the whole story, as it were, is being told. This point is relevant to all paramilitary groups and on both sides of the sectarian divide.

Further, local commanders in both republican and loyalist groups may want to retain some weapons for personal protection. They may have concerns about their safety in relation to their own communities particularly regarding the issue of how they have 'policed' them over the years. As paramilitary structures wind down the high levels of protection afforded by virtue of membership winds down also. During the conflict and in the post-Agreement period, antisocial behaviour was often met with a firm response from paramilitary groups. For those deemed by paramilitaries to have been persistent in their antisocial behaviour, rebuke did not always come in strong verbal form and punishment beatings were at times administered.

Of course, paramilitaries across the community divide have been persuaded to substitute the philosophy and methodology of restorative justice for the harshness of the retributive kind. Yet, a desire for revenge is a lurking menace for paramilitary commanders and we should not ignore its discomforting effects and the implications this might have for total decommissioning. These points are important to make because, although less noticeable, they nevertheless increase our awareness of some of the disquieting internal problems that organizations may encounter when efforts are made to decommission weapons.

Finally, at a symbolic level, loyalist decommissioning can be seen to be less difficult than it was for republicans. Protestant paramilitaries can claim that their strategic objective has been achieved and that after three decades of violence Northern Ireland remains an integral part of the United Kingdom. So decommissioning does not smack of surrender. Yet, although decommissioning may be less ideologically contentious to loyalists than republicans, it has taken the UVF eleven years to do so and as we near the end of 2009 it looks likely that a major move will have taken place within the UDA by 2010.

That the process of loyalist decommissioning has been delayed is in part due to the long drawn out process of IRA decommissioning and the length of time it has taken loyalists to become truly confident in the GFA. Loyalists needed to be sure that the Agreement was robust enough to last and that there would be no drifting away from its core principle regarding constitutional change. Finally, loyalists also needed to know that the IRA was committed to democracy and this required observing republican actions over a period of time. After all, Northern Ireland is not short on examples of failed experiments in conflict resolution.

Conclusions

When loyalists decided to step up their militant campaign in the early 1990s it indicated that personnel and weaponry were not in short supply. More importantly, the dramatic increase in loyalist violence also told us that the ideology, which justified the use of violence, was not showing signs that it was running out of steam. Of course, neither was it the case that republican volunteers were questioning the legitimacy of republican violence.

Political violence may be a nasty and destructive phenomenon (terrorism most certainly is) but it is nonetheless a powerful indicator of ideological conviction, which is foolish to ignore. So when the CLMC decided to call its ceasefire in 1994 it was not done from a position of ideological debilitation or operational weakness. Loyalists, however, were willing to respond to the opportunity for peace offered by the IRA's ceasefire in 1994.

Although they believed that their campaign of violence had greater legitimacy because it was conceived of as reactionary and contingent on the behaviour of republicans, loyalists did not feel that there was moral justification for a continuation of their violence. Yet, as we have seen, organizations that have been a response to violent conditions do not suddenly cease to exist once a political agreement has been reached. Protestant paramilitary organizations are powerful networks, which have been around for decades.

Uncertainty about the post-settlement situation *vis-à-vis* republican intentions did not help loyalists in their process of de-militarization. Arguably, the IRA only made clear its commitment to peace in it statement of 2005 which was followed by an act of decommissioning that satisfied the IIDC. That the IRA's statement and act of decommissioning came after a period when the republican movement had been put under immense pressure from the British and Irish governments (and the US administration), because of the Northern Bank robbery and the murder of Robert McCartney, caused loyalists to remain watchful and cautious.

However, with UVF/RHC decommissioning in 2009 (accompanied with a smaller act by the UDA) and the expectation that the UDA will have completed decommissioning in 2010, we are witnessing far-reaching changes within loyalism. Of course, for loyalists, that these changes be permanent is conditional upon the constitutional position of Northern Ireland being respected in line with the GFA and, not insignificantly, the absence of the kind of violent threat that loyalists might consider the security forces ineffective at dealing with.

Chapter 15
The Contemporary Politics of the Ulster Defence Association: In Discussion with Jackie McDonald

Graham Spencer

The following chapter is based on an interview conducted in late 2009, with Jackie McDonald, the UDA leader for south Belfast. The purpose of the interview was to try and assess the process of transition going on within the UDA at that time and to consider purpose and conviction towards non-violent change.

The UDA consists of six areas of strength and organization (north Antrim/ Londonderry, south east Antrim, north Belfast, south Belfast, east Belfast and west Belfast) and each area has historically tended to operate independently from the others. The end of conflict has meant that managing change requires effort to shift this independence in the direction of a more consensual way of thinking within the organization and this has created problems.

As the 'glue' and certainties of conflict have given way to a more fragile and uncertain approach to the prevention of conflict and its associated influences, attempts to manage transition have been inconsistent, with criminality and resistance higher in some areas than others. This poses significant internal problems of trust and confidence among leaders with regard to collectively transforming the UDA from a paramilitary organization to a community-development organization. This interview provides an insight into some of the current tensions and concerns for the UDA in the new climate of Northern Ireland and indicates the potential difficulties, which lay ahead as the need for reactive violence and paramilitarism increasingly lacks credibility (although this could change if dissident republicans hinder steps to transition and initiate a successful murder campaign).

Making that argument to volunteers and holding support for transition is especially problematic if the organization does not move as a unified whole, thus making the need for leadership consensus and commitment especially important. It remains to be seen how the UDA will continue to (re)construct itself as the roots of the peace process grow longer. But what is quite

clear is that transformation will continue to be difficult and that its successful implementation will only take hold if collective rather than individual
approaches to problems are taken.

In discussion with Jackie McDonald

GS: It's clearly been a pretty slow process of transformation for the UDA.
Are people still distrustful?

JM: Very much so, especially because of the dissidents. The paramilitaries are trying to move on but we need the PSNI [Police Service of
Northern Ireland] to succeed. People still come to the paramilitaries
for some sort of justice, should it be a family dispute, or because someone has had something stolen or because somebody has been beaten
up in the street. The paramilitaries are now telling people they must
go to the PSNI, but the PSNI are doing nothing about it because they
haven't got the resources. I've sat and talked to a policing board and
argued we should be lobbying for more resources for the PSNI to deal
with the problems that we have in our communities and they say
you'll not get it because per head of population, there's the equivalent
number of police officers in Belfast as they would be in Liverpool or
Manchester or Glasgow, even though those places are not coming out
of conflict. It is precisely because we are coming out of conflict that
we need more police officers on the ground. People have to have confidence in the PSNI, so they have to get results. It is going to be ridiculous if the whole peace process falls apart because the PSNI hasn't got
the resources to deal with the problems

GS: There have been press Reports that money has been asked for in
exchange for decommissioning. Is there any basis to this story?

JM: It's nothing to do with money for guns. The people in the organization wouldn't hear tell of that, it would be a non-starter. The only
way we can address the lack of community resources available, and
the same could be said for republicans, is by working with politicians.
Peter Robinson couldn't walk into a house in Sandy Row and deal
with somebody's problems, but I could. If it is east Belfast, Frankie
Gallagher could walk into any house. If somebody is suffering from
depression, or having a drink problem, or whatever the problem might
be, Frankie could walk in, sit and have a conversation with them and
try to help them out. But Peter Robinson couldn't do it, because politicians are working on a different level to us. We can go to places where
other people can't go. But we also know that only by getting rid of
the guns can we expect to be involved with politicians. We have to
get away from the idea of feeling protected with guns. If we are to
become the same as everybody else and if we want to be totally integrated with the community, there's no place for guns. A lot of people

in the communities are still talking about when I was quoted as saying couple of years ago that they were the people's guns. But I never said they were the people's guns, what I said was that people will tell you they're the people's guns and they would say 'You can't give your guns up, we'll be murdered in our beds'. I have heard those exact same words, 'We're going to be murdered in our beds'. Now that the loyalists have started decommissioning, there are people in Sandy Row saying those things again.

GS: When people see things on television like dissidents setting up a road block in Armagh does that create anxiety?

JM: The loyalist paramilitaries are trying to move on and they see this happening, and what obviously makes it worse is the fact that the police were on the scene and couldn't do anything about it, so they are seen as the inferior force. Part of the problem is that if there had been three land rovers of fully equipped police and they had shot dead three dissidents, they could be seen as making martyrs out of the dissidents. So is it better that you don't see it and the police tiptoe away and if that is the case where is the normality? If you don't do anything, then it will swell the ranks of the dissidents because it will seem to them that they can do whatever they like. It is a complex situation and there has to be a balance struck there somewhere.

GS: Is something like that likely to scupper your transition?

JM: Our people know that to be totally integrated with the community, with the politicians and with the government, there can't be any weapons as part of the equation. But when people are blatantly walking round with weapons and rocket launchers and being able to shoot soldiers and police and there is talk about weaponry being purchased, then this creates real problems for transition. There are more and more loyalists saying how can you give up guns when this is happening? It's all very well saying to the loyalist paramilitaries, you must do this or that, but other agencies and official bodies have to deal with the problems too.

GS: When Martin McGuinness called dissidents 'traitors', did that help at all?

JM: It did, but people still believe that the IRA is controlling the dissidents, because it seemed there were only so many bombs going off. There was only a certain level of violence and small rather than large bombs which didn't do a whole lot of damage. It was as if it was more a letting off some steam, but not going too far. That was the perception when they killed the two soldiers and the policeman. Then, people came to the paramilitaries and said we have to retaliate and kill somebody. But my response along with others was who are you going to kill? It's not the pan nationalist front anymore, so who are you going to kill? You're only going to alienate the nationalist community, who agree with the loyalist community and the unionist community that we need to move forward with. Dissident republicans really need loyalism to retaliate to give them the oxygen to carry on. But people still think that if you just leave it to the security forces to deal with dissidents, they will think they can do what they like and get away with it.

GS: Regarding the six areas of the UDA would you say that for the leader of each area their main commitment is to that area or to the organization?

JM: The violence bonded everybody together, so it was either kill or be killed, defend or attack and even ten years ago that was the basic principle. So everybody was connected the same way, everybody was under threat, everybody was retaliating, or everybody was responding. Since the violence has abated, individual characters and individual area characteristics are coming more to the fore and you can see the differences in opinion. As is well known, south east Antrim went their own way. Criminal elements are a real problem and confronting those who are and have been involved like Adair and Gray is important if we are to stop their influence. In the case of south east Antrim they didn't want to get involved or be part of that decision to change, so they separated from the rest of the areas and have not come back. With Londonderry, because it's close to the border and further away from the heart of north, east, south and west Belfast there are different opinions and concerns to deal with. These different pressures exist in all the areas and we have to respond differently to those pressures because the glue of violence is not there any more

GS: How do you diffuse tensions now? What is the chain of communication used to try to sort that out?

JM: There are all sorts of groups now working together and there are interface groups who are funded by the government also working together. Leading members of Sinn Féin will now sit with leading members from the loyalist community and they would try to pre-empt what might happen, because there is plenty of experience from what's happened in the past. But because of the INLA [Irish National Liberation Army] maybe, or because of dissidents playing the republican card, it isolates Sinn Féin a bit. If Sinn Féin are seen to work with the loyalists and the dissidents are encouraging kids to throw golf balls and petrol bombs or whatever, then it puts Sinn Féin in a very precarious position. If they are seen to allow a loyalist parade down a place where people don't want it any more, dissidents can try and use that to inflame the situation.

GS: Do loyalist people object to you working with Sinn Féin?

JM: We're trying to move on here, and people are asking me how I can talk to republicans who have murdered and bombed and shot people. But my response is that we have to move on. Many people want to forget about that and just leapfrog into the past, the glorious revolution and the uprising of 1916 and 1922 and partition and ignore how both sides contributed to conflict. But we can't cherry pick the past like that now because it prevents us from moving on. If I'm sitting down with a senior republican I'm not having a cup of coffee saying how great that person is. We are both trying to be objective and challenge each other's views. We're both saying each is wrong and this is the way it was. We're putting our view across and we have to be seen as more than we're portrayed, which is as villains and thugs.

GS: What have you learnt from republicans?

JM: Well we're learning from each other. I can understand them. I have done everything I could to prevent them doing what they did over the years, but looking back, you can see why they did what they did. All they were doing, we were doing the same back to them, or as near as damn it. You know, if we'd have had Semtex God knows what damage we would have done. If we had had the wherewithal the Provisionals had we would have bombed Dublin, we would have bombed so much of Dublin they wouldn't have wanted anything to do with it, because their infrastructure or their financial situation then would never have stood it. But at least there was nothing for their own pockets, they were dying and going to prison for the same things that UDA men were dying for and going to prison for.

GS: What are your thoughts on the problems of criminality?

JM: There are people who have been expelled from organizations and they are the professional paramilitary criminals. They don't belong to any organization any more, but they have the paramilitary experience and they're still selling drugs, they're still plying their trade and they don't care about our kids' future, or anybody else. The danger to both communities now comes from the gap when loyalist paramilitaries are moving away. I am totally opposed to drugs and criminality, I want people to have a normal life, for everybody to have their own individual ideas and aspirations but there are people who just want to come along and say I will have that man kneecapped for you if the UDA or the IRA won't do it anymore. There are dissident elements or criminal gangs who will kneecap people for money and offer a couple of inches of blow or coke as well. The financial crisis and a lack of jobs reinforce the situation. So you are getting people who will do kneecappings and sell you drugs at the same time. That is emerging as a real danger.

GS: Has this situation been made worse by a lack of effective policing?

JM: It's certainly got worse. A lot of the police who have been through the system and survived the Troubles and have all the experience have just resigned, or have been paid off, because they're not acceptable to Sinn Féin. So they have to bring these people out of college. There has to be so many Catholics but they haven't got the experience that the old RUC had. And if I was a Catholic, I would probably say well you have to get rid of the RUC, but there has to be this transition as well. It has to be part of a process. You can't just say right these people are in the bin and these are the people who are going to deal with the situation now, because they haven't a clue. Some of these young policemen coming along just don't know how to deal with situations they are faced with.

GS: Because of the conflict, most seem to have got their eye open and their ear to the ground in terms of what's going on. But is that a good thing or a bad thing when it comes to trying to create a transformed society?

JM: There are people here who, if you walked down the street and walked back up an hour later, could have told you that. They would know when a neighbour had last put their milk bottles out. The Troubles just made people like that, wary, observant and cautious. Without even thinking, people had a kind of sixth sense about them, especially if it was somebody who was a paramilitary or in the security forces, or somebody who might for one reason or another be under threat, or feel that they were under threat. They had sharpened senses. You know, even a wee granny would notice a strange car in the place, or if you asked a kid where so and so lived in an area he would say "I don't know" because it might be his uncle, his cousin, or his next door neighbour and that's what the Troubles did to people. In a normal society if somebody stopped and asked where so and so lives most people would say round the corner, but you would never say that here. It will probably take another forty years for that to happen, but we do need to try and take the benefits of peace into the second generation.

GS: Are the younger people listening to what you're saying, or ignoring it because they long for the excitement, as they see it, of a conflict they never took part in?

JM: They don't understand. There was a young man I was talking to the other day who was claiming that we should be doing this and we should be doing that and I said well that's okay if you want to carry a coffin down the street. And he didn't seem to know what I meant. So when I asked if he wanted to carry his mate or Dad down the street he didn't seem to be able to make the connection. Many young people only see one side of it and they don't realize how many casualties it creates. If they want to go and attack, shoot, or bomb Catholics, then someone's going to attack, shoot and bomb them back. It's getting that across which is the problem.

GS: Even if all the weapons are given up, presumably they will only be the weapons you know of. There's bound to be weaponry kept back.

JM: There are going to be weapons, which have been buried under a tree and now there are ten trees or shrubs grown up around it, so you'd need a JCB to get the stuff, if you knew exactly where it was that is. There are people who have left the country, and there's people in jail who would have left guns, but nobody else knows who or where. There was one particular person telling me there had been three guns buried in a field and when they went to get them somebody had built a shed on the field where the guns were. You could never account for every weapon, the UDA couldn't tell you, the UVF couldn't tell you, or the IRA couldn't tell you how many weapons they had.

GS: Presumably most loyalists would believe there is no way the IRA gave up everything?

JM: We talk to republicans all the time who say how are you going to get the AKA-47 off wee Paddy on the border? He's been killing policemen and soldiers for twenty years, how are you going to get it off him? They didn't get it off him, he still has it. They gave up the surplus stuff, the bunkers of stuff that were there for reserve purposes. We've spoken with republicans because we're working with them daily and they will tell you, not up a volunteer gave up a pearl handle revolver. We've said to the Secretary of State and we've said to the police if you and I drove down the Falls Road tonight and started shooting out the window do you think Sinn Féin would phone the police? You wouldn't get to the bottom of the street, simple as that. And in a way you can't blame them for that. If and when loyalism decides it is going to completely decommission, there's still going to be guns about. Every organization's got its magpies that are not going to give up guns and that's being realistic. But having said that, decommissioning has to happen, because in a normal society you can't sit down and talk if there are weapons under the table. We have to accept that there are doors open for us, but to open our own doors we need to get rid of the weapons. We have a contribution to make and need to show that we are not just thugs and gangsters, or bully boys and pimps. We don't need weapons for anything and I hope that the time when we did has gone forever.

GS: How do you take the strategies and the psychology of a paramilitary organization and over a period of a few years turns it into a community development/organization?

JM: When the Troubles started forty years ago, most of the commanders in the UDA or the UVF would have been ex-soldiers, because there were an awful lot of people that had been involved in the British Army, so people in their forties and fifties with British Army experience tended to get key positions. But many people don't understand events like Bloody Friday, when all the bombs went off in Belfast and where they were lifting body parts up on shovels to put them in plastic bags. Looking at that twenty, thirty, or forty years later and people rightly see it as terrible, but I saw it from a perspective of normality. Everything was to do attacking the other side, or trying to defend against the other side. Everything was about violence, one way or the other, either giving it or taking it. Then you get to the stage where you realize this is not the way to do it anymore, but there are no guidelines for moving ahead. The leadership in the paramilitary organizations, republican and loyalist are now taking people to a place where they've never been before. They're trying to tell young lads who want to be Michael Stone, or who want to be whoever on the republican side, that's not the way to do it anymore and that a vote is better than a bomb, or a bullet. But, you try telling that to some sixteen or seventeen-year-old, who hasn't got the right to vote anyway. They want to create a niche for themselves, they want to make a name for themselves and it's up to us to provide the sort of facility to try to take people away and say to them giving up a gun is not just giving up a bit of metal. A gun is something volunteers have cherished and it's like giving up an arm or a leg. You know, people defended this country with these guns, they might have killed somebody with a gun, it was there as part of looking after Ulster, part of our protection. So it's not just giving up a bit of metal. But we're saying that is not needed anymore, that we're going to prove to people that we're as clever as they are and that we have a right to have a part in the future of this country.

GS: What will happen though if the funding for community initiatives dries up?

JM: It would totally isolate a lot of people. Around the immediate area of Sandy Row there are about six hundred families living there which is nothing compared to what it used to be. We want this area revamped with shops apartments and new houses for people. This is a dead area for unionism, but we've an interest in this place. We have to be a part of this transformation, and the only way we are going to have a part of it is give up the weapons and move from one stage to the next. We're going to have to be part of politics and we're going to have to get our people to understand politics. People did what they had to do, but now they're going to have to move on otherwise we are going to be like dinosaurs, just left to whither and die. No right thinking person wants to go back to the bad old days, when they were carrying bodies down the street. I try to say to people that in the past, people like myself ran about with bombs and guns and the buzz and the excitement was fantastic, but John McMichael got carried down the street, Ray Smallwoods got carried down the street and people in Sandy Road got carried down the street and it's a hell of a price to pay. What are we going to do, match atrocities? Surely and hopefully those days are over.

GS: Are the lowest common denominator of the organization influential?

JM: No. Those people would have thrived on the Troubles and some of those people were expert killers. Even though they couldn't write their name and address they could go and kill somebody, or they could go and plant a bomb. And that gave them an identity they'd never had before. Now that's been taken off them and they're going to be back to being illiterate, you know. What you generally find is the people who have been there and done it are the ones who are saying move on. It's the ones who have never done anything, that don't understand the whole picture who are really the problem. If you just look at the statistics since the ceasefires, there is a significant number of people who have been killed because of drink.

GS: When you went around for two years telling the organization about the need to change were you coming up against similar objections?

JM: From north Antrim to south east Antrim to south Belfast, all the areas felt the same way. They were saying you can't trust the 'Taigs', you can't trust the IRA. But to an extent you have to try to trust them in order to move. The argument was about weapons putting you in a bracket, and if you don't move outside that bracket, then you're beat. I and others tried to make the case that there's no such a thing as standing still. You either go backwards or you go forwards.

GS: I suppose what you are talking about there is the siege mentality that arises when a community feels under attack

JM: In some areas like Toughmonagh people never went anywhere. There was only one way into the estate and one way out of it. If you went in one way and came out the other way there was far less chance of being attacked. But there was a club there, where people went to drink which was safe because of the insularity of the community. That has now changed and the club is struggling as people go to the nightclubs in the town. And in doing that they are not going into such places asking if there are 'Taigs' on the premises. They go there because there are women and men there who create a good atmosphere. Nobody is asking are you orange or green? Or, what are you?

GS: You have said previously that 2009–10 will be a crucial period for loyalism. Do you still think that?

JM: We're at a very crucial stage here. There have been acts of decommissioning, serious attacks on our community, with two soldiers and a policeman being killed, as well as the McDaid murder. But what is clear is that the PSNI had better get their act together, or they're going to endanger the whole thing. That's no reflection on any individual in it because this is government policy where cutting down resources is really putting the whole thing under severe pressure. But if we can get through to 2010 without any serious developments, I think we're well on our way.

GS: Why wasn't decommissioning all done in one hit rather an initial act to be followed by further stages?

JM: Some of the UVF membership is now asking why their own leadership didn't do it the same as the UDA. After the feud situation in the

Shankhill Road the UVF and the UDA fell out with each other. The UVF feared anarchy and now has no guns while the UDA has guns, so what happens if someone in the UVF falls out with somebody in the UDA and they start hitting each other over the head with bottles? Is it then a good thing that one side has guns and the other side hasn't? The sooner they all go the better. No doubt there'll be some people in the UDA asking why we didn't do it the same way the UVF did because dribs and drabs are no use and hardly count as a confidence-building measure. We've talked with the membership and local people about giving up guns and there's more people outside of the organization saying don't give up the guns than there are inside the organization. We did an initial act, will see that everybody is comfortable with it, and then move from there. The ideal situation from another act would be everything done and dusted.

GS: But do you think the idea of initial decommissioning and then more later just drags the pain out?

JM: I'm happy enough the way the UDA did it. They did it because they said they were going to do it. They said they would decommission partially, as a way of building confidence. If the UVF and UDA had given up all their guns at the same time this may well have assisted dissident republicans. But the sooner the weapons are gone the better if people's integrity is going to survive. I would rather have integrity than a gun. My integrity is going to do my community more good than any number of weapons.

GS: Was there fallout after the initial act? Did it go through relatively smoothly, or have people been angry?

JM: I was at a band parade shortly after and people were shouting 'Tell us it didn't happen'. This is not members of the organization, because they were all fully aware of it, but people in the street. But how can you have guns in a normal society? People don't understand because there is a ghetto mentality. I listen to all sorts of opinions and I have to try to understand why people feel the way they do and why they think the way they do. People keep saying 'You give up the guns and what happens if the IRA does this?' My response is that I believe the IRA won't do it, that dissident republicans might do it, but that's for the police to sort out. That's why the PSNI has to be a more efficient force than ever.

GS: Are you convinced that all the other leaders and areas are of the same mind as you there?

JM: Everybody's got different degrees of difficulty with it. But what sort of a society is it that still needs guns when war is over? Part of the decommissioning argument we have made comes from asking people if they can remember the last time a UDA and UVF gun was used to shoot a republican. In response those opposed will often point out that nobody ever told the Official IRA to decommission, although they are talking about it now, some forty years later, that maybe there is a possibility of at least agreeing in principle about decommissioning. But that's the sort of argument that's thrown in our face, even though they never gave anything up. Even though their weapons were put away, rotted, rusted, and were only used against other republicans.

GS: Is it the case that the biggest threat to loyalism today is loyalism itself?

JM: People say they're afraid to give up the guns because of dissident loyalists and dissident republicans. But people also don't want to give up their guns because they've made so many enemies within their own area, by bullying them, by terrorizing them over the last number of years, that they're afraid of what's going to happen if they haven't got guns to protect them, or to intimidate people with, or destroy people with.

GS: How confident are you that you have got the right set of leaders to deliver the change you want?

JM: Every area has its own identity now even though the violence to a large extent made every area the same. If you take the Shankill Road and the history of tensions because of the feuds there, how long is it going to take for those tensions to go away and people to forget? A good friend of mine was murdered by the UVF and by someone who I thought was a friend of mine. His wife knows who murdered her husband and she'll have to pass him, some time or another, maybe every day of the week in the same shop, or the same pub, or the same post office. How is she and others like her supposed to deal with that? And you can multiply that many times over, where the person who was your friend and ally is now your enemy because he murdered your husband.

As another example, the UVF are having their own problems with Mount Vernon where the supergrass thing is about to kick off again. What happens if three or four of these people turn supergrass and put twenty people in jail? How is the UVF going to pay for those people? If the UDA and UVF declare weapons are given up by a certain date and a member is caught with a gun what happens then? Was it his own gun or the UVF's gun and if they go to prison who is going to pay for them? It could be £40 a week and where is this going to come from? The danger is, if they don't take away all these threats and all the possible pitfalls and all the possible hazards, they may have to resort to extorting building sites again, or doing robberies and one way or the other, there's going be more prisoners. At that stage, you can see how the easiest way out is to sell drugs. But what's the point of somebody getting caught with a gun and getting ten years for it, if that gun has been lying dormant for ten years and if it hadn't been found it would lay there for another ten years? Whatever weapons the UDA has whether it be hundreds or thousands, the UDA did not use more than say ten or twelve in any one night during the conflict. So what is the case for needing all these hundreds or thousands of weapons? That is a point I make to support the argument for decommissioning. You can carry out the sort of war the UDA or UVF carried out against republicanism with that many weapons. You don't need hundreds and thousands of guns.

GS: How do they react to that?

JM: They've never thought of it before. That if you've got a thousand guns and there are a thousand people that have them, then that's a thousand potential prisoners you have. Or, if ninety-nine per cent of those guns are going to lie dormant, what is the point of having them? You know I started this whole discussion with some people who were asking us not to give up guns. When I asked them the last time they saw a gun, in most cases it was at least ten years ago. And when I asked them when it was the last time they handled a gun, it was fifteen years ago. But if you say to these people okay well you mind these guns for others they would object, saying they had a wife and kids. So I would say you don't want the organization to give up weapons and you want somebody else to take responsibility for them. Guns are a liability. How can you say you have moved on if you are found with a gun? How are you going to defend it? People know there is a cut off date in February 2010 and anybody caught with a gun after this has to take responsibility because it will not be a paramilitary weapon.

GS: That's a huge psychology to turn isn't it?

JM: It's a push against everything even I believed in a few years ago. But we have to have some sort of normality. What I'm trying to tell young people is that people like me did what we did, so they don't have to do it. Our sacrifices were made to provide a society that they could thrive in and flourish in, without being involved in the same sort of things that we were involved in.

GS: Are you confident that the situation is now irreversible or do you think it's too early?

JM: It's too early and it's too fragile at the moment. Loyalism has its problems, but it's closer than anybody else to putting them right. We are making progress, putting differences behind us, and coming together more than the politicians are. But we need five thousand more policemen to get us out of conflict for the next couple of years, to get to some sort of normality. It's only going to be normal when people feel at ease with fully armed police on the streets. That may sound strange, but it's the only way to neutralize the dissidents and gain public trust.

Chapter 16
'Bound by Oath and Duty to Remember': Loyalism and Memory

Kris Brown

According to Stephen Howe's influential and insightful analysis of the issue, one can discern an existential emptiness at loyalism's core. As modernity has dissolved once traditional but now outdated displays of Britishness, so an unanchored blue-collar constituency now assembles a bricolage identity, pasted together from local sectarianism and a reworked symbolic inventory borrowed from popular culture (Howe 2005).

The resulting 'bling and gun' culture as typified by the mural memorial to the UDA's John 'Top Gun' McKeag is one of the more obvious expressions of this, depicting the paramilitary leader with baseball cap, and pistol-shaped gold jewellery, the symbolism is as much borrowed from 'Gangsta rap' and American gang culture as it is from local traditions of communal conflict and public banding.

This postmodern crisis of loyalist organizations suggests a propensity to centripetal tendencies, lacking as they do a firm ideological centre to which activists and followers can firmly adhere. The history of feuding and schism within and between loyalist groupings through much of the peace process could be said to provide a bloody trail of empirical evidence that supports this notion of a loyalism beset by a crisis of identity and degeneration into vendetta and power jockeying.

Loyalist narratives of commemoration

But loyalism need not be as hollowed out as Howe's analysis suggests, or at least it has attempted to counter this by constructing a narrative for itself using commemorative practices and memory work. As Edwards and Bloomer note, loyalists, particularly those associated with the UVF, realize that the past is a 'bankable commodity' and have entered into 'an ideological battle to assert their claim to an historical and cultural lineage' (Edwards and Bloomer 2004: 15).

Howe's analyses of a cultural magpie promiscuity, counterbalancing a withering political identity, is the most recent expression of analyses, which seek to stress the contingent or ambivalent nature of loyalist identity (Miller 1978; Todd 1987). Others have sought to turn this assumption on its head and instead underline the attachments to concepts of Britishness and the effects on the wider unionist family of the state's irresolution (Aughey 1989; Coulter 1994).

There are certainly problems bedevilling modern post-Agreement loyalism, but rather than scrutinizing these under an umbrella term such as 'identity', it will be instructive to unpack this 'crisis' into component parts – which are in several cases interlocking and reinforcing rather than encapsulated. Once this is done, we may then see how loyalist commemorative practice acts both to vent, and compensate for, these concerns. We may unpick several broad themes of concern within contemporary Loyalism: *Structure, Environment, 'Family Relations'* and *Legitimacy*.

Structure

The organizational form and linkages within loyalism have contributed to its problems. Unlike Irish republicanism, in which the Provisional republican movement has predominated, loyalist influence is split down the middle between the UVF and the somewhat larger UDA. As underground illegal groups, Hugh Orde, the Chief Constable of the Police Service of Northern Ireland, considers them 'disorganized' and that they 'lack sophistication' in contrast to their republican counterparts (Edwards and Bloomer 2004: 18); they are also discerned to be 'shrinking' in terms of both number and quality of activists, and are correspondingly fractious (Bruce 2004: 518–19).

Internally, the organizations suffer from particular problems. The UDA remains a decentralized grouping at best operating as a federal body, at worst as an amalgam of fiefdoms, and although the UVF is more centralized in control and has benefited from the continuity provided by a long established core leadership, it has also suffered from the indiscipline and self-aggrandizing criminality which plague shadow 'armies' (Bruce 2004: 505). Irish republicanism has benefited developmentally from the growth of party political expression through Sinn Féin; a process, which has provided influence, prestige and access to a broader constituency. Loyalism has not.

The UDA-linked Ulster Democratic Party (UDP) has vanished, only partially replaced by the public face of the Ulster Political Research Group (UPRG). The UVF-aligned PUP is small and pushed to the electoral fringes; its organizational linkage to the UVF is in any case weaker than many suppose, and is virtually non-existent at the micro level (Edwards and Bloomer 2004: 44; McAuley 2004b). Post-Agreement loyalism is in a political sense a partial mute.

Environment

At micro level, loyalists have often viewed their urban environment as one of continued if transformed conflict, the peace process providing a 'methodological transformation of militant republicanism' into a form of cultural struggle, simply a 'different kind of war' involving mobilization over disputed parades and the display of material culture such as muralization (Southern 2008: 80).

This cultural struggle is seen by loyalists as being pushed into other arenas such as dealing with the legacy of the Troubles via inquiries and commissions; for many loyalists a vibrant sense of victimhood is seen as a component part of republican identity politics (Lundy and McGovern 2004: 57), one which impels renewed contestation. Cultural conflicts therefore require a degree of vigilance and counter mobilization on the streets and in the more abstract field of communal memory and narrative.

Regardless of the truth of these assertions of politicized victimhood and culture, it is not merely a fanciful invention cobbled together by an embittered foe. This view of republican memory and memorialization as war by other means, as a new phase of struggle, is also argued by some academic research (McAuley and Tonge 2007, 2009; McDowell 2007: 727) while victimhood is also underlined as being an important part of the political and cultural baggage of Northern Irish Catholics (Mitchell 2006: 105–6).

These viewpoints could be charged with essentializing nationalist identity; but what is not in doubt is that the proliferation of communal displays, the materiel of this cultural war, is a 'function of the tectonic grinding together of two communal blocs', a long pressure which has 'buckled and twisted' the political culture of rival communities in close proximity into forms which are both strident and often sensitized (Brown and Mac Ginty 2003: 87).

As Morrisey and Gaffikin note, when ethnic or cultural antagonisms are amplified by macro sovereignty disputes, a 'divided' city thus becomes a 'polarized' one (Morrissey and Gaffikin 2006: 875). Lacking substantial political representation, loyalists may feel cut off from these macro processes, leading to further mistrust at the local level of cultural conflict. Indeed when the focus on political activism has threatened to 'overshadow military prowess' [it is] 'looked upon scornfully by the rank and file' of loyalism (Edwards and Bloomer 2004: 42).

For many loyalists the micro political environment remains one of contestation while the macro environment is somewhat remote. But at this micro level, novelty can still be detected. Commemoration of the dead in working-class unionist communities is not simply in the hands of paramilitaries or their surrogates, and community groups and historical societies have in recent years begun a process of remembering the dead of the conflict, or constructing narratives tying historical conflicts with contemporary ones. These processes perform several functions, from that of mourning to education, but they are never divorced from the political struggles or cultural assertions – in this respect they are loyalist with a small 'l'.

Territory

A sense of territorial threat and encroachment cuts into the loyalist mindset in many urban areas, as demographic decline and residential retreat in the face of nationalist population expansion or entrepreneurial property developments is regarded as breaking up loyalist communal solidarity (Southern 2008: 75–6). The mix between territory and social capital is an important one in providing communal coherence. A strong sense of territoriality is needed to stabilize and mobilize politicized groups (McDowell 2007: 726) while landscapes, and their representation as part of a symbolic inventory, act as powerful identity resources (Graham and Whelan 2007). This is particularly marked in a society in which identity politics remains an evolving, vibrant force (Bean 2007: 155–6).

Territorial sensitivities are marked, and territory much valued, in a period of political deal making. The intensity and intimacy of micro political activity in contested spaces, expressed in the normalization of public banding and revenge on one hand, and the projection of victimhood on the other, has been perceptively surveyed (Morrissey and Gaffikin 2006: 876). Memory of the recent conflict has been telescoped back into these localities to the extent that what we have in Northern Ireland are multiple local pasts wherein ghettoized remembering occurs.

For Graham and Whelan, this encapsulated communalized memory is little short of poisonous, and Flint's terminology of 'spaces of hate' is used to label it (Graham and Whelan 2007: 480). As will be shown below, this is an oversimplification of loyalist memory practice, but there is no doubting the connection between territorial sensitivities and loyalist memory. Territory is a resource for its promulgation, and also a subject of remembrance.

'Family relations'

Relations with working-class communities, and also the wider unionist family are of concern to loyalists. There has been a degree of sidelining of loyalist working-class communities by mainstream unionism, but just as tellingly loyalist political parties have failed to capture substantial support (*Belfast News Letter*, 27 July 2009). To a significant degree harm done to these familial links has been self-inflicted.

As McAuley notes, feuds, hate crime and the day-to-day experience of living within areas subject to paramilitary control have all acted to 'constrict broader support' (McAuley 2005: 336). This may be an outworking of a quantitative shrinking and partial lumpenization in its cohort of activists (Bruce 2004: 505); but there are also structural reasons. Loyalism remains a strongly urban phenomenon and mid-Ulster excepted, most rural Protestant communities refused to respond to republican attacks with violent paramilitary retaliation, instead preferring to put their faith wholly in local security forces (Southern 2008: 71).

Recently, republicans have attempted to strengthen social contact between their political project and local communities by reworking republican combatant narratives to include politically valuable civilian deaths. This is problematic for loyalists, because as McDowell (2007: 731) points out, the unionist family operates a structured hierarchy of victims dividing victimhood into respectable (security force and civilian) and non-respectable (paramilitary). Loyalism seems hemmed in.

While loyalism remains pushed to the margins, it would be wrong to picture it as unattached to the wider unionist body politic. Its connection to this polity is undoubtedly organic as the 'vigilantism which spawned their growth was undoubtedly popular' (Rolston 2005: 196). While electoral success has been evasive, over the decades support for loyalist paramilitarism has been fluid, perhaps reflecting an ambiguity towards political violence that has been detected within opinion polls of the populace in Northern Ireland (Hayes and McAllister 2005: 605).

Although the gauging of support for illegal paramilitary groupings is fraught with methodological difficulties, in simple terms support can be 'best conceptualised as a spectrum' (Sarma 2007: 1075) one in which the depth of colouration is highly contingent. In times of relative quiet, popular street-level support for loyalists appears small, as acknowledged even by local community workers (Rolston 2006: 670) but experience of communal conflict, and circulating narratives of the same, can maintain a sense of victimhood and threat which leads to a degree of: 'communal legitimacy being afforded to paramilitary violence' (Southern 2008: 71–2).

The impression which emerges is of loyalism as a politico-cultural subculture which nevertheless is organically embedded within working-class unionist communities; its activity and popular support fluctuates with political uncertainty and level of violence, but it cannot be pictured as a mere criminal blister on unionist communities. At times, loyalists are frank in acknowledging the partial exceptionalism which their activity has endowed them with; at a Remembrance Sunday commemoration the oration noted that loyalists 'come from a close knit community which few from outside would understand' (*Combat,* January 1996). But this should not be overstated.

Other emotive commemorative activities such as funerals can see many thousands in attendance as supporters or spectators paying respect (*Sunday People,* 19 August 2001). It is within this strand of memory that loyalists can see a means to maintain coherence within their own inner group and also to reach into more widely circulating memorial tropes within unionism, shared by a wider constituency. Given the prevalence (and efficacy) of extra constitutional methods in Irish history, modern loyalist memory work can 'resonate' with historical themes and 'iconographic figures' of the past and this serves to compensate for a weakness in terms of contemporary legitimacy (Hayes and McAllister 2005: 615).

Legitimacy

Loyalist paramilitary groups and their supporters feel that loyalism's legitimacy is repeatedly challenged from a number of sides: the media; 'middle' unionism; the state; academia; and the traditional republican foe. PUP-elected representative Dawn Purvis feels that loyalists have become tabloid fodder and that a simplified 'negative stereotyping' distorts and diminishes the legacy of loyalism (Edwards and Bloomer 2004: 24).

Academics, journalists and politicians who claim that the loyalist campaign occupied a lower moral rung than republican violence are deemed to be 'more disgusting' than the republican perpetrators themselves (Mitchell 2003: 34). 'Middle' unionism is particularly lashed – the 'gross hypocrisy' of the 'so called respectable people' (*Combat*, September 1995) is ridiculed in loyalist commemoration, and the desire for a 'sort of clean living paramilitary group' to challenge republicanism, or a simple faith in the security forces and the rule of law, is presented as a naïve phantasm of mainstream unionist humbug (Mitchell 2003: 26). As such the recent history of the conflict becomes acutely sensitive.

Loyalists fear that attempts to deal with the legacy of the 'Troubles' via truth recovery will simply be used by those safe in their 'leafy, comfortable suburbs' to 'stigmatise' and 'isolate' them (EPIC 2004). The journalistic cliché of the garden centre unionist, a byword for passivity, is here transformed into an ideological threat. The corrosive threat of republican campaigning in further delegitimizing loyalism is also a theme within their discourse. Legacy issues of truth and justice are seen simply as 'republican issues' acting as a Trojan horse in a wider politico-cultural struggle. The projected republican assimilation of the victim agenda is seen as the 'latest phase of a political initiative', part of a comprehensive attempt by republicans to rewrite the past (Lundy and McGovern 2008: 53–4).

If all this may seem highly fretful and ideologically defensive, it is counterbalanced by a frank reflexivity. Loyalists, it is admitted have never enjoyed 'the same level of legitimacy within their areas as republicans have', thus making them 'particularly vulnerable' when it comes to memory (EPIC 2004). Their analysis of this is characteristically blunt. Because of the difficulty in striking at a shadow army, loyalist strategy was to take reprisals against Catholic civilians, by random assassination or no warning bombing.

Loyalists fully comprehend the damage this policy of reprisal caused them within unionist civil society. As a UVF-aligned document asserted:

> It was a harsh and ruthless strategy that was dictated by the nature of the conflict. It dehumanised members of the nationalist community and reduced them to the status of scapegoats who were forced to pay vicariously for the sins of its "secret army" (cited in Mitchell 2003: 29).

While loyalists understand their political and ethical vulnerability in terms of their actions, they nevertheless undertake a defence in depth of their strategy. Their institutional memory runs in this way: the UVF saw the conflict in terms of two communities engaged in a total war of psychological attrition; IRA bombings were less about economic sabotage than terrorizing Protestant communities and sapping morale; furthermore, the Catholic community provided 'political and moral cover' for the republican insurgency, and gained political leverage from 'armed struggle'.

Effective resistance against this ruthless, shadow foe is deemed impossible within the rule of law or conventional warfare. Terror is acknowledged as a tool of legitimate forces, and the firebombings of German and Japanese cities in the Second World War are cited as examples. Striking back at visible civilians, thus becomes moral, logical, pragmatic and a straightforward 'return of the serve' (Mitchell 2003: 25–9). But in the cultural struggle of 'dealing with the past', these counter-memories of 'community protection' via retaliatory violence need underpinning and periodic circulation. This is where commemoration comes in.

The uses of memory

In a society much structured by the identity politics, memory plays a crucial role. Barbara Misztal puts it thus:

> memory, especially traumatic memory, has established itself as a source of group identity due to the growing acceptance of memory as a criterion of authenticity of the collective selves, the vehicle for establishing collective rights and voicing collective demands. (Misztal 2004: 80)

Thus, memory is the necessary projector for victimhood, by transposing history for memory the past is reworked and a valuable 'sense of loss, deprivation, marginalisation' is sustained (Arthur 1997: 234).

Conflict and violence are seen as particularly potent in the creation of collective identity via collective memory, which itself is a 'kind of storage of ... violent blows, wounds and scars' (Ricoeur 1999: 8). These collective memories of violence can encompass active or passive tropes, can involve the lionization of the fallen, or the projection of innocent victimhood.

In a divided society, communities readily memorialize civilian casualties without going through the theoretical contortions of defining the 'complex' victimhood of those in a communal political system (Bouris 2007).[1] Agency is lauded too. Military sacrifice is often presented, with varying degrees of emphasis, as being part of the bedrock of modern political identity (Anderson 2006; Marvin and Ingle 1999).

The pitfalls of sustaining memories of political violence through rituals and memorials seem particularly dangerous. As Bar-Tal argues, they can both ideologize and concretize division (Bar-Tal 2003: 89), while for Misztal (2004: 80) memory can lead to 'an acceleration of intergroup conflict'. But commemorative rituals and the spinning of communal narratives have an enormous value for political actors, which may mean that they are always worth the risk. They perform several functions, they socialize new members to the values of the group, and 'sacralise the socio-political environment' creating a sense of higher purpose, of belonging to something that has gone before and will continue into the future.

Indeed, in terms of communal coherence, ritual activity is 'not simply one possible way of creating group solidarity; it is a necessary way. Only by periodically assembling together, and jointly participating in such symbolic action can the collective ideas and sentiments be propagated (Kertzer 1988: 29, 37, 45). Ritual, deepened by memorial, communal myths is of particular utility in that it can produce solidarity without a totalizing uniformity of political belief in the here and now. For Kertzer, what 'often underlies people's political allegiance is their social identification with a group rather than their sharing of beliefs with other members' (Kertzer 1988: 67).

Not only does the ritual of memory have a valuable cohering function, but it may also have a transformative one too. The dead, and their memory, can have a particular symbolic function in 'moments of system transformation'. Words can be put into their mouths, and their past actions reframed to fulfil the exigencies of the present. As such they are 'excellent means for accumulating something essential to political transformation: symbolic capital' (Verdery 1999: 125, 29, 33).

Continuity beds down with novelty in ritual forms. In times of transition, the symbols of commemoration can re-anchor authority and copper-fasten notions of continuity and longevity:

> Where a sharp change in policies takes place with the same leadership at the helm, leaders avoid attacking the old symbolism associated with past policies; rather, they attempt to appropriate those same symbols for their new political purposes. To challenge those symbols is to question the basis of their own authority. (Kertzer 1988: 45)

These functions go some way to explaining the importance of commemoration for loyalism in post-ceasefire society.

The form and function of loyalist commemorations

All loyalist groups engage in memorialization and commemorative activity, and while the organization with the richest symbolic capital and historic narratives is the UVF, the UDA has also recently adopted updated forms of memorialization. The process is not limited to paramilitaries. Community groups in loyalist areas such as the 'Bayardo Somme Association', and the 'East Belfast Historical and Cultural Society', have also adopted commemorative practices in remembrance of civilians killed by republican violence, or of special moments of communal mobilization in Ulster history (EBHCS 2006).

The canvas of physical memorialization takes in plaques, commemorative murals, physical monuments and plinths, and small gardens of remembrance. Numerous small monuments dedicated to fallen volunteers have arisen in recent years. Social events are organized too, but the focus of commemorative activity remains the parade. In these loyalists differ from republicans, in usually adopting a much more martial style, one that has been overtly militaristic, and despite softening continues to have a martial air.

While republicans may content themselves with a handful of marching bands, loyalists can utilize as many as 40, as in the case of the memorial for Trevor King, a high ranking UVF member killed by republicans.[2] Indeed, even less well-known loyalists, men *and* women, who die as a result of natural causes, often receive a militaristic 'farewell' with an armed guard of honour, and flag-draped coffin in what amounts to an extraordinarily hyper commemorative diligence. For larger affairs, the order of ceremony usually involves a wreath laying, an oration eulogizing the dead volunteer, followed by an accompanying political message.

Through much of the peace process, if the commemoration was of a dead loyalist paramilitary, armed and masked paramilitaries in the form of a guard of honour might appear in quasi-military uniform, such as the UVF 'black brocade', and fire a volley of shots in the air.[3] Loyalists seemed impervious to criticism that gunplay was threatening, or out of the spirit of the political process, instead underlining how commonplace the sight had become at commemorative parades and eleventh night bonfires, as a tradition cemented over the last few decades.

The use of armed paramilitary displays at memorials is not simply an attempt to emulate conventional military traditions, but as one loyalist wrote 'serves another purpose, for it delivers a strong and true message to our people, a message of reassurance, a message that we haven't gone away y'know. And one armed display, friends, is worth a thousand words' (*Combat*, August 2001).

The traditional aspect of this activity was a partial illusion; rather than being embedded within loyalist ceremony the use of masks and gunplay is perhaps best viewed as reaction to interface violence, conflict over parades and intra-loyalist feuding. Guns sent an obvious message to the grass roots of readiness and undiluted stridency, judged important in times of political uncertainty and street violence.

They were also useful in terms of *spectacle* – a parade in east Belfast to commemorate William 'Squeak' Seymour, a UVF member killed by the IRA in the 1980s, saw no less than 55 masked and uniformed UVF men form a circle at the end of the parade, providing a space within which armed paramilitaries displayed an array of weaponry and fired shots into the air (*Combat*, 14 July 2003); this activity reflects the development of what has been referred to as a 'hip paramilitarism' within working-class parading culture (Patterson and Kaufmann 2007: 255).

These militant displays have given way since 2005–06 following very conscious decisions by both the UDA and UVF to adopt a 'more civil and less sinister feel' in their commemorative rituals and memorial material culture; clothing was to be 'civilianised' (*New Defender*, December 2006) and commemorations that had since their inception featured armed honour guards and speechmaking by a masked 'officer of the day', now saw the oration given by a loyalist politician (*Combat*, July/August 2006).

The juncture reflected a clear form of conflict transformation and de-escalation, as the symbolic inventory was diluted, in parallel with moves in the political sphere to bring loyalists in from the cold and wind down their activities. Gun display militancy has given way to pseudo militancy. UVF commemorations best illustrate this. They have colour sergeants in uniform, shouting orders, straightening lines and carrying blackthorn sticks; their decorative cap badges and insignia reference paramilitary insignia over crossed rifles. An honour guard representing UVF companies wears a quasi uniform of black shirt, tie, and trousers; the floral wreaths they carry bear the names of illegal organizations.

At the moment when representatives are called forward to lay their tributes, photography by onlookers is loudly forbidden lest individuals be identified or misidentified as members of an illegal grouping, a process closely policed by vigilant stewards and spectators, and one which reinforces the sense of occasion, secrecy and illegality. But in this process of pseudo militancy, a strong attachment to the organs of the state is also displayed in the material culture and ritual form. The marching step and structure of the ritual closely resembles that of the British military tradition; buglers and bagpipers feature as they would in a typical regiment. Symbols such as Union flags and poppies are much used, and uniform trappings such as Sam Browne belts and ceremonial white gloves also reflect British military dress. The flute bands that make up the bulk of the parade similarly tap into British military tradition.

Far from being ill organized and lacking formal processes of ceremony (Graham and Whelan 2007: 486) participants in loyalist commemorations seem at pains to replicate disciplined marching amid the maze of back streets. Crowd applause is reserved for the most tightly drilled and presented bands. Ritual activity on Remembrance Sunday is particularly involved and extended, as field observation of these activities in Belfast demonstrates. Typically, a parade, in military formation, will lay wreathes at Belfast City Hall before re-assembling in their home districts for wreath laying, reading of the roll of honour, and speechmaking at paramilitary memorial sites studded across their environs.

During the day loyalists will also visit the graves of comrades killed in the conflict (these gravestones may themselves be ornamented with paramilitary insignia) and there may be further speechmaking in function rooms and indoor venues, whose walls may be lined with commemorative artwork, photographs of the dead, standards and paramilitary symbols. Flute bands often accompany commemorative parades and in recent years, many band colour parties have taken to wearing period British Army dress. The flags and standards, sometimes bestowed with paramilitary ceremony within loyalist social clubs (*Combat*, July 1998), relate to the local British army regiments and divisions of the First World War.

This marks a further seeking of legitimacy, of demonstrating connection with the institutions of the state and accompanies a display of pseudo militancy. The UVF and UDA often commemorate British forces killed in the world wars, as a means of underlining working-class unionist fealty to the British state, local participation in its conflicts, and as a means of identifying and conflating their own struggle to defend Ulster with wider conflicts involving the British Army, an obviously legitimate arm of the state. The loyalist attachment to the memory of the Somme, as a demonstrator of loyalty, legitimacy, sacrifice, and intrinsic communal virtues is much in evidence, as is its utility as a narrative that may be woven into modern discourses of conflict (Brown 2007).

Memorials and material culture

There has clearly been an increase in loyalist commemoration and memory work since the ceasefires of 1994. Loyalists have claimed that they are 'bound by oath and duty to remember' their dead (*Combat*, Special Edition 2001), a high blown phrase, but they are certainly backing up words with actions. Numerous plaques, commemorative murals, and gardens of remembrance dedicated to loyalists have sprung up in the years since 2000.[4]

The number of loyalist (and republican) memory sites is large and ever increasing. In an area that might be defined as 'Greatest Belfast',[5] which includes the city of Belfast, and several bordering housing estates and towns, there are 46 loyalist permanent or semi-permanent memory sites (built memorials, street plaques or murals with commemorative plaques) and 70 permanent or semi-permanent republican sites. Painted displays, such as commemorative murals are almost ubiquitous in working-class districts, and may be continually repainted and replenished.

If these less permanent memory sites are included the totals rise to 91 loyalist memory sites, and 102 for republicans. By way of contrast, there are only 21 permanent or semi-permanent memory sites on public display for the civilian dead in the same area, a figure, which only rises to 25 if commemorative murals are included.[6] Commemoration is thus a valuable public activity for loyalist groups. Loyalist memory sites serve not simply as graphic reminders of physical loyalist presence, but also act as focal points for ritual displays and parades.

Ritual commemorative events are commonplace, though scarcely reported in the media. The UVF has engaged in perhaps 113 acts of commemoration and remembrance, some large and some very small, between July 2000 and December 2006.[7] Memorial sites continue to feature the iconography of paramilitarism, including images of assault rifles and masked figures in contemplative repose – but more and more sites now show an image of the commemorated figure in terms of a simple head and shoulders portrait against a background of local or historic scenery, such as a battlefield.

Accompanying figures are often uniformed soldiers of the First World War, referencing the much venerated Battle of the Somme. The plaques on the memorials seldom have paramilitary imagery but instead opt for insignia and initials of the commemorated (and illegal) organizations; these are often supplanted with the insignia of the 36th Ulster Division, which fought at the Somme and was formed almost wholesale from the ranks of the old 'Home Rule' UVF.

These memory sites serve as markers of a degree of political transformation. Armies most readily commemorate when a conflict has ended, so the proliferation of sites serve as physical markers of a boundary in history, between something past and something new. This new setting is by no means devoid of violence or tension, as orations at commemorations themselves underline, but it amounts to something different, a different phase. Loyalist themselves have noted this difference when using these sites. Witness this oration:

> Only five years ago we could not commemorate Remembrance Sunday, we could not remember out dead in piece [sic]. We were forced to wear hoods, disguise ourselves. Our services were surrounded by hundreds of members of the security forces. Indeed some of us were arrested remembering our dead. Today we can remember them in peace and with dignity. (*Combat*, Millenium Edition, December 1999)

Cordite need not accompany commemoration. But are these ritual memorial sites also 'spaces of hate' creating a 'chauvinistic, intolerant and authoritarian reality?' (Graham and Whelan 2007: 492). This assertion is too blunt.

The material culture and symbolism of memorial sites is more nuanced and purposeful, despite its chafing effect on sections of civil society. Jarman dissects the utility and meaning of loyalist (and republican) muralism thus:

> Murals were used to situate the paramilitary political practices of loyalism and republicanism within the broader political bodies of unionism and nationalism. They were used to refine traditional beliefs in line with the changing circumstances of political and military conflict, to consolidate the support of the faithful and to give substance to an otherwise shadowy presence. (Jarman 1998: 86)

There is then a much more reflexive and adaptive side to these displays. In several cases, loyalists have trumpeted how their memorialization adds a 'fresh touch' to run down areas, and that their 'tastefully inscribed and cited' memorials contrast with the 'deliberately provocative nature of Republican monuments' (*The Loyalist*, May 2002; *The Loyalist*, September 2002).

This is not simple self-aggrandisement. Fred Cobain, an elected representative of the moderate Ulster Unionist Party felt that a newly opened UDA memorial garden 'lifts the whole tenor' of a neglected area in his constituency, and argued that such paramilitary memorial work was inevitable (and preferable to many other forms of paramilitary muralization) as such organizations were 'part of the furniture' in many neighbourhoods (*Belfast News Letter*, 11 June 2004).

Symbolic de-escalation and paramilitary 'gentrification'

A brief case study relating to a UDA commemorative site in South Belfast reveals an emerging process, in which militant memorial imagery is reworked to accommodate a more subdued, even gentrified form of commemoration. The gun is figuratively taken out of the symbolic inventory, and more legitimate signifiers inserted. Originally the small, unkempt UDA memorial garden in Roden Street, featured a mural of masked and armed UDA members and a black marble stone, commemorating the dead of the Ulster Freedom Fighters.[8]

A process of engagement between the local community regeneration group, loyalists, and the 'Re-Imaging Communities' project of the Arts Council of Northern Ireland led to the 'transformation and re-fashioning' of the memorial. The garden was rebuilt and enlarged, and featured a mosaic by artist Eleanor Wheeler and a sculpture by Alan Cargo, both designed with a poppies motif and entitled 'Reflect' (NI Arts Council 2009).[9] The colourful mosaic is non-traditional in its representation of the poppy emblem, and features a ring of the flowers, depicted in various stages of growth, and with a degree of botanical accuracy. Through the ring flies a white dove, trailing what appear to be olive branches. Lettering around the display gives some background to the symbolism of the poppy, including its reference in the poem 'In Flanders Fields' by John McCrae.

The sculpture too is highly modernistic and features hundreds of polished steel poppies arranged in the form of a tapering cone, halved down the centre. Embossed on many of the poppies are the words 'reflect' and 'remember'. Overall, the memorial site does not resemble a 'space of hate' – but interestingly neither does it jettison its loyalist purpose. The symbolism of British state remembrance and 'genteel' artistic forms have been drafted in to largely replace that of paramilitarism; but loyalist purpose is not wholly eclipsed. The black polished stone with its UFF insignia remains, although it is now less noticeable amidst the artwork. The sculpture is particularly subtle; on close examination many of the steel poppies have the names of the UDA/UFF dead inscribed on them, including well-known figures such as John McMichael and Joe Bratty.

A number of other loyalist memorials, although more traditional in form and unfunded by official initiatives, also demonstrate a divestment of traditional militant forms and their replacement with the symbolism of British soldiery or figures of impeccable, historic unionist legitimacy such as James Craig and Fred Crawford.[10]

The form and function of loyalist displays has played a role in both representing and compensating for tensions within the loyalist project; memory work has served a political utility over and above the remembering of dead comrades. Loyalists are explicit about the socializing purpose of remembrance of the dead. One oration noted that:

it is also important that we enshrine their names through murals on gable walls throughout the loyalist community they fought and died defending... In doing so future generations of young Ulstermen and women will have a visual and vivid reminder of who has gone before and the ultimate price they paid, as Ulster Volunteers to keep us free from Republican tyranny. (*Combat*, July 2001)

Street art is particularly acknowledged by loyalists for its use as 'methods of communication and Loyalist territorial markers' (*Combat*, September 1996). The rituals that take place at these sites also have a stabilizing function within peace process loyalism, partially ruptured as it has been by centripetal forces. At least in terms of the UVF, this perhaps had its genesis in the 'compound culture' of Long Kesh internment camp, which favoured military symbolism, discipline and the fostering of an esprit de corps.

As loyalist strategist Billy Mitchell noted: 'the uniform, drilling and the parades had a crucial role to play in maintaining a sense of purpose, of belonging and a sense of pride and discipline'; a martinet style 'playing at soldiers' was far from their thoughts (Fearon 2002: 27). Connecting this process to memory may deepen its effect. As Casquete notes in examining ceremonial protests, taking to the streets in a ritualized fashion is a useful means of 'coalescing and nourishing memories connecting individuals to their community'; activists, sympathisers and 'sneaking regarders' make up 'communities of remembrance' and thus 'communities of feeling' which catalyses group solidarity and engenders confidence (Casquete 2006: 290). Both are useful outcomes for Ulster loyalism.

To return to the concerns of loyalism outlined earlier, in terms of *Environment* anxieties, the occupation of space by memory sites, and their ritual use, is intended to counter fears of territorial shrinkage; commemorative function is important in terms of political environment too. Symbolism employed in this memory work can be varied over time to fit the required mood music; the symbolism may be strident when grass roots need assurance, but then softened as conflict transformation takes place. In terms of *Structure*, memorial activity and symbolism can provide some degree of coherence, purpose and identification – countering some centripetal tendencies.

These memorial demonstrations are also about fostering a sense of *'Family Relations'* within localized communities, and within the wider unionist circle. Loyalists attempt this via the parading band culture and the use of historical tropes and imagery that taps into more accepted sentiment, such as that surrounding original UVF and British military service. Difficulties surrounding *Legitimacy* are also screened behind the symbolism of the Home Rule Crisis and British military service.

A growing number of murals also represent memories of victimhood and feature representations of street fighting, attacks on Protestant homes, evacuation of residents, and incidences of the mass killing of Protestant civilians by republicans; this memory work is not necessarily directed by paramilitary groups, and indeed involves work by community groups and cultural societies in working-class loyalist districts; but in highlighting instances of threat and communal suffering, the practices are designed to create a sense of community, and the need for protection.

In terms of the political environment, they are also seen as necessary counter moves against republicanism in the cultural struggle over the meaning of the conflict. The Shankill Road's Bayardo bombing memorial features a framed essay, designed to undermine claims of republican legitimacy in using political violence; the Neill-McCurrie memorial on the Newtownards Road also decries the 'planned and unprovoked' nature of the IRA attack which 'introduced guns on to the streets of East Belfast'.

The sanctification of important messages

Commemoration also assuages grassroots support that the sacrifices of the fallen, the legitimacy of their cause, is not forgotten; this may have a mollifying effect on opposition to difficult decisions taking during the peace process, including perhaps the winding up of the organization itself.

Loyalists use memorialization and commemoration as a means to formulate and disseminate messages relating to the peace process. Current themes of import, from parades to internecine feuding, can be attached to political eulogies relatively seamlessly; this ensures a degree of augmentation of the message, as tropes of sacrifice and legacy are fed into it.

A detailed survey of loyalist orations via their mosquito press and observation at commemorations over several years,[11] reveals the following circulating themes used to articulate (and thus vent), or at least compensate for loyalist concerns relating to *Structure*, *Environment*, *Family Relations* and *Legitimacy*. Orations can highlight 'unwanted and unwarranted incursion' into 'our traditional boundaries' (*Combat*, July 2001) but frequently counterweight this with an affirmation of their willingness to provide *Communal Protection*.

This is further buttressed by their assertion that they were *Victors and Effective Fighters*. In the political environment, they underline their commitment to *Cultural Defence*, and highlight fallen members who were motivated by these matters, particularly around the issue of parades. They also stress the *Competency of the Leadership* in terms of its political vision, willingness to consult the grass roots, and unwillingness to be pressured by exogenous factors.

A commemorated leader such as Trevor King, is feted for his ability to take tough decisions, think politically and with intellectual rigour, and thus becomes an example of good leadership. His now eulogized ability to take tough decisions and the political long view is used to underpin further moves by the organization to consolidate the peace. The structure of the organization is sometimes envisioned as a *Family*, and the generational and neighbourhood links to loyalism of those commemorated is often stressed.

A sense of relationship with the wider community is also fostered by reference to the fallen as *Exemplars* – ordinary men, very much typical of their communities, who were motivated by a sense of patriotism or a need to defend against threat. Orations will also link in with the community by creating a sense of shared *Victimhood*, itemizing contemporary attacks made upon communities at interfaces and parades, and tying these in with the memories of the recent 'dirty little war'.

Victimhood is of course also cited to support the legitimacy of loyalist violence and mobilization as a necessary counter response; the legitimacy of the loyalist project is also presented as being underwritten by its *Historic Links* to previous incarnations of loyalist mobilization (less convincingly in the case of the UDA) and by *Links to the State* that loyalists have via familial or previous membership of the British armed forces. Legitimacy is also expressed via the theme of *Victors and Effective Fighters*. In 'defeating' republicanism, loyalism did what was needed and history will prove them right.

Loyalists can exhibit some inventiveness in using memorialization to recast strategy or policy shifts. The UDA, when initiating a return to ceasefire following a long series of attacks, referred to their proposals as the 'John Gregg Initiative' in memory of a UDA Brigadier assassinated in a feud with a rival faction within the organization. The use of Gregg's memory, a man who was anything but a political dove, was a move designed to mollify internal opposition to their proposals. It was also used, less successfully, to highlight a supposed shift in the UDA, away from drug-dealing activities, exemplified by the faction, which had killed him (*The Loyalist*, 4.5, February/March 2003).

The South Belfast UDA's Remembrance Sunday parade in November 2007 was used to announce the winding up of the Ulster Freedom Fighters, complete with a ritualized furling and retirement of the UFF banner. The oration itself underlined that the 'war is over' and that in a 'new dispensation' the UDA would undergo a 'process of transformation' which would lead to a shift in its activities towards 'retirement' and community work.[12]

Conclusions

Loyalist memory work is more than about reflecting on the dead. It is more even than implicitly drawing a line under the conflict, although it can serve that purpose. It has a particular utility. It can provide symbolic screens or wriggle room to allow loyalists to negotiate their way through an, at times difficult, ruptured, political, environment; linkages with past sacrifices, and blood letting, are stressed to provide overt proof of intrinsic ideological rectitude, legitimacy and continuity. Remembrance can thus serve to symbolically augment and contextualize messages relating to the peace process. It can even be used to insulate from criticism, by grafting on the name and memory of a veteran activist, a move, which adds to the legitimacy of political shifts.

Ceremonial commemoration allows increased political connection with the community, by providing spectacle and substance to a shadowy grouping and may enable history to be nuanced to suit both political continuity and the revamped project of conflict transformation. But there are obvious dangers. As Bruce notes, a desire for peace within loyalism was in part fuelled by a generation of loyalists who saw the reality of close quarter sectarian conflict (Bruce 2004: 518–19). If future generations of loyalists are reliant on the inherently simplified memory of murals, monuments and political orations, will they absorb only a sanitized view of ethnic conflict, in which paramilitaries are lionized with little understanding of the inevitable, bloody logic of gunplay in a divided society?

Notes

1. Bouris argues that 'the complex political victim can be understood as a victim who knowingly and purposefully supports certain discourses that contribute to the space of her political victimisation' such as voting along ethnic or communal lines (Bouris 2007: 84).

2. Field notes. Estimate of number of bands at Trevor King memorial parade, 8 July 2006.
3. It appears from field research that the custom of gunplay at commemorations has now been curtailed completely.
4. For a visual representation of the growth of memorialization in the Belfast City Council area in recent years see Elisabetta Viggiani's database 'Public Forms of Memorialisation to the Victims of the Northern Irish "Troubles" in the City of Belfast' at http://cain.ulst.ac.uk/viggiani/introduction.htm. Accessed June 2009. For a view across Northern Ireland and beyond, see http://cain.ulst.ac.uk/victims/memorials/index.html (accessed July 2009). It is a measure of the number of these memorials that not even the latter project could track all of them.
5. 'Greatest Belfast' comprises the Belfast Metropolitan Urban Area (population 579,276 according to the 2001 census) plus the town of Newtownards (population 27,821 in 2001), which has strong connections to east Belfast. For geographic and demographic details see http://www.nisra.gov.uk/statistics/financeandpersonnel/DMB/ur_gaz.pdf and the 'Newtownards' section on www.ninis.nisra.gov.uk.
6. Figures are drawn from my fieldwork survey of conflict-related commemorative sites carried out between February 2006 and February 2007. The figures are important given that 2074 civilians died in the Northern Ireland conflict, while the figure is 396 for republican paramilitaries and 166 for loyalists; see David McKittrick *et al.*, *Lost Lives* (Edinburgh; Mainstream, 2004: 1526). There are of course more memorials and commemorative sites relating to the loyalist, republican, security force and civilian dead of the modern 'Troubles' at roadsides and in towns across Northern Ireland. Many security force memorials are located within barracks or outside of public space.
7. Data compiled from survey of loyalist magazine *Combat*, local newspapers, and parades commission website. www.paradescommission.org.
8. See http://cain.ulst.ac.uk/viggiani/images/MEMORIALS/Belfast/Loyalists/UDA%20-%20Roden%20Street,%202006/P1020151.JPG. July 2009.
9. See http://www.artscouncil-ni.org/news/2008/new07032008.htm. viewed July 2009. Cargo and Wheeler also provided work for the RUC memorial garden, including another cone like sculpture.
10. http://cain.ulst.ac.uk/cgi-bin/AHRC/monuments.pl?id=404 and http://cain.ulst.ac.uk/cgi-bin/AHRC/monuments.pl?id=474. Viewed July 2009.
11. Publications surveyed included the UVF affiliated *Combat* and its successor, *The Purple Standard* (covering the years 1994–present); The UDA's *The Loyalist* and *New Defender* (covering the years 1994–2006, with a degree of publishing interruption). The author conducted field observation of 17 loyalist affiliated 'Troubles' related commemorations between 2006 and 2009.
12. Taken from field audio recording of speech by Jackie McDonald, 11 November 2007.

Chapter 17
Loyalist Perspectives on Apology, Regret and Change

Graham Spencer

If the Northern Ireland conflict is at an end, what place is there for apology and regret among those who orchestrated and carried out violence and what do attitudes about each of these areas from the protagonists tell us about moral responsibility in a 'post conflict' society? This chapter is a tentative attempt to explore such questions with specific reference to loyalists who engaged in acts of violence and murder. Although one might expect different reactions about apology and regret dependent on the extent of violence and murder perpetrated, it is evident that for most of the loyalists interviewed here a preoccupation with apology and regret is seen as counterproductive to the challenges of a changed political environment, as well as likely to entrench the interests of conflict rather than help move beyond that conflict. It is this perception and the understandings which surround it that I particularly want to explore in this chapter.

To do this it is important to sketch out some of the basic themes and issues, which inform understanding of apology, which stands as a manifestation of regret and remorse. For the purpose of this chapter we will take apology to be a public declaration of sorrow, while regret will be the reasons which shape that sorrow and prompt it. Or, to put it another way, apology is the act of saying sorry, while regret are the reasons as to why one is saying sorry and which determine its subsequent expression. Since the loyalists here appear to largely resist the idea of apology (at least on an individual level) we need to expand the emphasis further to consider why they are not sorry and what reasons they provide as justification for this.

In order to achieve this I draw from a small number of interviews with UVF and UDA ex-combatants, who because of the sensitivity of the subject, remain anonymous throughout. Interviewed in 2009, the respondents were candid and forthright in dealing with the questions asked and for their cooperation in this delicate and potentially difficult area I express considerable gratitude.

Apology

Although the loyalists interviewed here demonstrate resistance and even disregard towards individual apology, there has been one notably deliberate attempt in the past by loyalists as a group to apologize to those affected by loyalist violence. This example came in the combined loyalist ceasefire statement of October 1994, which included the comment:

> In all sincerity, we offer to the loved ones of all innocent victims over the past twenty five years, abject and true remorse. No words of ours will compensate for the intolerable suffering they have undergone during this conflict.

In comparison to apology on a one-to-one level between individuals, which often contains an element of spontaneity and improvisation and provides a direct, felt and intended articulation of personal regret and shame, group apology, or what Tavuchis calls the 'many to the many' mode of apology, is seen as more of a 'diplomatic accomplishment', and this is so because of 'adherence to formalities; which serve to underscore the group's honor and integrity' (Tavuchis 1991: 100). The intended effect of generating public attention for this kind of apology indicates that its prime objective is to not only reduce tension but avoid exposition or introspection about blame and responsibility (ibid.: 102). Though the group apology may have significant conciliatory implications, for Tavuchis, it adheres to a logic which 'has little to do with sorrow or sincerity but rather with putting things on a public record' (ibid.: 117).

Perhaps it is precisely because the group apology functions as a statement of organizational ambition rather than a personal expression of sorrow, which helps explain why, generally speaking, the group apology is likely to be tolerated more than the individual apology. Further, since such an apology is more political than individual, it can take on an ambiguity that allows for interpretive difference which the individual apology cannot so easily provide. Because of this, objections and sympathies can be contained within the organizational setting and be less prone to create schism or expectations for a series of potentially divisive individual apologetic acts or gestures.

But, there are other implications for the group apology, which require recognition. If credible, the group apology can offer potential for consideration of 'the roots and legacies of historical conflict as a first step towards dampening the discord and frictions that they produce' and, in this regard, provide as a step towards negotiation which can help to 'defuse tensions stemming from past injustices' (Barkan and Karn 2006: 7). The group apology can, to put it another way, present a moment of opportunity where the legacies of conflict can be conceptualized in terms of the past rather than the future and, as such, mark an end to the legitimacy of violence.

Having said that, it is also important to note one key implication of the group apology, which is that it is less about victims and more about perpetrators (Barkan and Karn 2006: 17). It is, as Barkan and Karn identify, an act of rehabilitation, which signifies a realization of the need to end rather than continue conflict, and as such stands as a strategic moment in the transformation of organizational goals and intent. Clearly, this is an emphasis not without value and significance since the collective apology, if genuine signifies the emergence of a new emerging narrative, which is itself representative of changed thinking in how the group operates and exists (Olick 2007: 147).

In this instance the group apology functions as a 'turning point' in the life of the group, symbolizing a possible new ethic of responsibility and so creating important expectations about cultural and organizational change (even if regret and remorse remain secondary to this aim) (ibid). Having said that, caution is also called for here as Smith reminds us: 'Because neither collective expressions of sympathy with blame nor collective expressions of sympathy with justification admit wrongdoing, they do not necessarily entail that the group will undertake reform or refrain from committing similarly justifiable acts in the future' (Smith 2008: 175).

An important qualification was included in the loyalist ceasefire statement, which was that the apology was for 'innocent victims'. Though one might assume that this notion of innocence meant those who were killed by mistake, it is also clear that the ceasefire statement is not a blanket statement apologizing for loyalist actions per se and as such, not an expression of general regret. Furthermore, in that innocent victims are not identified, the question arises which innocent victims is the statement referring to and what does innocence in this context mean? On the one hand, it could be argued that the most important aspect of an apology is that it admits responsibility for a wrongdoing and that through this admission may initiate a process of dialogue which could help improve relations between other groups and victims (Lazare 2004: 75), but the loyalist statement, through its assumed distinction between innocence and guilt, implies that there is no regret for those killed which groups did not believe were innocent.

In that sense, the apology is recognition of a mistake rather than an admission of regret and remorse for killing. Moreover, if for an apology is to have merit 'it is essential that the remorse conveyed is genuine' (Coicaud and Jonsson 2008: 78), then the distinction in the apology between undefined innocence and guilt raises problems for those who are supposed to accept it simply because the question of who they are is not known. Or, to put it more succinctly, if the apology is targeted at nobody in particular then its recipients remain nobody in particular and since the innocent victim is unknown, who is supposed to receive the apology and benefit from it?

Further, since the significance of apology derives from its dyadic nature, where apology offers interaction between perpetrator and victim (Tavuchis

1991: 46), it is apparent that without a discernible victim or identifiable group of victims the act of apology lacks meaning. Highlighting the import-ance of relationship in the apology process, Arendt raises an important point when she argues that to have effect apology needs dependence on 'plurality, on the presence and acting of others, for no one can forgive himself and no one can feel bound by a promise made only to himself; forgiving and prom-ising enacted in solitude and isolation without reality and can signify no more than a role played before one's self' (quoted in Tavuchis 1991: 47).

Perhaps there should be no surprise that the rather unspecific nature of the apology which, in separating victims into those who are innocent and those who are not and which therefore appeared to both legitimize and delegitimize violence simultaneously, caused differences of opinion among loyalists themselves, raising further questions about meaning and intent (Smith 2008: 165). For 'Alan' (UDA), talking about UVF leader Gusty Spence who announced the statement and other loyalist political leaders who were seen alongside him when the statement was televised, the apology was per-ceived as more reflective of leadership ambitions towards change than offer-ing a definitive expression of regret from those within the organizations generally:

> Did that man mean it for himself or the people at the table? He certainly wasn't representing everybody because there would have been people watching that saying 'I'm not remorseful, I don't think this should be happening at all. How can he say true and abject remorse when he's only speaking for a certain percentage of the people being represented?' So, many people did not feel he was speaking for them.

That the apology section of the ceasefire statement caused problems for some people was further reinforced by 'Darren' (UDA) who explained:

> There were people in my community who agreed with the apology but there were people I was apologising to who because they were not happy about it.

Alongside this contention 'Kevin' (UDA) saw the timing of the ceasefire statement as particularly difficult (itself indicating the importance of timing in the apologetic moment) and for him the statement was made too early. 'Kevin' believed that loyalists should have first retaliated against the PIRA for the murder of key loyalists in advance of the IRA ceasefire of August 1994:

> The problem was that just prior to the IRA ceasefire people were murdered and we didn't get the chance to avenge them. In the last few months of their campaign republicans clearly identified, targeted and murdered loyalists and this created some tension. My belief is that Ray Smallwoods

[a key political thinker in the UDA] was murdered to bring certain republicans on to the ceasefire bandwagon. Certain people would not have
gone into the IRA ceasefire without getting their revenge and the price of
that was that people had to die in order to get their support.

But for 'Andrew' (UVF), the idea of holding back because of a need to
account for previous losses amounted to a denial of the political realities,
which were clearly signalling a process of change:

To think about it in terms of needing to go on a bit longer to gain adequate
revenge seems a very callous way to look at things. What you are doing
there is personalising the conflict rather than basing your perspective
on a political judgement. That means working to a political solution that
everybody can sign up to rather than thinking in terms of a head count
of killings.

Highlighting that the main intention of the ceasefire statement was not
to discredit the past actions and reactions of loyalists and so was more
about organizational imperatives rather than victims' needs, 'Philip' (UVF)
described the statement as devised ostensibly to support political strategy
and calculation:

There was a clear shift towards acknowledging that by attacking a community you just drove more people into the hands of the IRA. But quite a
lot of people did not pick up on the intent of true and abject remorse and
did not see what was behind the words. For us it was clear that the war
was over and this statement was an acknowledgement of that.

If divergence in opinion exists over the merits of public apology, which was
couched in the loyalist ceasefire statement, there is far less of a divergence
when it comes to interpersonal apology and regret. Here, the respondents
collectively displayed a general resistance if not suspicion to any potential
advantages this might bring about. Though this resistance does not by itself
amount to a total denial of guilt, it needs to be seen in the context where
any gesture towards apology as a spoken act also becomes a revelation of
guilt and with that revelation there arises shame, which as Merrell Lynd
reminds us 'is based upon disapproval coming from outside, from other persons' (Merrell Lynd 1958: 21).

Although guilt may exist as an internalization of values which is kept private, while to become open to the possibility of shame is to make that guilt
known and risk ridicule (Merrell Lynd 1958), it is also important to note
that relations between shame and guilt are complex, with shame involving
'fairly global negative evaluations of the self' or who one is, and guilt involving 'a more articulated condemnation of a specific behaviour' or what one

did (Price Tangney and Dearing 2002: 24). This interaction between self and others (the individual and the social) is demonstrative of how relations with the self are inherently characteristic of relations with others (ibid: 52) and therefore how the personal acquires meaning through the social.

The decision to resist apologizing for the destructive impact of one's actions is not just representative of a distance between victim and perpetrator where the victim is depersonalized and reduced to an object, a dehumanised statistic of conflict, but also amounts to a denial of basic humanity and individual responsibility. In order to legitimize his own decision not to apologize (since to have merit, an apology must be made to a person not an object or statistic) the perpetrator must overlook personal responsibility and emphasize the influence of the social on his behaviour, for it was the conflict rather than he that made him do what he did. It was the conflict, which subsequently motivated his actions. Issues of personal responsibility become secondary from this vantage point, existing as not much more than inevitable expressions of living in a violent society.

Following on from this defensive and ultimately evasive logic it is not surprising for apology and regret to be seen as a threat, to be used by those who might (mis)represent or (mis)interpret both apology and regret as a confession of non-legitimacy, so discrediting the motivations of loyalist actions and bringing the loyalist tradition into disrepute. As 'Michael' (UVF) put it:

> Apology is a very dangerous thing to get into because then people want to individualise it and quote individual incidents or killings or actions which is very dangerous ground to get into. Inevitably you have the problem of people picking holes in it and saying it's not sincere.

For 'Darren' (UDA) it is action rather than apology, which constitutes a preferable response to victims (even if such action is unspecified and again fails to take account of the suffering inflicted), with apology seen as largely inconsequential in relation to ending conflict:

> I don't think apologies would serve any purpose. What value can be attached to an apology given what was done? You will have people saying 'How do we know you mean it, actions are more important than words'.

Though 'Kevin' (UDA) was not totally against apology, his case for resistance came from seeing apology as an isolated event rather than as part of a reciprocal process. Instead of viewing apology as an individually motivated action which is able to admit and to some extent confront wrongdoing, as well as offer potential benefit through that gesture (Coicaud and Jonsson 2008: 80), 'Kevin' saw apology as a move which has credibility only if other perpetrators from oppositional organizations do the same (discounting both how apologies differ and how the problem of apology as a choreographed and integrated cross-communal process would work):

> We have admitted on occasions we were wrong but once you start apologising you are into a minefield because people will say okay you have apologised for this but what about that. You have a monopoly of organisations in this country and it would be useless for them all to come out with an apology. Even if each did fall behind the other in doing so what would be the use of it? Can one imagine the British apologising and republicans following? Even though republicans will tell you on a personal basis this or that was wrong, collectively they will keep the party line. If certain people and organisations did come out to apologise it would create more problems because people would jump on the bandwagon and say you are not apologising for me and this would create friction. A more useful approach is to work so we don't have a repeat of what happened in the past and that we don't let history come back to haunt us.

Notably, 'Kevin's' response depicts apology as an act, which is political rather than individualistic. Here, apology is not taken as a straight one-to-one gesture, but seen through the prism of political conflict and interpreted in terms of general impact on a politically determined transformation process (rather than viewing individual change as the basis of political change (ibid: 85)). From this perspective, apology is likely to be received as an admission that violence was unnecessary, thus effectively discrediting any justifiable explanation for its purpose and consequences.

On this point, 'Alan' (UDA) also circumvented individual accountability in the conflict by viewing moves towards a changed political environment as evidence of successful non-violent initiatives, which are more valuable than comments about being sorry:

> Where would we be if we had not done what we did? I'm not apologising for that, which is over. I have moved on and have a contribution to make. I have an interest in the future of this country and I have a stake in this new society. I'm telling people that I would rather have integrity than a gun. The gun has served its purpose but I can do more good with integrity now.

Ignoring that apology is an acknowledgement of humanity, which, through a mutual recognition of the human consequences of violence, can assist steps towards potential reconciliation, unlike violent conflict that relies on dehumanization in order to continue (ibid: 90), 'Brian' (UDA) added:

> I worry about apologies because we are into that culture of apology. It used to be that nobody apologised but now you can apologise for

everything. To start expressing apologies now means a whole re-examination of everything you've done, supported, cheered for and so on. It means the deconstructing of a whole world view which leaves you pretty naked in terms of facing up to yourself on an awful lot of issues. I mean, it's a slippery slope.

For 'Philip' (UVF) there was some recognition in the value of apology but only if it is accepted rather than ignored or rejected. Here, the intimation is that apology only has worth if it is received with the intent given and that the victim offers a response to the apologizer which the apologizer finds acceptable. This conditionality clearly and problematically puts perpetrator and victim in an exchange where the response of each has mutual worth:

I think that whenever the war is over we should apologise for what we did but only in the context that people are prepared to accept the apology. What we can easily get in Northern Ireland is people using apology or lack of apology as an excuse to exclude people. For many it's repentance rather than apology that matters, but for me it's trying to build a better future that matters. Working with those who were your enemies and trying to put your differences aside. To do that speaks louder than any apology.

This response was also supported by 'Andrew' (UVF) who saw a more effective response to post-conflict transformation as coming from efforts to develop cross-community dialogue, the main intention of which is to close down the distance of misunderstanding between sides and inform each of the other's fears and desires:

The best thing is to encourage debate and dialogue between former adversaries to help undo the dehumanisation and demonization. When you meet your enemy, albeit still opposed politically, one can see that actually most have the same needs and aspirations as yourself. This realisation is most important in moving away from potential conflict and violence and preventing its return.

Regret

What might these responses possibly suggest about regret among loyalists who engage in violence? As one could expect from the responses about apology, regret here is understood primarily in relation to the immediate circumstances of the perpetrator rather than the victim and there is a tendency to look at the consequences of actions through the broader picture of social conflict than personal suffering. As 'Brian' (UDA) acknowledged, regret brings with it introspection which can throw past actions into a critical light. At the same time this examination is likely to intensify self-doubt and loathing, an inevitable result of confronting those actions:

> You would be less than human if you didn't have any regrets about at least some of the things that you were personally involved in, but, to start to go down that road leads to some very painful and difficult self-examination. I'm not so sure that there will ever be a group reflection as such. That will occur mostly at the individual level. I think the paramilitary knows that if he crosses the line into self-examination about his own history, his part in conflict, the things he has done, about the atrocities and whether they were unnecessary he will face some serious problems. So I think he hangs onto the traditional position because he is fearful of what he might do to himself and that position tells him that his actions were justified.

But as 'Brian' (UDA) went on to explain, any rejection of regret is unlikely to make that guilt disappear and particularly in a changed political environment, which has thrown conventional structures of influence and control within paramilitary organizations into question:

> There is a guilt complex with an awful lot of people and the stress of that is manifesting itself in all sorts of ways. Remember, there's the removal of a complete lifestyle and the power and the glory within communities is slowly collapsing. A lot of people did long stretches in prison and are now asking what it was all for. People who were elevated to senior positions within their organisations have been left high and dry, so worlds have been turned upside down.

Unlike responses over apology, which tended to emphasize the broader context of conflict as justification for actions, talking about regret has the potential to bring out recognition of the personal consequences of violence and in this sense returns us to the issue of individual responsibility. But for 'Alan' (UDA), regret was expressed more in relation to his own family than those affected by his paramilitary activities directly:

> I lost my family through having no emotions and just being 100 per cent involved in what I was doing. I got divorced twice and this was because I was totally immersed in terrorism. I would always be thinking I could die tomorrow or go to jail and this gave you license to do all sorts of wrong things. I used to go to bed at night thinking how to get a bomb into somewhere or how to assassinate somebody. I lived terrorism and fighting the enemy. That does not make you a nice person and there have been a lot of people who have been in and out of relationships or drug rehabilitation groups because of it. I regret what I put my family through

but I don't regret the rest. If I had been born 500 yards in another direction from where I was born I would have been in the IRA so there was
inevitability about being either a loyalist or republican paramilitary.

Again, 'Darren' (UDA) referred to regret more in terms of individual
circumstances rather than actions carried out. From that perspective, the
perpetrator becomes victim, looking at his own losses rather than those
inflicted on others:

I have known people within loyalism who have hung themselves because
of the regrets that they had. But the majority of people I would say don't
have regrets for what they actually did. They may regret losing a period
of their life in prison, not seeing their children grow up, that they got
caught and what they lost because of that. But as regards the actions
themselves, most would not regret that.

But, 'Kevin' (UDA) voiced regret less about what the violent campaign
had achieved and more about what it had not achieved. For him, further
action would have been beneficial to loyalist aims, as if more violence and
its impact would have provided a clear-cut advantageous outcome:

Certainly in the circles that I deal with people are not prepared at this
time to sit down and examine what was done wrong in the past 30 years.
I don't regret what I have done in the past but that does not mean that
I glorify it. I regret that the conflict went on for so long but we have to
live with that because life goes on. We were always told to remember two
things: you would either end up in prison or dead and I was fortunate to
end up in prison. One can't regret that too much because either of those
two outcomes was known beforehand, but maybe regrets will come later
and that it's currently too early for that. In a sense I regret the campaign
not carrying on for a couple of months and that we didn't 'clean up'
things that are now coming back to haunt us.

'Michael's' (UVF) response also sought to provide justification for actions
by looking at his role as a valid reaction to the violence of others, as well as
viewing conflict as a necessary precondition to the development of peace
and so making it less regrettable:

If someone attacks my home which they have, puts a bomb in my street
where the ceilings came down on my wife and children, attacks my place
of employment, blowing it up, if they attack my way of life, attack me
and issue me with 34 death warnings all of which have happened, then
I believe I am entitled to defend myself. If those people are attacking me
with force of arms and the only way I have of defending myself is through

force of arms then that is what I will do. I believe that if people like me had not committed to paramilitarism then Northern Ireland would not be in the position it is in today. The Brits would probably have got out with no misgivings of civil war breaking out. I wouldn't get myself in a position where I knew I could get 12 years in prison and regret it.

This position was further elaborated by 'Philip' (UVF), who similarly saw the actions of the past in the context of the present, but unlike 'Michael', 'Philip' admitted to using various coping mechanisms in order to avoid the self-destructive consequences of contemplating and reflecting on his own role in violence:

I regret every life that was lost but I always ask myself did we need to do that to get where we are now? For me the deaths are about the future not the past. Personally I have learned to put up a number of psychological barriers and to have answers in mind. What I went through could have destroyed me completely so I have had to develop coping mechanisms. For example, I have to tell myself that what I was doing was part of a war and that terrible things happened because of that. Other mechanisms might be found in doing various forms of exercise. But anybody who was involved as I and others have been who hasn't been scarred mentally must have something wrong with them. To not be mentally scarred would be inhuman. That is the reality of what violence does to you.

Contributing further, 'Andrew' (UVF) pointed out how community work has helped him to address the consequences of violence. Interestingly, his comments also prompt the question of whether apology and regret can be confronted through the unspoken as well as the spoken act (bearing in mind that apology is traditionally understood as a written or spoken expression of remorse or sorrow (Coicaud and Jonsson 2008: 78)):

In terms of the peace that we have now it's probably difficult to look back and understand all the motivations that led people to become involved in the conflict. I think that individuals in the UVF do generally take personal responsibility for what they do, whereas republicans tend to depersonalise the conflict and talk primarily in terms of the movement. Although for me there were legitimate reasons at the time for why I responded to republican violence in the way I did, I would certainly have had a much easier life if I had not done it. The hardship that I brought upon myself and my family is something I regret. My way of dealing with that is through reparation work and striving to make sure that the conflict is never resurrected. There is certainly little romanticism to be found in conflict and particularly not when you are laying in prison for a decade or more. Some people are seeking acknowledgment of the terrible hurt that has been visited upon them, whilst others are looking for revenge which is not available. People deal with it differently.

Change

So far the responses indicate a reasonably strong consensus about unease and resistance towards apology and express a general lack of regret for victims of violence. However, this does not mean that those interviewed do not have an inclination towards addressing in some way the consequences of conflict and the actions they have perpetrated. Perhaps the demonstration of a changed attitude and how one acts is a more useful indication that one is sorry than just saying so (although both of course would be preferable), and indeed, actually a more constructive way to confront the legacy of violence.

For 'Philip' (UVF), who viewed the nature of apology as a gesture which requires reciprocation by recipients of the apology, whatever response is chosen must be considered primarily both in the light of moves by opponents as well the complexities of political identity which shape attitudes and the endemic sense of inferiority and guilt that comes from a lack of communal confidence (see these comments in the light of Carroll's excellent study of guilt which highlights how the vulnerability it produces often leads to a situation where 'inferiority produces conformity, in order not to arouse the judgement of others' and where 'fear of criticism will drive a person to avoid any situation that might make him a target' (Carroll 1985: 14)):

> The point that the UVF have made and continue to make is that we are in business with republicans and we have to match their every move. We need to judge republicans on the ground, looking at what they are doing and building in their communities. It's about having some sort of social action and challenge against what they are doing as well as building joint relationships. As least we are saying things in the same room as them, which is a big difference from 10 years ago. But, one big problem, and it's a Protestant one, is that many will talk about collectivism but don't then practice it. They will use the word 'we' when things are going bad for them, but then use 'I' as a response. Problematically, as well, unionism is a political identity but it is not a political philosophy. That's part of the reason why so many buy into the idea of what they are not.

'Michael' (UVF) highlighted the conventional mode of reaction which shapes loyalist thinking, before going on to describe how the UVF has reacted to its own internal transformation and the problem of individuals seeking to hold on to power and influence within this changed environment:

> You draw the line when you realise the futility of what you are doing. We always said that when republicans stop so will we and we were

saying that to the police and anybody who had connection with the republican movement. But managing this transition when it comes is an internal matter. All dynamics come from within. If it comes from the outside it looks like you are being forced to do something that you don't want to do. It wouldn't matter what the suggestion was or how constructive it might be, there would be hostility right away because people will think we are being told what to do, as if we can't make up our own mind. There is considerable vigilance against being forced into anything. I believe there should be an evaporation where you go away and appear in a different form. If the climate changes then you can reappear in past form. The UVF should have left a kind of Pretorian guard and evaporated like steam. If it becomes necessary to return then you condense into rain and come back in the previous form. In my opinion there were too many frightened buffalos that didn't want to lose their position in life and were clinging on almost by the fingernails. There will, I think, be a natural process of withering on the vine, but the problem now, because the endgame was not dealt with decisively, is how that is managed and it's in that management that people cling onto positions.

'Michael' (UVF) was also critical of those within loyalism who, as he saw it, were using the argument of community development to maintain structures of power and organization and who were continuing to encourage young people to see value and significance in becoming part of a 'community based' rather than 'conflict based' organization:

There is no war anymore so others have developed this community influence where they continue to tell people what to do. Why in this day and age would anybody want to join a paramilitary organisation? It's like joining a gang. People are dribbling away because there is nothing for them to be there for. Again though you have these macho men who are going to hang on to the bitter end because it's the only status they have. A lot of people think the world owes them a living and it doesn't. It was freedom of choice in the first place whether you got involved in this or not, but now people are having problems getting their heads round the idea that they have to go away.

In contrast, 'Steven' (UDA) intimated in conversation that the UDA tends to operate as an organization of people with individualistic and regional inclinations rather representing a cohesive group psychology (collectively manifested through general reactions and feelings towards political enemies and the understanding of conflict). He went on to explain how the intensity of boundaries and borders at local level function to obstruct progressive change and how working towards eradication of the influences and conditions which contribute to violent behaviour presents the most important challenge ahead (within, it should be noted, those same border and boundary structures which are inextricably linked to the problems of insularity, isolation and fear) :

> There is a problem in who speaks on behalf of the organisation. Problems in north Belfast would not be the same as those in south Belfast and the leader of each area would find it difficult to manage another area because of that. We are now dealing with a lot of problems which people did not notice when the conflict was going on. Many took drink and drugs to deal with the conflict and we are now dealing with the impact of that which is devastating. In north Belfast there are plaques everywhere, which commemorate death and murder. Effectively people are living in a graveyard. If you live with that you don't expect to live too long and this has a very bad effect on the mindset of young people, which we are trying to address. We are trying to get our people to move on, trying to get them involved in building capacity skills, education and so on. We expel those who are involved in criminality and we inform the community of that.

'Darren' (UDA) similarly saw the continuing influence of paramilitary figures as a necessary response to political change and confronting the disadvantages created by conflict. For him, loyalism should now concentrate more on the future than the past and with that reorientation come to understand that those from within paramilitary organizations can continue in their efforts to 'defend' communities by seeking to create confidence and ambition through non-conflict expression:

> Personally I feel we should be putting the past behind us as much as possible. There is a danger that by concentrating on the past you recreate it. I understand why people can't let it go and there is a problem in pretending you are trying to be free of the past through drink and other destructive forms of escapism, which is going on quite a bit. There is also the problem of young people who think they have missed out on the conflict, who feel they missed that opportunity and want to get involved.
>
> More often than not those kids are the ones who become involved in criminality and we have to try and move them away from that. My argument is that if we look too much toward the past we will not want to create a better future. Most of the people I know wouldn't want to keep going over the past. They've raked through the ashes of their own past anyway and found that there is nothing to gain from that.

However, as 'Kevin' (UDA) indicated, the (re)education of those who might be particularly prone to the suggestions of violence and its dramatic appeal is something which older volunteers see as a key problem in the transformation of loyalist communities:

> The problem is that the older people want the new ways and the younger people want the old ways, which is frightening. The younger ones think conflict is glamorous but it's not. It's not glamorous when you can't stay at home, when you're being constantly arrested, living under the threat of being murdered by your enemies, the threat of going to prison, not having a social life and living under fear day in and day out. It's getting that across which is now a real challenge.

In comparison, for 'Brian' (UDA), now critical of the UDA, the 'image' of transformation is being used as justification for allowing those who wielded influence and control as paramilitary leaders to continue in that role but under another guise: that of reformed community worker:

> The only way that organisations can now maintain relevance is if, without them painting the picture, they can portray themselves as keeping the lid on a massive threat. As presenting themselves as moderates in that picture. In effect people need to walk away, question what they are paying money for and why they are being dragged to meetings for. There will be about 30 per cent that are 'dye in the wool', who have all sorts of personal agendas and interests riding on the organisation keeping together, keeping their clout and actually giving up weaponry because that would be the last shake of the orchard. The other 70 per cent would walk away in the morning and want out. Handing in weaponry means that any leverage that having it might provide is gone. A number are hanging on like grim death. What they see is power and influence evaporating. They don't have the means to gain any votes and they know that.

Although 'Brian's' comments dispute the legitimacy of the emerging picture of loyalist transformation being put forward by those he sees as having a personal interest to protect, 'Andrew' (UVF) nevertheless raises the important question about how efforts for community development (and the ambiguous forms of activity that might be camouflaged and defended through that term) and constructive change might take place given the absence of any moral agreement over the progress and change being pursued:

> In terms of dealing with the legacy of the conflict it's difficult to find any sort of concise mechanism, which will satisfy the diversity of needs out there. But rather than the conflict being resolved or transformed here it is being carefully managed and what we have is a benign form of apartheid. There's no internal community agreement on right and wrong and whilst some take a magnanimous approach towards their victimhood, others are looking for acknowledgement of the hurt visited upon them,

whilst others still are looking for retribution and revenge, which is not available.

Conclusions

What emerges from this series of responses about apology and regret? Perhaps to begin with it is important to move beyond any expected assumptions about a responsibility to apologize and display regret, towards acknowledging the sense of shame which apology and associated regret may produce and consider its implications. Most of the respondents here, in demonstrating similar objections to the possibility of apology know that with this apology comes the potential for shame where the conventions of identity, ritual, community organizational allegiance and self-esteem are exposed and opened to the attention of others (Heller 1985: 3). And because one is 'supposed to be seen' there is the added problem that if one 'is doing something which infringes the rules, or at least might be seen as something that infringes them, the affect of shame conquers or possesses the person' (Heller 2003: 1019).

From this perspective, shame can be seen as a regulatory device which presents itself as a 'failure to live up to expectations' (ibid: 1020) bringing with it the pressure of both internal (negative perceptions of the self) and external (isolation and harassment from the group or community which become undermined by possibility of further apologies) destruction for the person subject to shame. Significantly, a display of shame may be commendable on the one hand but also risks 'serious damage to social acceptance and a breakdown in a variety of social relationships' on the other (Gilbert 2003: 1205), and although it sounds reasonable to argue for individual demonstration of regret and shame, there is a need to also take into account the 'threats posed by others' (ibid) in this process.

The propensity for exclusion from the group which one's apology is seen to represent (and this is inescapable if one's actions emanated from belonging to that group) arises because 'stigmatization and ostracism are part of the process by which a group of others decide whom to associate and cooperate with and whom to exclude, reject and avoid' (ibid: 1216). Shame then can bring with it 'threats to the social order' (ibid) which can delegitimize the actions of the group and bring into doubt any credible reason for the group's existence and behaviour.

Taking the stigma of shame as one possible reason why apology and regret remain problematic for ex-combatants such as those interviewed in this chapter, we should appreciate that many tend to reject the idea of interpersonal apology because the conflict relied on depersonalization, where the individual was submerged within the category of 'enemy'. Reduced to 'the enemy', the person becomes the dehumanized 'target', an obstruction to be removed. To carry out this action effectively an absence of empathy is required (since empathy returns us to the personal), where violent actions and their consequences are understood not in the context of individual loss and devastation, but more in terms of how they contribute to success or failure in the conflict arena.

To expect those who adopted this psychology to apologize to those affected by violence is for them to admit that the process of depersonalization and dehumanization created by violence was illusory. Again this brings into question the legitimacy of the violent campaign and with that the justification of belonging to the groups and organizations which prosecuted that campaign. Once more we are returned to the social circumstances of the perpetrator if we are to grasp objections to apology and remorse.

But there is another point worth making here, which is that efforts to bring about social and communal transformation might be seen as a constructive and positive response to the effects of violence which amount not just to a rejection of that violence, but, through working to reduce communal tensions and stop a return to violence, in some way show acceptance of the destructive impact of past actions.

Expression of regret, in other words, can be manifest in works as much as words and have greater impact because of the wider social consequences that result. Actions which manifestly seek to draw people away from violence clearly also stand as a delegitimization of that violence. Might not efforts to prevent a return to violence be seen as a form of regret even if there are those involved who seek to hold on to power and status within communities by manipulating such efforts for personal gain?

This is a complex problem, which opens up a range of possible areas about the relationship between the self and society that will no doubt change as Northern Ireland moves to entrench structures and mechanisms of peace. But, for the time being, perhaps we might acknowledge that the public absence of apology and regret does not necessarily mean that neither exists. Maybe attitudes to both to some extent can be found in how those who committed past acts of violence now strive to live their life through deliberate acts designed to promote and help peace. And just as there seems to be some consensus around a general resistance to apology there also seems to be another consensus about not wanting to return to conflict and working to make sure through cross-communal and transformative projects that arguments for conflict are countered and neutralized. If such moves can be read as containing the seeds of apology and regret, then it is clear that each must be seen as a process rather than a stated position.

If that were to be the case, then perhaps there will come a time when those involved in that process will feel they have said sorry and tried to demonstrate regret but without direct public admission. And if that is so, then it is action rather than words which will have provided the means to reach that end.

Bibliography

Adair, J. *Mad Dog* (London: John Blake, 2007).

Adams, G. *The Politics of Irish Freedom* (Dingle: Brandon, 1986).

Adams, G. '"Protestants" future lies with the rest of us', *An Phoblacht/Republican News*, 20 May 1993.

Adams, G. *Free Ireland: Towards a Lasting Peace* (Dingle: Brandon Books, 1995).

Adams, G. 'An open letter to Drew Nelson', *An Phoblacht*, 6 August 2009.

Alison, M. 'Women as agents of political violence: Gendering security', *Security Dialogue*, 2004, 35(4): 447–63.

Alison, M. 'Gender, Small Arms and the Northern Ireland Conflict', paper presented to the International Studies Association Annual Conference, March, 2005.

Allen G. W. *None so Blind* (Chicago: Ivan R. Dee, 2001).

Allister, J. 'Get Marty's hand off the steering wheel', 25 June 2008. Archived at: http://www.jimallister.org/default.asp?blogID=1090; accessed 10 June 2009.

Anderson, B. *Imagined Communities – Reflections on the Origin and Spread of Nationalism* [revised edition] (London: Verso, 2006).

Anderson, C. *The Billy Boy: The Life and Death of LVF Leader Billy Wright* (Edinburgh: Mainstream, 2004).

Anderson, M. 'The great experiment', *An Phoblacht*, 16 October 2003.

Anderson, M. 'There's still only one rabbit', *An Phoblacht*, 7 June 2007.

Aretxaga, B. *Shattering Silence: Women, Nationalism, and Political Subjectivity in the North* (Princeton, New York: Princeton University Press, 1997).

Arthur, P. '"Reading" violence: Ireland', in D. Apter (ed.) *The Legitimization of Violence* (London: Macmillan, 1997).

Ashe, F. 'Deconstructing the experiential bar: Male experience and feminist resistance', *Men and Masculinities*, 2004, 7(2): 187–204.

Ashe, F. 'Gendering ethno-nationalist conflict in Northern Ireland', in Carol Coulter (ed.) *Northern Ireland Politics After the Peace* (Manchester: Manchester University Press, 2008).

Ashe, F. 'From paramilitaries to peacemakers: The gender dynamics of community-based restorative justice in Northern Ireland', *The British Journal of Politics and International Relations*, 2009, (11): 298–314.

Aughey, A. *Under Siege: Ulster Unionism and the Anglo-Irish Agreement* (London: Charles Hurst and Co, 1989).

Aughey, A. 'Britishness: An Explanation and a Defence', in G. Lucy and E. McClure (eds) *Cool Britannia? What Britishness Means to Me* (Lurgan: Ulster Society, 1999).

Bacevich, A. J. *American Empire: The Realities and Consequences of US Diplomacy* (Cambridge, MA: Harvard University Press, 2003).

Bacevich, A. J. *The New American Militarism* (Oxford: Oxford University Press, 2005).

Baggini, J. and Stangroom, J. (eds) *New British Philosophy* (London: Routledge, 2002).

Barkan, E. and Karn, A. 'Group apology as an ethical imperative', in E. Barkan and A. Karn (eds) *Taking Wrongs Seriously* (Stanford: Stanford University Press, 2006).

Barry, B. *Culture and Equality: An Egalitarian Critique of Multiculturalism* (Cambridge: Polity, 2001).

Bar -Tal, D. 'Collective memory of physical violence: Its contribution to the culture of violence', in E. Cairns and M. D. Roe (eds) *The Role of Memory in Ethnic Conflict* (Basingstoke: Palgrave Macmillan, 2003).

Bairner, A. 'Masculinity, violence and the Irish peace process', *Capital and Class,* 1999a, 23: 125–44.

Bairner, A. 'Soccer, masculinity, and violence in Northern Ireland: Between hooliganism and terrorism', *Men and Masculinities,* 1999b, 1: 284–301.

BBC. 'Orangeman slams cultural tourism', available at: http://news.bbc.co.uk/1/hi/northern_ireland/7503644.stm, 2008.

BBC News 'Community condemns "racist thugs" ', *BBC News Northern Ireland,* 17 June 2009a. Archived at: http://newsvote.bbc.co.uk/mpapps/pagetools/print/news.bbc.co.uk/1/hi/northern-ireland; accessed 28 August 2009.

BBC News, ' "These are criminals" Martin McGuinness', *BBC News Northern Ireland,* 17 June 2009b. Archived at: http://newsvote.bbc.co.uk/mpapps/pagetools/print/news.bbc.co.uk/1/hi/northern-ireland; accessed 28 August 2009.

BBC News 'Racism in Northern Ireland', *BBC News Northern Ireland,* 17 June 2009c. Archived at: http://news.bbc.co.uk/go/pr/fr/-/1/hi/northern-ireland/8104978; accessed 13 September 2009.

BBC News 'Parties briefed on justice plans', *BBC News Northern Ireland,* 15 October 2009d. Archived at: http://news.bbc.co.uk/go/pr/fr/-/1/hi/northern-ireland/8308441.stm; accessed 5 November 2009.

BBC News 'Prof quits over Ulster Scots fears', *BBC News Northern Ireland,* 1 July 2009e. Archived at: http://news.bbc.co.uk/1/hi/northern-ireland/8128299.stm; accessed 5 November 2009.

BBC News 'UVF Statement in Full'. Archived at: http://news.bbc.co.uk/1/hi/northern_ireland/6618365.stm; accessed 30 November 2009f.

Bean, K. *The New Departure: Recent Developments in Irish Republican Ideology and Strategy* (Liverpool: Institute of Irish Studies, University of Liverpool, 1994).

Bean, K. *The New Politics of Sinn Féin* (Liverpool: Liverpool University Press, 2007).

Bean, K. and Hayes, M. 'Sinn Féin and the New Republicanism in Ireland: Electoral progress, political stasis and ideological failure', *Radical History Review,* 2009, 104 Spring: 126–42.

Bell, C. 'Women address the problems of peace agreements', in R. Coomaraswamy and D. Fonseka (eds) *Peace Work: Women, Armed Conflict and Negotiation* (New Delhi: Women Unlimited, 2004), 96–126.

Berresford Ellis, P. (ed.) *James Connolly Selected Writings* (London: Pluto Press, 1988).

Bertridge Clarke, J. *The Tears and Smiles of Ireland; A Poem on the Death of the Right Hononrable John Hilpot Curran* (Dublin, 1817).

Billig, M. *Banal Nationalism* (London: Sage, 1995).

Bloomer, S. and Edwards, A. 'Bridging the militarist-politico divide: The Progressive Unionist Party and the politics of conflict transformation' in A. Edwards and S. Bloomer (eds) *Transforming the Peace Process in Northern Ireland: From Terrorism to Democratic Politics* (Dublin: Irish Academic Press, 2008), 97–113.

Bloomer, S. and Edwards, A. 'UVF decommissioning: A Pyrrhic victory?', *Fortnight,* 466 (August 2009): 6–7.

Borgonovo, J. *Spies, Informers and the ' Anti-Sinn Féin Society'* (Dublin: Irish Academic Press, 2007).

Bouris, E. *Complex Political Victims* (Bloomfield, CT: Kumarian Press, 2007).

Bowcott, O. 'Paisley and McGuinness mark new era', *The Guardian,* 8 May 2007.

Bowen, K. *Protestants in a Catholic State* (Montreal-Kingston: McGill-Queen's University Press, 1983).

Brennan, N. 'Compensating Southern Irish Loyalist after the Anglo-Irish Treaty, 1922–32', unpublished PhD thesis, University College Dublin, 1994.

Bridge, C. and Fedorowich, K. 'Mapping the British world' in C. Bridge and K. Fedorowich (eds) *The British World: Diaspora, Culture and Identity* (London: Frank Cass, 2003).

Brown, A., Donaghy, T. B., Mackay, F. and Meehen, E. 'Women and constitutional change in Scotland and Northern Ireland', *Parliamentary Affairs*, 2002, 55: 71–84.

Brown, G. *Speech to the Smith Institute*, 15 April 1999.

Brown, G. 'The golden thread that runs through our history', *The Guardian*, 8 July 2004.

Brown, G. 'The Future of Britishness', speech to the Fabian Society New Year Conference, 14 January 2006.

Brown, G. 'We must defend the Union', *Daily Telegraph*, 25th March 2008.

Brown, K. '"Our father organization": The cult of the Somme and the unionist "Golden Age" in modern Ulster Loyalist commemoration', *The Round Table*, 2007, 96: 707–23.

Brown, T. *Ireland: A Social and Cultural History, 1922-1985* (London: Fontano Paperbacks, 1985).

Brown K. and Mac Ginty, R. 'Public attitudes toward partisan and neutral symbols in post-Agreement Northern Ireland', *Identities: Global Studies in Culture and Power*, 2003, 83–108.

Brownie, 'Scenario for establishing a socialist republic', *An Phoblacht /Republican News*, 19 April 1980.

Bruce, S. *The Red Hand: Protestant Paramilitaries in Northern Ireland* (Oxford: Oxford University Press, 1992a.

Bruce, S. 'Victim selection in ethnic conflict: the case of Northern Ireland', *Terrorism and Political Violence*, 1992b, 9 (1): 56–71.

Bruce, S. 'Loyalists in Northern Ireland: Further thoughts on pro-state terror', *Terrorism and Political Violence*, 1993, 5(4): 252–65.

Bruce, S. *The Edge of the Union* (Oxford: Oxford University Press, 1994).

Bruce, S. 'Turf war and peace: Loyalist paramilitaries since 1994', *Terrorism and Political Violence*, 2004, 16(3): 1–21.

Bruce, S. *Paisley: Religion and Politics in Northern Ireland* (Oxford: Oxford University Press, 2007).

Bryan, D. *Orange Parades: The Politics of Ritual, Tradition and Control* (London: Pluto, 2000).

Buchanan, S. 'Transforming conflict in Northern Ireland and the border counties: Some lessons from peace programmes on valuing participative democracy', *Irish Political Studies*, 2008, 23(3): September.

Buckland, P. *Irish Unionism: The Anglo-Irish and the New Ireland, 1885-1922* (Dublin: Gill and Macmillan, 1972).

Buckley, A. D. *Symbols in Northern Ireland*. ([Belfast]: Institute of Irish Studies, Queen's University of Belfast, 1998).

Buckley S. and Lonergan, P. 'Women and the Troubles 1969–1980', in Y. Alexander and A. O'Day (eds) *Terrorism in Ireland* (London: Croom Helm, 1983).

Burton, F. *The Politics of Legitimacy: Struggles in a Belfast Community* (London: Routledge and Kegan Paul, 1978).

Butler, Lord. *Review of Intelligence on Weapons of Mass Destruction: Report of a Committee of Privy Counsellors, HC898* (London: TSO. Stationery Office, 2004).

Cadwallader, A. 'Romanians flee Belfast homes after racist attacks', Reuters,17 June: http://www.reuters.com/articlePrint?articleId=USTRE55G49U20090617 [accessed 13 September 2009].

Cairns, E., Van Til, T. and Williamson, A. *Social Capital, Collectivism – Individualism and Community Background in Northern Ireland* (Report to the Office of the First Minister and Deputy First Minister, Coleraine: University of Ulster, 2003).

Caldwell, J. and Robinson, J. (2006) *In Love with a Mad Dog* (Dublin: Gill and Macmillan, 2006).

Campbell, B. 'Has the Orange a future?', *An Phoblacht /Republican News*, 13 July 1998.

Canning, L. 'Stop the Orange madness', *The Guardian*, 15 July 2009.

Carlton, C. (ed) *Bigotry and Blood: Documents on the Ulster Troubles* (Chicago: Nelson-Hall, 1977).

Carroll, J. *Guilt* (London: Routledge and Kegan Paul, 1985).

Casquete, J. 'Protest rituals and uncivil communities', *Totalitarian Movements and Political Religions*, 2006, 7: 283–301.

Cavanaugh, K. 'Interpretations of political violence in ethnically divided societies', *Terrorism and Political Violence*, 1997, 9(3): 33–54.

Chandler, D. 'EU Statebuilding: securing the liberal peace through EU enlargement', *Global Society*, 2007, 21(4): 593–607.

Chandrasekaran, R. (2007) *Imperial Life in the Emerald City: Inside Iraq's Green Zone* (London: Bloomsbury, 2007).

Chrisafis, A. 'The Death of Doris Day', *The Guardian*, 12 October 2005.

Clancy, E. '100 Romanians flee homes after racist violence', *An Phoblacht*, 18 June 2009a.

Clancy, E. 'Sinn Féin meets UDA-linked UPRG in wake of killings', *An Phoblacht*, 19 March 2009b.

Clarke, L. 'Public spending is a jungle and we're lost', *Sunday Times*, 27 September 2009.

Clausewitz, C. V. *On War* [edited and translated by Michael Howard and Peter Paret] (Princeton, NJ: Princeton University Press, 1989).

Coakley, J. 'National identity in Northern Ireland: stability or change?', *Nations and Nationalism*, 2007, 13(4): 573–97.

Cochrane, F. 'Unsung Heroes? The role of peace and conflict resolution organisations in the Northern Ireland conflict', in McGarry, J. (ed.) *Northern Ireland and the Divided World. The Northern Ireland Conflict and the Good Friday Agreement in Comparative Perspective* (Oxford: Oxford University Press, 2001), 137–56.

Cochrane, F. and Dunn, S. *People Power : The Role of the Voluntary and Community Sector in the Northern Ireland Conflict* (Cork: Cork University Press, 2002).

Cockburn, C. 'Gender, armed conflict and political violence', *The World Bank, Washington DC*, 10 and 11 June 1999.

Cockburn, C. *The Space Between Us: Negotiating Gender and National Identities in Conflict* (London: Zed, 2003).

Cockburn, C. and Zarkov, D. (eds) *The Postwar Moment: Militaries, Masculinities and International Peacekeeping* (London: Lawrence and Wishart, 2002).

Coicaud, J. M. and Jonsson, J. 'Elements of a road map for a politics of apology', in M. Gibney, R. E. Howard-Hassmann, J. M. Coicaud and N. Steiner (eds) *The Age of Apology* (Philadelphia: University of Pennsylvania Press, 2008).

Colley, L. *Britons: Forging the Nation 1707–1837* (Yale: Yale University Press, 1992).

Community Foundation for Northern Ireland 2006, *Ex-prisoner Consortium - Dealing with the Past.* Archived at: www.communityfoundation.org/ ... 1/ Project520Descriptors.pdf; accessed 20 August 2009

Community Relations Information Centre *Community Development in Protestant Areas* (Belfast: Community Development in Protestant Areas Steering Group, 1992).

Conrad, J. *The Secret Agent: A Simple Tale* (Oxford: Oxford University Press, 2004).

Consultative Group on the Past, Report, www.cgpni.org, 23 January 2009).

Corcoran, M. *Out of Order: The Political Imprisonment of Women in Northern Ireland 1972-1998* (Devon: Willan Publishing, 2006).

Coulter, Carol 'Feminism and nationalism in Ireland', in D. Miller (ed.) *Rethinking Northern Ireland: Culture, Ideology and Colonialism* (Essex: Addison Wesley Longman, 1998), 160–78.

Coulter, Colin 'The character of unionism', *Irish Political Studies,* 1994, 9: 1–24.

Coulter, Colin. *Contemporary Northern Irish Society: An Introduction* (London: Pluto, 1999).

Coulter, Colin and Murray, M. *Northern Ireland after the Troubles: A Society in Transition* (Manchester: Manchester University Press, 2008).

Cowell-Meyers, K. 'Gender, power, and peace: A preliminary look at women in the Northern Ireland assembly', *Women and Politics,* 2001, 23(3): 55–87.

Cowell-Meyers, K. 'Women in Northern Ireland politics: Gender and the politics of peace-building in the New Legislative Assembly', *Irish Political Studies,* 2003, 18(1): 72–96.

Crawford, C. *Defenders Or Criminals? Loyalist Prisoners and Criminalisation* (Belfast: Blackstaff Press, 1999).

Crawford, C. *Inside the UDA: Volunteers and Violence* (London: Pluto Press, 2003).

Crenshaw, M. 'Theories of terrorism: Instrumental and organizational approaches', *Journal of Strategic Studies,* 1987, 10(4): 13–30.

Crenshaw, M. 'The psychology of terrorism: An agenda for the 21st century', *Political Psychology,* 2000, 21(2): 405–20.

Cronin, S. *Irish Nationalism: A History of its Roots and Ideology* (New York: Continuum, 1980).

Cunningham, C. 'A "War on Terror" in Northern Ireland? Northern Ireland perceptions of the war against terrorism and the war in Iraq', Paper prepared for the PSAI Postgraduate Conference Trinity College Dublin, 27–28 April, 2007.

Cusack, J. and McDonald, H. *UVF* (Dublin: Poolbeg, 1997).

Daly, J. 'The incompatibility of Green and Orange', speech at Republican Socialist Youth Movement Winter School, February 2008. Archived at: http://www.rsym. org/news/the-incompatibility -of -green -and organe.html; accessed 20August 2009.

Darby, J. *Intimidation and the Control of Conflict in Northern Ireland* (Dublin: Gill and Macmillan, 1986).

Dawar, A. 'Brown attacked for ignoring Ulster in article', *The Guardian,* 27th March 2008.

Day, P. 'Pride before a fall? Orangeism in Liverpool since 1945' in M. Busteed, F. Neal and J. Tonge (eds) *Irish Protestant Identities* (Manchester: Manchester University Press, 2008).

De Bréadún, D. *The Far Side of Revenge: Making Peace in Northern Ireland* (Dublin: Collins, 2008).

De Rosa, R. 'Explaining Ardoyne', *An Phoblacht /Republican News,* 13 September 2001.

Democratic Dialogue *Report Number 4: Power, Politics, Positionings: Women in Northern Ireland* (Democratic Dialogue, Belfast: Democratic Dialogue, 1997).

Democratic Unionist Party 'A bill of rights for Northern Ireland? A unionist vision', Policy paper 2003. Archived at: http://www.dup2win.com; accessed 13 October 2008.

Derrig, M. 'Outpost peoples', *An Phoblacht /Republican News*, 7 October 1999.

Derry Journal. 'McCausland must outline language strategy-Sinn Féin', *Derry Journal*, 27 October 2009.

Dixon, P. 'Political skills or lying and manipulation? The choreography of the Northern Ireland peace process', *Political Studies*, 2002, 50(4): 725–41.

Dodds, N. Speech by Deputy Leader to the DUP Annual Conference, Antrim, 1 November 2008.

Dodds, N. 'Deputy Leader's Speech to DUP Annual Conference', 3 November 2009.

Donaghy, T. B. 'The impact of devolution on women's political representation levels in Northern Ireland', *Politics*, 2004, 24(1): 26–34.

Dowling, B. 'The British presence, partition and Protestant privilege', *An Phoblacht / Republican News*, 22 October 1981.

Dudley-Edwards, R. *The Faithful Tribe. An Intimate Portrait of the Loyal Institutions* (London: HarperCollins, 1999).

Dunlop, J. *A Precarious Belonging: Presbyterians and the Conflict in Ireland* (Belfast: Blackstaff Press, 1995).

Eagleton, T. 'Afterword', in Terrence McDonough (ed.) *Was Ireland a Colony? Economics, Politics and Culture in Nineteenth-Century Ireland* (Dublin, 2005).

Earl of Moria. *The Speech of the Earl of Moria Delivered in the House of Peers on Wednesday March 9, 1803 on the Present Situation of Public Affairs. To Which is Added his Lordship's Speech to the Benevolent Society of St Patrick Last St Patrick's Day* (Dublin, 1803).

East Antrim Conflict Transformation Forum (EACTF). Minutes of Meetings, Strategic Guidance (2003–07), authors personal copies.

East Belfast Historical and Cultural Society. *Murder in Ballymacarrett: The Untold Story* Revised Edition. (Belfast: EBHCS, 2006).

Eccleshall, R. 'Anglican political thought in the century after the revolution of 1688' in D. G. Boyce, R. Eccleshall and V. Geoghegan (eds) *Political Thought in Ireland Since the Seventeenth Century* (London: Routledge, 1993).

Edwards, A. 'The UVF abandons its campaign of terror', *Fortnight*, 452, (May 2007a):12–13.

Edwards, A. 'Building relationships in the conflict transformation process?', *The Other View*, 2, (Autumn 2007b): 12–13.

Edwards, A. 'Abandoning armed resistance? The Ulster Volunteer Force as a case-study of strategic terrorism in Northern Ireland', *Studies in Conflict and Terrorism*, 2009, 32(2): 146–66.

Edwards, A. and S. Bloomer *A Watching Brief? The Political Strategy of Progressive Loyalism since 1994*, Conflict Transformation Papers, 8, (Belfast: LINC Resource Centre, 2004).

Edwards, A. and S. Bloomer *Democratising the Peace in Northern Ireland: Progressive Loyalists and the Politics of Conflict Transformation*, Conflict Transformation Papers, 12, (Belfast: LINC Resource Centre, 2005).

Edwards, A. and S. Bloomer 'Loyalism at the crossroads', *Fortnight*, 444, (May 2006): 7–8.

Elliott, M. (ed.) *The Long Road to Peace in Northern Ireland* (Liverpool: Liverpool University Press, 2007).

Elliott, M. 2009, *When God Took Sides: Religion and Identity in Ireland-Unfinished History* (Oxford: Oxford University Press, 2009).

English, R. *Armed Struggle: The History of the IRA* (London: Macmillan, 2003).

English, R. 'Sinn Féin's hundredth birthday', *Open Democracy*, 28 November 2005. Archived at: http://www.opendemocracy.net/democracy-protest/sinnfein-3068.jsp; accessed 4 November 2009.

English, R. *Irish Freedom: The History of Nationalism in Ireland* (Basingstoke: Macmillan, 2006).

Enloe, C. *The Morning After: Sexual Politics at the End of the Cold War* (Berkeley: University of California Press, 1994).

Enloe, C. 'Demilitarisation – or more of the same? Feminist questions to ask in the postwar moment,' in C. Cockburn and D. Zarkov (eds) *The Postwar Moment: Militaries, Masculinities and International Peacekeeping* (London: Lawrence and Wishart, 2002), 22–32.

Ervine, D. 'We have to start from somewhere', *Irish Reporter,* June 1996.

Etherington, N. 'Missions and Empire', in , W. R. Louis and Robin Winks (eds) *Oxford History of the British Empire; vol. V* (Oxford: Oxford University Press, 1999), 303–14.

Evans, J. and Tonge, J. 'Social class and party choice in Northern Ireland's ethnic blocs', West *European Politics*, 2009, 32(5).

Ex-Prisoners Interpretive Centre. *Truth Recovery: A Contribution from within Loyalism* (Belfast: EPIC, 2004).

Fairweather, E., McDonough, R. and McFadyean, M. *Only the Rivers Run Free: Northern Ireland: The Women's War* (London: Pluto, 1984).

Farrington, C. 'Unionism and the peace process in Northern Ireland', *British Journal of Politics and International Relations*, 2006, 8(2): 277–94.

Farrington, C. 'Loyalists and unionists: Explaining the internal dynamics of an ethnic group', in Edwards, A. and Bloomer, S. (eds) *Transforming the Peace Process in Northern Ireland: From Terrorism to Democratic Politics* (Dublin: Irish Academic Press, 2008).

Fearon, K. *Women's Work: The Story of the Northern Ireland Women's Coalition* (Belfast: Blackstaff Press, 1999).

Fearon, K. *The Conflict's Fifth Business: A Brief Biography of Billy Mitchell* (Belfast: LINC, 2002)

Fearon, K. and Rebouche, R. 'What happened to the women? Promises, reality and the Northern Ireland Women's Coalition', in M. Cox, A. Guelke and F. Stephen (eds) *A Farewell to Arms? Beyond the Good Friday Agreement* (Manchester: Manchester University Press, 2006), 280–301.

Finn, D. 'Community Relations', *London Review of Books* 27 August 2009.

First Minister and Deputy First Minister, *The Northern Ireland Act 1998*. Archived at: http://www.ofmdmni.gov.uk/index/equality/stautory-duty.htm; accessed 12 October 2009.

FitzGerald, G., 'New chapter of Irish history about to be written', *The Irish Times* 11 April 1998.

Fitzpatrick, D. 'Ireland and Empire', in A. Porter (ed.) *The Oxford History of the British Empire, Volume III: The Nineteenth Century* (New York: Oxford University Press, 1999).

Frampton, M. *The Long March: The Political Strategy of Sinn Féin. 1981-2007* (Basingstoke: Palgrave Macmillan, 2009).

Fricker M. 'Power knowledge and injustice', in J. Baggini and J. Stangroom (eds) *New British Philosophy* (London: Routledge, 2002).

Friel, L. 'A "Grand" night out', *An Phoblacht/Republican News*, 11 October 2001a.

Friel, L. 'Holy Cross and the victim discourse', *An Phoblacht/Republican News*, 20 December 2001b.

Friel, L. 'Wave of sectarian attacks', *An Phoblacht/Republican News*, 26 May 2005a.

Friel, L. 'Embracing cultural diversity', *An Phoblacht/Republican News*, 28 July 2005b.

Friel, L. 'War of words', *An Phoblacht*, 20 October 2005c.

Friel, L. 'Ballymena ethos fuels sectarianism', *An Phoblacht*, 18 May 2006a.

Friel, L. 'Poverty-the hidden war', *An Phoblacht*, 6 July 2006b.

Friel, L. 'Historic initiative heralds new political era', *An Phoblacht*, 31 May 2007a.

Friel, L. 'UDA claims end to all its violence and criminality', *An Phoblacht*, 15 November 2007b.

Friel, L. 'UDA-linked scheme funded by Ritchie', *An Phoblacht*, 16 October 2008.

Fourthwrite. 'Has the party died as well?', *Fourthwrite*, 2006/07.

Furedi, F. *Mythical Past, Elusive Future: History and Society in an Anxious Age* (London: Pluto Press, 1991).

Gallagher, C. and Shirlow, P. 'The geography of loyalist paramilitary feuding in Belfast', *Space and Polity*, 2006, 10(2):149–69.

Galligan, Y. *Women and Politics in Contemporary Ireland: From the Margins to the Mainstream* (London: Pinter, 1998).

Galligan, Y. and Wilford, R. 'Women's political representation in Ireland', in Y. Galligan, E. Ward and R. Wilford (eds) *Contesting Politics: Women in Ireland, North and South* (Oxford: Westview Press, 1999), 130–48.

Galtung, J. 'What if the devil were interested in peace research?', *Journal of Peace Research*, 1988, 25(1): 1–4.

Galtung, J. 'What peace research would be like if founded today', Speech delivered *on the occasion of the Peace Research Institute, Oslo-PRIO 50 Years*, Oslo City Hall, 5 June 2009. Archived at: http://www.transcend.org/tms/galtung_editorial_archive_detail.php?article_id=1355; accessed: 21 July 2009.

Garcia-Rivero, C., Coetze H. and Du Toit, P. 'Political culture and democracy: The South African case', *Politikon*, 2002, 29(2): 163–81.

Gaventa, J. 'Toward a knowledge democracy: Viewpoints on participatory research in North America', in O. Fals-Borda and M. A. Rathman (eds) *Action and Knowledge: Breaking the Monopoly with Participatory Action Research* (New York: Apex Press, 1991).

George, R. and Bruce, J. (eds) *Analyzing Intelligence: Origins, Obstacles and Innovations* (Washington, Georgetown: University Press, 2008).

Gilbert, P. 'Evolution, social roles and the differences in guilt and shame', *Social Research* 2003, 70(4): 1205–30.

Gillespie, U. 'Equality and the Good Friday Agreement: Fact or fiction', *Left Republican Review*, April/May 2006.

Gilmore, G. *The Irish Republican Congress* (Cork: Cork Workers' Club, 1974).

Godson, D. *Himself Alone. David Trimble and the Ordeal of Unionism* (London: Harper Collins, 2004).

Gordon, Rev. J. 'An Address to the People of Ireland' (Dublin, 1803).

Graham, B. and Whelan, Y. 'The legacies of the dead: Commemorating the Troubles in Northern Ireland', *Environment and Planning D: Society and Space*, 2007, 25: 476–95.

Graham, W. 'Addressing grievances first step to achieving peace: Chomsky', *Irish News*, 2 November 2009.

Grand Orange Lodge of Scotland website, Archived at: http://www.orangeorderscotland.com/; accessed 14 December 2009.

Grand Orange Lodge of England website, Archived at: http://www.gole.org.uk/; accessed 14 December 2009].

Grant, I. U202, Units 26 and 27 U202, 'Inquiry', (Milton Keynes: Open University, 1981).

Grieve, J. 'Sitting on the lid', *Policing Today*, 1994, 1.

Grieve, J. 'Intelligence as education for all', in L. O'Connor, D. O'Connor and R. Best (eds) *Drugs: Partnerships for Policy, Prevention and Education* (London: Cassell, 1998).

Grieve, J. 'Developments in UK criminal intelligence', in J. Ratcliffe (ed.) *Strategic Thinking in Criminal Intelligence* (NSW Australia: Federation Press, 2004).

Grieve, J. 'Lawfully audacious – a reflective journey', in C. Harfield, A. MacVean, J. Grieve and D. Phillips (eds) *The Handbook of Intelligent Policing, Consilience, Crime Control, and Community Safety* (Oxford: Oxford University Press, 2008).

Hadaway, P. 'The visual arts in Northern Ireland after the Good Friday Agreement', *Variant*, Winter 2009.

Hain, P. ' "Better than before" is not good enough', *The Guardian*, 29 July 2005.

Hall, M. *Seeds of Hope: Ex-Prisoners' Project* (Newtownabbey Co. Antrim: Island Pamphlets, 2000).

Hall, M. *'It's good to talk'; The Experiences of Springfield Phone Network* (Newtownabbey Co. Antrim: Island Pamphlets, 2003).

Hall, M. *At a New Crossroads? An Overview of Community Anxieties* (Newtownabbey Co. Antrim: Island Pamphlets, 2004).

Hall, M. *Loyalism in Transition (1): A New Reality* (Newtownabbey Co. Antrim: Island Pamphlets, 2006)

Hall, M. *Loyalism in Transition (2): Learning From Others in Conflict*. Report of an international workshop (Newtownabbey Co. Antrim: Island Pamphlets, *Island Pamphlets*, 2007a).

Hall, M. *Building Bridges at the Grassroots: The Experience of Suffolk – Lenadoon Interface Group* (Newtownabbey Co. Antrim: Island Pamphlets, 2007b).

Harland, K. *Young Men Talking – Voices from Belfast* (Belfast: YouthAction Northern Ireland, 1997).

Harris, L. 'Introducing the strategic approach: An examination of loyalist paramilitaries in Northern Ireland', *British Journal of Politics and International Relations*, 2006, 8(4): 539–49.

Harris, L. ' "Exit, voice and loyalty": Signalling of loyalist paramilitaries in Northern Ireland' in A. Edwards and S. Bloomer (eds) *Transforming the Peace Process in Northern Ireland: From Terrorism to Democratic Politics* (Irish Academic Press: Dublin, 2008a).

Harris, L. 'Duck or rabbit? The value systems of loyalist paramilitaries in Northern Ireland', in M. Busteed, F. Neal and J. Tonge (eds) *Irish Protestant Identities* (Manchester: Manchester University Press, 2008b).

Harrison, S. 'Are North and South Polls Apart?', *BBC News Northern Ireland*, 22 March. Archived at: news.bbc.co.uk/1/hi/northern –ireland/7307457.stm.; accessed 13 April 2008.

Hart, P. *The IRA and Its Enemies* (Oxford: Oxford University Press, 1999).

Hastings, M. 'The last writhings of a society left beached by history', *The Guardian*, 15 September 2005.

Haydon, L. 'Gangland glamour', *The Guardian*, 16 November 2005.

Hayes, B. and McAllister, I. 'Public support for political violence and paramilitarism in Northern Ireland and the Republic of Ireland', *Terrorism and Political Violence*, 2005, 17.

Heartfield, J. *The 'Death of the Subject' Explained* (Sheffield: Sheffield Hallam University Press, 2002).

Heller, A. *The Power of Shame* (London: Routledge and Kegan Paul, 1985).

Heller, A. 'Five approaches to the phenomenon of shame', *Social Research*, 2003, 70(4): 1015–30.

Hennessey, T. *A History of Northern Ireland* (Houndmills: Palgrave, 1996).

Hennessey, T. 'The evolution of Ulster protestant identity in the twentieth century', in M. Busteed, F. Neal, and J. Tonge (eds.) *Irish Protestant Identities* (Manchester, Manchester University Press, 2009).

High Court of Justice Queens Bench Division Divisional Court Case No. CO/9939/2005, delivered 19 January 2007.

Hill, M. *Women in Ireland: A Century of Change* (Belfast: Blackstaff Press, 2003).

Hill, A. and White, A. 'The flying of Israeli flags in Northern Ireland', *Identities: Global Studies in Culture and Power*, 2008, 15: 31–50.

Hinds, B. 'Women working for peace in Northern Ireland', in Y. Galligan, E. Ward, and R. Wilford (eds.) *Contesting Politics: Women in Ireland North and South* (Oxford: Westview Press, 1999), 109–29.

Hirschman, A. *Exit, Voice and Loyalty: Responses to Decline in Firms, Organizations and States* (Cambridge, MA: Harvard University Press, 1970).

HMSO *The Agreement: Agreement Reached in Multi-Party Negotiations* (Belfast: HSMO, 1998).

Horgan, J. *The Psychology of Terrorism* (London: Routledge, 2005).

Howe, S. 'Mad Dogs and Ulstermen: The Crisis of Loyalism (Part One)', Open Democracy, (2005a). Archived at: http://www.opendemocracy.net/globalization-protest/loyalism_2876.jsp; accessed: 12 July 2009.

Howe, S. 'Mad Dogs and Ulstermen: The Crisis of Loyalism (Part Two)', (2005b). Archived at: http://www.opendemocracy.net/democracy-protest/loyalism_2885.jsp; accessed 12 July 2009.

Howe, S. 'Loyalism's rage against the fading light of Britishness', *The Guardian*, 10 October 2005c.

Howe, S. 'Review of the IRA and its enemies', *Journal of Modern History*, 2006, 78: 710–13.

Howe, S. 'Questioning the (Bad) question: Was Ireland a colony?', *Irish Historical Studies*, 2008, 37(142): 1–15.

Hume, D. Speech to the County Grand Lodge of the East Commemoration at Grangemouth, Saturday, 28 June 2008.

Hume, D. Speech to Orange Society, Queens University, Belfast, 19 June 2009a.

Hume, D. Speech to Queens L.O.L. 845, 29 April 2009b.

Independent Monitoring Commission. 'Statement by the Independent Monitoring Commission (IMC) to clarify its role and the way it is going about its work', Press release, 9 March, 2004 (Belfast, IMC).

Independent Monitoring Commission. *Twenty-Second Report HC1085* (London: The Stationary Office, 4 November 2009).

Independent Monitoring Commission. *Reports Numbers 1–22 of the Independent Monitoring Commission [2004 – 2009]* (London: The Stationery Office).

Independent International Decommissioning Commission. Report of the Independent International Commission on Decommissioning to the Secretary of State for Northern Ireland and the Minister for Justice, Equality and Law Reform, 4 September 2009. Archived at: http://www.nio.gov.uk/iicd_report_26_sept_2005.pdf; accessed 30 November 2009.

Inter Action Belfast, *The Role of Ex-Combatants on Interfaces* (Belfast: Inter-Action Belfast, 2006).

IRA Statement. 'IRA statement in full' BBC News 2005. Archived at: http://news.bbc.co.uk/1/hi/northern_ireland/4724599.stm; accessed 30 November 2009

Irish Freedom Movement. *The Irish War* (London: Junius, 1987).

Irish Press Agency. *Ireland, Scotland and Ulster* (London: IPA, no date).

Irish Times 'Clare unionists, resolution supporting the government', 12 December 1921 [NAI S58].

Jacobson, R. 'Whose peace process? Women's organisations and political settlement in Northern Ireland, 1996–1997' (University of Bradford: Department of Peace Studies, Peace Studies Papers, 9/1997).

Jacobson, R. 'Women and peace in Northern Ireland: A complicated relationship', in S. Jacobs, R. Jacobson and J. Marchbank (eds) *States of Conflict* (London: Zed Books, 2000),179–98.

Jarman, N. 'Painting landscapes: The place of murals in the symbolic construction of urban space', in A. Buckley (ed.) *Symbols in Northern Ireland* (Belfast: Institute of Irish Studies, 1998), 81–98.

Jennings, S. (1999) 'Politics from women for women: It doesn't have to be a dirty word', *Women's News*, 1999, 100(January): 10–11.

Juett, L., Smith, R., Grieve, J. 'Open source intelligence – A case study: GLADA "London – the Highs and Lows" 2003 and 2007' in C. Harfield, A. MacVean, J. Grieve and D. Phillips (eds) *The Handbook of Intelligent Policing, Consilience, Crime Control, and Community Safety* (Oxford: Oxford University Press, 2008).

Kaufman, E. *The Orange Order: A Contemporary Northern Irish History* (Oxford University Press, 2007).

Kelman, H. 'Building trust among enemies: The central challenge for international conflict resolution', *International Journal of Intercultural Relations*, 2005, 29(6): 639–50.

Kennaway, B. *The Orange Order: A Tradition Betrayed* (London: Methuen, 2006).

Kennedy, L. *Colonialism, Religion and Nationalism in Ireland* (Belfast: The institute of Irish Studies, 1996).

Kenney, S. J. *Waving Goodbye to the Dinosaurs? Women, Electoral Politics, and Peace in Northern Ireland* (Belfast: Centre on Women and Public Policy, 2005).

Kerr, R. J. 'The perfect enemy. Reflections of an intelligence officer on the Cold War and today's challenges', in C. Harfield, A. MacVean, J. Grieve and D Phillips (eds) *The Handbook of Intelligent Policing, Consilience, Crime Control, and Community Safety* (Oxford: Oxford University Press, 2008a).

Kerr, R. J. 'The Track Record. CIA Analysis 1950-2000', in R. George and J. Bruce J. (eds) *Analyzing Intelligence. Origins, Obstacles and Innovations* (Washington, Georgetown: University Press, 2008b).

Kertzer, D. I. *Ritual, Politics, and Power* (New Haven: Yale University Press, 1988).

Kilcullen, D. '"Twenty-Eight Articles": Funamentals of company-level counter-insurgency', *Military Review*, (May–June 2006): 134–9.

Kilcullen, D. *The Accidental Guerrilla: Fighting Small Wars in the Midst of a Big One* (London: Hurst, 2009).

Kinealy, C. 'The Orange Order and representations of Britishness', in S. Caunce, E. Mazierska, S. Sydney-Smith and J. K. Walton (eds) *Relocating Britishness* (Manchester: Manchester University Press, 2004).

Kinealy, C. 'At home with the Empire: The example of Ireland', in C. Hall and S. O. Rose (eds) *At Home with the Empire* (Cambridge: Cambridge University Press, 2006).

Knaus, G. and Martin, F. 'Travails of the European Raj', *Journal of Democracy*, 2003, 14(3): 60–74.

Laming, Lord. *The Victoria Climbie Inquiry* (London: Stationery Office, 2001).

Lane, F. 'Banging the loyalist drum: A year of bigotry, attacks and censorship by unionists', *An Phoblacht/Republican News*, 16 December 1999.

Lane, F. 'Harold Gracey and King Lear', *An Phoblacht/ Republican News*, 10 May 2001.

Lawler, P. 'Peace studies', in P. D. Williams (ed.) *Security Studies: An Introduction* (London: Routledge, 2008), 73–88.

Lazare, A. *On Apology* (Oxford: Oxford University Press, 2004).

Lederach, J. P. *Building Peace: Sustainable Reconciliation in Divided Societies* (Washington, DC: United States Institute of Peace Press, 1997).

Lederach, J. P., Neufeldt R. and Culbertson, H. *Reflective Peacebuilding: A Planning, Monitoring, and Learning Toolkit* (University of Notre Dame: The Joan B. Kroc Institute for International Peace Studies, 2007).

Lister, D. and Jordan, H. *Mad Dog: The Rise and Fall of Johnny Adair and 'C' Company* (Edinburgh: Mainstream Publishing, 2003).

Londonderry Sentinel. 'Unionists urged to take a stand for Britishness', 12 July 2008.

Longley, E. 'Siege debate', Paper presented at *Irish Protestant Identities Conference, Salford*, November, 2005.

Lundy, P. and McGovern, M. (2004), 'You understand again: Testimony and post-conflict transition in the North of Ireland: The Ardoyne Commemoration Project, 1998-2002', *Words and Silences: Journal of the International Oral History Association*, 2004, 2(2): 30–5.

Lundy, P. and McGovern, M. 'Participation, truth and partiality: Participatory action research, community-based truth-telling and post-conflict transition in Northern Ireland', *Sociology*, 2006, 40(1): 71–88.

Lundy, P. and McGovern, M. 'A Trojan Horse? Unionism, trust and truth-telling in Northern Ireland', *International Journal of Transitional Justice*, 2008, 2: 42–68.

Lysaght, K. 'Dangerous friends and deadly foes – performances of masculinity in the divided city', *Irish Geography*, 2002, 35(1): 51–62.

MacDonald, J. 'Peace protests across Northern Ireland', *The Guardian*, 11 March 2009.

Mac Ginty, R. *No War, No Peace: The Rejuvenation of Stalled Peace Processes and Peace Accords* (Basingstoke: Palgrave, 2006).

Mac Ginty, R. and Darby, J. *Guns and Government: The Management of the Northern Ireland Peace Process* (Basingstoke: Palgrave, 2002).

Mac Ginty, R. and Richmond, O. *The Liberal Peace and Post-war Reconstruction: Myth or Reality?* (London: Routledge, 2009).

MacMillan, G. M. *State, Society, and Authority in Ireland: The Foundations of the Modern State* (Dublin: Gill and Macmillan, 1993).

McAuley, J. W. 'Cuhullian with an RPG7: The ideology and politics of the Ulster Defence Association', in E. Hughes (ed.) *Culture and Politics in Northern Ireland* (Milton Keynes: Open University Press, 1991), 44–68.

McAuley, J. W. *The Politics of Identity: A Loyalist Community in Belfast* (Aldershot: Avebury Press, 1994).

McAuley, J. W. ' "Not a game of cowboys and Indians": Loyalist paramilitary groups in the 1990s', in Alan O'Day (ed.) *Terrorism's Laboratory: Northern Ireland* (London: Dartmouth Press, 1995), 137–58.

McAuley, J. W. '(Re)Constructing Ulster Loyalism? Political responses to the "peace process" ', *Irish Journal of Sociology*, 1996, 6: 127–53.

McAuley, J. W. 'The loyalist parties: A new respectability?', *Etudes Irlandaises, Le Processus De Paix En Irlande Du Nord*, Special Volume on the Peace Process, (edited by Pierre Joannon), 1997, 22(2): 117–32.

McAuley, J. W. 'The emergence of new Loyalism', in John Coakley (ed.) *Changing Shades of Orange and Green: Redefining the Union and the Nation: New Perspectives on Political Progress in Ireland* (Dublin: UCD Press, 2002a), 106–22.

McAuley, J. W. 'Ulster unionism after the peace', in J. Neuheiser and S. Wolff (eds) *Breakthrough to Peace? The Impact of the Good Friday Agreement on Northern Irish Politics and Society* (New York and Oxford, Berghahn Books, 2002b), 76–92.

McAuley, J. W. 'Peace and progress? Political and social change among young loyalists in Northern Ireland', *Journal of Social Issues*, 2004a, 60(3): 541–62.

McAuley, J. W. '"Just fighting to survive": loyalist paramilitary politics and the Progressive Unionist Party', *Journal of Political Violence and Terrorism*, 2004b, 16(3): 522–43.

McAuley, J. W. 'Contemporary unionist understandings of the peace process', *The Global Review of Ethnopolitics*, 2004c, 3(1): 60–76.

McAuley, J. W. 'Fantasy politics? Restructuring unionism after the Good Friday Agreement', *Eire/Ireland: American Journal of Irish Studies*, 2004d, 39(1–2): 189–214.

McAuley, J. W. 'Whither new loyalism? Changing loyalist politics after the Belfast Agreement', *Irish Political Studies*, 2005, 20: 323–40.

McAuley, J.W. 'Two traditions in unionist political culture: A commentary', in C. McGrath and E. O'Malley (eds) *Irish Political Studies Reader: Key Contributions* (London: Routledge, 2007), 105–35.

McAuley, J. W. 'Constructing unionist and loyalist identities', in A. Edwards and S. Bloomer (eds) *Transforming the Peace in Northern Ireland: From Terrorism to Democratic Politics* (Dublin: Irish Academic Press, 2008), 15–27.

McAuley, J. W. *Ulster's Last Stand? Reconstructing Ulster Unionism After the Peace Process* (Dublin: Irish Academic Press, 2010, in press).

McAuley, J. W. and Hislop, S. "Many roads forward': Politics and ideology within the Progressive Unionist Party', *Etudes Irlandaises*, 2000, 25(1): 173–92.

McAuley J. W. and Tonge, J. '"For God and for the Crown": Contemporary political and social attitudes among Orange Order members in Northern Ireland', *Political Psychology*, 2007, 28: 33–54.

McAuley J. W. and Tonge, J. 'Faith, Crown and State: Contemporary discourses within the Orange Order in Northern Ireland', in 'Political discourse as an instrument of conflict and peace: Lessons from Northern Ireland', *Peace and Conflict Studies*, Special Issue, edited by K. Hayward and C. O'Donnell, 2008, 15 (1): 156–76.

McAuley, J. W. and Tonge, J. 'Still marching after all these years: Orange ideology and the culture war in Northern Ireland', in O. Coquellin (ed.) *Political Ideologies in Ireland/ L'Ideologie Politique en Irlande* (Cambridge: Cambridge Scholars Press, 2009), 299–316.

McAuley, J. W. and Tonge, J. 'Britishness (and Irishness) in Northern Ireland since the Good Friday Agreement', *Parliamentary Affairs*, 2010 in press.

McAuley, J. W., Tonge, J. and Shirlow, P. 'Conflict, transformation, and former loyalist paramilitary prisoners in Northern Ireland', *Terrorism and Political Violence*, 2010, 22: 22–40.

McCaffery, B. 'Former enemies' hard work brings end to interface riots', *Irish News*, 18 August 2008.

McCay, J. *Loyalty and Humanity: or a Variety of Scenes which a Clergyman of the Established Church and his Family, Evidenced and Came Through in a Disturbed Part of Ireland During the Late Troubles; with his Observations on Them* (Dublin, 1803).

McCloskey, A. 'Sectarian monster sated with blood', *An Phoblacht*, 27 July 2006.

McCoy, G. 'Women, community and politics in Northern Ireland', in C. Roulston and C. Davies (eds.) *Gender, Democracy and Inclusion in Northern Ireland* (London: Palgrave, 2000), 3–22.

McCready, S. *Empowering People: Community Development and Conflict, 1969–1999* (Belfast: The Stationery Office, 2001).

McDonald, H. (2009) 'Bridge over Troubles water', *The Guardian*, 29 July.

McDonald, H. and Cusack, J. *UDA* (Dublin: Penguin Ireland, 2004).

McDowell, J. *Godfathers: Inside Northern Ireland's Drug Racket* (Dublin: Gill and Macmillan, 2001).

274   *Bibliography*

McDowell, R. B. *Crisis and Decline: The Fate of Southern Unionists* (Dublin: Lilliput Press, 1997).

McDowell, S. 'Armalite, the ballot box and memorialization: Sinn Féin and the state in post-conflict Northern Ireland', *The Round Table*, 2007, 96: 725–38.

McDowell, S. 'Commemorating dead 'men': Gendering the past and present in post-conflict Northern Ireland', *Gender, Place and Culture*, 2008, 15(4): 335–54.

McEvoy, K. *Paramilitary Imprisonment in Northern Ireland: Resistance, Management, and Release* (Oxford: Oxford University Press, 2002).

McEvoy, K., O'Mahony, D., Horner, C. and Lyner, O. 'The home front: The families of politically motivated prisoners in Northern Ireland', *British Journal of Criminology*, 1999, 39(2): 175–97.

McEvoy, S. 'Women loyalist paramilitaries in Northern Ireland: Duty, agency and empowerment – a report from the field', paper presented to the International Studies Association Annual Conference, March 2007.

McEvoy, S. 'Loyalist women paramilitaries in Northern Ireland: Beginning a feminist conversation about conflict resolution', *Security Studies*, 2009, 18: 262–86.

McGarry, J. and O'Leary, B. *Explaining Northern Ireland: Broken Images* (Oxford: Blackwell, 1995).

McGregor, R. 'The necessity of Britishness: ethno-cultural roots of Australian nationalism', *Nations and Nationalism*, 2006, 12: 493–511.

McGurk, T. 'Attacks on Roma hint at Europe's last taboo', *The Sunday Business Post*, 21 June 2009.

McInnes, C. 'A Farewell to arms? Decommissioning and the peace process', in M. Cox, A. Guelke, and F. Stephen (eds) *A Farewell to Arms: From Long War to Long Peace in Northern Ireland* (Manchester: Manchester University Press, 2000).

McIntyre, A. (1995) 'Modern Irish Republicanism: The product of British state strategies', *Irish Political Studies*, 1995, 10(1): 97–122.

McIntyre, A. 'Gusty calls it a day? Britain's proxy warriors', *Fourthwrite*, Spring 2007.

McKay, S. *Northern Protestants: An Unsettled People* (Belfast: Blackstaff, 2000).

McKearney, T. Interview with author, 19 May 1998.

McKittrick, D. *Making Sense of the Troubles* (London: Penguin, 2001).

McKittrick, D. 'Hain resumes peace push after Northern Ireland elections', *The Independent*, 10 March 2007.

McWilliams, M. 'Women in Northern Ireland: An overview', in E. Hughes (ed.) *Culture and Politics in Northern Ireland: 1960-1990* (Milton Keynes: Open University Press, 1993a), 81–100.

McWilliams, M. 'The church, the state and the women's movement in Northern Ireland', in A. Smyth (ed.) *The Irish Women's Studies Reader* (Dublin: Attic Press, 1993b).

McWilliams, M. (1995) 'Struggling for peace and justice: Reflections on women's activism in Northern Ireland', *Journal of Women's History*, 1995, 7(1): 13–39.

McWilliams, M. 'Violence against women and political conflict: The Northern Ireland experience', *Critical Criminology*, 1997, 8(1): 79–92.

Magee, K. 'Beeb spotlight falls on dark side of loyalism', *Belfast Newsletter*, 28 January 2003.

Malinowski, B. *Argonauts of the Western Pacific: An Account of Native Enterprise and Adventure in the Archipelagoes of Melanesian New Guinea* (London: Routledge, 1932).

Marvin, C. and Ingle, D. W. *Blood Sacrifice and the Nation – Totem Rituals and the American Flag* (Cambridge: CUP, 1999).

Meaney, N. 'Britishness and Australia: some reflections', *Journal of Imperial and Commonwealth and History*, 2003, (31): 121–35.

Meintjes, S., Pillay A. and Thursden, M. (eds) *The Aftermath: Women and Post- Conflict Reconstruction* (London: Zed Books, 2001).

Merrell Lynd, H. *On Shame and the Search for Identity* (New York: Science Editions Inc, 1958).

Meyer, M. K. 'Ulster's red hand: gender, identity and sectarian conflict in Northern Ireland', in S. Ranchard-Nilsson and M. A. Tétreault (eds) *Women at Home in the Nation?* London: Routledge, 2000), 119–42.

Miller, D. W. *Queen's Rebels: Ulster Loyalism in Historical Perspective* (Dublin: Gill and Macmillan, 1978).

Miller, R. L., Wilford, R. and Donoghue, F. *Women and Political Participation in Northern Ireland* (Aldershot: Avebury, 1996).

Mills, C. W. *The Sociological Imagination* (Oxford: Oxford University Press, 2000).

Misztal, B. A. 'The sacralization of memory', *European Journal of Social Theory*, 2004, 7: 67–84.

Mitchell, B. *Principles of Loyalism – An Internal Discussion Paper* (Belfast: Progressive Unionist Party, 2002)

Mitchell, C. 'Civic society at city hall', *The Other View*, Winter 2002.

Mitchell C. 'Protestant identification and political change in Northern Ireland', *Ethnic and Racial Studies*, 2003, 26(4): 612–31.

Mitchell, C. *Religion, Identity and Politics in Northern Ireland: Boundaries of Belonging and Belief* (Aldershot: Ashgate, 2006).

Mitchell, C. 'The limits of legitimacy: Former loyalist combatants and peace-Building in Northern Ireland', *Irish Political Studies*, 2008, 23(1): 1–19.

Mitchell, G. J. *Making Peace: The Behind-the-Scenes Story of the Negotiations that Culminated in the Signing of the Northern Ireland Peace Accord* (New York: Alfred A. Knopf, 1999).

Moloney, E. *A Secret History of the IRA* (London: Allen Lane, 2002).

Moloney, E. *Paisley: From Demagogue to Democrat?* (Dublin: Poolbeg Press, 2008).

Morgan, V. 'Bridging the divide: Women and political and community issues', in P. Stringer and G. Robinson (eds) *Social Attitudes in Northern Ireland, The Second Report 1991-1992* (Belfast: Blackstaff Press, 1992).

Morgan, V. 'Women and the conflict in Northern Ireland', in A. O'Day (ed.) *Terrorism's Laboratory – The Case of Northern Ireland* (Aldershot: Dartmouth, 1995a).

Morgan, V. 'Peacemakers? Peacekeepers? – Women in Northern Ireland 1969-1995', Professorial Lecture, given at the University of Ulster, 25th October 1995b.

Morgan, V. 'The role of women in community development in Northern Ireland', in O. Hargie and D. Dickson (eds) *Researching the Troubles: Social Science Perspectives on the Northern Ireland Conflict* (Edinburgh: Mainstream Publishing, 2003), 245–58.

Morgan, V. and Fraser, G. *The Company We Keep: Women, Community and Organisations* (Coleraine: Centre for the Study of Conflict, 1993).

Morgan, V. and Fraser, G. 'Women and the Northern Ireland conflict: Experiences and responses', in S. Dunn (ed.) *Facets of the Conflict in Northern Ireland* (Basingstoke: Macmillan Press, 1995), 81–96.

Moriarty, G. 'PUP criticises ministers over slow progress', *The Irish Times*, 12 October 2009.

Morris, E. *Our Own Devices: National Symbols and Political Conflict in Twentieth Century Ireland* (Dublin: Irish Academic Press, 2005).

Morrissey, M. and Gaffikin, F. 'Planning for peace in contested space', *International Journal of Urban and Regional Research*, 2006, 30: 873–93.

Mulholland, M. 'The challenge to inequality: Women, discrimination and decision making in Northern Ireland', in C. O. N. Moser and F. C. Clark (eds) *Victims, Perpetrators or Actors? Gender, Armed Conflict and Political Violence* (London: Zed Books, 2005), 164–77.

Mycock, A. 'The enduring legacy of empire: post-imperial citizenship and national identity(ies) in the United Kingdom', in M. Dimova-Cookson and P. Stirk (eds) *Multiculturalism and Moral Conflict* (London: Routledge, 2009).

Mycock, A. 'British citizenship and the legacy of empire, in special edition of *Parliamentary Affairs* edited by A. Mycock and C. McGlynn, 2010, 63(2).

Mycock, A. and Tonge, J. 'The future of citizenship', in *Failing Politics? A Response to 'The Governance of Britain' Green Paper* (Political Studies Association, 2008).

Nagel, J. 'Masculinity and nationalism: gender and sexuality in the making of nations', *Ethnic and Racial Studies*, 1998, 21(2): 242–69.

Nairn, T. *Pariah: Misfortunes of the British Kingdom* (London: Verso, 2002).

Nellis, M. 'UDA's pay-off money', *An Phoblacht*, 5 October 2006.

Nellis, M. 'UDA's "how to spend a million"', *An Phoblacht*, 5 April 2007.

Nellis, M. 'The reality of "Traditional Unionism"', *An Phoblacht*, 11 June 2009.

Nelson, S. *Ulster's Uncertain Defenders: Protestant Political, Paramilitary and Community Groups and the Northern Ireland Conflict* (Belfast: Appletree Press, 1984).

Neumann, P. R. 'The imperfect peace: Explaining paramilitary violence in Northern Ireland', *Low Intensity Conflict and Law Enforcement*, 2004, 11(1): 116–38.

New Ulster Political Research Group. *Beyond the Religious Divide* (Belfast: NUPRG, 1979).

Northern Ireland Statistics and Research Agency. 'Labour Market statistics Bulletin: Women in Northern Ireland, February' (Belfast: Department of Enterprise, Trade and Investment, 2006).

Northern Ireland Women's Coalition. *Common Cause: The Story of the Northern Ireland Women's Coalition.* (1996?)

O'Broin, E. Interview with author, 20 August 2005.

O'Connor, F. 'Less fizz but politics lingers at Belfast Féile', *Irish Times*, 6 August 2009.

Ó Donnghaile. Sinn Fein-Keep Left, http://sinnfeinkeepleft.blogspot.com; accessed 23 September 2009.

O'Dowd. L. 'Church, State and women: The aftermath of partition', in C. Curtin, P. Jackson and B. O'Connor (eds) *Gender in Irish Society* (Galway: Galway University Press, 1987), 19–38.

O' Hamill, F. 'Republicans must win Protestant support', *Irish Democrat*, August/ September, 2005.

O' Leary, J. 'Orange Order Challenged', *An Phoblacht /Republican News*, 22 June 2000.

Olick, J. K. *The Politics of Regret* (London: Routledge, 2007).

O' Neill, B. (2001) 'A sectarian peace'. Archived at: spiked-online.com/Articles/ 000000002D219.htm; accessed 29 October 2009.

O' Neill, B. (2007) 'Paisley and Adams: The ghosts of politics past'. Archived at: spiked-online: http:www.spiked-online.com.index.php/site/article/3011/; accessed 12 October 2009.

Orange Order (2009c) 'Orange Culture Must Be Respected', 1 July, available at: http:// www.grandorangelodge.co.uk/press/PressReleases-2009/090701-orange_culture_ must_be_respected.htm

Orange Standard 'False information being spread', June 2008a.

Orange Standard 'Tampering with the constitution', November 2008b.
Orange Standard 'Commonwealth has a valued role to play', September, 2008c.
Orange Standard 'Renewal is the order of the day', August 2009.
Orr, P. (2008) *New Loyalties – Christian Faith and the Protestant Working-Class* (Belfast: Centre for Contemporary Christianity in Ireland, Belfast, 2008).
Ó Ruairc, L. 'Book review: Irish Freedom: The History of Nationalism in Ireland by Richard English', *Sovereign Nation,* January–February, 2007.
Page, E. 'Men, masculinity and guns: Can we break the link?' (London: IANSA – Women's Network, no date).
Patterson, H. and Kaufmann, E. P. *Unionism and Orangeism in Northern Ireland since 1945: The Decline of the Loyal Family* (Manchester: Manchester University Press, 2007).
Pearson, D. 'The ties that unwind: Civic and ethnic imaginings in New Zealand', *Nations and Nationalism,* 2000 (6): 91–110.
Pike, K. L. *Language in Relation to a Unified Theory of Structure of Human Behavior,* 2nd Edition (The Hague: Mouton, 1967).
Pike, K. L. *Talk, Thought, and Thing: The Emic Road Toward Conscious Knowledge* (Dallas: Summer Institute of Linguistics, 1993).
Police Ombudsman for Northern Ireland. *Statement by the Police Ombudsman for Northern Ireland on her investigation into the circumstances surrounding the death of Raymond McCord Jnr and related matters* (22 January 2007).
Porter, E. 'Diversity and commonality: Women, politics and Northern Ireland', *The European Journal of Women's Studies,* 1997, 4: 83–100.
Porter, N. *Rethinking Unionism: An Alternative Vision for Northern Ireland* (Belfast: Blackstaff Press, 1996).
Potter, M. and MacMillan, A. 'Unionist Women Active in the Conflict in Northern Ireland' (Belfast: Training for Women Network, no date).
Powell, J. *Great Hatred, Little Room. Making Peace in Northern Ireland* (London: The Bodley Head, 2008).
Power, M. 'Building communities in a post-conflict society: Churches and peace-building initiatives in Northern Ireland since 1994', *The European Legacy,* 2005, 10(1): 55–68.
Price Tangney, J. and Dearing, R. L. *Shame and Guilt* (New York: The Guilford Press, 2002).
Pritchett, L. and Woolcock, M. 'Solutions when the solution is the problem: Arraying and disarray in development', *World Development* 2004, 32(2): 191–212.
Public Record Office of Northern Ireland. *Introduction: Ulster Women's Unionist Council Papers* (Belfast: PRONI, 2007).
Pugh; M. 'Transformation in the political economy of Bosnia since Dayton', in D. Chandler (ed.) *Peace Without Politics? Ten Years of International State-Building in Bosnia* (London: Routledge, 2006).
Purvis, D. 'A vision for unionist working-class communities', *An Phoblacht,* 18 December 2008.
Purvis, D. 'Statement on UVF and RHC decommissioning', East Belfast Methodist Mission Hall, 27 June 2009. Archived at: http://www.pup-ni.org.uk/media/pr_read.aspx?a=59; accessed: 12 July 2009.
Purvis, D. 'Is abortion always wrong?' Archived at: http://www.pup-ni.org.uk/party/article_read.aspx?a=3; accessed: 12 November 2009.
Race Equality Scheme (2002) Manchester: Greater Manchester Police Authority.
Racioppi, L. and O'Sullivan See, K. 'Ulstermen and loyalist ladies on parade: Gendering unionism in Northern Ireland', *International Feminist Journal of Politics,* 2000, 2(1): 1–29.

Racioppi, L. and O'Sullivan See, K. 'This we will maintain': Gender, ethno-nationalism and the politics of unionism in Northern Ireland', *Nations and Nationalism*, 2001, 7(1): 93–112.

Ramsbotham, O., Woodhouse, T. and Miall, H. *Contemporary Conflict Resolution: The Prevention, Management and Transformation of Deadly Conflicts: Second Edition* (Cambridge: Polity, 2008).

Ratcliffe J. (ed) *Strategic Thinking in Criminal Intelligence* (Devon: Willan Publishing, 2009).

Redmond, J. E. *The Justice of Home Rule* (London, 1912a).

Redmond, J. E. *Mr Balfour on Nationality and Home Rule, A Reply by J. E. Redmond, MP* (London, 1912b).

Regan, D. 'Beyond the weariness: Finding consensus and moving forward', *The Irish Reporter*, 1996, June: 329–33.

Reid, C. 'Protestant challenges to the 'Protestant State': Ulster Unionism and Independent Unionism in Northern Ireland, 1921–1939', *Twentieth Century British History*, 2008, 19(4): 419–45.

Reynolds, S. *Kingdoms and Communities in Western Europe, 900-1300* (Oxford: Oxford University Press, 1984).

Richardson, L. *What Terrorists Want: Understanding the Terrorist Threat* (London: John Murray, 2006).

Richmond, O. *The Transformation of Peace* (Basingstoke: Palgrave, 2005).

Ricoeur, P. 'Memory and forgetting', in R. Kearney and M. Dooley (eds) *Questioning Ethics: Contemporary Debates in Philosophy* (London: Routledge, 1999)

Rolston, B. 'An effective mask for terror: Democracy, death squads and Northern Ireland', *Crime Law and Social Change*, 2005, 44: 181–203.

Rolston, B. 'Dealing with the past: Pro-state paramilitaries, truth and transition in Northern Ireland', *Human Rights Quarterly*, 2006, 28: 652–75.

Rooney, E. 'Women, community and politics in Northern Ireland: isms in action', *Journal of Gender Studies*, 1992, 1(4): 475–91.

Rooney, E. 'Women in Northern Irish politics: Difference matters', in C. Roulston and C. Davies (eds) *Gender, Democracy and Inclusion in Northern Ireland* (Houndmills: Palgrave, 2000), 164–86.

Rooney, E. 'Intersectionality in transition: Lessons from Northern Ireland', *Web Journal of Current Legal Issues*, 2007, 5. Archived at: http://webjcli.ncl.ac.uk/2007/issue5/rooney5.html; accessed 12 December 2009.

Rooney, K. 'Belfast: A tale of two cities', *Spiked*, 14 July 2008.

Ross, M. 'Ritual and the politics of reconciliation', in Yaacov Bar-Simon-Tov (ed.) *From Conflict to Reconciliation* (Oxford: Oxford University Press, 2004), 199–223.

Roulston, C. 'Equal opportunities for women', in A. Aughey and D. Morrow (eds) *Northern Ireland Politics* (London: Longman, 1996), 139–46.

Roulston, C. and Davies, C. (eds) *Gender, Democracy and Inclusion in Northern Ireland* (Houndmills: Palgrave, 2000).

Rowan, B. 'Loyalist chief appears at west Belfast festival', *Belfast Telegraph*, 6 August 2009a.

Rowan, B. 'Is UDA boss wavering over weapons?' *Belfast Telegraph*, 29 August 2009b.

Ryan, M. *War and Peace in Ireland: Britain and the IRA in the New World Order* (London: Pluto Press, 1994).

Ryder, C. *The Fateful Split: Catholics and the Royal Ulster Constabulary* (London: Methuen, 2004).

Rynder, C. B. 'The origins and early years of the Northern Ireland women's coalition', *New Hibernia Review*, 2002, 6(1): 44–7.

Sales, R. *Women Divided: Gender, Religion and Politics in Northern Ireland* (London: Routledge, 1997a).

Sales, R. 'Gender and protestantism in Northern Ireland', in P. Shirlow and M. McGovern (eds) *Who Are 'the People'? Unionism, Protestantism and Loyalism in Northern Ireland* (London: Pluto, 1997b), 140–57.

Sarma, K. 'Defensive propaganda and IRA political control in Republican communities', *Studies in Conflict and Terrorism*, 2007, 30: 1073–94.

Saulters, R. 'Three flagship Twelfths', *The Orange Chronicle*, 24 June 2009.

Schmid, A. 'Terrorism as psychological warfare', *Democracy and Security*, 2005, 1(2): 137–46.

Schulze, K. and Smith, M. L. R. 'Decommissioning and paramilitary strategy in Northern Ireland: A problem compared', *The Journal of Strategic Studies*, 2000, 23(4): 77–106.

Scotsman 'Orange Order ignites SNP over Union', 19 October 2009.

Sengupta, K. 'Irish Referendum May 22: Women who struggle seriously for peace but laugh at hecklers', *The Independent*, 5 May 1998.

Seward, W. W. *Collectanea Politica or the Political Transactions of Ireland from the Accession of His Majesty King George the Third to the Present Time* (Dublin, 1801).

Sharoni, S. 'Rethinking women's struggles in Israel-Palestine and in the North of Ireland', in C. O. N. Moser and F. C. Clark (eds) *Victims, Perpetrators or Actors? Gender, Armed Conflict and Political Violence* (London: Zed Books, 2001), 85–98.

Shirlow, P. 'Fear and ethnic division in Belfast', *Peace Review*, 2001, 13(2).

Shirlow, P. 'Why it's going to take two to tango', *Belfast Telegraph*, 14 March 2007.

Shirlow, P. and McEvoy, K. *Beyond the Wire: Former Prisoners and Conflict Transformation in Northern Ireland* (London: Pluto Press, 2008).

Shirlow, P. and Murtagh, B. *Belfast: Segregation, Violence and the City* (London: Pluto Press, 2006).

Shirlow, P., Graham, B., McMullan, A., Murtagh, B., Robinson, G. and Southern, N. *Negotiating Change: Sharing and Conflict Amelioration in Derry/Londonderry* (Belfast: OFMDFM, Equality Unit/Joseph Rowntree Charitable Trust, 2005).

Shirlow, P., Tonge, J., McAuley, J. and McGlynn, C. *Abandoning Historical Conflict? Former Prisoners and Reconciliation in Northern Ireland* (Manchester: Manchester University Press, 2010).

Silke, A. 'Drink, drugs and rock 'n' roll: Financing loyalist terrorism in Northern Ireland – part two', *Studies in Conflict and Terrorism*, 2000, 23: 107–27

Simpson, K. 'Untold stories: Unionist remembrance of political violence and suffering in Northern Ireland', *British Politics*, 2008, 3(4): 465–89.

Sims J. 'What is intelligence?' in A. Shulsky and J. Sims (eds) *What is Intelligence? Working Group on Intelligence Reform* (Washington: Consortium for the Study of Intelligence, Georgetown University, 1993).

Sinn Féin 'An appeal to unionists', *United Irishman*, March 1958.

Sinn Féin 'Disastrous approach', *An Phoblacht/ Republican News*, 3 May 1980.

Sinn Féin 'Report of Sinn Féin Ard Fheis', *An Phoblacht/ Republican News*, 10 November 1981.

Sinn Féin 'Constitutional manoeuvres in the dark', *An Phoblacht/ Republican News*, 25 August 1983.

Sinn Féin 'The Orange Maginot Line', *An Phoblacht /Republican News*, 30 September 1999.

Sinn Féin 'Brits armed loyalist beast', *An Phoblacht /Republican News*, 29 August 2000a

Sinn Féin 'Loyalism will eat itself', *An Phoblacht /Republican News*, 29 August 2000b

Sinn Féin 'Loyal to what?', *An Phoblacht /Republican News*, 29 August 2000c.

Sinn Féin 'One woman's story', *An Phoblacht /Republican News*, 26 April 2001.

Sinn Féin 'Debating Empire', *An Phoblacht /Republican News,* 21 February 2002.

Sinn Féin 'Report of Sinn Féin Ard Fheis', *Irish Republican News and Information,* 28 March 2003.

Sinn Féin 'Is deprivation the cause of unionist violence?', *An Phoblacht,* 22 September 2005.

Smith, M.L.R. *Fighting for Ireland? The military strategy of the Irish Republican movement* (London: Taylor & Francis, 1997).

Smith, N. *I Was Wrong* (Cambridge: Cambridge University Press, 2008).

Socialist Party. 'Socialist opposition needed!'. Archived at: http://spni.032.org.uk/Website/Northern%20Political/SPstandelectionsOct09.html; accessed 5 November 2009.

Southern, N. 'Britishness, "Ulsterness" and unionist identity in Northern Ireland', *Nationalism and Ethnic Politics,* 2007, 13(1): 71–102.

Southern, N. 'Territoriality, alienation and loyalist decommissioning: The case of the Shankill in Protestant West Belfast', *Terrorism and Political Violence,* 2008, 20(1): 66–86.

Southern, N. 'Post-agreement societies and inter-ethnic competition: A comparative study of the Protestant community of Londonderry and the white population of Pretoria', *National Identities,* 2009, 11(4): 397–415.

Spencer, G. *The State of Loyalism in Northern Ireland* (Basingstoke: Palgrave Macmillan, 2008).

Sriram, C. L. *Peace as Governance: Power-Sharing, Armed Groups and Contemporary Peace Negotiations* (Basingstoke: Palgrave, 2008).

Stapleton, K. and Wilson, J. 'Gender, nationality and identity: A discursive study', *European Journal of Women's Studies,* 2004, 11(1): 45–60.

Stapleton, K. and Wilson, J. 'Ulster Scots identity and culture: The missing voices', *Identities: Global Studies in Power and Culture,* 2004, 11(4): 563–91.

Steadman, S. J. 'Spoiler problems in peace processes', *International Security,* 1997, 22(2): 5–53.

Stoeker, R. 'Are academics irrelevant? Roles for scholars in participatory research', *American Behavioural Scientist,* 1999, 42(5): 840–54.

Sun-Tzu, *The Art of War* (Mineola, NY: Dover, 2002).

Sveinsson, K. P. *Who Cares about the White Working Class?* (London: The Runnymede Trust, 2009).

Tavuchis, N. *Mea Culpa* (Stanford: Stanford University Press, 1991).

Taylor, C. (ed.) *Multiculturalism: Explaining the Politics of Recognition* (Princeton, NJ: Princeton University Press, 1994).

Taylor, C. 'And don't forget to clean the fridge: Women in the secret sphere of terrorism', in G. DeGroot and C. Peniston-Bird (eds) *A Soldier and a Woman: Sexual Integration in the Military* (New York: Longman, 2000), 294–304.

Taylor, P. *Loyalists* (London: Bloombury Publishing, 1999).

Todd, J. 'Two traditions in unionist political culture', *Irish Political Studies,* 1987, 2: 1–26.

Tone, W. T. W. (edited by T. Bartlett) *Life of Theobald Wolfe Tone* (Dublin: Lilliput Press, 1998).

Tonge, J. *The New Northern Irish Politics?* (Basingstoke: Palgrave Macmillan, 2005).

Tonge, J. *Northern Ireland* (Cambridge: Polity, 2006).

Ulster Unionist Party (UUP). 'Positive progress for unionist identity', 29 May 2008. Archived at: www.uup.org.uk; accessed 17 November 2009.

Upper Springfield Development Trust. *Annual Report* (Belfast: Upper Springfield Development Trust, 2004).

Urquhart, D. 'In defence of Ulster and the Empire: The Ulster women's unionist council, 1911–1940', *UCG Women's Studies Centre Review*, 1996, 4: 31–40.

van Creveld, M. *Men, Women and War: Do Women Belong in the Front Line?* (London: Cassell, 2001).

Verdery, K. *The Political Lives of Dead Bodies: Reburial and Postsocialist Change* (New York: Columbia University Press, 1999).

Walker, G. *A History of the Ulster Unionist Party: Protest, Pragmatism and Pessimism* (Manchester: Manchester University Press, 2004).

Walker, L. *Godmothers and Mentors: Women, Politics and Education in Northern Ireland* (Belfast: December Publications, 1997).

Walsh, J. 'Orangemen, welcome to a united Ireland!'. Archived at: http://spiked-on-line.com/index.php/site/printable/7223/; accessed 28August 2009.

Ward, M. *Unmanageable Revolutionaries: Women and Irish Nationalism* (London: Pluto, 1989).

Ward, M. '"Ulster Was Different?" Women, feminism, and nationalism in the North of Ireland', in Y. Galligan, E. Ward and R. Wilford (eds) *Contesting Politics: Women in Ireland North and South* (Oxford: Westview Press, 1999), 219–39.

Ward, M. 'Gender, citizenship and the future of the Northern Ireland peace process', *Éire-Ireland*, 2005, 40 (3 and 4): 1–22.

Ward, M. 'The representation of women in public life in Northern Ireland since the Good Friday Agreement' (Belfast: Women's Resource and Development Agency, 2006).

Ward, R. 'Invisible women: The political roles of unionist and loyalist women in contemporary Northern Ireland', *Parliamentary Affairs*, 2002, 55: 167–78.

Ward, R. '"It's not just tea and buns": Women and pro-union politics in Northern Ireland', *British Journal of Politics and International Relations*, 2004, 6(4): 494–506.

Ward, R. *Women, Unionism and Loyalism In Northern Ireland: From 'Tea-Makers' to Political Actors* (Dublin: Irish Academic Press, 2006).

Ward, S. 'Introduction', in S. Ward (ed.) *British Culture and the End of Empire* (Manchester: Manchester University Press, 2001).

Wehr, P. and Lederach, J. P. 'Mediating conflict in Central America', *Journal of Peace Research*, 1991, 28(1): 85–98.

Weight, R. *Patriots: National Identity in Britain 1940–2000* (London: Macmillan, 2002).

Weiner, R. *The Rape and Plunder of the Shankill* (Belfast: Farset Co-operative Press, 1980).

West, L. A. (ed.) *Feminist Nationalisms* (London: Routledge, 1997).

Whalen, L. *Contemporary Irish Republican Prison Writing: Writing and Resistance* (London: Palgrave Macmillan, 2007).

Whelan, P. 'UDA fights on, for drugs and Ulster', *An Phoblacht,* 11 October 2007.

White, J. *Minority Report: The Protestant Community in the Irish Republic* (Dublin: Gill and MacMillan, 1975).

Wi'am. *Sulha Project at the Wi'am Palestinian Conflict Resolution Center.* Archived at: http://alaslah.org/sulha/; accessed 12 May 2009

Wilford, R. 'Women and politics in Northern Ireland,' in J. Lovenduski and P. Norris (eds) *Women in Politics* (Oxford: Oxford University Press, 1996), 43–56.

Wilford, R. 'Women, ethnicity and nationalism: Surveying the ground', in R. Wilford and R. L. Miller (eds) *Women, Ethnicity and Nationalism: The Politics of Transition* (London: Routledge, 1998), 1–22.

Wilford, R. 'Women and politics', in P. Mitchell and R. Wilford (eds) *Politics in Northern Ireland* (Boulder: Westview, 1999a), 195–219.

Wilford, R. 'Women's candidacies and electability in a divided society: The Northern Ireland women's coalition and the 1996 forum election', *Women and Politics* 1999b, 20(1): 73–93.

Wilford, R. and Galligan, Y. 'Gender and party politics in Northern Ireland', in Y. Galligan, E. Ward and R. Wilford (eds) *Contesting Politics: Women in Ireland, North and South* (Oxford: Westview Press, 1999), 169–84.

Wilford, R., Miller, R. and Donoghue, F. *Women and Political Participation in Northern Ireland* (Ashgate Press: London, 1996).

Wilkinson, P. *Political Terrorism* (London: MacMillan, 1974).

Wilson, R. 'Beyond ideology', *Fortnight*, October 1992.

Women into Politics (WiP). *Preliminary Submission to the Northern Ireland Human Rights Commission on A Bill of Rights for Northern Ireland* (Belfast: WiP, 2001).

Women into Politics. 'Statistics: Northern Ireland Assembly from March 2007 elections'. Archived at: http://www.womenintopolitics.org/index.php?option=com_content&view=section&layout=blog&id=11&Itemid=66; accessed 21 November 2009.

Wood, E. J. 'The ethical challenges of field research in conflict zones', *Qualitative Sociology*, 2006, 29(3).

Wright, A. *Policing: An Introduction to Concepts and Practice* (London: Cullompton, 2002).

Yougov/*Daily Telegraph*, 'The values of Britishness', Survey, July 2005. Archived available at www.yougov.co.uk; accessed 14 July 2009.

Young, D. 'PUP links with SF "for shared future"', *News Letter*, 18 September 2006.

YouthAction Northern Ireland. *Everyday Life: Young Men, Violence and Developing Youth Work Practice in Northern Ireland* (Belfast: YouthAction Publications, 2002).

Yuval-Davis, N. *Gender and Nation* (London: Sage, 1997).

Yuval-Davis, N. and Anthias, F. *Woman-Nation-State* (London: Macmillan, 1989).

Zalewski, M. 'Gender ghosts in McGarry and O'Leary and representations of the conflict in Northern Ireland', *Political Studies*, 2005, 53(1): 201–21.

Index